AF352713

MILITARIZED MASCULINITY IN SPAIN AND CHILE

Remembering Violence through Film and Literature

Militarized Masculinity in Spain and Chile

Remembering Violence through Film and Literature

LISA DIGIOVANNI

UNIVERSITY OF TORONTO PRESS
Toronto Buffalo London

© University of Toronto Press 2025
Toronto Buffalo London
utppublishing.com
Printed in Canada

ISBN 978-1-4875-6271-7 (cloth)   ISBN 978-1-4875-6273-1 (EPUB)
                                   ISBN 978-1-4875-6272-4 (PDF)

LATINOAMERICANA

Library and Archives Canada Cataloguing in Publication

Title: Militarized masculinity in Spain and Chile : remembering violence
    through film and literature / Lisa DiGiovanni.
Names: DiGiovanni, Lisa, author.
Series: Latinoamericana (Toronto, Ont.)
Description: Series statement: Latinoamericana | Includes bibliographical
    references and index.
Identifiers: Canadiana (print) 20250182432 | Canadiana (ebook) 20250182467 |
    ISBN 9781487562717 (hardcover) | ISBN 9781487562731 (EPUB) |
    ISBN 9781487562724 (PDF)
Subjects: LCSH: Violence in motion pictures. | LCSH: Violence in literature. |
    LCSH: Masculinity in motion pictures. | LCSH: Masculinity in literature. |
    LCSH: Motion pictures – Spain – History – 20th century. | LCSH: Motion
    pictures – Chile – History – 20th century. | LCSH: Spanish literature –
    20th century – History and criticism. | LCSH: Chilean literature –
    20th century – History and criticism. | LCSH: Violence in men. |
    LCSH: Militarization – Spain – History – 20th century. | LCSH: Militarization –
    Chile – History – 20th century. | LCSH: Militarism – Spain – History –
    20th century. | LCSH: Militarism – Chile – History – 20th century.
Classification: LCC PN1995.9.V5 D54 2025 | DDC 791.43/6552–dc23

Cover design: John Beadle

We wish to acknowledge the land on which the University of Toronto
Press operates. This land is the traditional territory of the Wendat, the
Anishnaabeg, the Haudenosaunee, the Métis, and the Mississaugas of the
Credit First Nation.

This book has been published with the assistance of Keene State College.

University of Toronto Press acknowledges the financial support of the
Government of Canada, the Canada Council for the Arts, and the Ontario Arts
Council, an agency of the Government of Ontario, for its publishing activities.

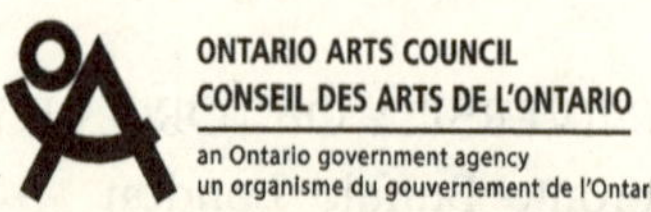

Canada Council   Conseil des Arts
for the Arts   du Canada

ONTARIO ARTS COUNCIL
CONSEIL DES ARTS DE L'ONTARIO
an Ontario government agency
un organisme du gouvernement de l'Ontario

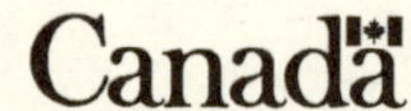

Canadä

Contents

Acknowledgments

I extend my deepest gratitude to the film-makers, authors, artists, activists, and survivors who have bravely challenged and continue to resist militarized forms of government and culture. Equally vital to my journey have been the faculty members, former advisers, and current mentors who nurtured my critical engagement with such important creative endeavours. I particularly wish to thank Michael Lazzara, Gina Herrmann, Robert Neustadt, Carlos Aguirre, Pedro García-Caro, Cynthia Enloe, Barbara Zecchi, Cristina Moreiras Menor, and Cecilia Enjuto Rangel for their invaluable guidance and friendship.

Since 2013, my wonderful colleagues at Keene State College in New Hampshire have been a tremendous source of support, and I extend my heartfelt gratitude to Brinda Charry, Patricia Pedroza, Amber Davisson, Sasha Davis, Greg Knouff, Taneem Husain, Ashley Greene, Emily Robins Sharpe, Jamie Landau, Kate DeConinck, Catherine Winters-Michaud, Tom White, Michele Kuiawa, Dana Smith, John Sturtz, Elisa Von Joeden-Forgey, Ted White, Jiwon Ahn, Jo Dery, Brandon Doherty, Martin Roberts, Taylor Dunne, and Sara Hottinger. I also continue to value the insightful conversations I shared in Eugene at the University of Oregon with Gabriela Martínez, Anuncia Escala, Sayo Murcia, Stephanie Wood, Meche Lu, Guadalupe Moreno, Lauretta de Renzo-Huter, Elena Espinosa, Mirtha Avalos, Roberto Galo Arroyo, and Adrea Bogle. Furthermore, the videographic scholarship community at Middlebury College has served as a rich source of inspiration in recent years. I extend my gratitude to Katie Grant, Jason Mittell, Celia Sainz Delgado, Will DiGravio, and my fellow participants in the 2022 and 2023 "videocamp."

The establishment of my joint appointment in Holocaust and Genocide Studies and Modern Languages and Cultures at Keene State College has been crucial in enabling new avenues of research, and I am deeply grateful to all who facilitated this arrangement, especially Kirsti Sandy and James

Waller. The Cohen Center for Holocaust and Genocide Studies has offered an invaluable environment for my work, reflection, and engagement with students at Keene State College, made possible by the generous support of Jan Cohen. For institutional backing, I extend my thanks to Melinda Treadwell, President, Keene State College; Celia Rabinowitz, Dean of the Mason Library; and the various selection committees that awarded me multiple faculty development grants in support of this monograph.

During my time as faculty at Keene State College, and in my previous roles at Indiana State University and the University of Oregon, my students have consistently served as a source of fresh perspectives and enduring optimism. While too numerous to list comprehensively, several individuals stand out: Elías Stowell Aleman, Jedidiah Crook, Jackson Caffrey, Danielle Dexter, Paula Durant, Melissa Frost, Eva Goodwin, Avery Honey, Teagan Hudzik, Cathleen Klem, TJ Lonergan, Kareema Maddox, Jackie Markle, Nora McIntyre, Paige Pribilla, Feride Eva Saribas, Daniel Scanlon, Jackie Sheean, Brook Elise Steppe, and Katie Woltner. It has been a distinct honour to serve as your professor and observe your growth into thoughtful individuals deeply engaged with the complexities of our world.

Over the past decade I have had the privilege of contributing to numerous publications and collaborating with scholars who have been instrumental in refining my arguments. I extend my gratitude to David William Foster, Ana Corbalán, Sebastiaan Faber, María José Gámez Fuentes, Rebeca Maseda García, Karen Boyle, Susan Berridge, Jordana Blejmar, Jaime Céspedes, Natalia Fortuny, Elizabeth Osborne, Vania Barraza, and Mark de Valk. I am particularly indebted to Lorraine Ryan at the University of Birmingham for her insightful feedback and unwavering encouragement throughout various phases of this project. Corey Sabourin has also been an invaluable editor of my work since 2020. Furthermore, I have benefited greatly from the perspectives of Leith Passmore, Fernando Blanco, Patricia Pérez Valdez, Pía Barros, Boris Hau, Jay Rosenblatt, Henry Theriault, Kerry Whigham, and the Institute for Genocide and Mass Atrocity Prevention at Binghamton University. Importantly, I wish to thank Patricio Guzmán, Lissette Orozco, Carolina Astudillo, and Marcela Said for their generosity in responding to my questions about their films. For his interest in my project and support throughout the review and publication process, I thank Mark Thompson, Senior Acquisitions Editor at the University of Toronto Press; Barbara Porter, Associate Managing Editor; and copy editor Angela Wingfield. The meticulous and perceptive anonymous peer reviewers also deserve a special acknowledgment although I cannot thank them directly.

My understanding of the Spanish Civil War and the Franco dictatorship has deepened significantly through conversations in Spain, not only with scholars and activists but also with my extended family, who generously offered their support and diverse perspectives during my travels to Madrid, Barcelona, and Galicia. Spain has become a cherished second home, and for this, I thank Emilio Vicente, Rosa Torras, Leopoldo Alvarez Sousa, Fina Pérez Sousa, Javier Barbi, Félix Echávarri, and Fani Yepes. Furthermore, El Archivo de la Guerra Civil Española in Salamanca and El Museo de la Memoria y Derechos Humanos in Santiago de Chile were fruitful resources in the development of this book.

I would also like to offer a deeply personal expression of gratitude for the relationships that shaped me before my professional life began. To my mother, Jacquelyn Button, thank you for your unwavering support and for the confidence you instilled in me as a young woman venturing out into the world. To my father, Sylvester DiGiovanni, this acknowledgment carries a unique weight. As the first example of masculinity in my life, you served as a powerful counter-example, clarifying the type of man I would actively avoid. Perhaps therein lies some of the inspiration in my search for understanding the different forms and significance of masculinity. My brother, Sebastian DiGiovanni, a war veteran, has also had a profound impact on my life. Though we inhabit different worlds – physically, psychologically, and emotionally – our love and respect for each other has remained constant. It is my sincere hope that the traumas you have endured as a result of war may one day find a powerful and healing expression through your own writing. To the Button family, thank you for your enduring love and support. I also extend sincere gratitude to the Holladay family – James, Diana, Myakka, Kisa, and Tyrone – for nurturing my curiosity and love of the arts. Thank you, Jim, for presenting a different model of masculinity and fatherhood to me – one marked by quiet generosity, kindness, and humility.

Above all, I am eternally grateful for Carlos Vicente, our daughters Belén and Sole, and our beloved Canela. Carlos, your unwavering love means the world to me. Sole, your humour and radiant spirit fill my life with joy every day. Belén, your brilliance and the profound bond we share are beyond words. With the three of you, I have everything.

Foreword

When *Militarized Masculinity in Spain and Chile: Remembering Violence through Film and Literature* first came into my hands, my immediate thought was, "Finally, a book that reflects intelligently and deeply on a part of contemporary cultural history without fear of theoretical conceptualization and of the use of complex thinking that supports, interprets, stimulates, and nourishes political, affective, and ideological processes from an entirely interdisciplinary and comparative perspective." Indeed, Lisa DiGiovanni's book uses cultural and historical analysis as instruments to open up knowledge and understanding, without hesitating to accompany that analysis with a well-argued theoretical reflection that is entirely in line with literary, cultural, and filmic readings.

Feminism and gender theory highlight hypermasculinities or militarized masculinities constructed on the unequivocal binary reality of sexed positions. These emerge as the foundational and basic axes of the repressive apparatuses of the two dictatorial states, Spain and Chile, as demonstrated by the author's magnificently presented, developed, and convincing arguments. Militarized masculinity, thus, reveals itself as the infrastructure supporting the functioning of these dictatorships and their instruments of torture and violence. In an original twist, the author takes us step by step through a detailed study of cultural expression in reference to a disturbing reality: power based on ideological violence is constituted through a socialization process in which a hegemonic practice is set in motion, giving undeniable reality to a binary sexualization that is predicated on the dominant idea of hypermasculinization. This hypermasculinization or militarized masculinity, as DiGiovanni terms it, becomes the signifier on which violence, torture, and repression are exercised as political acts of subjugation. DiGiovanni offers, from this premise, an innovative theory of violence that, from a feminist perspective, analyses instrumental forms of torture as intrinsically inseparable from the state apparatus.

Always understood from within a feminist theory of violence, the history of the Spanish and Chilean dictatorships takes on an essential intensity in this indispensable book. Reading the violence generated by sexual or gender positionalities as predicated on militarized masculinity leads to understanding these dictatorships and their power structures in a new and original light. Undoubtedly, the book offers an unparalleled contribution to cultural studies. It is respectful of previous studies on these two dictatorships while embracing sexuation as the structural origin of totalitarian machinery. Misogyny and gender violence are made invisible or visible in acts of torture, revealed both in the terror generated by the state through violence that contaminates society in general, and in the genocidal acts that structure and give political meaning to dictatorships in general. In this way, the book introduces gender as a foundational part of the ideological apparatuses of these two dictatorships, thereby providing a novel interpretation of the role of masculinity in regimes that use gender binaries as the basis for all political ideology. From this perspective, DiGiovanni presents a remarkably engaging book that is notable for its innovative analysis and comprehensive comparative archive. She persuasively and intelligently argues, both theoretically and analytically, that the gendered infrastructure that underscores terror was the prime political tool of the Franco and Pinochet governments.

I do not suppose this was an easy task, since the book uncovers an enormous archive of cultural, historical, literary, and theoretical work. In an original and constructive manner it follows in the footsteps of Nelly Richard in the interest of thinking politically about gender, sexism, misogyny, the dominant construction of masculinity and consequently of a subjugated femininity, together with the masculinist distortions that that subjugation produces. Alongside Richard, other authors such as Cynthia Enloe (the inaugural thinker of the concept of militarized masculinities), Walter Benjamin (a thinker of fascism), prominent historians of Chile and Spain (Balfour and Casanova, among others), and Judith Butler contribute ideas, critical discussions, and confirmations for DiGiovanni's arguments, which show the structural forms on which the exercise of power is based when it is instrumentalized through violence, torture, and the hypertrophy of sexed and gendered positions.

Militarized Masculinity will thus become an indispensable book among those dedicated to the study of military dictatorships, the study of gender as an instrument of domination and violence, and, above all, feminist work on cultural history in Hispanic studies. All of this would not have been successful without a first-rate cultural archive, and Professor DiGiovanni's book provides us with a well-selected corpus of films, literature, and graphic novels. Through the literary works of Roberto Bolaño, Nona Fernández, Antonio Muñoz Molina, Manuel Rivas, and Alberto Méndez; films by Jon Garaño, Aitor Arregi, Jose Mari Goenaga, Patricio Guzmán, Pilar Miró, Lissette Orozco, Marcela Said, Agustí Villaronga, and Benito Zambrano; and a graphic novel by Carlos Gimenez, the author examines and revises the relation that the Franco and Pinochet regimes established with torture and violence, as the structural foundations of politics and ideology.

In sum, *Militarized Masculinity in Spain and Chile* demonstrates outstanding scholarship, erudition in the Spanish and Latin American cultural and intellectual traditions, and sophistication in its cultural, historical, and political analysis. The book displays a marked commitment to grasping in a comparative way the subtleties of Spanish and Chilean reactionary thought. It will therefore be of much relevance for the fields of modern and contemporary Peninsular and Latin American studies.

Cristina Moreiras Menor

MILITARIZED MASCULINITY IN SPAIN AND CHILE

Introduction: Naming a Problem

One of the most jarring disclosures in Chile's official torture report is the extent to which sexualized violence was systematically exercised by the military regime (1973–90) to elicit information, assert power, and eliminate resistance to the implementation of a neoliberal counter-revolution. Women political activists were targeted for torture, along with the wives, mothers, and daughters of male dissidents. As Steve Stern points out, "The sexual aggressions and violence included not only vaginal, oral, and anal rape, but also sexualized insults, simulations of rape and forced witness of it, stripping and groping, forced sex with prisoners and relatives, and penetration by trained dogs, rats, and insects" (*Reckoning* 296). Beyond the official Valech Report, prepared by the National Commission on Political Imprisonment and Torture established by President Ricardo Lagos, Chile's recent history of brutality has generated many narratives by survivors, perpetrators, historians, writers, and film-makers. One of the earliest voices against gendered torture was Chilean feminist anthropologist Ximena Bunster (1931–2019) who examined the interlocking relationship between the military and the police forces, which functioned to control and punish dissident women in the name of national security under Augusto Pinochet.

The expansion of military power in Chile and its gendered methods of control were not entirely unique. The Chilean Armed Forces took cues from regional and international models and drew from a history of repressive practices. One of Pinochet's primary sources of inspiration came from Spain where the Francisco Franco regime (1939–75) conducted a forty-year "crusade" to destroy leftist opposition after the Spanish Civil War (1936–9). In the post-Franco period no truth commission was created as a means of democratic transition in the wake of the dictatorship. Nevertheless, testimonies by former political prisoners in Spain, similar to Chile, reveal that torture was routinized to dismantle underground rebel networks. Survivors also affirm that the demonstration of authority inflicted by the civil guard involved the assault of sexualized organs.

While these findings in Spain and Chile are eye-opening, it is also true that the creation of a militarized state that crushed leftist political opposition through surveillance, detainment, and torture was not an aberration in either place. The comparison of Franco's Spain and Pinochet's Chile is compelling on many levels. Both regimes emerged from societies that were steeped in military culture and shaped by egregious inequalities between men and women of different classes, races, and sexual orientations. Militarism, already deeply rooted, surfaced powerfully as a backlash to the economic and social reforms of the Second Spanish Republic (1931–9) and the Popular Unity government of Salvador Allende (1970–3). If patriarchy constituted the bedrock of militarism, then militarism served to buttress patriarchy at a time when the social order was in question.[1] In both Spain and Chile the military stoked conflict surrounding issues of gender and class while it simultaneously discredited the democratic political process and framed civilian leadership as weak.

The lionization of the armed forces and reverence for the figure of the all-powerful militarized male therefore went hand in hand with what Brian Loveman calls the "politics of antipolitics" (3). Military and civilian acceptance of this ideology, Loveman states, entailed "the denial of the legitimacy of labor protests, strikes, and political party claims of representing diverse interests" (5). The belief that politicians were incompetent and out of touch with the public had the potential to generate civilian-led social movements in Spain and Chile. However, in both cases, the rejection of politics meant the embrace of long-term technocratic military regimes that functioned as a bulwark of patriarchy. Accordingly, the typical features of antipolitics were inseparable from assumptions about gender. Under that anti-democratic model, the armed forces constituted the dominant body that enforced the implementation of decisions made by appointed economists, lawyers, and industrialists. In that narrative, "brave" officers and "efficient" businessmen were the only capable leaders.

---

1 Feminist Rebecca Johnson argued that patriarchy and militarism mutually reinforce each other. Thus, opposition to patriarchy necessitates anti-militarism, as demonstrated by the Greenham Common Women's Peace Camp (1981).

Given that the right-wing governments of Franco and Pinochet so vehemently defended patriarchal power and the authority of their respective armed forces to "clean up" and maintain order, it is crucial to understand the relationship between gender, dictatorial violence, and militarism. How might the social construction of the gender binary and militaristic socialization underlie and fuel acts of political persecution and subjugation? Where might we find insight into the juncture between militarized masculinity and violence? How might film and literature shed light on such connections? What strategies might film-makers and novelists use to unmask the ideologies underpinning torture? And finally, how might their counter-hegemonic depictions of militarized masculinity be meaningful today?

This book holds that until we connect the dots between masculinity, militarism, and violence, we cannot fully comprehend the causes and consequences of dictatorial brutality. Following a reciprocally beneficial line of inquiry, I argue that an exploration of gender helps us better interpret authoritarian atrocities, and a discussion of dictatorial brutality deepens our understanding of gender relations. Men make war and war make men, as the saying goes, but there is far more to the story than that simple axiom. Gendered violence is part and parcel of militarism, and literature, film, and feminist theory can play a key role in rendering visible the complexities of that overlooked relationship. With feminist tools of interpretation, we may sort through disruptive, or conversely conformist, representations of militarism in the arts. In so doing, we can map the lineage between commonly held notions of masculinity and a belief system that entails the adherence to hierarchical order and the suppression of opposition.

Drawing from a wide range of research, I develop a theory of violence grounded in feminist studies and focused on the sorely needed concept of *militarized masculinity,* originally coined by political scientist Cynthia Enloe. The term stands out in her study of US militarization and neo-imperialism in books including *Bananas, Beaches and Bases, The Morning After,* and *Maneuvers.* The content of militarized masculinity varies from one historical moment to the next, and from one cultural environment to another. However, the term constitutes an apt name for a wide-reaching problem given its cross-cultural link to violence and repressive asymmetrical power relations. Warrior conditioning was no small component in acts of torture and mass killing during the Franco and Pinochet dictatorships; it was central.

If militarism involves a set of beliefs that honour war and embrace the use of force as the most effective answer to political conflict, then militarized masculinity constitutes the gender identity at its core that is internalized through a process of socialization. Its effects are real, but the predestined existence of militarized masculinity is based on a lie. It is a long-standing collective fabrication that is kept alive through learned beliefs about the aggressive nature of heroic manliness (as epitomized by "hard" soldiers) in contrast with the powerlessness of femininity (perceived as "soft" and civilian). The faith in the inevitability of that rigid dichotomy built the core architecture of the Franco and Pinochet regimes and fortified their depths of cruelty. The construction of militarized masculinity fostered an emotional loyalty to national agendas and an idealized view of warfare. Through propagandistic language and images, they conceived of soldiering as a meaningful manly activity and sold the perception of the societal need of constant military preparedness against foreign and domestic enemies. With that doctrine and the necessary weapons to back it up, they further divided an already fractured populace. The diffusion of the idea that survival depended on military leadership bolstered the power of the armed forces and made resistance seem impossible, thereby making myth reality.

Even beyond Spain and Chile, the belief that societies must be ruled by strongmen stems from militarist ideology and patriarchal norms. While muscular physique can play a role, gender norms go far beyond anatomy. They associate masculinity with leadership, organizational skills, decision-making skills, charisma, and the ability to move the masses. Within that discourse, culturally constructed conceptualizations of the "other" hinge on binary comparisons of superiority and inferiority (us vs. them, strong vs. weak, good vs. evil, hard vs. soft, truthful vs. devious, male vs. female). The feminization of enemy men and the masculinization of enemy women serve to dehumanize the adversary since these are framed as unnatural. Meanwhile the virginal, feminine, or mother figure becomes the mythical icon to protect from corruption (Taylor 77).

That world view has cultivated societal structures that directly enable polarizing actions, dehumanizing language, and discriminatory laws – all recognized as key stages of genocide. Instead of recruiting and mobilizing human ingenuity for non-military forms of security, that narrative has fuelled government spending on weapons and war technology. What is lost is the creative potential to identify patterns and organize to find effective solutions to political division. By making change seem impossible and violence unavoidable, those convictions limit our imagination, curb our sense of responsibility to each other, and stop us from building more equal social relationships. Those militarized myths that celebrate violent masculinity have been a key component in nightmarish pasts and remain a dead-end road to a cynical future.

When it comes to analysing the origins and outcomes of violence, the setting of masculinity in parentheses or making it a footnote is dangerously short-sighted. Militarized masculinity is by no means the only cause of state violence, but it is an integral element that we must understand because it sustains the use of force as the most viable solution to political unrest. Militarized masculinity depends on oversimplified thinking bound up in, and weaponized through, a lexicon of fear. That narrative encourages armament and augments the influence of military-industrial-media networks. It teaches men to enforce conformity by policing difference and to justify hostile behaviour as unavoidable. This gender construct runs through and interacts with other causes of genocidal behaviour like authoritarianism, nationalism, religious fanaticism, and territorial expansionism. To ignore how these other causes are profoundly shaped by patriarchal and militaristic constructions of masculinity, obedience, and order is to assume a highly restricted view of violence. In the case of Spain and Chile, sexism, militarism, and nationalism functioned together to facilitate the creation of negative identities that were deemed corrupt and therefore less than human – that is, without bodily integrity or a legitimate claim to human rights.

I bring depth of analysis to the concept of militarized masculinity by illustrating how cinematographers and novelists in Spain and Chile present multiple ways of seeing the gendered dimensions of militarism and its relation to language and assault within and beyond the armed forces. They invite us to observe the main characteristics of the authoritarian agenda to militarize the social fabric through various incremental enforcement mechanisms. These include forced recruitment, military pageantry, widespread presence of civil patrols as permanent armed entities in communities, surveillance, the purging of military opposition, the inculcation of hierarchy, the repetition of dictums that equate militarism with patriotism, the normalization of a state of emergency as a way of maintaining order, the propagation of anti-democratic rhetoric, the burning of "subversive" books, the restructuring of universities, the humiliation of non-military men, the dissemination of stereotypes in the media, and the indoctrination of children through militarized discourse in textbooks, curricula, and other forms of socialization at school and home. Without these tactics, dictatorial regimes would cease to exist.

While I am guided by the valuable scholarship of historians and archival research, this book should not be read as a conventional historical study. It is an interdisciplinary work of feminist criticism that takes seriously the contribution of literature and film in provoking a deeper understanding of power and the perpetration of violence in connection with militarism and binary constructions of masculinity and femininity – that is, gender. Rather than strictly investigating testimonies of abuse and rape in prisons and clandestine torture centres, which has already been done, I put forward a broad definition of militarized masculinity through a feminist analysis of cultural production. My focus will concentrate on counter-hegemonic texts for their disruptive potential, but equally important is a critical investigation of media and other sources that create the tendency to see the world through a military lens.

Literature, Film, and Resistance

Resistance is commonly viewed as a physical act or a collective oppositional movement through strikes and other forms of public protest. But the refusal to obey authoritarian power comes in many forms, as the widely influential sociologist Gene Sharp (1928–2018) spells out in his writings on the weight of non-violent action to establish democracy in the face of authoritarianism. Methods range from the wearing of symbols, to the creation of caricatures, to economic boycotts, to mock funerals. Sharp never used the term *militarized masculinity* or explicitly discussed the role of literature and film as a form of resistance to the constructed warrior identity. However, anti-hegemonic art forms, and the feminist lens we use to analyse them, could be added to his globally instrumental list of 198 non-violent methods of resistance to war and tyranny.

"I write what I would never dare tell anyone" (Levi 184). This powerful quote is attributed to Primo Levi, the Italian author who survived the horrors of the Holocaust and documented his experiences in works like *If This Is a Man*, first published in 1947. His writing, like the works that I explore in this book, speaks to the power of literature and the importance of bearing witness to violence. The meanings people give to histories of state violence, as Lessie Jo Frazier puts it, "are transformed as they are rehabilitated and redeployed through multiple genres or containers of memory, such as songs, poetry, novels, and testimonies" (50). Writers may capture in words the nightmares that many readers will never know. Film-makers may hold an image so that we may contemplate its complexity. Both genres juxtapose contrasting experiences, upend our expectations, and raise a lantern to the dark corners of traumatic memories. These are among the many reasons that literature and film constitute the backbone of this book.

Narrative voice and perspective become crucial vehicles for writers and film-makers to probe learned behaviours like aggression and conformity.

In so doing, they prompt readers and viewers to see those behaviours anew. "The choice of the point(s) of view from which a story is told is arguably the most important single decision that the novelist has to make; for it fundamentally affects the way readers will respond, emotionally and morally, to the fictional characters and their actions," David Lodge writes in *The Art of Fiction* (26). Point of view, character development, interior monologue, narrating in different voices, irony, the rearrangement of syntax, repetition – these are all strategies that in the hands of astute writers and film-makers allow us to think in more nuanced ways about militarism, gender, and violence. Narrative structure constitutes another key strategy. Temporal shifts effectively underscore the process of remembering violence, as well as the relationship between memory and identity and the perpetual interjection of the past into the present.

Documentaries also transmit a point of view through narrative voice-over, interviews, the musical score, and dramatic reconstruction, all of which are carefully selected, edited, and pieced together to convey a message. To paraphrase Belinda Smaill in *The Documentary: Politics, Emotion, Culture*, where the expression of injured identities is concerned, documentary plays a small but important part in presenting avenues for imagining future possibilities of social transformation that further public debate (70). Viewing novels and films alongside non-fiction narrative and documentaries engenders a reflection on the parallels between the often-unrecognized strategies that communicate a critique of violence.

Polyphony or the inclusion of multiple viewpoints is a tool used by both novelists and film-makers to foreground complexity. By acknowledging the various perspectives at play, creators can explore the intersectionality of issues, highlighting how factors like race, class, and gender all intertwine. For instance, dominance becomes a key aspect of manhood, but how this has an impact on wealthy versus working-class boys varies. While wealthy boys are often encouraged to be assertive leaders, working-class boys might find themselves pressured towards physical displays of dominance. This difference can then influence how they view violence and their place in perpetuating it. The allure of weapons is also intertwined with militarization and social inequalities. Poverty can foster feelings of powerlessness, leading some to gravitate towards a hypermasculine militarized identity that seems to offer a path to respect that is otherwise unattainable. Furthermore, when a society ties a man's sense of worth to dominance over others, it creates a strong incentive and justification for cruelty.

The development of a critical theory of militarized masculinity requires an intersectional, interdisciplinary, and comparative approach.

I examine works produced by Spanish and Chilean writers and filmmakers over the last forty years (1981–2022). I include fiction and non-fiction films by Patricio Guzmán, Marcela Said, Lissette Orozco, Pilar Miró, Benito Zambrano, and Agustí Villaronga and a collaborative work by Jon Garaño, Aitor Arregi, and José Mari Goenaga. For the analysis of literature and creative non-fiction narrative, I investigate texts by Antonio Muñoz Molina, Nona Fernández, Alberto Méndez, Manuel Rivas, and Roberto Bolaño, as well as the graphic novels of Carlos Giménez. The films and novels under consideration provide rich material to explore how militarized masculinity exists on a gender spectrum with other masculinities.

Hegemonic masculinity is defined by R.W. Connell as "the maintenance of practices that institutionalize men's dominance over women and is constructed in relation to women and to subordinate masculinities" (*Gender and Power* 187–8). Hegemonic and militarized masculinity are not one and the same, but are not completely two either. Both involve assumptions about the naturalness of the patriarchal family, men's and women's "true natures," a division of gendered spheres, and the ultimate sign of manliness being dominance over women. Similarly, there is a homogenizing rejection of "complexity, plurality, inconsistency and ambiguity of subjectivity" (Mansfield 95). Nick Mansfield explains how this masculine norm is presented as inevitable: "Masculinity simultaneously advances and generalizes its priorities while concealing them" (96). Christopher Browning's acclaimed book *Ordinary Men* (1992) on Nazi perpetrators offers an example of this unconscious lack of attention to gender. While his study of Police Battalion 101 in the killing fields of Poland is compelling, it is limited to the extent that it disregards the social construction of masculinity and its performance of power. In Browning's conclusions about the "normal" middle-aged German man turned Nazi, he says nothing about the gendered expectations that contributed to coercive pressures to prove one's masculinity through physical strength, violence, and military rank. As a result, a deeper understanding of a range of matters like men's fear of castigation for cowardice, the existence of resistant and competing masculinities, and the unique processes that have shaped women perpetrators are all absent from the discussion.

Urgent is the need to elucidate "the language of gender in which the behavior of ordinary men is inscribed," as Stephen Haynes asserts. Following feminist scholars, Haynes links his own critique of Browning's blind spot to a wider problem: "Western discourse treats male experience as universal and ungendered … If women have been obscured from scholarly view by being relegated to the background of Western imagination, men have been distorted by being thrust into the foreground" (167). Responding to the problem of gender blindness is not merely a matter of style or methodology, as Haynes insists. It is necessary to gain a fuller picture of violence. Engaging with Spanish and Chilean novels and films enables me to unpack the conception of "ordinary" manhood and denaturalize the baked-in gendered expectations at its core. Only when we probe the learned normalization of violent masculinity and its link to militarism can we identify a unifying factor in the making of genocidal architects, rank-and-file perpetrators, and civilian bystanders.

By claiming that militarized masculinity was *integral*, not incidental, to acts of torture and mass killing during the Franco and Pinochet regimes, I am not suggesting that militarized masculinity was suddenly born with the installation of the dictatorships. Both regimes confidently glorified war and the militarized male at its core, but they strengthened established gender norms and ideas of the patriarchal family that the Second Republic and Popular Unity never truly overcame. Julie Shayne has written about the politics of gender and sexuality during the Allende years, arguing that despite the discourse of egalitarianism, socialist reform focused primarily on the male worker, while women were often supportive figures (mothers, daughters, wives). Citing the Chilean women's group Mujeres por la Vida, anthropologist Ximena Bunster explains how women mobilized in the early 1980s to address not only the human rights violations of Pinochet's government but also the shortcomings of the men in their own democratic parties ("Watch Out" 486).

Even earlier, trailblazing Chilean sociologist Julieta Kirkwood spearheaded organizations to demand transformation in power relations in the public domain and in interpersonal relations at home. But she was not the first; Chile already had a long history of feminist actors including Amanda Labarca (1886–1975). Fast-forward to present-day Chile, and the feminist collective LasTesis continues the hard work of its feminist antecedents. As Gwynn Thomas maintains, Chile's centre-left governments have a mixed record in promoting gender equality and LGBTQ rights, but they made "gradual progress, particularly in terms of legal reforms around violence against women and in improving women's socioeconomic position" (116). In the collective's words, the struggle goes on against "the darkest and most obsolete hate speech" of the right, but also the "machitos of the left" (*Set Fear on Fire*, 26–9). The collective calls out their double standard and denounces the false choice between class struggle and feminism as a short-sighted zero-sum view of the world. For this younger generation of feminists, the aspirant Che

Guevaras "can shove their anti-government, anti-systemic discourse wherever they want, because that incongruence has long been unacceptable" (29).

As Gina Herrmann illustrates in "Voices of the Vanquished: Leftist Women and the Spanish Civil War," that was also the case in Spain: "the social conservatism of the left circumscribed, to varying degrees, the potential for female political agency" (15). If some on the left posed a challenge to the dogged persistence of conservative gender relations and homophobia, still, leftist political parties and opposition groups largely remained patriarchal and heteronormative. In practice, this meant that most organizations ended up maintaining, albeit inadvertently, conventional norms and, by extension, hindering a more comprehensive move towards female empowerment. Pointing out this contradiction hardly invalidates attempts on the left to upend dominant forms of politics and culture; rather, it is a recognition of the pervasiveness of patriarchal ideology that frames men as political leaders and women as exclusively mothers and wives.

Roberto Bolaño, whose target was not only right-wing nationalism but also the hypocrisy of the left, often noted this incongruency in his fiction and non-fiction. In the story "Mauricio ('The Eye') Silva," he writes about a group of Chileans in exile who find sheer pleasure in denigrating gay men: "In spite of their left-wing convictions, when it came to sexuality, they reacted just like their enemies on the right, who had become the new masters of Chile" (*Last Evenings on Earth* 17). Likewise, Pedro Lemebel challenged the oppressive militarized masculine ideal that characterized both the right and the left. In *My Tender Matador*, Lemebel depicts the experience of a transgender woman in Pinochet's Chile among members of the Marxist-Leninist Manuel Rodríguez Patriotic Front. One passage succinctly captures the invisibility of trans and queer people in the anti-Pinochet resistance. As Queen (the protagonist) contemplates leaving Chile, she knows that her sorrow will be ignored because "a fairy's tears have no identification, no color, no taste; they have never watered any garden of illusions" (154). Carl Fischer is keen to observe in *Queering the Chilean Way* that Lemebel poignantly brings out the atrocities of the right, as well as the sexist, homophobic, and transphobic betrayals committed by the left. More on this later.

Emphasizing the centrality of militarized masculinity in acts of violence, furthermore, does not reduce normative masculinity (cisgender and heterosexual) to a singular violent identity. Gender, as a social and cultural construction, is performative, multiple, relational, and dynamic as it shifts over time. The idea is not to conflate normative and militarized masculinity; rather, it is to trace the threads between these masculinities and to spotlight acts of resistance. As Enloe explains, militarism and patriarchy are systems of ideas and practices in which we all participate to some degree. As they permeate politics and popular culture (movies, slang, toys, video games, camouflage, etc.), war and violence are normalized or de-normalized. Concurring with Enloe, I argue that to embrace militarized masculinity requires one not to wear a uniform but to adopt a certain world view. If we only look to militaries to understand military culture, we see a partial picture. In fact, some of the military's most fervent proponents are civilians, and many are women. The selection of authors and film-makers in this book demonstrates that just as militarism is not an entirely male domain, anti-militarism and resistance to toxic masculinity are not inherently female endeavours.

A feminist comparison of Spain's and Chile's histories of dictatorial violence allows us to track the similarities and differences between patriarchal norms, the social engineering of identities, and their relationship to militarism, state terror, genocidal violence, and economic exploitation. As Rosa Luxemburg observed, militarism itself is deeply intertwined with processes of self-expansion of wealth, serving a "very definitive function in the history of capital, accompanying as it does every historical phase of accumulation" (130). Recognizing, with Luxemburg, the historical use of militarism to subjugate colonies and dismantle social structures for resource appropriation, this book investigates the multifaceted nature of these relationships. I extend this understanding to contexts after Luxemburg's assassination by Freikorps paramilitaries in 1919, examining how such processes unfold in relation to gender. This involves addressing specific dimensions of violence, including the gendered socialization of boys under dictatorial rule, the nexus between misogynistic ideology and war, the sexualized torture of political detainees, civilian complicity and collaboration in politicide, and the enduring traumas associated with mandatory military service. Although taking on all these topics might seem overly ambitious, I explain how they are interwoven. To deal with them separately is to perpetuate the inability to associate pressing problems.

Forging New Paths

Many cultural critics have written about the ways in which literature and film represent traumatic memories and play a part in the ongoing debates about the legacies of the dictatorships in Chile and Spain. Some critics have looked at the intersections of gender and violence in the context of the Franco and Pinochet regimes, albeit separately. Particularly fruitful for my own thinking about the case of Spain has been the work of historians and cultural critics like Jo Labanyi, Mary Nash, Helen Graham,

Gina Herrmann, Cristina Moreiras Menor, and Paul Preston. For Latin America, I have taken cues from Jean Franco, Elizabeth Jelin, Diana Taylor, Michael Lazzara, Nelly Richard, and Rita Segato. In *Cruel Modernity* Jean Franco explores testimonies by victims and perpetrators of torture and uses the term *extreme masculinity* to describe a constructed gender identity that plays a role in the making of violence (15). She shows why it is important to expose the bonds between misogyny, extreme masculinity, and the practice of rape as a form of torture. In deciding to use the adjective *militarized* rather than *extreme*, I underscore the link between militarism and violent masculinity. Before entering the armed forces, men are already exposed to the myth that equates "real" masculinity with "hardness." After they enter the domain of uniformed men, that myth becomes all-consuming under the pressure of combat training, competition, conformity, and comradeship. As such, we must comprehend the significance of the process of militarization in the perpetration of mass atrocity crimes.

My intention is to provide the first book-length comparative treatment of militarized masculinity in terms of its typical features, from the subtle to the obvious, as well as its depiction in two interconnected historical and cultural contexts: Spain and Chile. Examining recent and under-explored fiction and creative non-fiction narrative as well as film with new interpretive tools allows me to capture the gendered complexities of militarism under Franco and Pinochet, and additionally to provide a definition of a concept that applies to other contexts. Without collapsing difference, the arguments in this book dialogue with anti-imperialist critiques by scholars such as Judith Butler, Cynthia Cockburn, Sara Ahmed, and Chandra Mohanty among others. Their responses to the hypermasculinity of the US army and its workings in the perpetration of abuse globally have provided insight for my analysis. In its interdisciplinary and transnational approach, *Militarized Masculinity* charts common patriarchal discourses, strategies of militarization, and torture techniques that cut across regional and historical specificity.

Through contextualized analysis of works by well-known and emerging writers and film-makers, I seek to counteract the normalization of militarized masculinity. I distinguish between strategies that resist the ideological pillars that safeguarded dictatorial rule in Spain and Chile and those that continue to shape belief systems today. Instead of reinforcing the view of rape and other acts of gendered humiliation as "other," I expose their pervasiveness, recasting them as integral in what Cockburn calls a "continuum of violence" ("Don't Talk"). They allow me to make the larger claim that although rape, harassment, and femicide exist outside military institutions, they occur inside patriarchal cultures that embrace the militaristic model of masculinity. As Ian

Winchester puts it, "Militaries are not hermetically sealed from society, and in modern history, militarized masculinities have been integral to conditioning general cultural and societal conceptions of masculinity" (233). Bound together, toxic civilian masculinity and militarized masculinity feed each other on a scale that typically goes unnoticed.

Some novels and films in this corpus complicate the common perception that exclusively equates gendered abuse with women. By listening to men's testimonies of torture, we might not only acknowledge the existence of male-on-male sexual abuse but also interpret the misogynist and homophobic notions in its development. Militarized masculinity harms both the men that become victims of violence and those who are inducted into organized militaristic culture. Literary representations of perpetrators can shed light on the conflict between hypermasculine expectations of the ideal militarized male and the real experience of vulnerability, fear, and shame felt by men. Conversely, they may also reveal the torment that can follow the reaching of such expectations through violence.

Other authors and film-makers turn to the ways that non-conforming men and boys are dehumanized for not performing their presumed role in patriarchal militarized society. Jokes are an inherent aspect of the system of disciplinary enforcement. Cruel laughter and other forms of ridicule serve to intimidate, belittle, and extinguish empathy in the process.

A complete picture of militarized masculinity necessitates not just the highlighting of this negative dynamic but also an examination of counter-narratives. Although research on military opposition to abuse is lacking (Kelly 61), films, novels, and memoirs offer valuable insights into non-violent masculinities. When we explore that cultural terrain, we can appreciate how some recruits have struggled to make sense of their identities during obligatory military service. In the memoir *Ardor guerrero*, Antonio Muñoz Molina gives us a complex picture of the ways in which militarized masculinity is embraced or rejected. My chapter on that memoir sharpens our vision of the resemblance between military barracks and prisons and therefore adds to our conception of Michel Foucault's metaphor of the panopticon and the forming of regulated "docile" bodies. Since Foucault did not have a comprehensive theory on the military, this book makes inroads into his critique of power relations and disciplinary practices that are exercised through oppressive structures and institutions. Whereas Foucault focused on how these techniques are embedded in prisons and hospitals, this study examines how disciplinary power operates in the military, focusing on the normalization of militarized masculinity through constant observation to ensure compliance. I explore how the ideology of militarism permeates not only military academies and barracks but also civilian schools where students must demonstrate patriotism and pride through conformity and hostility towards the nation's enemies. Since they never know when they are being watched, students monitor themselves and their fellow classmates.

An awareness of the ties between militarized masculinity and misogyny also enriches our understanding of dictatorial and genocidal violence. Aptly described by Jack Holland as "the oldest prejudice" (7), misogyny has "profoundly shaped our consciousness" and institutions, not the least of which involve the military. Instead of ascribing to the conventional definition of misogyny as the hatred of women, I draw from Kate Manne's theory of misogyny in *Down Girl*. Interpreting literature and film through a nuance-revealing lens sheds light on the distinction between sexism as a set of beliefs and misogyny as an enforcement mechanism. We see how the contempt for women surfaces as an act of control when women depart from the gender expectations that keep them beneath men. Militarized masculinity enforces misogyny and vice versa. The pressure to dominate women and other men breeds a hatred of feminism, while making it harder for others to intervene when they see sexism happening. The subordination of women makes men feel they must constantly prove their masculinity through stereotypical behaviours and reject any expression of female autonomy, agency, or anger.

Representations of militarized violence, misogyny, and torture run the risk of reinserting exploitive modes that capitalize on suffering through gratuitous scenes of rape, nudity, and mutilation. The novels and films that I discuss effectively go against such exploitive modes and what Judith Butler calls the restricted "frames of war" that disallow the recognition of exclusionary and destructive institutions in the fuelling of hostilities. Butler wants "to consider the way in which suffering is presented to us, and how that presentation affects our responsiveness" (*Frames of War* 63). The portrayals that I have selected de-normalize the narratives that structure our understanding of violence. Through unsettling perspectives they interrupt the unconscious repetition of norms originating in patriarchal and militaristic culture that result in the acceptance of violence. They help us perceive the limiting scope that shrinks our expectations of what could be non-violent coexistence.

Transatlantic Connections

The transatlantic comparative approach teases out the parallels between histories and their representations that would not be visible if they were studied from an exclusively nationalist perspective. Kirsten Weld, a historian who has documented the links between

Franco and Pinochet, explains how Chilean conservative political parties closely watched the Spanish Civil War and hoped that the Nationalist militarized efforts would bring an end to the progressive agenda of the Second Republic. Weld argues that "the Falangist strain of Spain's insurrectionary coalition had an explicitly transnational dimension, encouraging the strengthening of cultural ties between Spain and erstwhile colonies and appealing, in a clearly racialized fashion, to those Latin Americans who defined their heritage as peninsular" (84). Later, during the 1970s, Pinochet looked nostalgically to the Franco regime as a model authoritarian corporative state. As Weld observes, "The Civil War – or at least one interpretation of it, in which the military had purged Spain of communism in a kind of Christian reconquest – was a key component of the paradigm that some anti–Salvador Allende revanchists used to understand their world" (77). John Bawden also emphasizes this association in his book *The Pinochet Generation*: "In the 1980s Nicanor Díaz said that Generals Roberto Viaux and Augusto Pinochet – classmates of his at the Military Academy from 1933–1936 – both wanted to be 'the Franco of Chile'" (48).

One of the forerunners to compare Spain and Chile was Felipe Agüero in his book *Soldiers, Civilians, and Democracy: Post-Franco Spain in Comparative Perspective*. By putting Spain and Chile in a comparative framework (along with other Latin American and Southern European post-authoritarian nations), Agüero recognizes the similarities between them but also the key differences. He emphasizes the important stabilizing role of civilian leadership in Spain's transition to democracy, which he contrasts with its Latin American counterparts. Agüero's comparative study resists the impulse to homologize, while appreciating the parallels and intersections between contexts. Martín-Estudillo and Ampuero take a similar approach in *Post-Authoritarian Cultures: Spain and Latin America's Southern Cone*. Indeed, a useful comparison does neither flatten difference nor simply yield a series of anecdotal historical and ideological coincidences. A constructive comparison produces what the editors of *The Iberian and Latin American Transatlantic Studies Reader* envision as a meaningful exploration of patterns, relations, configurations, contexts, and texts that challenge the confines of national or state boundaries (Enjuto Rangel et al. 9). One of those patterns involves a nostalgic right-wing discourse that mythologized the military and served to subjugate the political left in Spain and Chile.

As Leith Passmore observes, "The groundwork for an understanding of the coup as the salvation of the patria (fatherland) from ruin and civil war was set in the rhetorical buildup to September 11, 1973. After the coup, the military junta – using heavy-handed symbolism and aided by a controlled media – established salvation as the dominant narrative" (*Wars* 6). In *El peso de la noche: Nuestra frágil fortaleza histórica*, historian Alfredo Jocelyn-Holt Letelier describes how the Pinochet regime also evoked the strong-handed state influenced by Diego Portales (1793–1837), the conservative authoritarian Chilean minister of the interior and statesman. Portales and his successors governed through the 1860s, frequently enforcing violent repression to control the opposition. Fast-forward to the 1970s when Pinochet revived Portales along with Franco and eliminated the voices of constitutionalists like General René Schneider, General Carlos Prats, and General Alberto Bachelet who believed in the apolitical role of the armed forces and firmly opposed military interference in the democratic process. A nostalgic interpretation of the Portalian state and the Franco regime became one of the unifying tools to assuage the uneasy alliance between the landed elite, the military, the technocrats, and the powerful Opus Dei. As in the case of Spain, a disdain for the left outweighed power struggles and resentments among groups on the right.

Upon the Spanish dictator's death on 20 November 1975, Pinochet travelled to Madrid and was received by King Juan Carlos and representatives of the right-wing newspaper *Pueblo*. In an interview he stated, "I came to Spain because I wanted to pay tribute to a man who also fought against communism." The newspaper article brings out the alignment between the monarchy and the Spanish and Chilean military dictatorships, as well as the intersections between political agendas and nostalgic discourses. Pinochet was quoted as stating: "If the Communists, who always lurk in the shadows, do not cause problems, Spain will achieve great goals and once again be a great country as it was in the past" (*Pueblo*, 24 November 1975). One year later, in 1976, Pinochet explained to the former US secretary of state Henry Kissinger that the Chilean regime was a participant in a long-term transatlantic struggle: "It is a further stage of the same conflict which erupted into the Spanish Civil War" (Weld, 78).

Francoist thought also played an influential role in the development of the political ideology of Jaime Guzmán, one of Pinochet's closest advisers and author of Chile's 1980 constitution, which gave the armed forces a "tutelary role" over national security, granting them the authority to intervene in political affairs if they deemed it necessary. "Gremialismo, Guzmán's philosophy turned political movement, was central to the anti–Salvador Allende opposition and explicitly rooted in the military nationalism, conservative Catholic social thought, and mythology of a glorious Hispanic cultural inheritance that had undergirded the Nationalist uprising and that Franco had used to legitimate his rule" (Weld, 78). As Guzmán played a pivotal role in the construction of neoliberal ideology in Chile, it is important to also note, as Michael Lazzara does in the book *Civil Obedience: Complicity and Complacency in Chile since Pinochet*, that another one of Guzmán's key influences was José Antonio Primo de Rivera, founder of the Spanish fascist party the Falange. His charismatic militarism and actions – specifically, his promotion of divisive symbols, dehumanization, and organized violence – were critical factors in the lead-up to mass political killings in Spain. He had a profound and far-reaching impact on the radical right in Latin America. "Such early influences resulted in a special mixture of conservative Catholicism and right-wing ideology that would lead Guzmán to reject the tenets of Liberation Theology that had taken root throughout Latin America in the 1960s" (59).

The focus on heteronormativity is also crucial when examining the similar nostalgic discourses of Spain and Chile. In her book-length essay *Courtship Customs in Postwar Spain*, Spanish novelist Carmen Martín Gaite (1925–2000) renders visible the nostalgia that shaped Spain's post-war political discourse and served to define perceptions of family, gender, and sexuality. She cites Franco's 1945 speech that venerated Spain's "blessed backwardness," in which he proclaimed, "Our revolution made it possible for Spain to return to her true essence" (21). Franco sought to "restore" traditional Catholic patriarchal values by eliminating divorce, and religious and political freedoms, which he exclaimed were things of "the reds," a pejorative term for anyone associated with the political left wing. The vindication of "backwardness" also unconvincingly justified Spain's economic crisis that disproportionately affected the working class.

The Franco regime's negative reading of modernity was inconsistent. To paraphrase Labanyi, the wealthy landowners, the Catholic Church, and the monarchists embraced tradition and religion. Dissimilarly, the Falange, industrialists, and bankers tended to advocate for social modernization within totalitarian structures, inspired by Italian fascism (Labanyi, "Memory" 92). These right-wing groups came together through their hostility towards the Second Republic's agenda to "better the economic and legal positions of the working classes and women" (92). If the left lacked congruence on women's rights and held onto sexist and homophobic views of the family, supporters of the Franco regime brazenly cultivated patriarchal attitudes that ensured the militarized male's dominance over women, children, and non-heteronormative men.

The echoes of the Spanish fascist discourse and practice in Chile are hard to ignore. The consolidators of the Pinochet regime compared the nation under Allende's Popular Unity to a diseased body, sick from the foreign infection of Marxism. At the same time, they depicted the nation as a family in crisis that required the leadership of a strong father figure who would return health to Chile's progeny. These metaphors came together in a moralizing story, as Alice Nelson observes: the regime's narrative emphasized the "sacred" military-technocratic mission "to purge Chilean society of the base temptations of the Allende period, in order to restore Chile to its pristine spiritual grandeur supposedly existent before the 'fall'" (40). Aspects of modernity, like social change and individual freedom, became synonymous with a corrupted female body (i.e., Eve) in need of salvation. The comparison of Allende's democratic socialism and humanity's fall from grace reflects the misogynistic and anti-democratic character of the regime. The subordinate and self-sacrificing maternal figure is the flip side to the same coin. So long as women followed traditional female roles, including those of housewife, servant, nurse, schoolteacher, and mother, they were authentic and worthy of the being called *chilena*.

By seizing the right to delineate the nation and gender roles, the military insurrectionists in Spain and Chile justified the purging of non-conformist, revolutionary women who were masculinized through the regimes' rhetoric while dissident men were conversely degraded as "unmanly" or *maricón*, a pejorative for homosexual. Diana Taylor explains a similar process in Argentina where non-conforming and single (non-military) men were "grouped together in a feminized zone of deviancy" (40). Homosexuality, as a reality rather than a metaphor for weakness, was treated as a vile aberration and a direct threat to the traditional family. Both cases exemplify Eve Sedgwick's contention that the rules and regulations that oppress women are products of the same patriarchal system that suppresses homosexuality ("Between Men" 2437).

This gendered discourse resonated strongly in Chile with the neo-fascist paramilitary group Patria y Libertad (Fatherland and Liberty), which emerged as a nationalist faction calling for the return of a caudillo state. Like the Falange in Spain, Patria y Libertad believed in a powerful patriarchal state with a strong executive in command. It also had in common a need for scapegoat enemies seen in its hatred of communism, socialism, and feminism. The group had an appeal among some middle- and working-class men who were discontented and disenfranchised. If the Movimiento de Izquierda Revolucionaria (MIR, Revolutionary Left Movement) aimed to create class consciousness and prompt structural, economic, and cultural change, Patria y Libertad emphasized the counter-revolutionary language of authoritarian patriotism and tradition (Ensalaco 19). This vocabulary, coupled with Patria y Libertad's clandestine operations of infrastructure sabotage, instilled fear and radicalized many Chileans, convincing them of the need to "return" to order and support military intervention. The Chilean paramilitary was one of the many groups that contributed to the erosion of the democratically elected Popular Unity party. Later, the official Secretaría Nacional de la Juventud, 1973–91; National Secretariat for Youth) became the official organization created under the Pinochet regime to cultivate a positive attitude towards the armed forces. In *Los más ordenaditos. Fascismo y juventud en la dictadura de Pinochet*, Yanko González Cangas brings out the influence of the Spanish fascist youth on their right-wing Chilean counterparts.

In 1974 a Chilean sociologist living in exile anonymously penned a lucid essay that recorded the ideological influences of Chile's counter-revolution. The essay, titled "The Military as Agent of a Fascist Revolution" and printed in a dossier of documents compiled by Gary MacEóin at IDOC (International Documentation), states: "The associated specters of external intervention and internal subversion, reinforced by the international implications of McCarthyism in the United States, set the terms of the Chilean military's understanding of its role" (MacEóin 20). That role was to be an instrument and shaper of an anti-communist order characterized by hierarchy and the use of state-sanctioned force to maintain lawful behaviour as defined by the military regime. How that was accomplished is at the heart of this book, but journalist Philippe Labreveux gave us some clues as early as 1974. Published in *Le Monde* and reproduced in the IDOC dossier, Labreveux reported that influential generals and right-wing civilians who were hostile to Allende sought to prevent constitutionalist neutrality among the officer corps. Strategies included immersive schooling in anti-Marxist propaganda and training in counter-insurgency tactics at special bases in the United States and Panama (MacEóin 23). That article also points to a façade of military unity and emphasizes attempts made by figures like General Prats and General Schneider to respect the democratically elected socialist government. Both generals were assassinated. As Labreveux remarks, "The breach of the Constitution and the downfall of the Allende government was certainly opposed by elements within the armed forces, which had to be, and were, neutralized" (MacEóin 25).

In Spain and Chile national security and unity became a major justification for the military coups and later a maxim for ongoing self-legitimization. The Spanish insurrectionists claimed that the Republican government posed a grave danger to the nation by aligning itself with the Soviet Union, and the Chilean military insurgents argued that Allende's socialist government created economic chaos and anarchy. Both provided a convenient mask for Cold War power struggles and a cudgel against the democratic process. By painting the left-leaning governments as puppets of the Soviet Union and themselves as the sole protectors against anti-patriotic threats, the military leaders justified their own strong-arm takeovers. They also sought to rationalize the military's actions by claiming the illegitimacy of the previous governments led by the Popular Unity and the Popular Front.

Wearing military uniforms in public was a defining characteristic that Franco and Pinochet shared. Their military-style dress changed over time, showing their long history with that institution and signalling the degree to which it shaped their lives from youth in military academies to death. Just before Pinochet was born in 1915, Franco was transferred to Spanish Morocco where he gained combat experience and status in the Spanish Army of Africa. The image of Franco dressed in a military tunic with decorations befitting his high rank must have deeply impressed Pinochet who graduated from the Chilean Army War Academy in the 1930s. He would later become commander-in-chief of the Chilean army and don uniforms based on Prussian styles, featuring elements like spiked helmets and caps with visors.

Dressing in uniform played a key part in a larger performance of power, which was put on show in military marches and salutations and with combat vehicles, gatherings, grandiose speeches, and masses. Military attire codified the vigour of the patriarchal system and the military establishment's institutional power. Franco and Pinochet, by means of badges and decorations, visually manifested their pre-eminence over civilians and the rank and file, signifying accomplishments rooted in domination. It was a conscious choice indicative of their absolute identification with the armed forces and the highest rank they held within that hierarchy. It was a non-verbal statement that conveyed the politics of antipolitics. These displays of militarized masculinity were photographed and regularly disseminated in news outlets like the fascist *Arriba*, and *El Mercurio*, which became instruments of the armed forces. Such photographs revealed that the spectacle of military pomp and ceremony was a male-dominated affair, with women positioned as onlookers or simply out of view. Virginia Woolf eloquently addressed these very points in *Three Guineas*, a work I will revisit later.

The Post-Dictatorial Spain–Chile Nexus

When one traces the relationship between Spain and Chile, Pinochet's arrest stands out as another key moment of connection. In early 1998, after a referendum, Pinochet stepped down as commander-in-chief and became senator for life; later that year, in London, he was arrested on a Spanish warrant regarding charges of genocide and torture of Spanish nationals in Chile. Among the duelling actors in the Pinochet case were Spanish judge Baltazar Garzón, Valencian attorney Joan Garcés (one of Allende's former advisers), and José María Aznar, conservative prime minister from 1996 to 2004 and a former fascist youth. Aznar had the choice of either sympathizing with Pinochet and allying himself with the ex-dictator's wealthy Chilean business brotherhood or endorsing Garzón's petition for Pinochet's extradition to Spain, an appeal with strong Spanish support, particularly within the Partido Socialista de Chile (PSOE, Socialist Party of Chile).

Strengthening ties between the Spanish and the Chilean right, Aznar ultimately discouraged Pinochet's extradition and trial. Despite Aznar's position, Pinochet was indicted in October 1998 and placed under house arrest in England for a year and a half before being released to return to Chile in 2000. Although he was summarily charged in Chile by Judge Juan Guzmán Tapia, he died before any conviction, in 2006. Like in Spain after Franco's death in 1975, Pinochet's passing gave rise to a sense of sorrow in some parts of Chile, while elsewhere people marked the moment with celebrations. In Spain over the following decade Judge Garzón would turn his attention to Franco-era crimes until conserva-tive leaders suspended him from judicial activity in 2011 amid heated debates surrounding Spain's amnesty law.

The legal challenges of this transnational case and the disillusionment that they brought to the survivors are mapped in Luis Martín Cabrera's *Radical Justice: Spain and the Southern Cone beyond Market and State*. Written as the events were unfolding, Martín Cabrea's book reflects on popular culture, including the political documentaries of Patricio Guzmán and the detective fiction of Roberto Bolaño. He sees them as "a mode of response" to "a series of silences, rumors, half-truths, and even denial regarding acts of violence committed by terrorist states on both sides of the Atlantic" (3). The interconnected topics of militarism and masculinity never come up, but Martín Cabrera's valuable comparative study of impunity leaves no doubt about the relevance of the Spain-Chile comparison.

Going beyond these mentioned transatlantic connections, which I also explained in my previous book *Unsettling Nostalgia in Spain and Chile*, here I bridge boundaries between Spain and Chile to facilitate an understanding of militarized masculinity and the social conditioning that perpetuates patterns of violence and the acceptance of militarism. What is the nature and function of militarized masculinity inside the armed forces, and how has this aggressive gender construct been at the centre of the enactment of violence both within the barracks and outside their boundaries? How can militarized violence occur even in the absence of military structures? The Spain-Chile juxtaposition encourages reflection on related processes of conformity and collaboration, as well as the paradox between developments in human rights after the military dictatorships and the persistence of social policing, rape, and the tacit approval of violence. A heightened awareness of the multiple phases of mass atrocity crimes and the underlying factors that shape them contributes to larger efforts to counter the single-minded notion that "hard" force is the only effective response to political conflict.

The Chapters

By organizing the chapters thematically rather than chronologically, I draw out common threads, broadening and webbing together the many facets of militarized patriarchal systems. Chapter 1 offers a theoretical framework that goes beyond the introduction. It lays a foundation of language and descriptions that distil the underpinnings of violence. I use several of Roberto Bolaño's short texts to shine a light on the glorification of male authority over women and children, the murderous defence of heteronormativity, the cold rationalization of armed intervention to resolve social unrest, and the veneration of bloodshed in war. I conclude with a reflection on the ongoing problem of violence that makes this examination of militarized masculinity still relevant today.

Chapter 2, titled "Boot-Camp Brutality," illustrates the making of militarized masculinity through various social processes including obligatory military service. First, I focus on the Spanish writer Antonio Muñoz Molina and his memoir of conscription in Spain, titled *Ardor guerrero* (first published in 1995). By leading with an analysis of Muñoz Molina's memories of boot camp and beyond, I explore the initiation and conditioning tactics used to train soldiers. The analysis makes clear the link between militarism, gender norms, and the use of violent force. After discussing the most relevant aspects of *Ardor guerrero*, I turn to traumatic memories of conscription in Chile under Pinochet and draw a link between the methods of military socialization that created perpetrators of violence. Although conscription was instrumental, I also explain how the military camps were not the only site for combative conditioning. By discussing *El mocito* (*The Young Butler*) directed by Marcela Said and Jean de Certeau, I argue that it is necessary to gain a panoramic view of military culture that goes beyond an analysis of the military institution itself. My analysis tracks down the links between civilian and military violence and throws into relief the leading role that gender plays in both.

In chapter 3, titled "Perpetrator Memory and Masculinity," I offer insight into the ways that literature might make a meaningful statement about the torment that afflicts rank-and-file perpetrators. In a transatlantic framework I compare Nona Fernández's *La dimensión desconocida* (2017; *The Twilight Zone*, 2021) to Manuel Rivas's *El lápiz del carpintero* (1998; *The Carpenter's Pencil*, 2000) and Alberto Méndez's *Los girasoles ciegos* (2004; *The Blind Sunflowers*, 2008). Fernández's creative nonfiction text follows the author as she tries to interpret the testimony of a former military conscript who, amid the dictatorship, gave a public account of the covert raids and executions in which he participated.

With Fernández's book in mind, I draw out common threads in *The Carpenter's Pencil*, a novel set in Galicia during the Spanish Civil War (1936–9) and the post-Franco present. I pay particular attention to the characterization of a prison guard for Franco's fascist forces, who personifies the victors but transmits a discourse of defeat. Through his confessions, readers learn that he executed a Republican painter and suffers from the haunting traumas of a perpetrator's past. Finally, I turn to Alberto Méndez's hybrid novel *The Blind Sunflowers*. The book encompasses four interconnected stories of "defeats" that took place between 1936 and 1942. Méndez's portrayal of a Nationalist deserter in the first story asks readers to consider how practitioners of cruelty might also suffer from the hostile forms of masculinity to which they feel obligated to conform. The parallels between these seemingly disparate texts are striking. By comparing the works of Fernández, Rivas, and Méndez, I show how writers complicate the victim-perpetrator binary and wrestle with the ramifications of militarized masculinity on the regimes' henchmen.

Chapter 4, titled "Militarizing Children under Franco and Pinochet," provides a comparative analysis of childhood memories of the Franco and Pinochet regimes to understand better the relationship between gender socialization, militarized masculinity, and violence. For Spain, I analyse the autobiographical visual narratives *Todo Paracuellos* and *Todo Barrio*, first released in 1981 during the transition to democracy and republished twenty-five years later during Spain's memory boom (2007; translated into English in 2016). This grim series by Carlos Giménez was inspired by the author's lived experience in an orphanage managed by the Auxilio Social (Social Aid). Established in 1936 with the patronage of the women's branch of the Spanish Fascist Party, the Auxilio became a site of indoctrination for children abandoned as a consequence of the right-wing military coup and the class inequalities at the heart of the conflict. I place this graphic novel in dialogue with Nona Fernández's creative non-fiction life narrative *Space Invaders* (2013, English 2019). Born in early 1970s Chile, the writer explores her own schoolday memories of growing up under the watchful gaze of the Pinochet dictatorship. She interweaves recollections of the regime's discourse of national security alongside nightmares of collective terror. Fernández thus subverts the myth that militarization provided security and the antidote to social upheaval.

Both Giménez and Fernández draw our attention to a continuum of violence by representing emotionally alienating spaces in which religious and military figures instil fear in children through militaristic language and the constant threat of draconian forms of punishment for transgressing the rules and regulations of the state. They redefine children's experiences of militarism by rendering visible the gender formations that the Franco and Pinochet regimes imposed through intersecting institutions (education, religion, military, media). These works allow us to understand better how the enforcement of gender norms was pivotal in the creation of militarized states. They are examples of how autobiographical narrative in its many forms can expose the institutions that sustained militarized masculinity within the construction of an ultra-Catholic, misogynist, and homophobic national identity.

Chapter 5, "Militarized Masculinity, Misogyny, and Mass in Spain and Chile," underscores the role of religious doctrine and misogynist myths in the perpetration and justification of militarized violence in Spain and Chile. First, I return to Mendéz's *Blind Sunflowers* to examine the ways in which it elucidates the regime's use of gendered dogma as a weapon to enforce the supremacy of the militarized male. I focus on the last story, which is set in Madrid in 1942 and revolves around a family of four living in fear of reprisal for its support of the republic. The chief militarized figure is a Catholic schoolteacher and former fascist soldier who attempts to indoctrinate the family's son and later rape his mother. I trace the links between Méndez's story and Roberto Bolaño's *Nocturno de Chile* (2000; *By Night in Chile*, 2003), a short novel that consists of a monologue by a priest who mingled with ultra-right-wing writers under Pinochet and secretly taught military generals about Marxism for counter-intelligence.

What these stories have distinctly in common is the narrative voice of a tormented Catholic collaborator. Both writers use that perspective to explore the justifications of dictatorial violence shaped by religious, military, and patriarchal discourse. The comparison also brings out the Janus-faced nature of misogyny. The same misogyny that fuels attacks on women who challenge power also drives their systematic removal from view. It is what Manne calls "herasure" (209). Unlike Méndez's militarized priest for whom the female body becomes a sexualized obsession, women are mostly nameless and absent for Bolaño's protagonist. The juxtaposition thus enables a deeper awareness of misogynist logic whereby women either are seen as threatening or are unseen. Their agency, creative capacity, and complexity are denied in both cases. By comparing these apparently different texts, this chapter adds new breadth to our understanding of the ties between masculinity, militarism, and the misogynistic vision of Christianity. It shows how these played a role in the broader goal of internal colonization in Spain and Chile, which meant the domination over or exclusion of women and the restoration of the hegemony of the military, the Catholic Church, and the economic elites.

Chapter 6, "Cinematic Scenes of Gendered Torture and Resistance in Spain," compares three narrative films that depict torture in Spain to demonstrate how militarized masculinity shaped interrogation and prison violence. *Crimen en Cuenca* (*Crime in Cuenca*, 1981) by Pilar Miró centres on the alleged murder of a shepherd in the province of Cuenca in 1910. Based on a real account, the film-maker reconstructs the systematic torture of two anarchist tenant farmers who were falsely accused of the crime by powerful oligarchs. Although the film is set in the pre-Franco past and was produced after the transition to democracy, Miró's explicit depiction of interrogation enraged authorities, who banned the film and threatened the film-maker with a court martial for insulting the civil guard. The inclusion of this film allows me to delineate a longer trajectory of torture and its legitimization in the regime's wake. Another film that deals directly with Francoist post-war reprisals is *La trinchera infinita* (*The Endless Trench*, 2019) by Jon Garaño, Aitor Arregi, and José Mari Goenaga. It journeys into the stories of men who supported the republic, were driven into hiding during the civil war, and then were forced to live underground as *topos* (moles) during the dictatorship.

In contrast with these two films that signal the impossibility of resistance within militarized culture, I deal with Benito Zambrano's adaptation of the novel *La voz dormida* (*The Sleeping Voice*, 2011) by Dulce Chacón. The film opens viewers to the world of female political prisoners in Franco's Spain. Blending fact and fiction, the film-maker stages gruesome interrogation scenes that stress the severity of the regime's sustained attempt to fracture and neutralize guerrilla bands. However, equally important is the principled resistance of the women detainees. The film presents a creative challenge to militarized masculinity through the female protagonists who overturn the regime's logic. Rather than reinscribe the patriarchal notion of women as submissive objects of male hostility, Zambrano characterizes them as politically engaged actors struggling against fascist forms of government and culture. Taken together, these films widen the audience's perception of torture by illuminating the context in which it emerges, and also how it is defied.

In chapter 7, "Torture and the Language of Subjugation in Chilean Documentary," I analyse the underpinnings of torture through an analysis of four documentaries: Patricio Guzmán's *The Pinochet Case* and *My Imaginary Country* , Marcela Said's *I Love Pinochet*, and Lissette Orozco's *Adriana's Pact*. These documentaries allow me to discuss how torture is shaped by wide-reaching systems of power that celebrate male domination and sanction militarized tactics of social policing. *The Pinochet Case* foregrounds the victims whose stories provide a window into the gendered ideologies and sexual core that sustain interrogation and torture. It also unsettles assumptions that associate gendered abuse exclusively with female victimhood. Guzmán accomplishes this by featuring one man's account that gives clues to the nature and implications of sexualized degradation of male bodies. In *My Imaginary Country* Guzmán focuses on the *estallido social* and how Chilean women continue the struggle against militarization.

The juxtaposition of Guzmán's documentaries with Said's *I Love Pinochet* and Orozco's *Adriana's Pact* is instructive given that the protagonists of the latter two convey problematic perspectives of the dictatorship. Whereas Guzmán records the voices of the victims, Said and Orozco observe the pro-Pinochet establishment and reveal the barefaced admiration of authoritarian masculinity that makes sexualized violations possible. Said and Orozco unearth the emergence of torture from ingrained misogynist and militaristic ideologies. They accomplish this by including dialogues with Pinochetistas that display the quotidian use of a lexicon of war and the way in which the glorification of bellicose masculinity is internalized by men and women.

Chapter 8, "Unmasking Civilian Complicity in Chilean and Spanish Film," explains the various ways in which Chilean and Spanish film can confront the topic of civilian complicity in violence and also unmask the normalization of toxic masculinity undergirding rape and torture. I return to the film-maker Marcela Said, this time to examine her narrative film *Los perros* (*The Dogs*) alongside the Catalan film *Pa negre* (*Black Bread*) by Agustí Villaronga. Both explore dark secrets of collusion in violence that make visible the interwoven connections between gender, sexuality, and torture. The plot of *The Dogs* circles around the world of an upper-class daughter of a family that benefited from the injustices upheld by the Pinochet regime. The dramatic tension arises after she begins a sexual relationship with an unapologetic former secret agent who is under investigation for human rights violations.

Torture, murder, and complicity also pervade nightmarish secrets in Villaronga's *Black Bread*. The film takes place in post-war Catalonia and follows an adolescent son of a persecuted family as he is socialized into a world of toxic masculinity, homophobia, and cruelty. The exploration of political and sexualized brutality unfolds in progressively expanding layers throughout these films. They reveal the perpetration of violence and complicity as learned acts bound up with pervasive assumptions about gender and sexuality. They indite a broader ideology of power, which hinges upon the assertion of hypermasculine and heteronormative violence. Both film-makers give these attitudes screen time, but they challenge them by showing their destructive consequences.

Drawing parallels between past and present, the conclusion highlights how investigating creative expressions in film and literature can expose the gendered discourses and institutional forces that facilitate torture. These explorations also offer pathways to envision courage and cultivate hope. Crucially, the concepts we articulate through language act as catalysts for change, enabling us not only to perceive what is ignored but also to transform our thinking, discourse, and behaviour.

As Nelly Richard so elegantly expresses it, "Highlighting sexual gender as representation (in other words, as effect of discourse and a mediation of codes) [...] has been critically helpful in denouncing the work of concealment that cultural ideologies enact when they disguise as *natural* the *conventional* manners in which hegemonic masculinity fixes its interpretations and valuations of the sexual as if these were not what they are: interpretations and valuations that are historically constructed and therefore can be deconstructed and opened to rearticulation" (*Cultural Residues* 135). Societal change can only be achieved if we heed a warning: unless we understand the ways in which gender and militarization are propagated, disrupted, and transfigured, our attempts to stem a continuum of violence that underpins torture and war will remain highly deficient.

1 Militarization, Myth, and Masculinity

Assessing militarized masculinity in a transnational framework and defining it as a pre-existing condition for mass atrocity crimes helps us not only to break down the brutalities of the past but also to detect elements that accelerate violence in the present. The key difference between a *pre-existing* condition and a *predestined* condition lies in causation and control. The latter leans towards the religious idea of fate or scientific determinism and therefore ignores agency. Militarized masculinity is not predetermined but rather a man-made warrior identity that emerges in concrete historical contexts. This learned identity not only catalyses aggression but also hinges upon it and is emboldened by it. Domination constitutes both its raison d'être and its general guiding logic.

It was precisely the logic of militarism that united European and Latin American strongmen of yesteryear and continues to unite them today. In 1937 George Orwell wrote, "It was easy to laugh at fascism when we imagined that it was based on hysterical nationalism, because it seemed obvious that the fascist states, each regarding itself as the chosen people and patriotic contras mundum, would clash with one another. But nothing of the kind has happened" (148). Militarism was fascism's mainspring. Orwell described the fascist ideal not as a beehive but rather as a "world of rabbits ruled by stoats" (148). The small but fierce weasel-like animal manages to dominate prey ten times its size by chasing them relentlessly, grabbing their windpipe, and choking them to death. Orwell's powerful image evokes the small but fierce figures of Mussolini (five feet five inches) and Franco (five feet four inches). The rabbit, a characteristically docile creature, stands no chance against the fierce stoat. Orwell's analogy of the fascist objective to dominate docile bodies conjures Foucault's description of the role of discipline and punishment as "a general formula of domination" (*Discipline and Punish* 137).

Mythologies of war, as Suzanne Hatty explains, "circulate throughout society sanctifying the killing and destruction of warfare" (127). For

Emma Goldman, patriotism was a myth "artificially created and maintained through a network of lies and falsehoods" that urged "obedience and readiness to kill father, mother, brother, sister" (119). Broadly speaking, the word *myth* can be described as an imaginative collective construction that has been used to understand natural phenomena and human behaviour in order to influence social organization. In his enquiry into the word, Raymond Williams posits: "From mC19, the short use of myth to mean not only a fabulous but an untrustworthy or even deliberately deceptive invention became common, and has widely persisted" (176–8). Indeed, the word *myth* has evolved over time, and its meaning continues to shift. An in-depth definition remains incomplete if we leave out the gendered hallmarks of myths, which reflect the societal norms and power dynamics of the cultures that create them.

By definition, myth-making is a group activity, as is war-making. Both played a part in the development of various brands of authoritarianism across the globe in the first half of the twentieth century. In Europe and Latin America these brands coalesced in a shared observance of a trinity that included patriarchy, anti-liberal nationalism, and the militarist mythology of battle as a source of renewal. Militarized masculinity was at the epicentre of this unholy trinity.

In *Strongmen*, Ruth Ben-Ghiat reminds us that fascism emerged out of the First World War's matrix of violence and attracted disenchanted veterans who turned the humiliation of defeat into a rallying call and a defence of total war where civilian and military boundaries erode: "Bringing the mentality and tactics of the war home, these combatants regarded persecuting domestic enemies as a patriotic duty" (*Strongmen* 20). The mantra "Believe, Obey, Fight" was instrumental in the Italian nationalist fervour that shaped brutal anti-communist street fighting. More recently, the far-right political party Brothers of Italy and its current leader, Giorgia Meloni, won elections in 2022 with the Mussolini-era slogan "God, Homeland, Family." Like before, the slogan is widely used to rally support for xenophobic, homophobic, and anti-socialist policies in the name of national security.

In Spain the founders of fascism are still highly regarded among some Spanish right-wing hardliners who sublimate violence, like Primo de Rivera did, as sacrifice for a rightful cause. Cristina Moreiras-Menor states that the centrality of violence and the cult of masculinist leadership, or *caudillismo*, in the Spanish and Italian fascist agendas cannot be overstated and that looking at them side by side is instructive (128). In the words of Franco himself, "Las revoluciones alemana, italiana, y española son fases del mismo movimiento" (Sueiro and Díaz-Nosty 166; The German, Italian, and Spanish revolutions are phases/forms of the same movement).[1] With this affirmation Franco made Spain's fascist ties clear to the Cuerpo Diplomático acreditado in Madrid in December 1942. As Sueiro and Díaz-Nosty point out, it was one of the last declarations of the fascist alliance since the allies had begun to show the vulnerabilities of the axis forces. As such, the Franco regime would soon try to rebrand itself, but many of the similarities remained.

The parallels are on full display in Guillermo del Toro's extraordinary films. We can trace thematic and aesthetic through lines in *The Devil's Backbone*, *Pan's Labyrinth*, *The Shape of Water*, and *Pinocchio*. These films are set during the Spanish Civil War (1936–9), the post-war Franco dictatorship (1940s), the 1960s Cold War era in the United States, and fascist Italy (1922–43). The Mexican director offers a path to think about militarized masculinity comparatively over time and across national and geographic boundaries. His plots foreground the pervasiveness of acts like interrogation, humiliation, and torture, and how such acts were positioned on a continuum of violence. Del Toro's fascist characters justify violence as inevitable and enforce the subjugation of women, children, and non-conforming males. In those resistant characters (non-violent boys and girls, black and deaf women, amphibian-humanoid creatures) the director depicts models of gentle courage. That creative task is also undertaken by Elena Ferrante in her Neapolitan novels beginning with *My Brilliant Friend*. The quartet offers a compelling exploration of the relationship between misogyny, fascism, and homophobia in post-war Italy. Ferrante explores how violent masculinity is woven into the fabric of society but also how non-conforming characters work to unweave the fascist fabric. Almudena Grandes's six-volume saga, *Episodios de una guerra interminable*, also provides a compelling exploration of the deep-seated connections between militarism, masculinity, and violence from the rise of fascism through the duration of the Franco dictatorship, as I have addressed elsewhere.

These contemporary portrayals of the past subvert the militarized masculine discourse that was prevalent across Europe in the 1930s and 1940s where fascist leaders attempted to diminish the division between the state of war and the state of non-war. To that end, they organized nationalistic pageantry and fully integrated military culture on the home front through education and conscription. In "War and Critical Theory" Max Pensky explores how the Frankfurt school of German philosophers worried particularly about the integration of war in politics. Anti-fascist theorists like Theodor Adorno and Walter Benjamin offered damning critiques of the vanishing distinction between the military combatant and the civilian non-combatant. The blurring of that separation was part and parcel of the

---

1 All translations are mine unless otherwise stated.

process of militarization that unfolded in Nazi Germany in the interwar period. Pensky summarizes the value of these philosophers' efforts: "Theorizing war as one facet of a larger totalizing, interlocking system of social domination [offered an] illuminating perspective on the nature, meaning, and implications of armed conflict" (69). At the core of that "interlocking system of social domination" exists an alliance between militarism, masculinity, and violence. In *Three Guineas*, Virginia Woolf theorizes that alliance when she writes: "What connection is there between the sartorial splendors of the educated man and the photograph of ruined houses and dead bodies? Obviously, the connection between dress and war is not far to seek; your finest clothes are those you wear as soldiers" (21).

Woolf refutes the conviction that the biological essence of masculinity inevitably involves military might. As an author of *Virginia Woolf and Fascism* explains, Woolf's rejection of the adherence to a natural gender order was linked to her critique of the learned language and pageantry of the military (Gättens). Although her critique of fascism preceded the Spanish Civil War, the consequences of fascism in Spain directly affected her writing. Julian Bell, the son of Woolf's sister, Vanessa Bell, joined the International Brigades as an ambulance driver and died defending the republic in 1937. As Gayle Rogers argues, the connection between fighting Spanish fascism and dismantling the English patriarchal system constitutes the subtext of *Three Guineas*. Woolf never used the term *militarized masculinity*, but *Three Guineas* makes a powerful statement on the damaging consequences of societal views that frame the soldier as the quintessential embodiment of masculinity.

Similarly, Walter Benjamin's illuminating essay "Theories of German Fascism," first published in 1930, dissects the militaristic discourse that associates masculinity with heroism, fate, and machine warfare. He identifies Ernst Jünger's harmful role in the glorification of war as a force that gives men meaning. Jünger (1895–1998) was a decorated German soldier and intellectual known for his First World War memoir *Storm of Steel*. Whereas Jünger deemed war's "education" as necessary and even life giving, Benjamin lamented the destruction produced by "warscapes" and their lessons of bombs and barbed wire. Jünger had his critiques of Nazism, however, as Benjamin points out; the writer and war veteran shared with the unified armed forces of Nazi Germany (the Wehrmacht) the view that the uniform represents men's "highest end, most desired by all their heartstrings, and that the circumstances under which one dons the uniform are of little importance by comparison" ("Theories of German Fascism" 313). Benjamin does not mention the words *militarized masculinity* directly, but he spurns the stories that reinforce stereotypes equating manhood, courage, and violence. He sums up his disgust with the fascist cult of war when he calls it "nothing other than an uninhibited translation of the principles of *l'art pour l'art* to war itself" (314).

In the 1934 text "Hitler's Diminished Masculinity," Benjamin communicates an understanding of the gender performance in which militarized authoritarians invest great effort to exert charisma and seduce their followers. In that short text he lauds Charlie Chaplin for his ability to see the artifice in displays of power and ridicule them through a counter-performance. "Chaplin shows up the comedy of Hitler's gravity" (792). Laughter at the seriousness of Nazi Germany's supreme commander-in-chief effectively deflated his authority. If Hitler's show of virility through military might swayed the fascist public, for Benjamin and Chaplin it was a farcical performance that betrayed his own insecurity. "Chaplin has become the greatest comic because he has incorporated into himself the deepest fears of his contemporaries" (792). The actor's performance not only mocked one tyrant but also invalidated the power of aggressive masculinity on both sides of the Atlantic.

Like their European counterparts, Latin American "strongmen" shared a conception of military force as necessary to establish order and maintain power hierarchies in war and peacetime. From a transnational perspective, Federico Finchelstein draws parallels between the mythologies of war in Europe and in Latin America and how they functioned to endorse military takeovers throughout the twentieth century. In *Fascist Mythologies* he perceptively writes of the "displacement from the classical myth of the hero to the modern mythification of the leader" (viii). This valuable claim, however, takes for granted the constructed hypermasculine identity of the classical hero and fascist leader. It is true that "in fascism the legitimacy of myths is the basis of politics" (ix), but that equation remains incomplete without an acknowledgment of gender. The basis of fascism's politics of domination is the legitimacy of the militarized male myth.

Finchelstein directs our attention to Argentine writer Jorge Luis Borges and his 1946 short story "Deutsches Requiem," which is told from the perspective of a fictional commandant of a Nazi concentration camp, named Otto Dietrich zur Linde. In a monologue following a trial that found him guilty of torture and murder, the character describes war as sublime, happy, and not unlike love. His unabashed devotion to violence and his lack of remorse motivate his narrative attempt to be understood rather than pardoned on the night before his execution (Borges 142). Borges's character pontificates about the reason for living: "For each man that justification must be different; I awaited the inexorable war that would prove our faith. It was enough for me to know that I would be a soldier in its battles" (143). In the same breath Otto Dietrich zur Linde refers to war and glory as *"facilities"* (desirable and useful features of life), and Nazism as "an act of morality, a purging of corrupted humanity, to dress him anew" (Borges 144). He describes mercy as a sin and the destruction of one's compassion as a goal.

As Finchelstein notes, the mythical imaginary put forward by the fascists (as brilliantly depicted through Borges's character), "was based on fantasies of total domination" (*Brief History* 19). Those fantasies were inseparable from the social construction of gender and the idealization of the militarized male leader. When Borges's Nazi narrator concludes that "the history of nations also registers a secret continuity" (Borges 146), he refers to the teachings of "violence and the faith of the sword" (146). How can we interpret these words without regarding the weight of masculine myths that shape them?Borges's fictional last testament of a Nazi killer likely influenced Roberto Bolaño's magnum opus *2666*, which features the story of Hans Reiter, later known as Benno von Archimboldi. He comes from a long line of military men, a lineage that shapes his character and actions. It may not be explicit, but Reiter's military heritage inextricably connects to the sprawling and cyclical nature of violence that culminates with the murders committed by his "femicidal" nephew near the Mexican *maquiladoras* (manufacturing plants). The novel masterfully delves into the parallels between the mythologies of war in Europe and those in Latin America by exposing the interlacing brutalities that have emerged from the glorification of militarized masculinity in both contexts and which endure today. The Nazi characters in Bolaño's and Borges's fiction manifest a perspective of violence that echoes Hitler's world view. Timothy Snyder, the author of *On Tyranny* reminds us in an earlier work that Hitler saw Eden not as a garden but as a trench (Snyder, "Hitler's World"). Synder emphasizes Hitler's belief in the power of the natured (biological) over the nurtured (learned) in the formation of subjectivity and the innate urge to commit violence. In his assessment of the finite amount of land and resources Hitler embraced the anti-Enlightenment thinking that "races should behave like species, like mating with like and seeking to kill unlike" (Snyder).

The Nazis were convinced that questioning hierarchies, binaries, and behaviours was a tendency of the Jews not unlike that of Marx, Freud, Benjamin, and Luxemburg: "For Hitler the bringer of the knowledge of good and evil on earth, the destroyer of Eden, was the Jew. It was the Jew who told humans that they were above other animals, and had the capacity to decide their future for themselves. It was the Jew who introduced the false distinctions between politics and nature, between humanity and struggle" (Snyder, "Hitler's World"). Any non-racist or anti-war attitude was deemed Jewish. "The planet had nothing to offer except blood and soil, and yet Jews uncannily generated concepts that allowed the world to be seen less as an ecological trap and more as a human order. Ideas of political reciprocity, practices in which humans recognize other humans as such, came from the Jews" (Snyder, "Hitler's World"). In other words, Jews were guilty of challenging the violent nature of the human animal.

Similar ideas about the eminence of violence as a fascist principle are conveyed by the Italian feminist author Michela Murgia, but from a satirical perspective. Her "manual" titled *How to Be a Fascist* cleverly uses the voice of a brazen right-wing populist to ridicule authoritarian creed: "Multiple contradictions run through the veins of democracy, and all can be exploited by fascism. The biggest of them all, however, is non-violence [...] Democracy still insists on rejecting violence as a way of doing politics, which makes as much sense as training tarantulas by only feeding them lettuce" (57). That statement would be humorous if it lacked transnational relevance. Through satire Murgia also urges readers to remember the relationship between anti-democratic dogma, language, and power: "Why would anyone need to overthrow institutions if all you need to do in order to seize them is to change the referent of a word and make sure everyone speaks it?" (7).

Murgia reflects Hannah Arendt's concept of the "banality of evil" as described in *Eichmann in Jerusalem*. The Italian feminist never refers directly to Arendt, because Murgia's *How to Be a Fascist* is pure satire; however, she shows the concept's enduring relevance through the exposure of the ways in which fascism can manifest in subtle, everyday actions, often through seemingly innocuous beliefs and behaviours. When studied through a feminist lens, Murgia's book can help us develop further Arendt's influential concept. The satire ridicules the links between gender conformity and violence and how these links play a constitutive role in the rise of authoritarian regimes. When we listen to the perspectives of Murgia, Arendt, Finchelstein, and Snyder with the knowledge of the significance of militarized masculinity, we may better articulate a transatlantic reflection on the features of fascism and the threat of what Finchelstein calls post-fascist populism adapted for democratic times (*Brief History of Fascist Lies*, 6).

Words from Outer Space

In order to define militarized masculinity, it is instructive to turn to a concrete example of its description in literature by Roberto Bolaño. He has gained iconic status for his investment in themes of violence and impunity, but insufficient attention has been paid to how his characters and plots help us conceptualize military masculinity. Later in the book I will discuss *By Night in Chile*, but here a brief analysis of "Palabras del espacio exterior" ("Words from Outer Space") contributes to my theoretical framework. It is a two-page text that forms part of a chronicle written by Bolaño after one of his trips to a post-Pinochet Chile in 1998.[2] His reflections speak volumes about the pervasiveness of violence and militarism that did not simply appear with the coup and disappear with the transition to democracy.

Republished in the collection of essays and speeches *Between Parentheses*, "Words from Outer Space" refers to "Interferencias secretas," a tape recording in which a series of military orders and counter-orders were transmitted on 11 September 1973. The aged audio recording has been digitized and may be accessed online with a click of a button, but most listeners would not know how to decipher it. It is warped, but its magnetic surface preserves a series of terse, chilling orders issued in a military cadence. Bolaño must have listened attentively and repeatedly to the ninety-minute-long tape to make sense of it. That tape is analysed in depth by Patricia Verdugo, a Chilean journalist, writer, and human rights activist. What stands out about Bolaño's remarks on the commanders' expressions is the way that he traces the links between so-called ordinary masculinity, militarized masculinity, and violence.

He writes that the voices of the commanders were vaguely familiar, like "echoes of a nebulous fear located in some parts of our bodies" (Bolaño, *Between Parentheses* 84). State violence is not depicted as "other" but troublingly familiar. He identifies it in the pranks of schoolboys, the teacher's punishing rod, the discourse of national security, and the laughter of militarized men: "Some orders are unequivocal: there's talk about killing on sight, arrests, bombings. Sometimes the men who're talking make jokes: this doesn't bring them any closer to us, in fact, it sinks them deeper into an abyss, they're men who emerge from invisible and imperceptible pits and who, in vaguely military terms, promise to establish order. Despite it all, the humor they flaunt is familiar. A humor that one recognizes and would rather not recognize. The man who's talking could be my father or grandfather" (84). Bolaño does not just probe the line between military and civilian brutality; he rips it open, revealing a festering legacy of suppressed emotion and learned aggressive posturing.

He points to a military discourse shaped by patriarchy and bent on the restoration of "order," a euphemism for repression and persecution. Corporal punishment, in both the domestic and the public spheres, reinforces hierarchical and patriarchal power structures. In making these connections, Bolaño breaks down the ground-in conditioning

---

2 Also see Ignacio Rodríguez de Arce, "'Estrella distante' de Roberto Bolaño."

and expectations that permeate the construction of "ordinary" men: "There's no getting around it: these are the voices of our childhood," he writes with a certain disgust (86). The personal and the political are explored alongside each other.

Bolaño's work counters the common neglect of "slow violence," a concept initially developed by Rob Nixon to depict environmental devastation. Clair Bielby expands this idea into perpetrator studies, demonstrating its relevance to gendered violence. Slow violence, characterized by its gradual, often hidden, and spatially dispersed nature, aptly describes forms of abuse like domestic violence, stalking, and psychological manipulation, all of which disproportionately have an impact on women. Furthermore, this type of violence suffers from a representational bias, often overlooked due to deeply ingrained patriarchal norms that obscure its insidious nature.

Bolaño notices slow forms of violence in his many novels, short stories, and vignettes that blur lines not only between fact and fiction but also between subtle and obvious forms of aggression. *Antwerp*, a 2002 collection of short prose set in Barcelona and the Costa Brava, offers a fitting example. In the piece called "Occasionally It Shook," Bolaño conjures a disturbing scenario of concealed destruction that takes place in a dark hotel room. There a policeman rapes a "nameless girl" who was lost in the metro (37). As he is an authority figure, the "risk of the gaze was partly overcome by the exercise of his profession" (37). Training for the urban police force, like the civil guard or the carabineros (Chile's militarized police), produces a sense of power, privilege, and immunity. But the word *partly* in Bolaño's text is significant because it reminds us that, in comparison to women, men already disproportionately hold power. Sexual assault is regularly perpetrated by "ordinary men." It is what Kate Manne calls "the banality of misogyny" (211). A "nameless girl" lost in a metro cannot be raped, Bolaño concludes is the imagined policeman's line of reasoning.

On that continuum of violence, sexual brutality is central, not just another topic. In "Words from Outer Space," Bolaño writes: "The tape rolls and little by little the voices become familiar, as if they'd always been there, talking to us, threatening us. The image is redundant. In fact, they were always there. They're the men who ordered a father to sodomize his own son if he didn't want them both to be killed, the bosses who put live rats into the vagina of a twenty-two-year-old Mirista they called a whore" (*Between Parentheses* 85). This jarring reference to the use of rats to terrorize women also appears in Nona Fernández's *The Twilight Zone*, a title that bears a striking resemblance to "Words from Outer Space." Both authors add complexity to the nightmarish image of men using rats for torture by also considering some soldiers' hesitancy, fear, and nervousness. Bolaño knows that group pressure is critical to understanding how and why foot soldiers participated in mass atrocity crimes. It is part of the social and psychological process that conditions men to perform acts of cruelty. The results of that process are horrific but not far from home: "No matter how many unbelievable deeds accumulate, the picture we're left with is tinged with a familiar vulgarity, taken to a sickening degree. At some point in our lives, we knew the people who are talking" (Bolaño, *Between Parentheses* 86).

Militarized masculinity, as Bolaño illustrates, is pervasive and performative, to use Judith Butler's term in *Gender Trouble*. Butler maintains that gender "is produced as a ritualized repetition of conventions, and that this ritual is socially compelled in part by the force of compulsory heterosexuality" ("Melancholy Gender" 31). The idea that gender is a performance, also supported by the trailblazers in masculinity studies, challenges the common belief that male violence is natural. According to Raewyn Connell, the standard argument is that males are inherently more aggressive than women and they cannot be trained otherwise. "There is often an appeal to biology, with testosterone in particular, the so-called 'male hormone,' as a catch-all explanation for men's aggression" (*The Men and the Boys* 215). But, as Connell explains, hormone levels are far from being a clear-cut source of behaviour. "Cross-cultural studies of masculinities reveal a diversity that is impossible to reconcile with a biologically fixed master pattern of masculinity" (215). Butler sums it up well: "The paradox of human nature is that it is always a manifestation of cultural meanings, social relationships, and power politics; not biology, but culture becomes destiny" (Butler, qtd. in Kirk and Okazawa-Rey 67).

Like Bolaño and Butler, the film-maker Jay Rosenblatt understands that in civil society boys discover that acts of violence (bullying, abuse) are ordinary occurrences that shape boys' lives. Hearing, seeing, and smelling violent masculinity guide Rosenblatt's audio-visual narrative in the short film *The Smell of Burning Ants*. Through voice-over and a black-and-white montage of archival footage from 1950s United States, he makes evident the cycle of fear, shame, collaboration, conformity, and competition that forms or deforms boys into men and leads to self-destruction. "Boys become boys by not being girls. The ones that don't figure this out are the ones that get beaten up" (Rosenblatt). In slow motion, a boy throws a crying child to the ground. "He learns early about the power and protection of a mob." His desire for domination prompts his declaration of war on insects that he traps, dismembers, and kills. "In a frenzy he burns ant after ant and will not stop until there are no visible signs of life remaining" (Rosenblatt).

If cruelty is not foreign to men before they enter the military, it becomes a language in which they are well versed in that setting. In the familiar voices of the commanders, Bolaño dares to say, "We can contemplate ourselves, at a remove, as if watching ourselves in a mirror" (*Between Parentheses* 85). It isn't Stendhal's mirror, he notes, thereby suggesting that the image is a refraction, not an exact reflection. That said, "it could be, and for many who hear the tape it surely will be precisely that" (85). Bolaño, like many men, is repulsed by hypermasculine theatrics and sickened by killing; however, he is careful to recognize that such acts are not from another world but uncomfortably close to his own.

Militarized masculinity is assimilated and enacted through gestures, words, intonation, postures, and corporeal displays. Connell reminds us, however, that even while such social conditioning is pervasive, "we must not slide into the inference that therefore all men are violent. Almost all soldiers are men, but most men are not soldiers. Though most killers are men, most men never kill or even commit assault" (*The Men and the Boys* 215). For the boys and men who end up embracing militarized masculinity, either voluntarily or unwillingly, arrogance, intolerance, and intransigence are not considered imperfections to overcome but rather qualities to hone. They accept that it is better to inspire fear than to provoke cruel laughter.

The pressures to become "hard" increase dramatically in the military, and the presence of women soldiers does not inherently change the ethos of that environment. For instance, in the United States, "ninety percent of women on a Veterans Administration study reported harassment, and a third said they had been raped by military personnel" (Kirk and Okazawa-Rey 499). As Gwyn Kirk points out, "Despite the existence of policies against sexual harassment and assault and an increase in sensitivity training for military personnel, entrenched military culture has blocked the systematic implementation of such policies" (500).

All soldiers encounter hypermasculine battle rhetoric, competitive training, and the threat of humiliation, but the extent to which these staples of military culture transform them tends to vary. The soldiers in Bolaño's "Words from Outer Space" appear particularly disturbing because of their sense of amusement at the time of the infliction of violence. Readers may well imagine their laughter. It contrasts with the kind that Chaplin produced by mocking Hitler. Laughter is a social act of shared amusement and group cohesion, but cruel laughter is often a performance of power and aggressive masculinity. In such cases, it is not a subversion of social norms but rather a reinforcement of them. Cruel laughter, rather than merely being associated with the trivialization of violence, is fundamental to it. Cruel laughter constitutes an integral part of the normalization of militarized masculinity, or, figuratively speaking, it provides its chilling soundtrack. The two influence and reinforce each other in a cyclical manner.

In the essay "Gendering the Perpetrator," Clare Bielby observes that the perpetration of violence is "a dynamic process, a form of *doing* (perpetrating) rather than *being* (the perpetrator) and a form of *doing* intimately bound up with many others, not least the *doing* of one's gender" (163). Those military commanders captured on tape, Bolaño writes, "are performing for us as if in a radio serial, but mostly they are performing for themselves" (*Between Parentheses* 86). Militarized masculinity is learned and expressed in the interactions that happen between men. These interactions operate on two fronts: the public display of power through ceremonies, aerial shows, parades, combat manoeuvres, and so on; and the hidden realm of unabashed sexual subjugation, sometimes filmed for pleasure. "Pornography, snuff movies. At last, they've found the roles of their lives. Finally, the soldiers have their war, their great war" (86). Having been prepared for combat, rather than peacekeeping, those military men want to observe the implementation of their training, and they want to be praised for it. Bolaño ends this brief but impactful text with an unsettling commentary on bystander inaction: "before them we stand, unarmed but watching and listening" (86).

"Words from Outer Space" captures in brief evocative descriptions how military men and "ordinary" civilian men can occupy similar positions in patriarchal society. Bolaño wishes that those military agents captured on tape were from outer space, but he knows they are not. Violent masculinity was not produced in 1973 by the Pinochet regime, nor was militarized masculinity unique to the barracks. As Bolaño indicates, military culture is far from being confined to a single space. It percolates through patterns of child-rearing and gendered education in which boys are taught that domination over others is manly, war is meaningful, and patriotism through military or police "service" is a masculine ideal. Often for working-class and poor men with few career opportunities, the military offers not only the most viable economic option but also, as Leith Passmore suggests, "a male rite of passage in terms of social and familial responsibility, discipline, education, employment, and physical toughness" (*Wars* 106). The making of militarized men through cruel hazing practices often physically and psychologically destroys recruits. The process draws from the existing gender binary and magnifies it. Through that process, bravery is conflated with the capacity to kill while both are endowed with revered status.

To survey another example, in Bolaño's short story "The Colonel's Son," from *The Secret of Evil*, the horrors of militarized violence are depicted through an allegorical tale of zombies. Set in contemporary Spain, the narrator describes a B-grade American horror flick that he watched on television. The film that he describes features a military man's son whose girlfriend (Julie) becomes a zombie. The character in this low-budget slasher movie who fears the zombies the most is the colonel. His mission becomes to protect his son from the female zombie, destroy the other contaminated bodies (Mexican gang members and Black homeless laborers), and extinguish the zombie rebellion. The police and armed forces persecute the colonel's son and Julie. Plenty of blood is shed in the film, as the narrator explains in gory detail. All the zombies are captured, tortured, put in cages, and subjected to experiments by the military scientists at a labyrinthine army base. The colonel's son manages to free the zombies, now a band of survivors, but ultimately their only escape is a fiery furnace.

Looking beyond the far-fetched plot line, it is hard not to read this zombie story as a parable of militarism. Whereas Bolaño uses a real recorded tape of military orders from 11 September 1973 to begin "Words from Outer Space," he uses a zombie movie as an entry point to explore the militaristic justification of the subjugation of humans who are seen as corrupt, dangerous, and "other." It is a caricature of a military man and his desire to establish order through violence in the face of a threat, namely an uprising of flesh-eating women and people of colour. It is an unusual and thought-provoking way to explore how militarist logic depends upon the act of envisaging the enemy as threateningly subhuman.

The zombie trope and narrative tone appear absurd, but, as in the case of "Words from Outer Space," killing is both alien and familiar to the narrator. It is significant that he sets the stage for the story in this way: "You're not going to believe this, but last night, at about four a.m., I saw a movie on TV that could have been my biography or my autobiography or a summary of my days on this bitch of a planet. It scared me so fucking shitless I tell you I just about fell off my chair" (Bolaño, *The Secret of Evil* 19). Something equally, if not more, horrific than ravenous zombies and aliens exists among us, Bolaño suggests. The real monsters, described as frighteningly recognizable in "Words from Outer Space," are the agents of the military regime who raped and mutilated leftist women's bodies in the name of national security, patriotic duty, and honour.

One more useful example from Bolaño can be found in *Nazi Literature in the Americas*, first published in 1996. In what appears to be a biographical encyclopaedia Bolaño creates a web of far-right literature connecting European and Latin American fascists of many stripes. He does not portray them as mere automatons, but they share an admiration for war violence in its many forms. Some are ex-combatants or fervent admirers of them, including their sons, daughters, and wives. While they are fictional and often absurd, the scenarios are plausible and positioned in the context of real events and historical figures. Bolaño traces the transatlantic crossings of ideologies and actors, like the tale of a Colombian Falangist for whom the Spanish Civil War was a defining moment. He recounts his battle memories in the Spanish Blue Division, while also marvelling at his own sexual potency and the "length of his member" (Bolaño, *Nazi Literature* 38). Bolaño leaves us in no doubt that gender and sexuality play a role in war, torture, and other acts of brutality.

Fictional and non-fictional narratives like these exemplify the kind of literature that offers an unsettling view of the connections between violence, masculinity, and militarism. The aim is not only to interpret the complexity of texts like Bolaño's, as many literary critics have already done, but also to expand and develop the concept of militarized masculinity as a tool for a compelling critique that can be applied to other texts and contexts where militarized violence has been exercised.

Concepts as Tools

In militaristic jargon, sexism abounds to teach, measure, test, and celebrate violent masculinity. In the United States some soldiers refer to their first combat experience as "popping one's cherry," thereby making killing and sex analogous. The message is clear: the initiation into a brotherhood of militarized men involves domination and bloodletting. The virginity metaphor also implies that killing is an inevitable and desirable rite of passage in the movement towards full adulthood. In the process, weapons become personified as a soldier's best friend and an extension of the phallus. Sexual innuendos leach through talk of cleaning, lubricating, holding, discharging, and making the rifle sing. The relationship between discourse and practice is evident in the omnipresence of wartime rape and sexual exploitation. Misogynist and homophobic slurs have their equivalents in Spanish and are widespread to degrade non-combat soldiers framed as weak. The nuances of this range of insults in Spanish could be discussed here and compared to their English counterparts, but I have consciously decided to keep that catalogue unlisted.

Words are powerful weapons used to militarize and desensitize, but they can also be designed to do just the opposite. The term *militarized masculinity* is one that we are missing in our working vocabulary as activists, students, and scholars committed to building a more just world. In the book *The Big Push*, Cynthia Enloe insists on the value of feminist concepts: "They can make the invisible visible and, in so doing, enable people to move beyond either denial or self-blame, toward collective action and meaningful change. 'Date rape,' 'glass ceiling,' 'domestic violence,' 'double day,' 'feminization of poverty,' 'mansplaining,' 'systematic wartime rape'" – these are all "accurate conceptualizations for effective action'" (127). Such terms have given names to problems and have changed the way we think and work towards social change. Coining new terms, as well as redefining existing ones, pushes the conversation about violence forward and causes a ripple effect.

To define and refine words is to shape narratives that travel and transform in translation. Using new or reimagined terms in a global frame and in different languages can have numerous outcomes, as Judith Butler explains in *Who's Afraid of Gender?*. As a response to the feminist constructive expansion of vocabulary and theory worldwide, many right-wing leaders and their followers have popularized a movement against "gender ideology." In Spain the far-right Vox party considers gender theory as part of a broader attack on national identity. Antifeminist movements in Latin America have associated the word *gender* with US neo-imperialism. In so doing, they have created a false dichotomy that discourages ideological shifts and new conceptions of society. Conveniently, they disregard the large anti-gender theory movement in the US neo-imperial north.

Using the term *gender* as a cultural construct detached from the biological, as Butler demonstrates, "represents a wide range of political struggles that its opponents seek to shut down in their effort to restore a patriarchal order for the state, religion, and the family" (*Who's Afraid of Gender?* 248). Targeting and demonizing that word is part of a larger reactionary attempt to limit social change, maintain heteronormative control, and reinforce traditional gender roles that solidify existing power structures. Rejection of "foreign" terms and the recalcitrant defence of "culture" is often a front rather than a thoughtful denunciation of colonialism. It involves selective outrage stemming from nationalist agendas that appeal to cultural purity. That rejection ignores the interconnectedness of languages and how they evolve.

In the collectively written text *Barbarismos, queer y otras esdrújulas*, R. Lucas Platero, María Rosén, and Esther Ortega explore how Spanish speakers can understand and use neologisms, many of them Anglicisms, while being aware of colonial processes and assimilation. Seeing that the promise outweighs the danger, they embrace words that have emerged from feminist and sexuality studies, activism, and artistic practices. Their fifty-three definitions involve imperfect and unfinished travelling words between languages and cultures. Some translated and others not, the terms are meant to provoke curiosity and provide a starting point for a debate in which social movements can converge with critical, cultural, and artistic studies. Likewise, the term *militarized masculinity*, or its Spanish translation *masculinidad militarizada*, also arises in activism and develops with nuances as we use it. Like Butler suggests, coinage and translation can initiate constructive conversations among users of different languages and can become "not only a practice but also a way of developing a multilingual epistemology" (*Who's Afraid of Gender?* 230).

Militarized masculinity is a term that contributes to our understanding of other terms like *homosociality* coined by Eve Sedgwick. In her groundbreaking book *Between Men: English Literature and Male Homosocial Desire*, Sedgwick uses this term to refer to non-sexual interpersonal attractions between persons of the same sex. Sedgwick differentiates between homosocial relations between women and those between men, defining the latter as intense emotional bonds that exclude women through discrimination and harassment. In her analysis of military discourse Liz Kelly observes the omnipresence of sexual imagery in the homosocial spaces of the barracks. Metaphors reveal a combination of homoerotic excitement, the pleasures of group identity, competitiveness, and heterosexual domination (50). Sedgwick posits that the threat of same-sex desire can surface within homosocial bonds, leading to anxiety, violence, and rivalry over a woman that blocks any inkling of homoeroticism. Such fear can lead men to distance themselves from each other, further solidifying rigid notions of masculinity that emphasize stoicism and emotional suppression.

In "Welcome to the Men's Club," Sharon Bird expands on the concept of homosociality: "Through male homosocial heterosexual interactions, hegemonic masculinity is maintained as the norm to which men are held accountable despite individual conceptualizations of masculinity that depart from that norm" (120). Bird uses the metaphor of the "Men's Club" to emphasize emotional closeness between men, while simultaneously excluding women, devaluing feminine qualities, and limiting women's opportunities for advancement. When we directly address the specifics of militarized masculinity, we add to Sedgwick's and Bird's valuable theoretical conclusions. Military culture, with its emphasis on male camaraderie and the exclusion of civilian traits, reinforces larger male-dominated kinship systems based on gender subordination and derision of the feminine.

The redefinition of the concept of misogyny is equally relevant in discussions of militarized masculinity. In *Down Girl*, Kate Manne redefines misogyny by bringing out the fine-grain distinction between sexism (as a belief system) and misogyny (as an enforcement mechanism). Misogyny becomes the manifestation of sexism and emerges in acts like blame, mockery, vitriolic shaming, and violence to punish women who refuse to play their assigned role as caregivers to men. Manne's redefinition of misogyny has been instrumental in my own understanding of the relationship between militarized masculinity and torture in the context of Spain and Chile. Beyond Manne, I draw from the rich bibliography of feminist literature on the topic of masculinity and heteronormativity (R.W. Connell, Kimmel, Katz) and intersectionality (Crenshaw, Hill Collins).

If it is crucial to emphasize the role of Enloe's research on militarized masculinity, it is equally as important to recognize the Latin American feminist scholars that contributed to Enloe's theorization of the topic. The notion that militarized masculinity is cultivated by both men and women and that "most of the people in the world who are militarized are not themselves in uniform" (Enloe, *Globalization and Militarism* 4) echoes the work of Bunster, whom Enloe credits in *The Big Push* (127–8). Living in exile and working with Enloe at Clark University in the 1980s, the Chilean anthropologist paid attention to patterns of torture and their link to gender and militarism, when others were treating these issues separately. Early on she carefully observed the unabashed interest of military regimes to "secure and defend the patriarchal structure and the privileged status of "masculinity" (Bunster, "Surviving Beyond Fear" 102).

Argentine-Brazilian anthropologist Rita Segato is also situated in this influential community of transnational feminist scholars working to create and rethink concepts to clarify complex issues of violence and to galvanize action. In researching the Ciudad Juarez killings, Segato reframes feminicide as a language communicated among powerful men in a call-and-response style. Her emphasis on the "expressive dimension" of violence is evocative of Bolaño's "Words from Outer Space": those military men "are performing for us as if in a radio serial, but mostly they are performing for themselves" (Bolaño, *Between Parentheses* 86). In a succession of tests performed to gain admission to the brotherhood of militarized men, rape is synonymous with conquest. As Segato reminds us, *"rapiña*, the Spanish word for pillage, and *rapinagem*, the Portuguese word for voracious looting, share a root with *rape*" ("Territory" 87). For the militarized male, sexual dominance and the capacity to kill have united perpetrators, providing proof of virility and access to territorial control. However, the supreme act of domination, Segato argues, "is not the power of death over the subjugated but, rather, the psychological and moral defeat of the subjugated and their transformation into a receptive audience for the dominator's exhibition of its discretionary death power" (75). Feminicide, re-evaluated through this lens, requires us to stop thinking of killing as a consequence of impunity but rather as a producer and reproducer of impunity (79).

Concepts are thus valuable tools forged out of cultural, geographical, theoretical, and disciplinary border crossings. From the field of Holocaust and genocide studies, one of the most influential terms for my own research has been *post-memory,* a concept developed by the feminist Holocaust scholar Marianne Hirsch to describe how the children and grandchildren of genocide survivors experience trauma. Looking beyond the Holocaust to other mass atrocities in *Rites of Return*, Hirsch and Nancy K. Miller claim that if we are "attentive to hierarchies of gender and sexuality and the power dynamics of contested histories, we find that hidden within what appears to be a universal narrative of rights are uneven and gendered smaller stories, forgotten and submerged plots" (7). A trailblazer in the field, Hirsch has long recognized the relationship between gender, violence, and memory.

As Adam Jones observes in the canonical text *Genocide: A Comprehensive Introduction*, most genocide studies scholars have missed the question of gender: "The gender dimension of genocide and other crimes against humanity has only recently attracted sustained attention. Leading the way were feminist scholars, who paid particular attention to rape and sexual assault against women, and pressed for such crimes to be considered genocidal" (625). Yet so much work remains to be done. Most studies associate genocidal thinking with nationalism, fascism, racism, xenophobia, colonialism, and totalitarianism without recognizing how these are shaped by patriarchal constructions of dominant masculinity. Even when rape and harm to the genitals are pinpointed as acts perpetrated to bring about the destruction of a group, questions surrounding the learned performance of combative manhood pass from sight. When women perpetrators are discussed, questions regarding the making of militarized civilian womanhood and how the process differs from the making of militarized manhood often go unasked. Footnotes abound with naive conceptions of gender that carelessly equate the word *gender* with women, usually female victimhood. In so doing, they inadvertently uphold the male position of privilege by maintaining its normative status. Some identify gender inequality as a risk factor in genocide and war, but the topic is often dealt with in a cursory fashion or as token.

Texts that count as part of the canon of perpetrator studies and that provide its conceptual tools "seldom address gender, taking the male subject as universal," explains Bielby ("Gendering the Perpetrator" 155). Browning's work on "ordinary men" exemplifies this oversight. He paints Nazi perpetrators in broad strokes without interrogating the social process through which violent masculinity and militarism emerge. That is not the case in Leigh Payne's *Unsettling Accounts*, which takes the question of gender seriously. In her examination of the reception of perpetrators' remorseful confessions in post-dictatorial Chile and Argentina, she explains that the confessors were often met by the regimes' supporters with insults like "crybaby" (49). The language that infantilizes and feminizes vulnerability is hardly veiled. Payne identifies two other types of perpetrator confessions, namely the heroic and the sadistic. In the first, former military officials (like Alfredo Astiz in Argentina) took pride in their martial lineage and glorified their role in the military regime (79). They fashion themselves as versions of James Bond by boasting of the risks they had to take to "save the nation" from the internal threat (75–105). The second is the dark shadow of the first. In sadistic narratives, agents enjoyed recounting depraved details of torture. The Chilean DINA agent Osvaldo Romo Mena justified such acts by insinuating "that women prisoners deserved violence because they neglected their traditional roles" (115). Both heroic and sadistic confessions, Payne argues, "provide investigators and the public with clues about events previously shrouded behind silence and denial" (105). Building on these observations, we must explicitly identify and understand the core role of militarized masculinity within these perpetrator narratives.

It is not that gender is *deliberately* treated as an afterthought or, worse, explicitly rendered irrelevant. Rather, it seems that a theoretical foundation in gender studies among scholars remains uncommon. Instead of seeing a gender perspective as a stark necessity, it is viewed as an optional extra (Cockburn, "The Continuum of Violence" 24). For this reason, volumes like *Genocide and Gender in the Twentieth Century*, edited by Amy Randall, and *Sexual Violence and Armed Conflict* by Janie Leatherman are so valuable. They place long-overdue attention on the nature, function, and implications of gender in genocide. Such scholars grasp the need to expose the cultural, economic, political, and legal practices that uphold male authority, undergird subjugation, and sanction killing. These are not the only examples, and fortunately the field is expanding. As Elisa Von Joeden-Forgey insists, the analysis of gender is the future of genocide studies (298–320).

Among the list of scholarly works focused on dictatorial violence in twentieth-century Spain and Chile, many authors examine the role of neoliberal capitalism and competition for economic control in the destruction of human rights. A smaller, but significant, number examine the role of gender in such destruction. The pivotal work of Nelly Richard on gendered political violence is being expanded upon by multiple generations of voices, including Bernardita Llanos and Brandi Townsend. Historians Hiner and Castro perceptively distinguish different kinds of narratives about sexualized violence broadcast on Chilean television in the last decade. They shed light on the great import of those testimonies by torture survivors that are both told from and analysed through a feminist perspective. They also elucidate not only the typical right-wing backlash to such empowered interviews but also the pushback from the "center-left that do not 'see gender' in human rights abuses" (115). Townsend takes a similar approach by interpreting oral testimonies of women political prisoners from a cutting-edge feminist perspective. She brings out the complexities of narratives that give voice to collective experiences of political imprisonment but that also reflect threads of internalized misogyny rooted in ingrained discourses of power. As a literary and film scholar, Llanos focuses on how the prose fiction of authors like Diamela Eltit and Fátima Sime probe the gaps in the historical record and unsettle any universalist ungendered perspective of violence.

The scholarship of critics like Jean Franco and Elizabeth Jelin has been indispensable to me and many others working to address the gendered dimensions of torture, not only in Spain and Chile but in other areas, particularly Argentina, where socio-political patterns and responses to those patterns have crossed borders. Argentina has been at the cutting edge of research regarding gender, genocide, and torture, as evident in pioneering works like *Disappearing Acts: Spectacles of Gender and Nationalism in Argentina's "Dirty War"* by Diana Taylor, *A Lexicon of Terror: Argentina and the Legacies of Torture* by Marguerite Feitlowitz, and more recently in *Surviving State Terror: Women's Testimonies of Repression and Resistance in Argentina* by Barbara Sutton. These studies contribute to our understanding of the roots, effects, and meanings of torture and provide impetus to explore further its relation to militarized masculinity.

To develop the definition of this concept, it is important to consider not only Enole's enormous contribution to the topic but also similar thinking about the gendered dynamics of militarization that have been posed by Seungsook Moon in *Militarized Modernity and Gendered Citizenship in South Korea*, Maya Eichler in *Militarizing Men: Gender, Conscription, and War in Post-Soviet Russia*, and Erica Fraser in *Military Masculinity and Postwar Recovery in the Soviet Union*. Their treatments of how disciplinary tactics have been enforced to "remold individuals into useful and docile members of the nation" (Moon 18) or to establish soldiering as the ideal form of masculinity (Eichler, Fraser) reveal common patterns. Some short essays have also wrestled with the topic of militarized masculinity, like Milena Abrahamyan's "Tough Obedience," which finds sources of violence in masculinity within the Russian and Swedish armies. Cockburn, however, stresses the *continuum of violence* between brutality in military culture and civilian society. In Latin America, Passmore's *The Wars inside Chile's Barracks* and Bawden's

The Pinochet Generation are insightful contributions that expand our understanding of obligatory military service under Pinochet and how it shaped violence workers.

Generative new ground can be cultivated through a transatlantic comparative framework and interdisciplinary approach that uses film, literature, and feminist theory to expose the tenets of militarized masculinity at the core of dictatorial regimes. In the spirit of Bolaño, I aim to detect patterns and provoke new questions. I agree with Ignacio Echevarría, who suggests that Bolaño's work is largely compelling for its "narrative openings" (Bolaño, *The Secret of Evil* viii). The goal is to open ways to conceptualize the behaviours that militarism entails, and to observe acts of resistance. Militarism and toxic masculinity have been so intertwined and widespread for so long as to be almost unnoticeable. Drawing attention to their function, against the backdrop of other intersecting forms of oppression, constitutes an act of resistance of its own.

The Ongoing Problem of Violence

The examination of the past is most compelling when there is an eye on the present. Chile has recently experienced a human rights crisis, and the effects of that crisis are ongoing. As a response to student protests in October 2019 against the unsustainable rising cost of living, the state provoked grave human rights violations, including massive detentions, beatings, and the use of rubber bullets that caused ocular mutilations among other traumas. The violence unleashed by the right-wing government of then president Sebastián Piñera (1949–2024) stems from a longstanding culture of impunity shaped by the deep-seated conviction that military intervention is the only response to political upheaval.

At the same time, Chile has recently witnessed the mobilization of a massive movement against militarized masculinity and misogyny as exemplified in performances by the collective LasTesis. The artistic intervention called *Un violador en tu camino* (A rapist in your path) has animated movements worldwide to change attitudes towards rape. The global dissemination of the production attests to the ubiquity of rape culture and the need for societal transformation. The energy around movements for change, to which LasTesis contributed no small part, precipitated the creation of Chile's first feminist party in January 2020 (Partido Alternativa Feminista). Such occurrences underscore the relation between politics, art, and non-violent revolution.

The building momentum in Chile, and the right-wing backlash against it, only grew the following year when José Antonio Kast (b. 1966) ran in a presidential election against Gabriel Boric (b. 1986). Kast, the son of Michael Kast Schindele (1924–2014), a German Nazi lieutenant who fled to Chile after the Second World War, validated a pro-Pinochet narrative, praising the former dictator's economic legacy. The younger Kast pledged to "restore" order after the 2019 protests (labelled by him as terrorism) and to use a strong hand to tackle tensions with Indigenous Mapuche in the south, which also reflected a performance of masculinity reminiscent of the Pinochet regime. In *A la sombra de los cuervos*, journalist Javier Rebolledo dedicates a chapter to the Kast clan and its relationship to the Pinochet regime, an association that the politician does not deny. Needless to say, Kast's unbending views on sexuality (opposition to same-sex marriage and other LGBTQIA+ rights) align with the past regime's stance. Although he is a lawyer and politician, his support of the military seemed to play a role in his public appearance and appeal among right-wing, nationalist, anti-choice, Catholic, and retired military groups.

Even so, it is important that, in December 2021, Chileans elected as their new president Gabriel Boric of the newly established leftist Social Convergence party. In the run-off vote the far-right Kast received 45 per cent while the thirty-five-year-old former student leader won with 55 per cent. In the hip-hop jingle "Nuevo Chile," the Boric campaign conveyed an agenda that recognized the valuable intersections between social and economic justice.[3] The colourful audio-visual montage was widely disseminated on YouTube and reached progressive voters by highlighting environmentalism, feminism, LGBTQIA+ rights, Indigenous rights, educational reforms, and a universal publicly funded health-care system. "Nuevo Chile" featured many faces accentuating Chilean diversity, while another campaign video, called *Granja de Boric, te invitamos a votar!*, focused on Boric. Using animation techniques, the video presented the presidential hopeful dancing an unconventional cueca with farm animals.[4] The use of traditional attire, including a *chamanto* (poncho) in red, white, and black with the *huaso* (hat), together with rhythmic moves alongside animated roosters, cows, and horses was a light-hearted way to celebrate Chilean customs while breaking norms. His victory reveals not only that militarized masculinity is not the *only* form of masculinity in Chile but also that alternatives to that version are strongly credited by a major part of the population. Boric

---

3 *Jingle – Nuevo Chile*, posted by Gabriel Boric Font, https://www.youtube.com/watch?v=PVYDOGU2SxQ.

4 *Granja de Boric, te invitamos a votar!*, https://www.youtube.com/watch?v=3dJxWa7RtaM.

was a vocal critic of Piñera's response to the 2019 student protests, but he remained committed to non-violent solutions even in the face of criticism from his supporters.

The establishment of the Constitutional Convention to write a new progressive charter came out of that context. In 2020 nearly 80 per cent of voters elected to rewrite the Pinochet-era constitution, and that agenda became the cornerstone of Boric's presidential bid in December 2021. As the new constitution was mapped out in 2022, a right-wing fear campaign united conservatives and moderates against a so-called plan to end homeownership, allow abortions up to the moment of birth, and make non-Indigenous people second-class citizens. The rejection campaign was strong and effective. In September 2022, 61 per cent of the population voted no. Although the referendum was not approved, the process to revise the constitution will continue. Boric broadcast a speech in which he emphasized his plan to listen to public concerns and never to succumb to violence and intolerance.

There has been a resurgence of fascist ideology in Spain, too. In late 2019 the far-right Vox party became one of the largest political forces in the country. Like the myth of the American conservative "silent majority" popularized by Richard Nixon to bolster support for the Cold War, Vox refers to the so-called people without a voice that represent the "true" views of most Spaniards. Those who celebrated Vox's victory were captured in media coverage openly raising their arms in the fascist salute in a brazen vindication of the return of Francoist ideology. The racist and militaristic lexicon of the Reconquista – which hearkens back to the expulsion and conversion of Jews and Muslims in fifteenth-century Spain – has given the Vox party a weapon to galvanize reactionary sentiment, reverse reforms made since democratization, and dehumanize immigrants and refugees. This is one way in which race continues to intersect with gender and nationalism in Spanish militarized masculinity. With the Basque neo-fascist Santiago Abascal at the helm, the party also pushes an anti-feminist agenda that threatens to turn back the clock on women's rights, including access to abortion.

Although endorsements of Pinochet's brutality might not be explicit in Spanish politics, old and new alliances suggest that admiration of the Chilean dictator is shared by members of the Spanish right wing. Kast and Abascal have shown public mutual support in televised conversations (see #KastConAbascal). In 2020 they joined forces in an anti-communist organization called the Madrid Forum with the goal to unite ultra-conservative politicians from Latin America, Spain, and the United States. Around the same time, in a challenge to the Popular Party's Pablo Casado, the leader of Vox tweeted an image of himself wearing a *morrión* worn in the sixteenth century by Los Tercios españoles (a military unit of the Spanish Army). It was part of a larger nostalgic narrative of transatlantic militarized masculinity in an allied "Iberosphere" of nations. Abascal fashioned himself as the true conquistador compared to the mainstream right-wing party (Partido Popular, PP) and therefore better equipped to battle Spain's internal "enemies" and garner respect from a transatlantic brotherhood. The gesture implies a common Spanish and Spanish American collective memory of a golden age of militarism in the colonial and revolutionary eras in the Americas that shaped modern military masculinity. Of course, that selective memory virulently rejects the implementation of Spain's Historical Memory Law (Ley de Memoria Histórica), which acknowledges the brutalities committed by the fascist insurrections during the Spanish Civil War and subsequent dictatorship.

These performances of militarized masculinity stand in sharp contrast to feminist acts of collective power and defiance. Over the last decade Spain has seen a surge of public forums, films, novels, and other creative outlets that voice clear-eyed critiques of the present-day version of Francoism. Thousands of feminists regularly gather on International Women's Day (8 March) in solidarity to celebrate victories and carry on the struggle in cities and towns across Spain. Recently, in Madrid's Plaza Mayor, three hundred Spanish feminists joined their fellow Chilean feminists to sing the transnational anthem "A Rapist in Your Path." These performances and counter-performances underscore the timeliness of this book; however, the larger problem of militarized masculinity unfortunately has a timelessness or obstinacy about it that will survive beyond the news of the day.

Matchsticks for Mass Atrocity

A comparative approach strengthens both educational and prevention work even beyond the particular social and cultural contexts in question. To rephrase Connell, in view of the concentration of weapons and brutality perpetrated by men, a strategy for prevention must include a strategy to change notions of masculinity ("Masculinities, the Reduction of Violence" 33–40).[5] Extending Connell's assertion, masculinities are multiple, taught, historically and culturally situated, and shaped by

---

5 The essay was republished in *The Criminology of War* (2014), edited by Ruth Jamieson. It was originally published in 2002 in Cynthia Cockburn and Dubravka Žarkov, *The Postwar Moment*, pp. 33–40.

both men and women through children's socialization. However, just as boys, men, civilians, and soldiers are desensitized to violence and learn through institutions and cultural production that dominance over women and other men is a true sign of masculinity, they can unlearn such notions through critical organizations and expressions.

This approach to the problem of violence offers what is missing from what genocide scholar James Waller calls "upstream, midstream, and downstream efforts" to confront genocide (124). Militarization must be considered both a trigger and an accelerant for mass atrocities. An analysis of the understudied topic of military conscription and the normalization of cruel hazing practices that aim to eliminate empathy and vulnerability (framed as feminine) and turn recruits into weapons of war adds a vital piece to upstream prevention efforts or the "before" analysis of risk factors. A midstream strategy must recognize the links between de-escalation and demilitarization since the logic of militarization fuels the dehumanization of the "other" and serves to justify armed domination.

Examining militarized masculinity is also essential when considering the rules of engagement (ROE) during war. The pressure to conform to a culture of stoicism and aggression is the hallmark of the armed forces, and the demands to be considered "tough" lead to recklessness, disregard for civilian safety, and a reluctance to admit mistakes, ask for clarification, or question orders. Militarized masculinity fosters a view of the enemy as "less than human," making it easier to justify torture, indiscriminate killings, and other war crimes. The desire to be a hero or avoid appearing weak clouds judgment and leads to poor decisions. In that environment, violations are not only tolerated but often celebrated.

A theoretically nuanced examination of the perpetration of violence and its intersections with gender also contributes to downstream prevention or the "after" efforts to foster resiliency in post-atrocity societies because this approach attempts to transcend simplified binary accounts of perpetrators and victims. When young conscripts are forced to commit acts of violence, many suffer from perpetration-induced traumatic stress. The lack of policies and incentives for their reintegration into civilian society creates a scenario that gives rise to hate groups and organized crime buttressed by paramilitary ex-combatants. Only downstream efforts informed by a gender analysis can adequately address these problems, as well as the challenges facing traumatized survivors of masculinized violence. The anthropologist Kimberly Theidon has long recognized this in the case of Colombia, arguing that transitional justice requires "a gendered analysis that includes an examination of the salient links between weapons, masculinities, and violence" (2).

A feminist lens also identifies rape as a weapon of control and emphasizes the need to shift resources to support survivors, investigate violations, map patterns, document sexual abuse, and hold abusers accountable.

By placing in conversation voices of writers, film-makers, and theorists that uproot the large-scale belief systems that contribute to violence, we can address what has repeatedly been ignored. Rape and other forms of gendered abuse have been at the nucleus of a patriarchal and militaristic culture in which masculinity is defined in terms of dominance and aggression. It is at the intersection of literature, film, feminist studies, history, and genocide studies that we may discover unexpected inroads in the study of violence. By using these fields to interpret the operations, management, and reinforcement of militaristic culture and gender norms, we can identify key factors that escalate political crisis, trigger conflict, and then frame violence as inevitable.

Franco's Spain and Pinochet's Chile offer arresting examples that allow us to deconstruct the glorified narrative of "national reorganization." We observe how militarized masculinity became a matchstick in the outbreak of unsparing suppression of human rights and the flame for long-term maintenance of social control. More broadly, we gain critical tools to substantiate the bold case that sexual harassment, anti-gay abuse, genocidal violations, toxic masculinity, and militarism are all related issues. Treating them as mutually constitutive must become a cornerstone in the work of human rights to learn from the past and achieve meaningful change in the present.

This connective framework also makes possible the exploration of the tensions between optimism and despair. As the ensuing chapters will show, some writers and directors weave hope through stories of resistance, while others project a dim portrait of the impact of violent masculinity and its ongoing place in discourses and institutions long after the transitions to democracy. As concerns the latter, the unmasking of male brutality and complicity constitutes a sufficient response. The effects of these differences matter, but, in the end, these works complement each other. Analysed together they become a helix-like response that extends our comprehension of how militarism, misogyny, and homophobia have characterized the roots that produced the Franco and Pinochet regimes and that remain cooked into societal views in the regimes' wake.

2 Boot-Camp Brutality: Making Militarized Masculinity

Militarized masculinity is a construction of manhood associated with physical strength; discipline; a religious zeal for the hierarchical, patriarchal nation; and the ability to voluntarily use violence to solve problems. It is a gender identity that dictatorial regimes around the globe have imposed through intersecting institutions (education, religion, government, military, media) to shape men into disciplined members of a hierarchical and heteronormative state (Moon). In many contexts over time, militarized masculinity has been fomented within larger constructions of anti-liberal, ultra-Catholic, misogynist, and homophobic national identities. To paraphrase Moon, the indoctrinatory apparatus that institutes the ideal of militarized masculinity spans childhood to adulthood through gendered propaganda, but also through conscription, which summons men for military service, while young women are expected to serve the state through biological reproduction and domestic management. These gender formations serve the greater political goal of cultural colonization and economic imperialism by upholding the hegemony of the military and the economic elites whose privilege is framed as natural and necessary.

The process of militarization depends on assumptions about the value of gender hierarchies, separate domains for men and women, and military service to the state. Enloe observes that the more militarization transforms society, the more society sees militaristic imperatives as necessary to ensure security against presumed enemies (*Maneuvers* 3). Patriarchal assumptions about men's natural duty to defend women feed into the notion that war is a male endeavour and that violence is hardwired. Military service is therefore viewed as a normal development of expected masculine gender roles and behaviours. This form of masculinity parallels normative hegemonic masculinity to the extent that both are associated with values including competitiveness, strength, and heterosexual virility. In the escalation of political conflict, authoritarian discourse serves to blur the distinctions between militaristic, nationalistic, and patriarchal beliefs. At the intersection of these belief systems, armed intervention and war are framed as the only effective response to social upheaval.

To embrace militarized masculinity is to conceive of a binary biological opposition between men and women, with the former as predisposed to using force to protect the patriarchal family and the latter as apt to mothering and caregiving. This understanding of gender configurations coincides with Enloe's arguments in *Bananas, Beaches and Bases* that women are often relegated to secondary or symbolic roles in nationalist movements, either as icons of nationhood, to be elevated and defended, or as the spoils of war, to be denigrated. In either case, the protagonists are men who defend freedom, honour, homeland, and women (Enloe qtd. in Nagel 112).

Enloe maintains that militarized masculinity requires both men's and women's acceptance, yet it privileges masculinity (*Maneuvers* 4). Such insights were gained, in part, through dialogue with Bunster who examined the role of right-wing women in the expansion of militarization in Chile. Bunster observed that the Pinochet regime used the ideology of femininity to sustain a doctrine of national security ("Watch Out"). In *Right-Wing Women in Chile*, Margaret Power also emphasizes how militarization relies on women who support patriarchy: "The right's identification of women as mothers and housewives dovetailed with many Chileans' ideas about gender" (45). Enloe, Bunster, and Power agree on the need to look beyond militaries to militarism and patriarchy in order to find the gendered dimensions of torture as well as its justification in the present.

Men's education in Spain and Chile under Franco and Pinochet aimed to produce patriotic professionals, while male military service reinforced the imperative of "national unity," which, as Moon suggests, constitutes a euphemism for the unmitigated elimination of internal political opposition (55). Patriarchal ideology and militarism in Spain and Chile framed war as natural and necessary. Slogans and terminology such as "Fight against Subversion," "National Reorganization," and "Moral Purification" drew from a history of ruthless domination and became a means to bolster support for the military takeovers, to disguise acts of terror, and to dehumanize the opposition. As Stern explains in *Remembering Pinochet's Chile*, words like *subversive* "enabled regular-army soldiers to compartmentalize responsibility and establish mental distance" (98). The goal for the regime's architects was to justify the coups and the subjugation of the leftist resistance, thereby capturing political power and material resources to ensure ultimately the hegemony of the economic and military elites.

Although Chile and Spain both had a long history of armed intervention in political conflict, the Franco and Pinochet regimes arose from a reaction to the social change that gave rise to the Second Spanish Republic (1931–9) and the Popular Unity government (1970–3). The military regimes demobilized the societal transformation that had been spearheaded by historically marginalized groups. For four decades in Spain and two decades in Chile, Franco and Pinochet, together with their civilian proponents, wielded a right-wing discourse that framed inequalities based on gender, race, class, and sexuality as prescribed and deserved. The suppression of political and economic choices was depicted ad nauseam as the military's heroic duty to save the nation from social and economic disorder.

Thinking through militarized masculinity requires a panoramic view with multiple angles. There are many entryways to broach the topic and thread together these two contexts. A chronological approach would raise questions about the origins of the military dictatorships before their official establishments in 1939 and 1973 and would call attention to the important sequence of events and influences. While that approach is valuable, I will work from the lens of memory with texts written after the dictatorships to emphasize the legacy of militarization and the ongoing imposition of aggressive masculinity. In both Spain and Chile a central way to cultivate militarized masculinity has been through obligatory service, which continues in Chile and was abolished in Spain as recently as 2001. In the ensuing pages I will take up the topic of conscription, followed by boys' socialization, the militarization of civilian women, misogyny, sexualized torture, and resistance.

Antonio Muñoz Molina's memoir *Ardor guerrero* (*Warrior Fervour*) provides an illuminating first-person perspective of compulsory military service and the ways it functioned in Spain to normalize militarized masculinity and violence. Leading with an analysis of the initiation and conditioning tactics to train soldiers clarifies the link between militarism, gender norms, and the brutal use of force. After discussing the most relevant aspects of *Ardor guerrero*, I will turn to traumatic memories of conscription in Chile under Pinochet and draw a link between it and the methods of military socialization that created perpetrators of violence. While conscription was instrumental, I will also explain how the military camps were not the only site for combative conditioning. To paraphrase Cockburn, boys and men learn in everyday life to be aggressive, use their bodies as forces of coercion, manoeuvre their fists, heads, boots, and penises as weapons to exert dominance, and obtain the respect of other males and the sexual submission of women ("Don't Talk"). Extending these ideas, I argue that it is vital to gain a panoramic view of military culture that goes beyond an analysis of the military institution itself. A more perceptive analysis tracks down the links between civilian and military violence and articulates the leading role that gender plays in both.

The decision to explain boot-camp brutality is a decision to foreground the deadening experience of soldiers as a precursor of perpetration. Such an approach runs the risk of exempting individual soldier torturers from responsibility for acts of violence in the service of the regimes. Nevertheless, it is a constructive line of inquiry that provides necessary scaffolding to comprehend militarized masculinity and its violent effects. Focusing on boot-camp brutality allows us to understand better past atrocities, which by extension contributes to the prevention of state violence. It is a long view that considers the role of conscription in the process of militarization and an important, but not the only, site in the solidification of misogynistic and heterosexist beliefs that fuel acts of gendered violence.

Zealous Warriors: Antonio Muñoz Molina's *Ardor guerrero*

Since militarized masculinity is an acquired rather than an innate identity, it is important to examine the sources of its reproduction, including conscription. Compulsory military service in twentieth-century Spain and Chile became an instrumental tool in the shaping of national and gender identity throughout the dictatorships. As historian Leith Passmore maintains in *The Wars inside Chile's Barracks*, from 1973 to 1990 approximately 370,000 young men in Chile – most of them from impoverished backgrounds – were conscripted and forced to serve the Pinochet dictatorship (3). Many were funnelled into clandestine detention centres to monitor and often participate in the torture and execution of political detainees.

In Spain, during and after the civil war, conscription was a normalized practice and became a primary tool in the National Catholic regime's indoctrinating mission. Conflicted memories of compulsory military service and its harmful effects in Spain are still vastly understudied, and as such, ferreting out critical accounts of conscription gives us new clues about the training grounds for violence. For its rare and compelling illustration of the army, its relation to violence, and its role in post-Franco society, Antonio Muñoz Molina's memoir of conscription greatly contributes to the theorization of militarized masculinity. Written in 1995, six years before the end of obligatory military service in Spain, *Ardor guerrero* (Warrior fervour) reflects a cultural environment shaped by competing masculinities.

The book takes us back to 1979, a time of transition just after the twilight years of the Franco regime. The power of the military remained intact, and conscription was still mandatory even for university students like Muñoz Molina, who opposed the regime and was even arrested for participating in a student protest. Without the power to opt out, the author was forced to endure over a year of military service in one of the most high-risk areas for violence at the time, San Sebastián. That location was the site of the increasing radicalization of ETA (Euskadi Ta Askatasuna), the armed leftist Basque nationalist and separatist organization that was founded in 1958 and dissolved in 2018. Muñoz Molina departs from the genre of fiction, for which he is most well known, to explore the many facets of military culture and to narrate the impact that conscription had on his own life.

The memoir is a remarkable account of military service that sheds light on how violence emerges from the larger systems of patriarchal power that celebrate male domination and militarized methods of control. In inquisitive rather than prescriptive prose, the author manages to condemn violence while contemplating how and why it occurs. While Muñoz Molina's book does not name militarized masculinity directly, it reconstructs the regulation of male bodies, the shaming of weakness to reinforce aggressive male norms, and the authorization of extreme punishment for the violation of rules of conduct. He illustrates what James Dawes, author of *Evil Men*, calls the step-by-step process by which men are made into war criminals. As Dawes explains, first, recruits are removed from their families, friends, and educational structure in order to be re-educated. This is a deeply gendered process since separation from civilian society usually involves separation from women and children. Then recruits are taught to regard the world in binary terms of weak versus strong, us versus them, clean versus unclean, safe versus unsafe. Again, the question of gender, as well as sexuality, cannot be neglected because the oppositional division between masculine and feminine is crucial in the militarization of men.

The reduction of nuance facilitates acts of violence by framing forceful domination as not only the easiest but also the *only* solution to social and political problems. The third step, as Dawes describes, involves the physical, emotional, and psychological breakdown of the recruits through exposure to extreme elements and fatiguing activity. Pushing recruits beyond their imagined boundaries also involves subjecting them to a system of arbitrary rewards and punishments that makes them feel disempowered. This step is also gendered because physical strength is viewed as masculine and weakness is framed as feminine. The feeling of disempowerment and shame subsequently creates an intense craving for power and domination over others. The fourth step involves the desensitization to violence, which Dawes points to in stating that recruits often begin by bayoneting dummies, then bayoneting corpses, and finally killing prisoners. To my mind, each of these steps must be understood in relation to the reproduction of gender roles. Even in militaries that accept women, soldiering is a gendered experience, and those who uphold the structures and culture of militarism not only expect the capacity for violence but also glorify it.

If gender socialization in civilian society involves a process of learning the socially acceptable behaviours associated with being a boy or a girl, then militarization involves violent enforcement of such norms and the exaggeration of hypermasculine subjectivity. The binary view of men as naturally commanding, physically strong, and sexually virile becomes built into recruits' sense of self-worth and identity. What is so remarkable about Muñoz Molina's military memoir is his clear-eyed views on continuities, namely between the outward expression of militarized masculinity within the army, on the one hand, and dominant gender relations within civilian culture, on the other. He probes violent characteristics of boys' socialization and prompts reflection on how aggressive masculinity may be enacted by civilians in the absence of dictatorial governments and outside the barracks. The defence of violence as a method of control depends on civilians whose support of militarized masculinity goes unquestioned. Muñoz Molina's memoir sets the stage to expand later on Marina Lazreg's premise that torture and terror feed one another, and that systematic torture is "not just an instance of violence committed by uncontrolled soldiers" but rather "part and parcel of an ideology of subjugation" (Lazreg, *Torture and the Twilight of Empire* 3).

To be clear, Muñoz Molina's account of conscription is firmly set after the dictatorial context of subjugation, and yet it is extremely relevant for its rendering of the crucial links between the normalization of violence during the Francoist past and the ongoing views of the essential role of the military in the wake of the regime. He does not take for granted what Enloe calls the "symmetry between masculinity and militarism" (*The Morning After* 73). By reflecting on how military service is presented through family expectations, heroic narratives, and popular culture, he renders visible how the nexus between masculinity and militarism is hammered out. Notions of manhood and womanhood become uncovered in his narrative of military service. He also illustrates the multistep process that Dawes describes earlier, first by depicting the segregation from the outside world, followed by nationalist indoctrination, deprivation of control, and desensitization to violence.

The militarizing process of separation and dispossession begins with a general sense of grief and terror that is followed by despondency produced by the loss of a familiar appearance, name, and civilian clothing. Muñoz Molina spells it out: It was "as if we had lost our individual consistency to become a malleable substance, in a crowd with herd-like passivities" (*Ardor guerrero* 58). He goes on to write: "The shaved skulls accentuated the clone-like effect of the uniforms, further reducing us to a collective and numerical identity" (76). The author explicitly describes the experience as a banishment shaped by "a monotony of orders" that recruits began to fulfil "with the daze of automatic obedience" (59). The image conjures Foucault's critique of various regulating and punitive practices in bureaucratic institutions like prisons that shape identities and produce docile bodies. The abuse to which Muñoz Molina was subject in public, in front of other recruits and instructors, was, in his words, "an embarrassing test of my incompetence, not of the cruelty of the norms to which we obeyed" (91). Therein lies a lucid critique of the conditions that preserve the continuity of both gender norms and violence within the military institution. The insufficient performance of masculinity results in punishment, while brutality maintains its normative position. The message is clear: the fault lies with the victims, not the perpetrators. The outcome is fear and silent acquiescence.

The non-fiction narrative also weaves together thought-provoking segments on the ways in which military indoctrination reduces historical, social, and political nuance to create binary and hierarchical thinking. "One had to become familiar with an infinitely detailed universe of values and gestures, signs, moral codes, tasks, and rites that structured and configured the hours" (Muñoz Molina, *Ardor guerrero* 61). Military identity, as the text reveals, is constructed through discourse and recycled through language over time: "It was necessary to go backward ideologically in time not only to the still recent years of Francoism but much further back. To return to a dusty archeology of heroism and sacrifice and everything for the country. We had to forget our recently acquired fragile civil rights and learn to resign ourselves again to absolute obedience" (61–2). Writing against military indoctrination, the author deconstructs the cultural landscape in which gender and national identity are viewed as fixed. Dualistic oppositions of male and female are reinforced as natural through language. His critical departure constitutes a negation of the exclusionary Francoist vocabulary of the militarized patriarchal nation with its gendered norms and customs. It also responds critically to the conformism that remained ingrained in societal views in the Franco regime's aftermath.

Muñoz Molina sheds light on the initiation that marks recruits and gives them a gendered language that shapes their world view and futures beyond the barracks as civilians. "The vocabulary of rural young men with which they arrived at the camp was quickly enriched with the murkiest words of urban marginality. After graduating from the military, they would return to their towns and use their new language with pride to tell the young boys about their military adventures" (*Ardor guerrero* 209). He reveals the role of military language in gender socialization that categorizes and conditions military and civilian men and boys.

Military conditioning, as Muñoz Molina illustrates, involves a system of arbitrary rewards and punishments that result in uncertainty and terror: "At no time was anyone safe from punishment, since we couldn't know and comply with the infinite number of rules without ever making a mistake. Even more damaging was that no one was ever safe from shame and ridicule" (*Ardor guerrero* 82). The mental breakdown from contemptuous mockery, and the physical exhaustion from extreme conditions and strenuous activity, produce a sense of disempowerment, which has violent consequences: "They told us, and we also ended up saying it ourselves, that we had to be cruel to survive. But often survival was an excuse or an alibi for cruelty, which was exercised universally and systematically from top to bottom" (82). This statement unmasks the constructed nature of violence and the way that cruelty is framed as inevitable. By recasting violence as learned and normalized, the text scrutinizes the narrow simplicity of biological essences and the notion that male violence is innate. Gender socialization is exacerbated by military socialization within the barracks and comes to constitute one of the root causes of violence.

Military structures hinge upon hierarchies of power and gender norms that are more visible and strictly observed than in other social institutions. Such asymmetries are integral in a hostile and competitive environment where recruits become increasingly deprived of agency and stripped of empathy. In raw and vulnerable recollections of boot camp Muñoz Molina asks readers to consider how the feeling of disempowerment creates an intense craving for power over others: "We were the plagued and outcasts, the untouchables, the bottomless pit of all cruelties that descended from rank to rank from the pinnacle to the base of the military structure. Yet those who treated us most viciously were not the officers, but the corporals and the instructors who perhaps had only spent three months more than us in the army" (*Ardor guerrero* 82). As an illustration, the author describes a notably disdainful instructor: "He looked at me with an expression of hatred that I don't think I've seen in anyone's eyes, with a fierce contempt that seemed to satisfy his need to abolish in me any residue of human dignity" (90).

These details sharpen our awareness of how militarism reinforces power hierarchies not only through the deprivation of power but also through cut-throat competition and the derision of civilian identity. Milena Abrahamyan observes in the article "Tough Obedience": "According to militarized masculinity, a peaceful civilian is someone who has feminine traits, from which it is required to move away if one is to acquire a 'true' masculine image. As a result, one of the main focuses of military training is the destruction of a soldier's civilian identity" (4). If new recruits possess the most visible civilian traits deemed feminine, then those recently promoted soldiers seek to accentuate their own difference as more authentic militarized males through acts of humiliation and violence towards the novices.

The experience of segregation, masculine inadequacy, and ridicule, from Muñoz Molina's perspective, produces self-loathing and a desire for power rather than mutual support or identification among the marginalized. It created "a constant hotbed of hierarchies and evils [...] There was no mercy for those who fell or stumbled, for those who lost their step, for the one who was so fat that he couldn't climb the rope or jump the colt, for the extravagant, the effeminate or the lunatic" (*Ardor guerrero* 83). Fear of harm contributes to either enthusiastic conformity or passive acceptance of the imposition of an aggressive male identity. The ubiquity of fear "was the gravitational force that prevented military life from collapsing" (194).

Acquiescence to uniformity and military affiliation end up erasing otherwise complex alignments of the self and constitute steps in the path of least resistance. Muñoz Molina admits that the last thing he wanted was to be like the outcasts or join them to defend their damaged self-respect: "What I wanted was to be exactly like the others, to join their normality, to blend in, to secure myself within the crowd" (*Ardor guerrero* 91). He preferred one improbable smile or a friendly gesture from a bully over an act of kindness from an underdog: "Just like most victims, what I wanted wasn't to end up like the executioners, but rather to deserve their benevolence. When at last I managed to keep up the pace without making mistakes and to synchronize my arm movements, I was freed from the threat of the clumsy squad. I began to look with a certain disdain on those who didn't have the same skill or the same luck as me" (91–2). In these passages the author calls attention to the gendered process of shaming through which the violent world view of the dominant militarized male becomes the world view of the dominated.

Adaptation to the hostile military domain and compliance with the gender norms at the crux of that domain become a strategy of survival, as Muñoz Molina suggests: "it was clear to me that the only secret was to endure, that one endured, not out of cunning or courage, but out of the sheer instinct to adapt to everything, to anesthetize oneself or harden in adversity, and to reduce their world to the small-minded environment in which for now one had to live" (*Ardor guerrero* 149). If Muñoz Molina underscores the inertia to adapt, he also questions the normalization of violence and the assimilation of gender norms that frame aggression as the quintessential feature of masculinity. Painfully forthright, he admits the great difficulty of going against the grain. At one point he, too, vigorously raised his arm in the nationalist salute and took pleasure in the unmistakable unanimity of the soldiers in formation: "it's possible that once a maximum degree of saturation has been reached in the endlessly reiterated uniformity of gestures, no member of a crowd can withdraw from full identification with it, even if they seek refuge in secrecy and misanthropy" (100).

In that "overwhelming world in which nothing but blind obedience and physical brutality mattered" (*Ardor guerrero* 162), one could still refuse to take the path of least resistance and disrupt prevailing gender norms. However, as Muñoz Molina makes clear, in so doing, he who challenges gender norms becomes part of a subordinate masculinity (i.e., akin to femininity) and therefore not only risks depriving himself of certain privileges but also exposing himself to harassment and physical harm. Conformity provides a safe haven and a sense of pride in belonging to a dominant masculinity, even if that identity simultaneously inspires reluctance, disgust, or shame. Not unexpectedly, militarized masculinity becomes a tool of power.

Weapons constitute symbols of authority that emerge from societal veneration of militarized masculinity. In Muñoz Molina's case, the submachine gun initially overwhelms him "with its evident condition as a killing machine" (*Ardor guerrero* 106). Under the watchful eyes of his superiors he learns to wield the weapon to force his opponents into submission. Firing the gun and brandishing the bayonet suddenly inspire a feeling of power. He explains that once he managed to exercise control over his adversary, he felt a combination of rage, aggression, embarrassment, and self-ridicule. His own battle cry, he recalls, became even louder as he gazed into the eyes of the other. His eyes "no longer reflected complicity or humor, but hatred. One's soul becomes taken over by the cruel anger of a stranger that until that moment had not been regarded as part of the self" (152). If Muñoz Molina asserts that the military machine spares no one, he also undermines the notion that aggressive masculinity is natural. Unlike the soldiers and officers that he observes, he does not confuse the ideological and the learned with the biological.

What Muñoz Molina describes is a painful self-discovery of his own shared capability of perpetrating violence. He does not characterize that capability as an instinctual impulse, rather as one that results from the conditioning practices of the military institution. Suddenly, he explains, he felt "a fascination with weapons, the drunkenness or elation of exercise and physical strength, which for the weak can reach paroxysms of delirium, dreams of vengeful arrogance" (*Ardor guerrero* 153). Written as both a fraught acknowledgment and a warning, the author unearths the gendered process by which soldiers are trained to become militarized men capable of carrying out murder, torture, and rape. "I fired a pistol and saw with surprise and a sudden sense of pride that the dark shape of a bullet hole was marked on the human silhouette in front of me" (154). Revelations like this one illustrate a key contention in this book, namely that perpetrators of violence are not born but made through a multistep process that cannot be disentangled from gendered power relations.

The role of language in the making of militarism and violence cannot be overstated. Throughout his book Muñoz Molina reflects on the pervasiveness of sexist jokes, self-praise regarding sex with women, pornography that objectifies women, and sexualized taunts that humiliate non-aggressive males. All of these contribute to the normalization of violent masculinity. He relates an encounter between soldiers and a woman during a convoy: they "whistled, screeched like apes, shouted hypotheses about how she would wet her panties upon seeing us. As that solitary woman would push the cart trying to get ahead of the vehicles, they competed to suggest the most diverse sexual positions and possibilities" (*Ardor guerrero* 147). Similar to Bolaño, he recognizes his own bystander behaviour: "Had one of the women looked up and seen my face among those in the back of the truck, there would have been no reason to distinguish my face from the others. Nor would there be reason to exempt me from the anger and shame she undoubtedly felt" (148). He seems to understand that to dismiss these catcalls as mere compliments is to ignore their place within a larger framework of sexist and homophobic language, a framework that ultimately supports sexualized violence. As Jean Franco indicates, women have been routinely insulted as prostitutes or animals during rape, "as if the verbalization confirmed the degraded state of the victim and helped spur on the perpetrator to more acts of violence" (86).

The objectification of women's bodies and the consumption of their sexuality is linked to the consumption of meat, argues Carol Adams in

The Sexual Politics of Meat. Muñoz Molina's military memoir makes that link evident. Meat is a component of camaraderie and masculine identity. He discusses a heavy combination dish consisting of pork chops, steak, fried eggs, potatoes, bread, and wine. It was popularly called the Urtain, a nickname for the legendary Basque heavyweight boxer José Manuel Ibar who ate large quantities of meat. As Muñoz Molina explains, soldiers doing military service would go to Vitoria to have sex with women and consume the famous Urtain, both of which they had dreamt about throughout the week (*Ardor guerrero* 115). "The Urtain, as much for its size as for its composition and texture, was more than a dish; it was the materialized dream of hunger" (116). The dual lust to "devour" female and animal flesh is explicit, but the author alerts us to the societal messages producing and driving those desires: "In the recruit's imagination, in the artificial paradises that we all ended up sharing, the dream of the Urtain was in a position as privileged as the dream of a girlfriend with which the most unleashed carnal ambitions were to be satisfied during our designated leave" (117). "Artificial" aptly describes that socially constructed paradise in the minds of militarized men. The underlying anguish plaguing the real Urtain (the boxer) revealed that masculine bravado failed to provide him genuine fulfilment. After distancing himself from boxing, he committed suicide by throwing himself off a ten-storey building in 1992 at the age of forty-nine.

The association between meat consumption, masculinity, and power also becomes visible in the threats among men in the militarized hierarchy. Sergeants would threaten lower-ranking corporals with the nightmarish assignment of guard duty in which soldiers became vulnerable "pieces of meat" (*Ardor guerrero* 134). "You're fresh meat for the watch tower" (210). One particularly cruel sergeant named Valdés threatened "to make meat of us" if certain duties were not performed (173). This kind of language functioned to objectify, intimidate, and humiliate lower-ranking men while elevating the speaker to a higher status. The meat metaphor was used to convey a message of strength and dominance. In that setting, recruits learned that strength was synonymous with a disregard for human and animal life and with a willingness to inflict pain and suffering.

To this point, I have used Muñoz Molina's memoir to examine the gendered discourses, operations, and management of militaristic culture in Spain and the ways in which boot-camp training reinforced the belief in the inevitability of violence. As it is set in the wake of the Franco regime, it attests to the continuity of an ideology of subjugation that had previously authorized the detainment, abuse, and execution of the regime's political opponents. One additional example will illustrate that an examination of the spectacle of military life with a focus on the construction of masculinity deepens our understanding of violence.

The case revolves around the dreaded military prison and Sergeant Valdés who had the power to send recruits there as punishment. First, the author recalls how the sergeant court-martialled one recruit who ended up serving a year in the dungeon and came out a different person: "When he returned to the barracks, his head was shaved, and he was missing half his teeth. He was swollen, with a livid whiteness of the deceased, as absent from everything, as if moving through the paved and trellised corridors of a psychiatric hospital" (*Ardor guerrero* 302). This recollection calls to mind Foucault's critique of the similarities between prison-like institutions – hospitals, prisons, the military – where subjects are under constant surveillance and disciplined for any misstep. Muñoz Molina describes something like a panopticon, in which soldiers, like prison inmates, are always in view. The combination of panopticon and the zombie-like image of the disciplined soldier was highly effective in instilling an overwhelming fear that kept all soldiers in a perpetual state of self-regulation.

The brutal beating of another recruit at the hands of the same sergeant further develops a picture of the prison-like character of the military setting. The assault that the author witnessed reveals the psychological and physical torture to which recruits were subject and the homophobic language at the centre of militaristic shaming:

> Valdés knocked him down with a slap. We all saw him place his knees and palms on the gravel to stand up and we heard the sound of his breathing as he got up. Valdés waited for him to stand up to punch him in the stomach. The veins in his neck had swollen and he was screaming, getting very close to the face of the other, who had a hunched back and seemed unable to support himself on his knees. He called him a faggot and a drunk, ordered him to stand up, hit him on the chest with his clenched fist, kicked him in the ankles, increasingly out of control, challenging him, telling him that if he had balls, he would defend himself, come on, he said, if you're so brave, hit me, drunk, faggot, you're all faggots. And then he kicked him with even more force, sticking out his chest with his shirt open. Come on, answer me, ask your friends for help, look at them. He shouted at us now. Nobody comes to your defense, they're all faggots like you. His own sadism excited him, and he could no longer contain himself, he was drunk and maddened by the evidence of his strength and the helpless weakness of the soldier in front of him, because nothing inflames the cruelty of the depraved more than the absolute helplessness of their victims, the power that this gives them to abuse them until they are exhausted. (Muñoz Molina, *Ardor guerrero* 303–4)

While the violent posturing that Muñoz Molina describes is as remarkable as it is revealing, we know that such acts are extremely common.

The scene is reminiscent of a long list of American military films (or anti-militarist films) like Stanley Kubrick's classic *Full Metal Jacket* or *Jarhead* by Sam Mendes. The pattern reveals shared gendered ideologies and indoctrinating practices. For the enraged sergeant who haunts Muñoz Molina's memory, the recruit's refusal to play his assigned role (i.e., obey, conform, respect hierarchies) was not a mere misstep; it was grounds for annihilation. As he becomes increasingly intoxicated with power, the militarized male no longer sees the humanity in the other.

Hostility directed at his subordinate contained explicitly homophobic language that dehumanized the other specifically through feminization. Voicing and repeating certain words like *faggot* catalysed an escalation of violence. While the physical damage of such brutality was conspicuous in the recruit's bandaged wounds, Muñoz Molina regrets that no one denounced the violence. It was already clear that the military institution not only implicitly excused such demonstrations of authority but also condoned them. When he discovered months later that the sergeant in question was found dead, "lying on the bed, naked, with his head destroyed by a bullet" (*Ardor guerrero* 305), it was hard to not feel "the relief of a delayed revenge" (302). The case ended in a mystery, and the pistol was never found. This story is not simply about an individual sergeant and the soldier that he tormented, but rather about the systemic oppression cultivated in the military that spills out into society and also is fed by a pervasive culture of toxic masculinity that breeds violence. The memoir lays bare the gendered dimensions of militarism, the role of conscription in socialization, and how these have contributed to violent subjugation of political, gendered, or sexual "others."

Becoming Dogs of War in Chile

The tortured memories of former conscripts in Chile reveal the extent to which obligatory military service fortified the repressive political apparatus of the Pinochet regime. In *The Wars inside Chile's Barracks: Remembering Military Service under Pinochet*, Passmore catalogues memories of physical and psychological abuse performed inside military camps to break, indoctrinate, and shape young men into "dogs of combat" (118). The phrasing is significant as the recruits underwent a process of animalization meant to produce vicious yet obedient fighters. The term *dogs of combat* also recalls numerous accounts that reveal the routine utilization and butchery of dogs as part of initiation. Conscripted men were forced to train canines, develop a relationship with them, then slaughter them, and eat their raw flesh. Conditioned to see the animals as internal enemies, soldiers were forced to drink their warm blood in survival drills. Those who questioned the practice were humiliated and beaten until they conceded. The goal was not only submission but also the desensitization of the conscripts and making them into militarized "hard" men capable of destroying those framed as enemies. The brutality inflicted upon animals, mirroring the patriarchal oppression of women as theorized by Carol Adams, is demonstrably intensified by militarization.

Whether it is the often-invisible cruelty towards animals, or aggression towards women and other men, the common denominator is militarized masculinity. Gendered hazing and sexualized punishment, such as forced nudity, homophobic insults, and attacks on the testicles, were all reported by former recruits as routine practices. Such violent acts were standard in the barracks and "equated falling short of military hardness with femininity and homosexuality" (*Wars* 118–19). Passmore explains that former conscripts remember being beaten with a plank or broomstick called *la nena* (the little girl) or *la flaca* (the skinny girl). The tool was used as a form of chastisement in combination with electricity applied to the teeth and the testicles. One recruit who underwent this particular type of torture was forced to "sing over and over 'my corporal rapes my mother and my sister while I hold them down'" (119). The gendered nature of such violence inflicted by military men on other men must give us pause. What is the function of sexual humiliation and misogynistic vitriol in the process of militarization? What kind of harmful impacts does it have?

Conscript accounts in Chile attest to the centrality of misogyny and anti-gay hate in the process of making militarized masculinity. Ritual abuse functions to safeguard hierarchies of power, reinforce sexism and heterosexism, normalize masculine myths of strength, and produce fear of deviation from gender norms. Soldiers are conditioned to equate femininity with emotional and physical weakness and, by extension, as a source of contempt. As Milena Abrahamyan holds, desensitization must be viewed in light of the imposed imperative to eradicate any sign of the feminine: "Femininity – perceived as the total opposite of masculinity – becomes the 'enemy other,' which needs to be dominated and destroyed" (5). Passmore exemplifies the point: "Making men hard meant conditioning draftees via a series of mutually reinforcing, and often overlapping processes of desensitization. It implied deadening the body to physical suffering, severe weather conditions, and its own instincts, as well as instilling blind obedience, numbing recruits to compassion, and making them indifferent to the pain of others [...] Basic training lasted for the first three months and is characterized in ex-conscript testimony by the physical brutality and psychological degradation, often administered in a place called 'the valley of tears'" (*Wars* 117).

Conscription was an essential tool in Pinochet's offensive on human rights to secure the hegemony of the military establishment. For conscripts already serving and those who would join the ranks, the message of civil war was normalized. The fabrication of Plan Z, which alleged that Allende supporters were plotting to kill generals and admirals, fuelled fear within the barracks. Some recruits, as Passmore contends, enthusiastically participated in the perpetration of violence to suppress the leftist opposition, while others endured physical and psychological torment, political persecution, and forced labour. The 1994 film *Amnesia* by Chilean director Gonzalo Justiniano depicts just such torment. Released four years after the end of the Pinochet dictatorship, the film is told from the perspective of a guilt-ridden former soldier who searches for the army sergeant who forced him to guard and take part in the brutal treatment of prisoners in the Atacama Desert. The film explores how militarized masculinity has oppressed not only the regime's enemies but also those forced to sustain the regime's violence.

After the regime had been institutionalized, the most violent political repression took place in clandestine torture centres and became the focused work of the DINA (Dirección de Inteligencia Nacional). Beginning in 1974, the secret intelligence service (sometimes referred to as Pinochet's Gestapo) included some civilian agents like Michael Townley, but most of the actors were active or former members of the military network. Some of the most notorious, like Manuel Contreras, Miguel Krasnoff, Marcelo Moren Brito, and Basclay Zapata, were colonels or officers, some of whom had been trained at the US-run School of the Americas. From 1977 the CNI (Central Nacional de Informaciones) and the militarized carabineros took the place of the DINA, but the connective tissue between torture and militarized masculinity remained strong. That is, most perpetrators of human rights violations emerged in some way from the armed forces, including those who have come forward to acknowledge wrongdoing and those who lack any sense of remorse. Military conditioning was part of their experience and influenced the wider culture of the DINA's chain of command. Such a statement in no way attempts to exempt individual agents from blame, but rather to bring nuance to the analysis of violence by tracing its longer trajectory.

It is hard to overstate the role of military training and its gendered dimensions in the creation of conditions for soldiers to torture civilians. The kind of abuse that many soldiers perpetrated on political detainees in Chile was precisely the sort of abuse that they suffered in boot camp. Testimonies show that torturers consistently integrated sexual injury into their treatment of female prisoners; however, the Valech Report reveals that the torture of men also involved sexualized violence (Stern, *Reckoning* 296). Stern notes that "men testified less often than women about sexualized violence. But enough did so to make clear that the climate for them, too, included sexual humiliation and assault" (296). Sexualized torture of men is part of a larger attempt to guarantee the centrality of aggressive militarized masculinity. The act of framing the civilian political prisoner as the enemy "other" and the act of conceiving of him as unmanly through misogynist and homophobic language and violence must be viewed as two interconnected acts. They have a mutually constitutive relationship that facilitates the normalization of torture and politicide.

Militarism in *El mocito* by Marcela Said and Jean de Certeau

Examining the relationship between boot-camp brutality and the torture of political prisoners must not be confused with an attempt to merely conflate experiences between Pinochet's victims and his henchmen. It is about posing uneasy questions about responsibility and complicity, while steering clear of what Michael Lazzara calls "a generalized notion of victimhood that can dangerously morph to encompass just about any subject position" ("Uncovering"). Referring to the context of the opening of the Museum of Memory and Human Rights in Santiago, Chile, in 2010, Passmore emphasized the need to make space for conscript memories: "The ambiguous figure of the uniformed recruit – potentially a witness to, participant in, or victim of human rights, or all three – blurred the line between victim and perpetrator and could not be accommodated within any of the grand narratives of the coup and military rule" (*Wars* 11–12).

El mocito (*The Young Butler*, 2010), directed by Marcela Said and Jean de Certeau, explores the story of an accomplice named Jorgelino Vergara who, forty years after the 1973 military coup, gave a public account of the torture and executions that he had witnessed. Recruited as an adolescent boy by the notorious General Manuel Contreras, Vergara was responsible for serving coffee to the secret police during interrogation sessions. Later he stayed within the realm of the regime's henchmen and worked for years concealing the dead bodies of political prisoners. Both Michael Lazzara and Ana Ros use the documentary to discuss the way in which some perpetrators in Chile have come to see themselves as victims. Lazzara warns that interpretations of stories like Vergara's must not lose sight of the agency of accomplices and their active decisions to back the military junta. Ros focuses more on how *El mocito* allows us "to reflect upon the structures, situations, and interactions that bring common, morally adjusted individuals to support a repressive system rooted in the harassment and annihilation of others" ("El Mocito" 121–2). My discussion will place *El mocito* alongside Muñoz Molina's *Ardor guerrero* to raise questions about when, where, and how militarized masculinity is made, who it harms, and how it continues to shape beliefs about the Pinochet regime.

From a young age, Vergara worked in clandestine torture centres and, like a recruit in boot camp, internalize military language and learned to resign himself to absolute obedience. In that environment dominated by military men, naming conventions were part of protocol and reflected each man's place in the power hierarchy and his progress through training. Naming conventions served as constant reminders of the chain of command and the recruit's duty to respect it. The most obvious example is the use of military ranks like "private" or "sergeant," but new recruits were also assigned derogatory nicknames that denoted childishness, which later might be replaced by their proper names or "earned" nicknames, showing a gain in respect. Muñoz Molina recalls the process of learning a "new classification of human beings" (*Ardor guerrero* 61–3). He emphasizes the embarrassment of being called an *empanao*, meaning "clueless, dimwitted, oblivious, and inexperienced."

As the diminutive form of *mozo* in Spanish, *mocito* suggests "young man." Using *El* (the) before *mocito* emphasizes two defining characteristics: Vergara was the designated poor "little boy" meant to serve within the context of military men and secret agents with formal titles, surnames, and terms of respect. The name Jorgelino is also a diminutive and portrays Vergara, even as an adult, as lacking the qualities associated with being a "real man." It is through naming that we witness how Vergara's critique of the dictatorship exists alongside continued support of the military and idealization of the repressive model of militarized masculinity that fuelled political persecution. While he distances himself from past human rights abuses, his behaviours and language bespeak an ongoing acceptance of militarism and reverence for militarized men. This is particularly evident in one scene in which Vergara speaks with Juan Morales Salgado, an ex-operative who was under investigation at the time of filming. Vergara's deferential treatment of his former military superior speaks volumes. From his perspective the ex-military captain is an authoritative man and a leader who continues to command respect. This exposes how the Pinochet regime was predicated upon military ideology and how it continues to be profoundly gendered and accepted by both soldiers and civilians. It also reminds viewers that class and military hierarchies functioned together to target poor young men by ostensibly offering a path out of poverty and into the ranks of a dominant brotherhood.

Like Muñoz Molina's memoir, another important aesthetic choice in *El mocito* involves the foregrounding of weapons. The documentary opens in rural southern Chile where Vergara hunts small game for survival and routinely practises martial arts with nunchakus. As others have noted, the hunting and nunchakus sequences compel viewers to consider Vergara's capacity to kill (Lazzara, *Civil Obedience* 127). I interpret these scenes as a window into the learned performance of aggressive masculinity and the role of weapons in that performance. The veneration of weapons is a recurring trope. In one scene Said follows Vergara on the street where a gun on display for sale catches his eye. He handles it and discusses the price with the vendor. In another scene the image of the weapon is foregrounded at a shooting gallery within an amusement park where Vergara teaches his estranged daughter to shoot. Finally, his relationship to weapons is captured in a series of dictatorship-era photographic stills featuring an emboldened Vergara brandishing a pistol and wearing a black beret. His tough-guy pose indicates a feeling of power that seems to be missing in the present. His gaze at the photographs looks tinged with nostalgia. When the film-maker follows Vergara to a former torture centre where he once guarded political prisoners and watched as they were brutally tortured, viewers are prompted to connect the dots between the present-day weapons-wielding man and the boy who grew up under the guardianship of ruthless military officials.

The fascination with weapons cannot be detached from the process of militarization as well as the socio-economic structures of a profoundly unequal society. When poverty creates a sense of powerlessness, the appeal of a hypermasculine identity can increase because such an identity appears to command the respect that is otherwise denied. When a man's ability to dominate others becomes a valuable feature of his identity, his motivations to inflict violence increase. To recognize this is not to offer an apology for violence workers but rather to gain a better understanding of how dominant narratives of manhood become instrumental in perpetration and collaboration in mass atrocity crimes. When we take an intersectional approach, we can understand further how factors like class, race, and gender all intertwine to create a range of militarized masculinities. We can use Said's film to sharpen our view of a continuum of violence and therefore move beyond the micro-level interpretations of violence that miss its entrenched and continuing macro-level social sources.

When we view accounts of conscription in Pinochet's Chile in relation to accounts from Spain, we gain insight into how militarized masculinity is reproduced through powerful institutions, violent practices, misogynist language, and anti-gay hate. The comparison also raises questions regarding militarized masculinity's targets, victims, and supporters. If we ask ourselves how men in Spain and Chile became perpetrators of violence at the command of the regimes, we must recognize that obligatory military service is part of a violence-spawning system that teaches men to transform their bodies into powerful weapons of subjugation in the name of national security.

Toy Soldiers, War Stories, and the Continuum of Violence

The Círculo de Bellas Artes in Madrid hosted an exhibition of Antoni Miralda's photography called *Cowboy's Dream* from 29 May to 17 September 2023. It included the photographic series called Soldats Soldés (1965–73), in which the Spanish multidisciplinary artist treats playfully the serious topic of militarization. Born in Terrassa, Catalunya, in 1942, he served his mandatory military conscription during the Franco regime. Although his perspective on the experience is not explicitly documented in a definitive statement, his artistic output provides insights into his critique of militaristic culture and the dehumanizing effects of war. In Soldats Soldés little plastic soldiers are transformed into comical figures, roaming in platoons on the naked bodies of women. By enlisting unlikely elements, Miralda expands the boundaries of meaning. One photograph features a close-up of a breast, and another a hip, which are meant to appear as sloped landscapes that the toy soldiers traverse and conquer. The seemingly incongruous setting and distortion of elements is a visual juxtaposition that allows Miralda to compare critically the conquest of women's bodies to the conquest of lands. Other photographs feature apparent incongruities that invite spectators to bridge the gaps. The curator's statement at the exhibition summed it up succinctly:

In Nightmare's Chappelle, sixty-one vintage photographs belonging to the Soldats Soldés series (1965–1973) are on display, images that document the public interventions created by the artist with plastic soldiers. The series, incorporating hundreds of white soldiers joined together, was a kind of visual symbol of Miralda's work during the early years of his career. A pacifist plea, a personal exorcism, a parody of the mythologies of violence and the archetypes of patriotism, Soldats Soldés is an obsessive variation on the same image, repeated to the point of paroxysm and, to some extent, disengaged from its original meaning. Toy soldiers, attached to the gravitational centre of our culture, constituted a first approach to the ideas of seriality, accumulation, and archiving, characteristic of later works.

Militarized masculinity, as Miralda's photographs suggest, is persistent and pervasive beyond the institution of the military. The armed forces constitute one piece, albeit paramount, in the process of cultural militarization. The weight of militarist culture becomes minimized when the military is designated as the only source of militarized thought and action, as Enloe argues. Cockburn agrees, placing militarized violence on a *continuum of violence*, a term for which she is cited. She discovered the expression in the pamphlet *Piecing It Together*, written in 1979 by women associated with War Resisters' International who stressed the association of violence against women with international military abuse of power (Cockburn, "Don't Talk"). Since then, feminist scholars and activists like Cockburn and Liz Kelly have developed the notion of the continuum of violence to give a name to the correlation between a spectrum of gendered brutality spanning sexist jokes, misogynist threats, sex trafficking, rape, and femicide. The concept of the continuum is part of a larger theory of violence, threaded and developed throughout *Militarized Masculinity*, that looks beyond simplified and gender-blind assessments of individual acts of violence. Recognizing the interconnectedness of different forms of violence prevents a societal disconnect: domestic abuse is common, yet femicide and homophobic murders shock, revealing a failure to link everyday abuse to its extreme forms.

The notion of the continuum sharpens our awareness of the process through which violent thoughts and actions come to be seen as "normal." Cockburn argues: "Violence in our everyday cultures, deeply gendered, predisposes societies to accept war as normal. And the violence of militarization and war, profoundly gendered, spills back into everyday life and increases the quotient of violence in it" ("Don't Talk"). Extrapolating these ideas and applying them to Spain and Chile, one sees that militarism, inextricably bound to the glorification of aggressive masculinity, has been so omnipresent in culture and language as to be invisible to the uncritical eye. If violence was normalized under Franco and Pinochet and enabled the repression of political and gendered "others," then dissecting the everyday outlets for its normalization (i.e., language, popular culture), as well as critical depictions of subjugation (counter-hegemonic representations), becomes a strategy to disrupt the continuum.

As I shall explain later, within the Spanish Civil War (1936–9) and post-war context, visual culture in general and the comic book (*el tebeo*) in particular became effective media for political propaganda and militaristic socialization aimed at children. Fascist comics such as *Flechas y*

Pelayos and *Chicos* conveyed gendered, colonial, and ultra-right-wing Catholic discourses that, in turn, played the role of legitimizing certain acts of aggression and violence. In question is the process of children's socialization and identity formation. In the years after Franco's death, Carlos Giménez inserted the comic genre into the still-ongoing process of collective memorial reconstruction. His graphic novels, which I analyse in chapter 4, challenge the superhero archetype of hegemonic masculinity and instead depict physically and emotionally vulnerable boys struggling to navigate the limited terrain of militarized masculinity.

In tracing the continuum of violence in Spain through time (from the dictatorship through the transition) and in space (from the barracks to the playground), it is instructive to return to Muñoz Molina's memoir because it depicts the way in which militarized masculinity relates to violence beyond the military. The author explores how the idealization of the soldier is transmitted to the imagination of young boys both within their families and through cultural production. He writes: "The *'mili,'* as we heard it being told by adults, was an attenuated kind of war in which no one died. It was […] a world so novelistic and alien like that of the movies, but with a dense emotion of reality: pistols, bayonets, machetes, machine guns, cannons, all the words that we had learned in war films or famous comics" (*Ardor guerrero* 21). Muñoz Molina joins the dots between gendered narratives of military service in media and those told by fathers and retold by sons and so on. For him, however, "fear was stronger than the attraction to the aggressive and ruthless world of men" (29). Muñoz Molina's unheroic narrative breaks away from recycled stories of boot-camp bravery and allows readers to imagine the destructive ramifications of gender norms.

Without collapsing difference, we can connect Muñoz Molina's reflection with Marc Feigen Fasteau's *The Male Machine*. Written against the backdrop of anti-militarist movements in the United States during the Vietnam War, the book critiques the ideal of manhood, which is "the most fundamental standard, the yardstick against which we measure ourselves as men. To the extent that we fail to meet its injunctions, even by deliberate choice, we are likely to see ourselves, at least at times, as inadequate" (2). As in Fasteau, the picture that Muñoz Molina develops involves the humiliation produced by the aggressive male ideal: "The oldest, the strongest, the most lively and agile, always abused the weak, that is, those who were like me. On my street, like in the army, war was played, and there were violent heroes who scared the weakest and staked battles, launched screams and stones away from which some of us fled with an anticipated feeling of ignominy and shame" (Muñoz Molina, *Arbor guerrero* 33). When acts of violence are retold in this critical light, the links between military hazing and boyhood games become clear. Rather than solidifying the myths of masculine superiority and dominance, Muñoz Molina provides an example of how men can oppose violence not just as people but as men in that gender identity. To quote Cockburn from a 2017 speech in Istanbul, men need to engage as men "resisting the complicity, the exploitation of masculinity for war" (Keynote video address).

Such recollections confront violent masculinity at the centre of boys' socialization and foreground its relation to militarism. One final quote illustrates the point: "I couldn't know then to what extent my intuition was true: the military, when I arrived, wasn't going to be like the false stories that my uncles and father had told me, but rather a story of anguish, limitless and monotonous sadness of childish cowardice. It was the story of the vulnerability of not daring to go out on the street for fear that the older boys would hurt me" (Muñoz Molina, *Arbor guerrero* 33–4). Muñoz Molina's representation of this microcosm of violence invites reflection on the continuum of violence and the convergence of gender, politics, and subjugation. Militarized masculinity is bound to the fascist pillars of the Franco regime that justified the forcible suppression of the opposition during the dictatorship. The basis of those pillars predates Francoism, however, and they have endured beyond Franco's death in 1975. Reading Muñoz Molina's memoir provides insight into a continuum shaped by patriarchy, the military, and the state through which boys' and men's bodies have become sites for violence and control.

Women's Recruitment Roles

In *The Morning After: Sexual Politics and the End of the Cold War*, Enloe explains that "militarization relies on distinct notions about masculinity, notions that have staying power only if they are legitimized by women as well as men" (3). Women play a key role in disciplining and regulating gender norms or, conversely, in challenging them. Drawing from Connell and Theweleit, I note that men predominate in warlike conduct, rape, and other forms of violence; however, while women are less involved in the actual physical violence, they will help organize, speak with the same hatred, witness, and applaud at the sight of brutality.

As has been well documented, right-wing women in Spain and Chile played a key role in the defence of gendered hierarchies of power and gender norms during the Franco and Pinochet regimes. In 1973 a massive movement of right-wing Chilean women took to the streets to oppose the Allende government and explicitly call for a military coup. The strategies that these women used were clearly gendered, as Margaret Power observes: "In order to encourage the military to take action, the anti-Allende women questioned their masculinity. They threw corn and feathers at them to suggest that they were chickens and therefore 'sissies' not real men" (246). Striking kitchen pots and pans with spoons also became a gendered action against Allende that patriarchal women embraced to protest progressive reforms. As Ximena Bunster points out, by 1987, right-wing women's organizations "had branched out from the established military government bureaucracy, further infiltrating civilian life with military values" ("Watch Out" 487). The CEMA Chile (Chilean Mothers' Centres) and the Secretaría Nacional de la Mujer (Women's National Secretariat) became the most important right-wing women's organizations and brought together all social classes. She estimates that during the ten-year period 1973–83 the secretariat's activities had involved more than two million women (497).

For some women who helped provoke the coup, the social and economic programs of the Popular Unity represented a threat to their class privilege. It is also true, however, that many anti-Allende women were only positioned to lose from the economic policies of the regime. Many supported the right, based on the assumption that the revolutionary milieu of the 1960s was an unnatural transgression of gender norms and a betrayal that undermined their roles as mothers and wives. Conservative women with various identity positions shared assumptions about the predominance of the patriarchy and men's and women's "true natures" as ordained by God. Deviation from that model became a source of resentment and blame. Right-wing women thus saw themselves as part of a cultural battle that was waged during the Allende years and won with the military coup. Their mission, paradoxically, was to support the imposition of a regime that vigorously sought to continue the asymmetrical power relations that kept women in an inferior position in relation to men. In their support of the regime, upper-class women protected their class privilege, no matter that in the long run they had to face discrimination as women compared to their male counterparts.

While many middle- and upper-class anti-Allende women supported the military takeover, it is important to note that many of their sons avoided military service through connections or access to higher education. Most of the men who were called up and who entered the barracks were from the popular sectors of society, and therein lies the intersection between class and gender and the making of militarized men. In both Chile and Spain, working-class and poor women often supported military service as a valuable option for their sons and husbands. Even beyond Spanish and Chilean borders, Connell suggests, "working class boys, who don't have the other resources that will lead to a professional career, become the main recruits into jobs that require the use of force including the police, the military, and private security" (Connell and Pearse, *Gender: In World Perspective* 5). However, the economic rationale cannot be divorced from societal views of masculinity (Passmore, *Wars* 20). Many believed that the armed forces offered the necessary discipline and education required to make boys into men, a notion that is bound up in gender norms. It was not only that those recruits and their families understood that soldiers had to endure abuse as a price to pay for better work prospects after leaving the barracks, but also that withstanding punishment and being able to carry it out as militarized men was an asset that garnered respect. The narrative, as Muñoz Molina put it, of the military being "literature and epic poetry, cinema and tourism of the poor" (*Ardor guerrero* 32), was widely accepted by mothers, girlfriends, and wives.

In Chile the pro-Pinochet establishment depended on women to celebrate militarized masculinity throughout the dictatorship. As I discuss later, Marcela Said provides in her film *I Love Pinochet* a window to view the discourse of militarized masculinity through the voices of women ranging from the working class to the elite. By offering an image of what we can call militarized civilian womanhood, the film-maker challenges the notion of militarism and war as exclusively male zones. Said's exploration of right-wing women's perceptions of Pinochet provides a wealth of insight into binary constructions of masculinity and its presumed opposite, femininity. Such social constructions, as the film reveals, depend on specific institutions that extol the virtues of the militarized male (the military, the Church, the media, and the state) in the name of patriotism and capitalist modernization.

Internalized social mores and the long-standing celebration of militarized manhood also governed the political position of conservative women in Spain. As I explain later, Pilar Primo de Rivera, leader of the Sección Feminina (the women's branch of the Falange), was instrumental in upholding the belief in the biological distinction between the creative male and the simple-minded woman. In her words, "El hombre es rey; la mujer, los hijos, las ayudas, los necesarios complementos para que el hombre alcance su plenitud" (qtd. in Sueiro and Díaz-Nosty 363; The man is king; the wife, the children, the aids, they are necessary complements for the man to reach his full potential). She defined women entirely in terms of lack and disseminated that inferior view of Spanish womanhood for over four decades (1934–77) through magazines, radio shows, and in obligatory programs of domestic training considered as a social service. Such training, involving instruction on cooking, cleaning, and mothering, amounted to the female counterpart to conscription and was enforced by the women's branch of the Falange.

Obligatory domestic training is a primary example of gender socialization and an integral component in the creation of militarized civilian womanhood, which at the same time preserved the supremacy of militarized masculinity. Like the military, official domestic training was a highly regulated institution as it constituted one of the requirements for obtaining a passport, a driver's licence, and educational titles. Another requirement was written permission from a male figure. Significantly, the institution greatly devalued women's creative capacity. Primo de Rivera's comments describe men and women as innately opposite. Women, as a group, were seen as subordinate to men, deficient in physical strength and intellectual aptitude. Women's primary role was caregiving. This construction of gender roles and biological distinction shaped expectations of both women and men under Franco.

Some of the worst victims under these circumstances were politically active, leftist, proletarian, and middle-class women who digressed from their expected role as mothers and caregivers. Broader societal inequalities and masculinist conventions fed into the process of militarization that shaped the structures of violence perpetrated against progressive women. The regime's champions framed non-conforming women as the ultimate transgressors of societal norms. This will be discussed in more detail in chapter 5.

Conscription and Militarized Masculinity Today

On 23 February 1981 Antonio Tejero Molina (b. 1932), lieutenant colonel of the Guardia Civil, entered the Spanish parliament with approximately two hundred civil guard members and held congress hostage. The attempted military coup, which took place against the backdrop of elections for a new prime minister after the resignation of Adolfo Suárez, constituted a desperate response from the hard right to the social and political changes that had grown in the wake of Franco's death. Among the factors that generated tensions, prominence was given to the legalization of the Communist Party in 1977 and the statutes to increase regional political autonomy. However, the newly established democratic government was also associated with the legalization of contraception, feminist demonstrations, demands to legalize divorce, universal suffrage, and a growing conscientious-objector movement. Such social changes clearly bespoke shifting conceptions of gender roles that the guardians of Francoism were unwilling to accept. In a strategically planned move a state of emergency was declared by the military insurrectionists who appealed to King Juan Carlos to abolish the Cortes Generales (congress and senate) and re-establish a military dictatorship. For thirty-five minutes shots were fired in the chamber while live television captured the dramatic moment. No one was killed, but the fear and uncertainty that many Spaniards felt was rooted in the memory of 1936. Within a period of under twenty-four hours other army units failed to join the coup, and King Juan Carlos gave a nationally televised address denouncing the action and, in so doing, safeguarded the crown as democracy's champion at a moment of insecurity for the monarchy.

Much has been written about the failed coup; what is relevant here is the confluence of gender and militarism in Tejero's discourse, his admiration for Pinochet and Franco, and the relationship between the failed coup and the anti-conscription movement. The trial in the aftermath of 23-F (known in Spain by the numeronym or as "el Tejerazo") proved to be a public humiliation for the armed forces. Tejero and his fellow conspirators stood by a seemingly contradictory line of defence that, on the one hand, they were simply following orders, and on the other, they had a moral obligation as patriotic guardians to save the nation and leave it to their progeny in the same condition in which it was left to them by military leadership. Contradictions and conspiracy theories aside, it is important to note the long-standing junction between nationalism, militarized masculinity, and patriarchy that shapes the saviour discourse of the *golpistas*. They declared a determination to protect the achievements and values of the Nationalist victory through military rule and to re-establish order and unity. Overturning the "chaos" of the transition to democracy by force, from their perspective, was the only viable response to the weak, liberal, and unpatriotic civilian-led democracy.

The hope for the survival of the dictatorship after the dictator's death, however, was not shared by everyone in the military. Ultimately, the nostalgic military hardliners were outnumbered, and

Tejero surrendered in 1981 within one day of the Tejerazo. He went on to serve a fifteen-year prison sentence before he was released in 1996. In less than two years of the unsuccessful coup, the Socialists gained power and undertook a series of measures to change the composition and focus of the military. Many of the most fanatical Francoists in the army's senior ranks (mostly veterans of the civil war and the División Azul) retired definitively after 23-F, but they remained unapologetic. Following the death of Pinochet in 2006, Tejero attended an homage to the Chilean dictator in Madrid, showing his unwavering backing of the military regimes in both Chile and Spain. The symbolic funeral was organized by the Círculo de Amistad Hispano-Chilena and was attended by figures linked to the Franco regime, as well as the new Spanish ultra-right ("'Viudos de Franco'").

According to Javier Cercas in *The Anatomy of a Moment*, the attempted coup "was the most efficient vaccination against another coup" (371). While it seems unlikely that an infallible inoculation exists, it is true that the *golpistas* were discredited as outdated sabre rattlers, and the debate around conscientious objection and social service as an alternative to the *mili* began to grow exponentially. If Tejero represented those policemen and soldiers that longed for the old regime, Pepe Beúnza became a leading figure in the Insubordinate Movement (Movimiento Insumiso, or Movimiento de Insumisión). Whereas in the 1960s and 1970s, conscientious objection was based mostly on religious grounds (e.g., by Jehovah's Witnesses), it was not until the early 1980s that men began to object in large numbers to military service for political reasons. The minimum penalty was a year in prison, which some objectors did not avoid as increasing the numbers of prisoners of conscience placed more pressure on the government to abolish the *mili*.

The anti-conscription movement was decentralized and non-partisan although it was associated with the left and included anarchists, anti-fascists, anti-imperialists, and separatists (Basque, Catalan, Galician). Some denounced the military presence in their regions, while others rejected military culture as a relic of Francoism. It was part of a larger debate about cultural norms, gender expectations, and the nuclear family with a male head as the social and economic ideal. Collective objection, coupled with calls for tax resistance to military spending, non-violent marches for demilitarization, and hunger strikes in military prisons first engendered the establishment of civil social service as an alternative, followed by the reduction in service time, then the decriminalization of insubordination, and ultimately the abolition of conscription in 2001. The now all-professional armed forces in Spain, including women who as of 1999 made up about 12 per cent, has approximately 133,300 active personnel.

The death of conscription in Spain constitutes one of the multiple ruptures with Francoism; however, as in the case of many contexts without compulsory enlistment, militarized masculinity remains alive. Still woven into pieces of the cultural fabric, militarized masculinity re-emerged powerfully in the last decade with the founding of the ultra-right-wing, anti-feminist, and anti-immigrant Vox party led by Santiago Abascal. He is the grandson of Franco-era politicians and a fervent supporter of the military, fashioning a soldier-like image in photographs and political campaigns. Since he avoided military service himself, he has been criticized across the political spectrum, but nonetheless he has led the increasingly popular Vox since 2014.

In Chile twelve to twenty-two months of military service is still obligatory; however, in the post-dictatorial period this mandatory draft has been mostly unnecessary because sufficient volunteers have filled the ranks. In an army of 80,000 men and now women, approximately 9,200, or 11 per cent, are conscripts, and about 15 per cent of the total are women. Recently the number of volunteers has decreased, which involves multiple factors that may, though not inherently, include a decrease in the cultural presence of militarized masculinity. The lack of educational opportunities, as we know, has often driven men into the military as a means of economic survival and social mobility. If the number of volunteers has fallen in recent years, one contributing factor likely involves an increase in access to higher education and a simultaneous stagnation in conscript pay.

In understanding conscription in Chile, it is also important to consider the mobilization of groups critical of the armed forces. In 2017 the group Ni Casco Ni Uniforme (Neither Helmet nor Uniform) marked its twentieth anniversary of bringing together anti-militarists, anarchists, pacifists, feminists, students, and workers to condemn the legacies of the military regime and to denounce conscription and military spending. Many ex-conscripts have called for recognition as victims of the military regime and demanded reparations. As Passmore explains in *The Wars inside Chile's Barracks*, many conscripts frame service as a fundamental rupture in their lives: "They felt haunted by 'ghosts': changes in their personalities, recollections of atrocities committed against detainees or fellow conscripts, the constant fear on the streets and in the barracks, the shame or guilt of participating in the abuse of civilians or their fellow conscripts, or the powerlessness to respond to their own mistreatment or that of others" (165).

Ex-conscript testimonies demonstrate how militarized masculinity has oppressed not only the regime's enemies but also those sustaining the regime's violence. Even so, as Passmore suggests, the ex-conscript movement more broadly is neither entirely anti-military nor anti-conscription. "Most ex-conscript groups emerged initially around the issue of unpaid pension payments and wages that former recruits felt they were entitled to (2006–2009). Their demands for retroactive payments were soon to be complemented with calls for health and education benefits and compensation for damages" (*Wars* 18). Transnational truth-and-reconciliation processes and the memory boom also influenced the ex-conscript movement; however, anti-militarism or a political identity does not unite them. Some have compartmentalized the dictatorship as a deviation in the long history of the institution. As Bawden and Passmore point out, public confidence in the military recovered shortly after the dictatorship. This only reaffirms the notion that many Chileans have been able to separate their view of the military from the Pinochet years and either look back to the heroic narratives of a more distant past or focus on the military's work in disaster relief.

To close this chapter on militarized masculinity in relation to conscription, gender socialization, and resistance during and after the Franco and Pinochet dictatorships, I would like to circle back to Antonio Muñoz Molina's memoir and consider how the book was received in Spain at the time of its publication. We should recall that the author finished his obligatory service in 1979, two years before the attempted military coup. The book was written in 1996, six years before the end of obligatory military service. At that time, Fernando Savater predicted at a book launch that the memoir would serve as an instrumental anti-militarist text. It is true that during the five years after its publication the number of conscientious objectors increased until the *mili* was abolished in 2001. But anti-militarist music (ska, punk, pop rock), protests, marches, and hunger strikes were arguably more visible and influential in shaping political action than was Muñoz Molina's book. In fact, the author has been hesitant to identify himself as altogether anti-militarist. On the day of the book launch he stated that he felt an even greater hostility towards religious education than towards the army and added that his children would have to choose for themselves. Muñoz Molina is only clear that "democracy has to defend itself" ("Antonio Muñoz Molina revela"). Referring to the fight against Nazism, he suggested that there was a place for some form of military in a democratic society.

Muñoz Molina's hesitant position towards the military does not undercut his scathing assessment of the way it functions. Rather, it adds a layer of sobering nuance to his judgment. Furthermore, regardless of the author's official statements about his work, the texts themselves reveal the damaging gendered pressures working within the military and how they relate to a matrix of social relations in society at large. What the memoir itself reflects about the military is damning, therefore arguably anti-militarist, albeit never dogmatic or simplistic. At the time of the memoir's release a reporter asked Muñoz Molina if he was afraid that a story of military service would seem too "heavy," which was, she assumed, a viewpoint held by most women. He reacted by saying that he was not afraid because by telling his story he could also discuss many other things. Indeed, the memoir represents an intervention into a much wider debate than one on the military alone. It allows readers to connect cultural constructions of masculinity and sexuality to militarism and violence and to cut through heroic myths that only conceal the inner workings of the armed forces and obscure the interconnections between combat zones and home fronts. It is only with the wide exposure of cutting perspectives of militarism, like Muñoz Molina's, that there will be a chance of radically transforming the institution and diminishing violence more broadly.

3 Perpetrator Memory and Masculinity: Breaking Ranks in Chile and Spain

It became known as the Slit-Throat Case (Caso degollados), one of the most notorious state crimes in Chile's second decade of politically motivated violence under the Pinochet regime (1973–90). In March 1985 three members of the Communist Party – Manuel Guerrero (teacher, age 36), José Manuel Parada (sociologist, age 34), and Santiago Nattino (artist, age 63) – were kidnapped in Santiago by agents of the military and the national police force (carabineros) and ruthlessly murdered. Their mutilated bodies were dumped into a ditch near the airport; a memorial (Tres Sillas, or Three Chairs) was built there in 2006 to commemorate their struggle. A small memorial was also inaugurated in 2016 in Providencia, at the spot where the men were taken. Parada was head of the analysis department at the human rights organization known as Vicaría de la Solidaridad, which was protected by the Catholic Church. Six months before his gruesome murder, Parada met with Andrés Valenzuela (age 28), alias Papudo, who had deserted the military after working as a soldier in the Fuerza Aérea de Chile (FACh) (Chilean Air Force) and as an operative of an ultra-secret group called the Comando Conjunto (Joint Command) created by General Gustavo Leigh. In the midst of ongoing dictatorial repression, Valenzuela first contacted the journalist Mónica González and later the Vicaría to give detailed information about the persecution, detainment, torture, and execution of the Pinochet regime's political opponents.[1] Since

---

1 See "Confesions de un agente," by Mónica Gonzalez, http://www.casosvicaria.cl. Also see "El hombre que olía a muerte," by Andrea Insunza and Javier Ortega, http://www.casosvicaria.cl.

Valenzuela's life was at risk after he provided evidence that incriminated a network of perpetrators, the Vicaría helped him escape to France in December 1984.

The Slit-Throat massacre that ensued after Valenzuela's escape was a brutal act of control and retribution against the human rights organization and Papudo, the perpetrator and defector. His testimony, which helped to unravel scores of disappearances, was published first in Venezuela in December 1984 and six months later in Chile in the magazine *Cauce*, one of the few oppositional media outlets that operated during the dictatorship. On the cover Papudo's photo appears in black and white next to the large headline "I Tortured."

The novelist Nona Fernández (b. 1971) grew up in a neighbourhood not far from the site where the infamous Slit-Throat Case abduction took place. At the time of the massacre she was around the same age as the victims' children, Manuel Guerrero (age 14) and Javiera Parada (age 11). In *La dimensión desconocida* (*The Twilight Zone*), Fernández dissects that violent crime and others; she also interrogates the world that produced them. Her exploration expands in concentric circles with a common centre – the story of Papudo. Who was he? What did he do? How did he change direction? Written in reflective prose, her creative non-fiction book presses readers to consider the perspective of a rank-and-file perpetrator of torture who denounced the system in which he was deeply involved. In telling the story of Papudo, she describes a cultural and political web, showing the interconnections between seemingly disparate topics such as military conscription, education, the emergence of consciousness, the links between memory and identity, and the multiple legacies of militarism. *The Twilight Zone* illustrates how these are best understood in relationship to one another.

This chapter considers how literature might move beyond the static faceless image of soldiers to address the *shaping* of perpetrators of violence. I demonstrate how fiction and creative non-fiction can unpack the complexity, tensions, torment, and antecedents to violent acts without merely producing an apology for torturers. This analysis provides insight into the ways that literature might make a meaningful statement about the making and unmaking of violence workers who served the Pinochet and Franco regimes. In a transatlantic framework I compare Nona Fernández's *La dimensión desconocida* with Manuel Rivas's *El lápiz del carpintero* (*The Carpenter's Pencil*) and Alberto Méndez's *Los girasoles ciegos* (*The Blind Sunflowers*). The parallels between these seemingly dissimilar texts from Chile and Spain are fruitful in helping us understand militarized masculinity, violence, and the emergence of consciousness. By comparing the works of Fernández, Rivas, and Méndez, we can complicate the victim-perpetrator binary and deepen our understanding of the ramifications of militarized masculinity on the regimes' henchmen.[2]

Beginning with *The Twilight Zone*, I probe the ways in which Fernández chronicles her attempt to interpret the motivations of a former military conscript who, amid institutionalized state terror, gave a public account of the covert raids, torture, and executions in which he participated. Fernández's portrayal asks readers to consider how practitioners of cruelty might also suffer from the hostile forms of masculinity to which they feel obligated to conform.

To draw out the common threads of the effects of militarism in the Spanish and Chilean contexts, I turn to *The Carpenter's Pencil* by Manuel Rivas. The Galician author opens a window for readers to view contrasting forms of masculinities during the Spanish Civil War and to imagine the pressures to obey military protocol. The novel also explores how normalized toxic interactions among men inform power dynamics between men and women. Rivas accomplishes this by juxtaposing two male characters and the significant figures in their lives. One of the characters is a low-ranking prison guard for Franco's fascist forces, and the other is a progressive doctor imprisoned for his defence of the Second Republic. I pay particular attention to the militarized figure who personifies the side of the Nationalist victors, yet transmits a discourse of defeat. Through his confessions readers learn that he executed a Republican painter and suffers from the haunting traumas of a perpetrator's past. Rivas offers a disruptive and valuable commentary on the hypermasculinity of military culture by disassociating it from bravery and instead linking it to physical and mental suffering.

To bring further nuance to the claim that the violence of militarization also oppresses the military men that uphold it, I return to Alberto Méndez's extraordinary hybrid novel *Blind Sunflowers*. Whereas in a separate chapter I look at the links between militarized masculinity and misogyny, here I focus on two different stories in the book to chart how the author connects the dots between masculinity, war, and violence. The first story is told from the perspective of a wealthy captain of the Nationalist army who comes to understand the full implications of his participation in the military uprising against the republic. The third story leads readers into the dark territory of a Francoist prison in 1941 where an anguished Republican prisoner reflects on the cruelty of war

---

2 In this chapter I draw some insight from Nicole Beth Wallenbrock's article "An Apology for French Torturers: L'Ennemi intime."

and seeks a new language to express his feelings and recuperate his humanity as he awaits his execution. Through these stories Méndez captures the horrors of war and militarism from the vantage point of military men who have experienced them.

"I Tortured," in *The Twilight Zone*

In Chile the attempt to visualize the atrocity of torture with a focus on the perpetrators is a powerful component in a larger reckoning with the past in the post-dictatorship. As Lazzara reminds us, an expansive bibliography exists on the experience of victims and their children, but stories of perpetrators and their families remain largely underexplored (Lazzara, "Familiares). Recent documentary films like Andrés Lübbert's *El color del camaleón* (*The Color of the Chameleon*) and Lissette Orozco's *El pacto de Adriana* (*Adriana's Pact*), both from 2017, foreground voices of the children and relatives of collaborators and, as Lazzara maintains, reveal how perpetrators and collaborators represent themselves. They also shed light on how their descendants confront political and ethical dilemmas associated with their family bonds.

The documentary *¡Viva Chile Mierda!* (*Long Live Chile, Damn It!*) by Adrian Goycoolea is particularly relevant to my analysis of Nona Fernández's *The Twilight Zone* because it features an interview with Andrés Valenzuela, the same figure at the centre of Fernández's book. Goycoolea interweaves the interview with the story of his aunt, Gabriela Goycoolea, a former schoolteacher and political prisoner now living in Spain. She is also at the centre of Carolina Astudillo's short documentary *The Unspeakable*. The link between Gabriela Goycoolea and Valenzuela is significant: she was held in captivity and tortured for three weeks, during which time she was guarded by Valenzuela. Since he recognized her as one of his neighbours from the coastal village of Papudo (the place that lent Valenzuela his nickname), he secretly helped her to survive by giving her food and information. The documentary *¡Viva Chile Mierda!* broke new ground by putting before the public a present-day interview with the soldier who had splintered the regime's secrecy after the original interview in 1985 and then vanished from sight. The film was released not long after the first season of the television series *Los archivos del cardenal*, which fictionalized Papudo's confession and the subsequent Slit-Throat Case in several episodes. As one of the scriptwriters, Nona Fernández carried out meticulous research for the series and gained insight that she would later use for her 2017 non-fiction narrative about Valenzuela and the crimes in which he was implicated.

As a work of creative non-fiction, *The Twilight Zone* is told from the first-person perspective of a narrator who is also the author. She renders visible her subjective position as a researcher, an artist, a scriptwriter, and a civilian woman whose gaze primarily at men is inquisitive and self-consciously intrusive. By looking at men's lives and their various positions in society as soldiers, activists, victims, bystanders, deserters, sons, fathers, brothers, and husbands, she encourages readers to see anew an entire structure of gender relations that cannot be divorced from the context of militarism in which they play out. Readers gain access to the curious gaze of a woman who never claims to understand fully the trauma of the victims or the motives of the perpetrator in question but tries to glimpse the pain that emerges from Valenzuela's testimony, his trajectory, and the people whom he harmed.

Andrés Valenzuela was a rank-and-file agent of the Joint Command who participated in kidnappings, torture, clandestine killings, and disappearances. Unlike many prominent military officials, he attempted to look critically upon his involvement in mass atrocity even though it meant risking his life. Valenzuela's confession in 1984 to the journalist Mónica Gónzalez about the repression aided human rights activists and alarmed the armed forces. La Vicaría de la Solidaridad, the organization founded by Cardinal Raúl Silva Henríquez, protected the former agent (facilitating his exile in France) and delivered his testimony to lawyers of the institution.

On the surface the impact of his testimony reveals that exposure was a powerful countermeasure to violence as it provided information to unravel a network of torture centres. But when we go beyond that initial step, like Fernández does in her creative treatment of the case, we find uneasy questions about perpetration and responsibility. Fernández's *The Twilight Zone* prompts thought on conscription and militarized masculinity and the significance of these in the process of creating perpetrators of torture. It also sheds light on the tensions and contradictions within the military and exposes it as "less impermeable, more fragile" (Enloe, *The Morning After* 99). If the military is an institution that forges men into violence workers, it is a man-made system that requires military and civilian acquiescence, without which it would deteriorate.

Fernández begins *The Twilight Zone* around 2015, thirty years after the author first saw the 1985 cover of *Cauce* that featured the photograph of Valenzuela and his confession. Fernández attempts to reconstruct the atmosphere of constant danger surrounding the former conscript when he gave his account to Mónica González. By moving the perpetrator's experience to the centre, the author brings human complexity to the image of a soldier, yet she never loses sight of the atrocities that he has committed. One of the gruesome torture scenes that she describes constitutes the frame for the book and first appears in the opening pages after we are introduced to the figure of Valenzuela. The story that she evokes was told by a former political prisoner, specifically a sixteen-year-old woman, who had been stripped naked, covered in excrement, and tormented in a dark interrogation room by rats. Giving such detail reveals an attempt to expose the specificity of sexual terror and to raise questions about its link to domination and politicide. As the author grapples with the horror of gendered violence, she consistently turns back to the perpetrator of such acts. In so doing, she opens a path to consider the person who committed the acts and the gendered conditioning that shaped conscripts like Valenzuela.

By braiding pieces of information from the torturer's story with survivors' testimonies, the author reconceptualizes state violence within a broader framework of power relations where dominant masculinity is learned and enforced. The act of naming is part of the author's strategy to explore a broader social framework. She consistently refers to Papudo as "the man who tortured" rather than "the torturer." With that move she conceives of violence as an act that a man performed rather than as an inborn impulse or character trait. Violence was systematic and produced in social contexts and in the service of a military regime that justified the elimination of political "others."

Violence did not emerge spontaneously, aberrantly, inevitably, naturally, or uncontrollably, as naive explanations would have it. The author's use of the moniker "the man who tortured" instead of Papudo (his nickname) or Valenzuela (his surname) is also a way to express the existence of patterns in soldiers' collective experiences rather than a focus on the individual. This point is further developed as the author identifies the man who tortured with conscription. She explains that in 1974, one year after the military coup, he was conscripted into the air force and separated into a unit that would train in a military academy and guard political prisoners. That was the beginning of his initiation into what he would later call the machine of death.

Drawing upon Papudo's admissions, the author delves into uncommon aspects of the conscript experience, tracing the transformation into a torturer and the unexpected instances of camaraderie between prisoners and their captors. One such moment of personal humanity is recounted: "Before I tied him up he shook my hand and held it for a moment. I gave him a cigarette and he thanked me for it" (Fernández 104). This singular act of kindness by a torturer towards a prisoner illustrates a rejection of the military's rhetoric and conditioning, which encouraged soldiers to view the prisoners as non-human. Papudo's superiors would interpret his empathy as fraternizing with the enemy, which would have severe repercussions. Papudo's internal conflict is evident as he acknowledges both his grief and his descent into callousness, noting, "We had been innocent conscripts. Dumb. Naïve. Now we were able to eat sandwiches while gawking at a dead body" (104). Why bring out these details? For Fernández, telling this story is a response to a larger frustration with oversimplified narratives that reduce violence and suffering, as she states, to "one big massacre, a fight between good guys and bad guys who are easy to tell apart because the bad guys are in uniform and the good guys are civilians. There is no in between" (Fernández, *Twilight Zone* 32).

Fernández, using Papudo's narrative as a central thread, brings to light the devastating impact of torture and forced collaboration. He spoke of his duty as a guard over political prisoners held in the War Academy's basement, which led to his meeting with the Flores brothers. He witnessed the collapse of many prisoners, including those brothers. Under torture, one brother became a collaborator to save his siblings, returning a transformed man (*Twilight Zone* 70–7). The discussion of military-induced collaboration then prompts Fernández to reflect on the profound psychological impact of fear, recalling Chris Marker's *Level Five*. This essay film about the 1945 Battle of Okinawa and mass suicides includes one man's testimony of killing his own mother upon the emperor's orders (78). When Fernández recalls the man saying that he became his own worst enemy, she uses an associative strategy. She places different kinds of suffering side by side in her narrative. In some way, the elderly Japanese man mirrors the submission, conformity, and regret forced upon individuals in Chile during the military regime. Fernández poignantly asks, "How many faces can a human being contain?" (84). She then personalizes the narrative by introducing her own family, reflecting on the innocence of her adolescent son and envisioning him in comparable circumstances. By doing so, she intensifies the analysis of perpetrators, urging readers to confront the possibility of their own involvement in such scenarios.

The Twilight Zone heightens readers' awareness that the dictatorial control in Chile involved not only the murder of anti-Pinochet resisters but also an atmosphere of widespread fear. It was a context in which conscripted soldiers could be tortured and killed for insubordination. The book prompts readers to take a long view, connecting the dots between the making of perpetrators of violence and a process of militarization in which conscripts are considered property of the state. The author walks a fine line between making an apology for violence workers and tracing the toxic roots that shaped their experience. Ultimately *The Twilight Zone* offers a springboard to discuss both how the process of militarization creates violent masculinity and how men and women participate in that process or defy it. The book opens new pathways to thinking about the structural and social breeding of terror and how it is sustained. The author accomplishes this difficult task through meticulous research and by setting up a narrative structure that is interrogative by nature instead of prescriptive.

Perspectives of Perpetration in Spain

In *Reluctant Warriors*, historian James Matthews emphasizes the complexities of the Spanish Civil War by reassessing the significance of conscription in the making of Franco's army. He demonstrates that although the Second Republic galvanized communist, socialist, and anarchist volunteers and the Nationalist side motivated Falangist and Carlist participants, as the war ensued, the number of volunteers decreased significantly. The magnitude of conscription on the Nationalist side, he argues, is evident in the fact that at the beginning of the war Franco's rebel army had under 100,000 men, but as the army gained ground and forced conscription, Franco's forces grew to 1.26 million by 1939 (Matthews 3). After the war, conscription continued as a normalized practice under Franco and became a key tool in the National Catholic regime's indoctrinating mission. As was explained in chapter 2, Muñoz Molina's *Ardor guerrero* offers a deeply critical view of the damaging effects of military indoctrination and its promotion of male brutality. Through the lens of memory he sheds light on how the punitive practices of military service endured beyond the Franco regime and left men's bodies deeply etched with the constricted notion of masculinity as synonymous with aggression.

Conflicted memories of military service in the context of dictatorial rule in Spain, still vastly understudied, are key to understanding the perpetration of violence and its numerous consequences. Historian Paul Preston suggests in the prologue of Matthews's *Reluctant Warriors* that when one considers the massive bibliography on the Spanish Civil War and the Franco regime, conscription is one of the most important subjects that remains obscure. Paying attention to conscription leads to a more nuanced understanding of the ways in which militarism is part and parcel of broader systems of violence that police and punish those who do not conform.

Narratives that involve men's experiences as actors in war and political persecution have the potential to deepen our understanding of the ways in which gender norms, and specifically the internalization of intersecting discourses of aggressive masculinity and passive femininity, fundamentally shape the process of socialization, militarization, war making, and mass atrocity crimes. As Stephen Haynes suggests, "masculinity is often constructed around images of strength, hardness, firmness, etc. and this has had the effect of normalizing conformist, aggressive, and asocial behavior" (169). Haynes goes on to argue that the socialization of soldiers is a form of hegemonic masculine socialization in patriarchal society (168–9). Amina Mama upholds a similar view when she states, "It is not that 'masculinity' generates war, as the question has been put, but rather that the process of militarization both draws on and exaggerates the bipolarization of gender identities *in extremis*."[3]

Reluctant Executioners in *The Carpenter's Pencil* by Manuel Rivas

The novels of Manuel Rivas (b. 1957) and Alberto Méndez (1941–2004) disrupt simplified accounts of victims and victimizers by imagining soldiers' deeply ambivalent attitudes about violence. These authors at once recognize the agency of Nationalist soldiers, while acknowledging the role of historical processes and gendered social conditioning that affected their choices. In doing so, they give rise to new perspectives on the Spanish Civil War and the Franco regime, namely the ways in which militarized masculinity was used to uphold a broader system of hierarchical power that oppressed not only civilian women and the gender non-conforming but also military men.

The Carpenter's Pencil is set in Galicia during the Spanish Civil War and in the post-Franco present. The story revolves around two contrasting figures: Daniel Da Barca, a Republican doctor and political prisoner; and Herbal, an uneducated man from rural Galicia who served as a prison guard for Franco's fascist forces. The narrative begins around 1998, when the number of first-hand witnesses to civil war has begun to dwindle. In that context a Galician journalist named Carlos Sousa receives an assignment to interview the aging Dr Daniel Da Barca, now in his eighties. Sousa's political disenchantment and ignorance of the war set up what becomes his own process of critical consciousness through attentive listening. The novel highlights the ambivalences and gaps in memory through temporal shifts from the present to the past and through differing perspectives of alternating narrators. Such

---

3 Amina Mama is a Nigerian-British writer, feminist, and academic. Her main areas of focus have been postcolonial, militarist, and gender issues. https://www.opendemocracy .net/en/5050/challenging-militarized-masculinities/.

narrative shifts involve a third-person omniscient narrator who relays the present-day interactions between the journalist (Sousa) and the erstwhile Republican (Da Barca), as well as an omniscient narrator from the civil-war years who chronicles events as they unfold.

Running parallel to the story of Da Barca is an alternating one that depicts the Nationalist side and produces a thought-provoking contrast between masculinities. This parallel narrative is set on the present-day border between Galicia and northern Portugal in the oppressive setting of a brothel. There the former Nationalist soldier (Herbal) tells his own life story to María da Visitação, a lusophone African woman who was sold into sex slavery and was living on the extreme margins of society. She becomes the interlocutor for Herbal on the day that he reads Da Barca's obituary in 1998, presumably shortly after Sousa's newspaper interview with the doctor. Herbal recounts his fraught relationship with the Republican figures of his past, including Da Barca. Born into a family of executioners, Herbal is socialized to view domination over women and male enemies as the true reflection of masculinity.

The representation of Herbal speaks volumes against the Franco regime's discourse through the way of victory. His voice reveals the negative influence of militarized masculinity on those who are socialized to perform it. His traumatic memories of acts of violence, and specifically the execution of political prisoners, serve to reveal how military brutality leaves deep scars on those who participate in it. After he executes a Republican painter, the only physical remnant that the victim leaves behind is a carpenter's pencil, which Herbal salvages and places behind his ear. This object symbolizes the spectre of the prisoner, a sort of artistic soul inside the breast of an executioner. Similarly to the case of Valenzuela in *The Twilight Zone* by Fernández, Herbal in *The Carpenter's Pencil* becomes a kind of prisoner. The pencil "speaks" to Herbal throughout the narrative as a voice of beauty and truth in a land of aggression, competition, and conformity.

Haunting memories of perpetration are powerfully conjured through the literary device of the pencil. For Herbal, the object becomes a relic that beckons the image of a particular non-militarized character (the painter), as well as the Republican civilian resistance generally. It is suggestive that the pencil originally belonged to a Republican carpenter named Antonio Vidal, a man whose profession signifies creation rather than destruction. The pencil was later given to Pepe Villaverde, a self-confessed humanist who "would open his speeches on the factory floor talking of love" (Rivas 24). The pencil's third owner was the painter, and finally the fourth was Herbal. The author's nostalgia for the Second

Republic manifests itself in characterizations and symbols (the pencil) that reflect a certain form of non-violent masculinity in opposition to militarized masculinity. At its core the pencil is a life-giving tool. The painter would use the pencil to record "almost feverishly" the identities and humanity of the Republican prisoners (25): "The painter wanted to capture the invisible wounds of existence" (27). The ghostly figure of the artist symbolizes the haunting presence of the murdered Republic. The phantom constitutes a literary manifestation of unsettling nostalgia, one that summons the lost creative potential of that period and subverts the violent patriarchal structures and practices of the military victors (DiGiovanni, "Return to Galicia").

The contrast between the militarized prison guard and the non-militarized painter offers a window into multiple masculinities and the ways in which gender plays a role in acts of political persecution, subjugation, and murder. Non-violent masculinities associated with civilian identities were simultaneously feminized and framed as threatening by militarized men. During the republic the painter is blacklisted for two primary causes: his creation of posters promoting the loyalists and his public disavowal of all acts of violence. His honesty is matched only by his compassion, particularly towards those suffering from mental illness, as well as women forced into sex work. The painter's interest in capturing on paper the anguish and hope of the disenfranchised attests to his deep sense of empathy. Standing in opposition to aggressive masculinity at every turn, he is finally executed by Herbal, who immediately feels remorse and becomes forever tormented by the painter's spectre. When Herbal is once again in the role of executioner, this time with the medical doctor Da Barca, he must repress the voice of the painter to fulfil his orders to kill. As he puts the barrel of the gun in Da Barca's mouth, he says, "One queer less" (Rivas 51). This language stems from broader gendered discourses of masculinity and sexuality that have become instrumental in the transformation of some men into dehumanized objects and others into perpetrators of violence.[4] It reiterates the idea that the theme of wartime and dictatorial violence cannot be separated from issues of gender and sexuality.

Through the portrayal of the soldier in *The Carpenter's Pencil* the author makes a powerful statement about the affliction produced by hostile forms of militarized masculinity. Herbal is socialized to view violence as the true reflection of masculinity, a view that is compounded

---

4 For an excellent analysis of the role of masculinity in mass atrocity see *Genocide and Gender in the Twentieth Century*, edited by Amy E. Randall.

as he works with the "Iron Man," one of the leading Nationalist figures. Through these characters the author shows the hostilities between conflicting masculinities and the enormous influence of dominant ideologies. An example of this takes place after Herbal executes the painter and finds himself caught between the phantom voice of the Republican victim and the despotic voices of his fellow victimizers. The painter suddenly disappears from Herbal's conscience, leaving him momentarily without this "voice of reason" and, as a consequence, under the influence of the Iron Man: "From the moment the painter left, and as he feared, Herbal noticed the sense of unease return [...] The Iron Man made the most of the painter's absence. Herbal listened to what he had to say" (Rivas 87). In what ensues, Herbal acts aggressively towards the Republican prisoners and seeks to assert male dominance over them. Guilt always follows such acts as Herbal remembers the painter and Da Barca, whose intellectual and social lives he covets but can never fully understand.

Militarization in Spain enforced the adherence to the traditional family unit and the centrality of the father figure. Patriarchal myths about control over a woman being the true manifestation of manliness helped silence not only Republican women who sought to change patriarchal-driven societal structures but also all women generally, even those supporting the conservative ideals of the regime. For Herbal, one of the leading female figures (the doctor's fiancée, Marisa Mallo) comes to represent an object of desire, possession over which would signify a certain form of triumph. Herbal's engrained views of gender and sexual relations contrast sharply with those of the leading Republican figures, who view women as subjects rather than objects. However, it is also true that Herbal differs from his brother-in-law, the misogynistic and physically abusive Zalo Puga, whom Herbal later kills after he discovers the extent to which Puga tormented his sister. Her story points not only to how some military wives faced extreme brutality but also to how the military as an institution shielded aggressors. Later Herbal is found guilty of murder, expelled from the civil guard, and imprisoned, ultimately becoming a social outcast.

Through this plot line the author depicts how stories of violence against military wives are silenced and how such silence feeds into the military's toxic culture. It also reflects the conflicts within Spain's barracks, as well as the ingrained nature of socially constructed views of gender. On the one hand, as Folkart suggests, by killing Puga, Herbal defies the established order. On the other hand, Herbal maintains the view that women must be rescued by men and that violence is the only method to achieve that goal. It is therefore unsurprising that after

Herbal's release from prison he spends the rest of his life working as a bouncer at a borderland brothel. This salient choice of setting invites readers to consider the relationship between past injustices and present-day exploitation of women and cultural minorities. Setting, characterization, and plot work together to illustrate how militaristic ideology in Spain is part and parcel of a broader patriarchal order that celebrates heterosexual militarized men as the true protectors of women and then sustains a culture of toxic masculinity in which women become the targets of violence without any recourse to social, legal, or economic justice.

The Carpenter's Pencil deepens our understanding of the links between war, dictatorial repression, and the persistence of repressive gender norms in the past and present. The author imagines the scope and longer trajectory of exclusionary projects of patriarchal power and the social invisibility that they produce. He calls forth a reflection on the significance of memory in current constructions of oppositional identities that recognize the relationship between militaristic, colonial, and capitalist legacies and their incompatibility with social and economic justice (Mohanty 8–9).

At the end of the novel Herbal entrusts the carpenter's pencil to brothel worker María da Visitação – a gesture whispered to him by the phantom painter. With this narrative move, the novel signals new forms of resistance to hegemonic power. Yet María's story remains on the horizon as her voice is largely inaccessible to readers. From one perspective she and Sousa (Da Barca's interlocutor) form a new generation that might gain necessary insight from the histories of civil-war survivors and bring them forward into the future. Yet Rivas complicates this optimistic message in the final scene when María is called to attend to a melancholic journalist, who readers can only assume is Sousa. His very presence in the brothel points to the enduring gender and economic inequities in the present. Rivas sets a present-day story of marginalization over another from the past, so that both are evident. Gender, class, and nationhood all form part of Rivas's critique that bears witness to the ongoing repressive structures that effectively segregate, exploit, and disrupt even the lives of those who support them.

"If the Heart Could Think It Would Cease to Beat" by Alberto Méndez

The hybrid novel *Blind Sunflowers* by Alberto Méndez contains four interconnected stories that capture the traumatic consequences of military conflict. The focus here is on the first and third stories, which complicate images of the Nationalist soldiers by showing how the war became a point of fracture for many who originally supported it. The title of the first is thought provoking: "If the Heart Could Think It Would Cease to Beat." Emotions (associated with the heart) and logic (linked to the brain) seem to be at odds. But the narrative reveals that logical thinking, clear-eyed seeing, and emotional feeling are all crucial parts of human experience and work together. Initially protected from the sight of bloodshed, the protagonist coldly calculates war's economic cost. Once he witnesses its human cost, however, his heart becomes driven by both emotions and logic, which ultimately paralyse him.

His critical reflections become entirely incompatible with the Francoist discourse of courage and victory. Méndez's descriptions of the disconnect that the protagonist experiences resonate with one of Emily Dickinson's poems: "The world feels dusty, when we stop to die. We want the dew, then honors taste dry. Flags vex a dying face, but the least fan stirred by a friend's hand cools like the rain" (Dickinson 199). Just as the flags, symbols of militaristic patriotism, become irritating and irrelevant to the dying in Dickinson's verse, so too do the grand pronouncements of Francoist courage become meaningless against the protagonist's personal reflections. External, idealized, symbols and discourses lose their significance when confronted with the intimate and honest realities of war and suffering.

The story takes place in 1939 in Madrid when the war was near its end. The author imagines an unusual scenario in which a captain on the winning Nationalist side surrenders to the Republican army despite the fact that Franco's victory was in clear sight. It is the story of Carlos Alegría, a former law student and military captain from a family of wealthy farmers who live on the outskirts of Burgos. With this character Méndez asks, "What is someone who is defeated by the defeated?" (8). The story is recounted from the perspective of a third-person narrator who attempts to piece together the events leading up to a life-changing turning point for the protagonist. The account is based on the testimonies of those who knew Alegría, as well as on official documents and personal letters. As a story in Méndez's larger historical novel, it blends fact and fiction, thereby inviting readers to imagine the inner world of a military man, his trajectory in war, and his links to broader oppressive social structures.

The author makes visible the historical social structures, like gender and class, that shape military men; he also imagines the varying degrees to which men change and resist the reproduction of norms. Coming from a life of privilege, "Alegría joined the rebel army in 1936 in order to defend what had always been his" (Méndez 9). War for him meant "administering anything and everything that others might need to help kill, be killed and defeat an enemy he never even saw close up" (9). His surname, Alegría (happiness), is indicative of the affluent lifestyle that he had led before the war, but the name contrasts sharply with the description of his despondent frame of mind at the war's close, which is when the story begins. "I'm a prisoner," he shouts to a disbelieving Republican enemy (3). The narrator explains that "he probably rejected the idea of saying 'I surrender' because that would have suggested a fixed moment in time, whereas in reality he had been surrendering for a long, long time. First, he surrendered, then he turned himself over to the enemy. When he had the chance to talk about it, he defined his gesture as 'a victory in reverse'" (3). The author's depiction of this character subverts common perceptions of war, victory, and conquest. For the protagonist, complicity in violence only produces defeat. In the narrator's words, the act was not a "narrow, selfish gesture" but rather one "full of complexity and moral ambiguity" (8).

If, as Enloe suggests, militarization is a step-by-step process by which a person or a thing gradually comes to be controlled by the military (*Maneuvers* 3), then Méndez offers clues into the process by which a militarized man becomes demilitarized. The protagonist rejects the legitimation of war when he states in a letter written to his fiancée in January 1938, "We have to choose between winning a war and conquering a cemetery" (Méndez 3). But as the narrator suggests, "We know now that unconsciously he had already rejected both" (3). Instead of depicting the way in which civilians or soldiers become cruel or come to depend on the military for their well-being, Méndez illustrates the unmaking of that process.

The story captures the unravelling of the tightly woven relationship between masculinized pride, violence, and military identity. From his barricade the Nationalist captain had observed the Republican enemy and initially "thought it was an army entirely lacking in warlike spirit, and therefore deserving of defeat" (Méndez 4). After further observation of the Republican side, however, "he came to a different conclusion (and this was reflected in his letters). It was a civilian army, 'which is like being a bird underground or an angelic weasel'" (4). The captain comes to view militaristic ideas and actions as the source of anguish, decay, and shame rather than pride.

What is at stake is a military ideology and its core belief that armed force is not only the best solution to political conflict but synonymous with real manhood and bravery. Revealing the dynamic structures of gender identity, the militarized man in Méndez's story becomes profoundly estranged from such notions. "With time violence and pain, rage and weakness all bond together in a religion of survival, a ritual of waiting where the same melody is sung by killer and killed, by victim and executioner. The only language spoken is that of the sword, the only tongue that of the wound" (Méndez 4). These are the words that Alegría wrote in a letter two months before he surrendered to the Republican army. Whereas Borges's Nazi narrator (mentioned in chapter 2) espoused a doctrine of violence and the faith of the sword, this character's journey involves dismantling his emotional nationalism stoked through symbols. As a quartermaster he had not seen the pain of war up close, but he knew that his role in the military machine created the conditions for brutality. He comes to see himself as a cog in a killing machine with which he ultimately refuses to identify.

While it seems irrational to those who witnessed it, the captain's act of turning himself in to the Republican army constitutes a congruous and logical act that emerged from a longer process of gaining critical consciousness of the individual and collective suffering produced by violence and injustice. As such, he insists that he is a prisoner, not a deserter. The act appears so incongruous to his disbelieving Republican captors that he stays silent even though "he would have liked to explain exactly why he was quitting the army that was about to win the war, why he was surrendering to a defeated army, why he wanted no part in the victory" (Méndez 6). He struggled to find the words to convey the life-affirming nature of his decision to break away from the Nationalists' death-focused environment. Leaving that side, in pursuit of life, was even harder than expected, reflecting Bolaño's views on military culture's grip. "There was a martial air to their footsteps, the rhythm of power and obedience, submission and hierarchy. Captain Alegría recognized the sound as familiar, the voice of his own kind. But this recognition brought him no comfort. On the contrary, it was like going back to a world to which he had no wish to belong" (Méndez 10). When he cryptically describes in a letter to his fiancée that his situation was like one of "Leibniz's monads," he signals his state of isolation among the "usurers of war" (11–12). In the trial record he explained that as the quartermaster who tracked key signals, he knew that the strategy was not to end the war but "to kill them all" (14).

The military man at the centre of the story accepts responsibility for his role in the destruction of lives in a public act of self-recognition that involves great danger. He not only risks a death sentence or imprisonment for desertion but also jeopardizes his own status as a "real" man. It is not merely that he would rather face a death sentence than continue to serve those who kill. It is about rejecting the entire masculinized notion that glory entails killing and that cowardice involves non-violence. The war came to an end, he understands, but it did not resolve anything (Méndez 18). In his military record he concludes to the military prosecutor that "the defenders of the Republic would have caused Franco's army greater humiliation had they surrendered on the first day of the war" because every death in the war "only served to glorify whoever did the killing. Without any dead, or so he claimed, there would have been no glory" (5). The reaction by Alegría's military superior is revealing: "you're a fool and a traitor" (11). The betrayal ostensibly refers to the captain's political disloyalty, but the subversion also involves gender identity because he breaks with the dictates of militarized masculinity. By finely sketching the captain's radical shift in identity, Méndez approaches the perpetration of violence as a learned act that is yoked to the performance of masculine identity.

The story illustrates the limitations of language to convey the traumas created by war and the fractures of identity produced by complicity in killing. In a letter again to his fiancée Alegría captures the shortcomings of language by writing that he must use "other people's words to speak for himself." This statement not only points to a distrust of heroic narratives that erase the messiness of war but also alerts readers to the patriarchal nature of language that celebrates battle and justifies suffering. The historical ramifications of war vocabulary are evident in the documentation of Captain Alegría's trial, which displays the Nationalist army's euphemisms for the civil war that framed bloodshed as a "Crusade" and the mass killing of leftists as "glorious deeds" (Méndez 14). The hegemony of militarized masculinity under Franco also perpetuated the image of loyalists to the republic as foreign enemies of the fatherland.

By juxtaposing the trial record with the narrator's reconstruction of Alegría's story, the author makes readers aware of the multiple ways of seeing and understanding. He also prompts thought on the patriarchal social relations that remain deeply embedded in language. In turn, language is used to shape discursively the meaning of violence. War is a gendered reality that is described with a gamut of gendered words that link a vision of combat with masculine bravery. In the Nationalist lexicon during the Spanish Civil War and the Franco regime, hegemonic views of men's and women's roles were inscribed in institutions and repeated ad nauseum. The absence of words to describe non-binary thinking, as well as complex gender performances like militarized masculinity, thus blocked such realities from collective understanding. In *Blind Sunflowers* the author acknowledges the disconnect between the scope and subtleties of experience on the one hand and the inadequacies of language on the other. Such an acknowledgment constitutes an act of resistance against the enforcement of patriarchal culture and militarized violence.

The unspeakable anguish of war is made clear in the captain's sense of relief when he faces the Nationalist death squad on the day of his execution for treason. Alongside a multitude of condemned Republican prisoners, Alegría is ushered into "the community of the defeated" (Méndez 15) where he simultaneously experiences a sense of solidarity and shame. A bullet creases his skull, and after he is knocked unconscious, his body is covered in a few shovels of earth. When he emerges from a mound of dead bodies and becomes the only survivor of that mass execution, he experiences what he would call a resurrection or a rebirth. Nearly dead, he is nursed back to health by an elderly Republican woman who shows him compassion and humanity despite the political affiliation made evident by his uniform. In his attempt to return home to Burgos he must scale a mountain range that splits Spain in two. It "was yet another way of ignoring all that separates things, of wanting more than anything to be on both sides" (18). This may be read as an attempt to move beyond political division, but it can also be interpreted as an act of defiance against the reductive confinements of socially defined behaviours associated with gender.

The story of Captain Alegría comes to an end with a damning portrait of war and the repressive structures of militarized masculinity on which it depends for its fulfilment. After he reaches Somosierra, where the Nationalist troops have taken control, Alegría observes their lifeless, mechanical gestures as an absurd parody indicating defeat rather than victory (Méndez 19). He understands them far more than they understand him, and possibly far more than they understand themselves. This is evident in the letter that is found on his body at the time of his real death sometime later. Those soldiers were men for whom life would be strange after the war, he wrote. They would be absent from their own worlds and would slowly turn into vanquished flesh fused with those they defeated (19). After he has approached the guard house, crawling on all fours, he chokes back his sobs and says, "I'm one of you" (20). The story ends with these words, but readers learn in the third interconnected story that Alegría is taken into custody once again. When the prison officials ask for his details, he replies, "My name is Carlos Alegría, I was born on 18 April 1939 in a mass grave at Arganda, and I have never won a war" (61). Not long after that, "he blew his brains out with a rifle seized from a prison guard" (19). Before he put the tip of the barrel under his chin, he "shouted out that he had never killed anyone and yet here he was, about to die a second time" (62). He pulled the trigger and "paid his debt" (62). For his complicit role in the war he had become his own enemy. Seen through this lens, armed conflict produces only negative effects.

"The Language of the Dead" by Alberto Méndez

Whereas the military coup of 1936 enabled the unleashing of violent force as a method of social control, post-war Spain saw the militarization of the state. That involved the implementation of detention and torture of the remaining Republican population as a means of political consolidation, cultural erasure, and revenge. Méndez's third story, "The Language of the Dead," sheds light on the ways in which masculinity, violence, and language affected each other in the post-war context. It takes place in 1941 and focuses on the prison experience of Juan Senra, a cello teacher and Republican detainee who delays his execution by lying to Judge Eymar. Eymar, who is also a colonel, discovers that Juan met his son when he was held captive and later executed by the Republican army in Porlier Prison in Madrid.

The author gives insight into multiple masculinities, including those that are militarized, complicit, and marginalized, by depicting several male characters and the friendships and conflicts between them. While Juan awaits the judge's final verdict, he befriends a young Republican named Eugenio and a former Nationalist captain who had surrendered on the day the war ended. When we discover that the captain has a scar on his forehead as a result of a bullet wound, it becomes evident that the characters in the first and third stories intersect. Carlos Alegría is a secondary character in this story and the protagonist of the first. With both men Juan begins to develop a friendship, but after a while Alegría takes a weapon from one of the prison guards and commits suicide. A couple of days later young Eugenio is executed. After these events Juan decides to stop creating falsehoods to delay his execution. He tells Eymar the truth about the judge's son: he was an opportunist, a thief, a trafficker of stolen and contaminated goods, a criminal gang leader, a traitor, and a killer of civilians. The day after Juan refuses to disingenuously glorify the dead soldier, he is called to climb on board one of the lorries of death.

Both characterization and setting in the story emphasize the intersections between institutions that facilitated and justified the perpetration of violence. "General Franco, wearing his military cap, stared fiercely down at them from that back wall of the courtroom, next to a wooden crucifix. The empty room [...] must once have been used for classes" (Méndez 44). The military, the Church, the legal system, and the education system worked in tandem in the process of militarization and the persecution of dissenting voices. Through the description of that setting, the author also subverts the militarized ideology that lionizes soldiers: "Three guards stood at the back like statues, although their frozen poses suggested weariness rather than any warlike or epic qualities" (44). Méndez also further underscores the complicity of the Church in militarization and politicide when he explains that one of the roles of the army chaplain was that of censor. Juan's letter to his brother is rejected by the censor for including phrases "about the cold, his poor health, how kind and gentle their mother had been, or the poplars in the avenues at Miraflores. There was no room for anything human" (47).

The description of Colonel Eymar is particularly salient as it outlines the beliefs and behaviours characteristic of militarized masculinity as well as its connection to language and violence. "The colonel's habit of reducing court proceedings to a minimum meant he never stopped to consider subtleties. Military justice is only black and white, and yet he found himself flushing as he told the prisoner that Miguel Eymar was his son" (Méndez 43). This passage dramatizes James Dawes's argument that military men are taught to regard the world in binary terms of good versus evil, us versus them, pure versus impure, safe versus unsafe (MacTalks). But Méndez also brings out the conflicted and complicated nature of gender and identity. The process of militarization aims to inscribe violent masculinity on men's bodies, but it is not inevitable. It is a gender performance fraught with anxiety and fragility. When questioning Juan, the colonel tries "to conceal his anxiety that gripped his throat and made his stern voice tremble" (Méndez 43).

The description of the protagonist, Juan, is also essential to our understanding of the author's de-normalization of militarized masculinity. He was a member of the Republican nursing corps during the war and is depicted in sharp contrast to Colonel Eymar. He allows himself to be vulnerable and comfort those in need of physical and emotional support. "He helped delouse a smooth-cheeked youngster who was scratching his head so much it was full of sores" (Méndez 47). That youngster was Eugenio Paz, whose character is also juxtaposed with the image of the militarized and misogynist male. "He was sixteen, and was born in Brunete. His uncle owned the only bar in the village, where his mother served. Despite being the owner's sister, he treated her like a dog [...] When war broke out, the youngster waited to see which side his uncle was on, and chose the opposite. That was how he came to swear allegiance to the Republic" (48). The author portrays Eugenio as humble, compassionate, and gentle, which are characteristics deemed feminine (i.e., inferior) by militarized men.

By emphasizing Eugenio's sensitivity and fortitude through evocative vignettes of his prison experience, the author transmits a critical commentary on gender norms that equate real masculinity with stoicism, aggression, and strength. The depictions of both Juan and Eugenio differ not only from Colonel Eymar but also from the guards and lieutenants whose arrogance and displays of authority dissolve into "unctuous submission" when they are in the presence of their superiors (Méndez 50). These details illustrate militarized masculinity as a learned gender performance that is bound to hierarchies of power. But, to reiterate, the author's portrayal of the other characters who are at odds with the armed men suggests that neither fervent obedience nor acquiescence to repressive norms is inevitable. When Juan and Eugenio share memories and acknowledgment of their fears, or when Juan discovers "a similarity between writing and caresses, words and affection" (53), readers envision an alternative to militarized masculinity.

The relationship between language, consciousness, and nonconformity to militarism and violence is also central to this story. In a letter to his brother, Juan explains that in his dreams he imagines "a world where everyone speaks a foreign language" that he cannot understand, but in that world he does not "feel like a stranger" (Méndez 58). As his body wastes away, his consciousness increases and the language of his dreams becomes more accessible to him (65). In the letters that he writes to his brother, he conceptualizes new words like *amortesía*, combining *amor* (love) and *cortesía* (courtesy) (65). He had also "learned how to catalogue sadness, to distinguish between all the different kinds of despair, to recognize fear mixed with hate, hatred on its own, and fear in its pure state" (65). In his search for a new discourse to capture the dimensions of love and pain, he nurtures a compassionate self while denouncing the horrors of violence. In so doing, he disrupts the gender order and offers an antidote to militarized masculinity. But when the young Eugenio is executed, Juan concludes, "The language I dreamt in order to create a happier world is in fact the language of the dead" (68). No longer willing to perform for his captors by upholding a false image of military heroism, he speaks honestly to Eymar. It is his final act of resistance. As the lorry takes him and the other condemned men to the cemetery, he thinks with some satisfaction "that the smug look of triumph must have disappeared forever from Colonel Eymar's face" (71). And yet he manages to stop "hating when he thought of his brother" (71).

The characters in Méndez's stories are blind sunflowers, searching but not finding the light. Unlike the image of life that the sunflower usually evokes, Méndez's sunflowers seem dead, not knowing in which direction to reach for illumination. Some of Méndez's blind sunflowers are followers, passive bystanders, allowing militarization and the repression of the opposition to become the norm. In the story of Capitan Alegría, we witness how a Nationalist sunflower becomes profoundly disillusioned and foreign to himself when he comes to understand his own responsibility in the production of violence. Similar to Herbal in *The Carpenter's Pencil* and Papudo in *The Twilight Zone*, Alegría comes to grasp his place in a war machine that ultimately sinks both victors and the vanquished into a dark abyss. In the case of Juan Senra it is the line that separates the perpetration of violence and acquiescence that is explored. In the end the protagonist comes to see that line as dangerously thin and ultimately chooses death over submission.

Blind Sunflowers, *The Carpenter's Pencil*, and *The Twilight Zone* parallel each other in significant ways, all shedding light on how violent masculinity is inscribed on men's bodies through militarization – and also how it is contested. Transcending conventional forms of historiography as well as narrative fiction, these writers illuminate how militarized masculinity was, as Cockburn has suggested, not casual but *causal* in the perpetration of violence in Spain and Chile, and how it oppressed not only the victims but also the victimizers. What makes these books so compelling, however, is their inquiry into the process through which militarized men gain critical consciousness and push against the inertia of conformity.

4 Militarizing Children under Franco and Pinochet

In 1978 Argentine film-maker Maria Luisa Bemberg interviewed seventy girls and boys to investigate behaviour patterns.[1] Her short documentary *Juguetes* sheds light on how children are educated in specific ways so that they act in specific ways. As Hilda Ocampo succinctly wrote, the conclusion is clear: toys are not innocent; they are the first material form of cultural conditioning (184). Fifty years earlier Walter Benjamin wrote in the 1928 text "Toys and Play": "The fact is that the perceptual world of the child is influenced at every point by traces of the older generation. It is impossible to construct them as dwelling in a fantasy realm, a fairytale land of pure childhood or pure art" (118). Benjamin observed that "even where they are not simply imitations of the tools of adults, toys are a site of conflict, less of the child with the adult than of the adult with the child" (118). Compared to all others, toy soldiers, war comics, and battle games have the most pernicious effects because they militarize children's minds, normalize violence, and glorify aggressive masculinity.

Adult-made and -purchased forms of children's entertainment tell stories that contribute to the myth of war. Such fabrications idealize combat skills, dominance, and physical strength, while concealing war's unmythical morally gray decisions, fear, shame, and indelible images of death. Some boys will be inspired to enlist, but most will probably never wear a uniform or use a weapon. Nevertheless, militarized "play" creates indifference to bloodshed and propagates the notion that dominance over women and other men is the true sign of

---

1 Sections of this chapter have been previously published in DiGiovanni, "Militarized Masculinity."

masculinity. Death-obsessed toys and warmongering discourses shape warscapes in children's minds whether or not they join the military. As Cynthia Enloe comments, militarized narratives shrink children's gender understandings and measures of what could be a genuinely fair, open, and non-violent adulthood (Enloe, personal communication with author, 11 December 2023).

In Spain and Chile some writers and film-makers have recognized these connections. In literature and film about the Franco and Pinochet dictatorships, children have been depicted as the inheritors of political conflict who struggled to make sense of division during and after the military coups. Throughout the 1950s and 1960s Ana Maria Matute published novels and short-story collections like *Doce historias de la Artámila* that foreground the violent environments that shape young lives. The novel *Si te dice que cai* by Juan Marsé also stands out for its depiction of the relationship between comic book, war "play," and socialization in the poor districts of post-war Barcelona. More recently, the orphanage and the fatherless child have become salient cinematic tropes as featured in films like *El espinazo del diablo, El laberinto del fauno, Los girasoles ciegos*, and *Pan negro*. In Chile, *Machuca* stands out for its representation of children's under-examined experiences of political violence and militarization. These films require viewers to consider the regimes' mission to appropriate and re-educate the progeny of the opposition.

Guillermo del Toro has received international acclaim for his portrayal of violence and its significance in young lives in *El espinazo del diablo* and *El laberinto del fauno*. In these films Del Toro denaturalizes the structures of power and histories of violent masculinities underpinning the Franco regime. Through the representation of contrasting masculinities the film-maker subverts the myth that militarization provided security and unmasks the human cost of embracing militarized masculinity. While Guillermo del Toro's work is the focus of many academic and non-academic studies, his brilliant juxtaposition of militarized and resistant masculinities has been overlooked. Likewise, scant attention has been paid to one of Del Toro's influences, the graphic novelist Carlos Giménez (b. 1941). A crucial distinction between *El espinazo del diablo* and its model, *Paracuellos*, involves the context. Whereas the film is situated during the Spanish Civil War in a Republican-run orphanage, *Paracuellos* takes place during the Franco regime in the state-run boys' orphanage, the Auxilio Social. The implications of this shift are significant because the original offers valuable insight into the systemic injustices of the National Catholic apparatus.

In a comparative framework this chapter examines the graphic novels *Paracuellos* and *Barrio* by Carlos Giménez alongside Nona Fernández's creative non-fiction life narrative *Space Invaders* to shed light on the history of children's socialization and militarism in the context of dictatorial repression. Although Carlos Giménez was born in 1941 in Madrid, and Nona Fernández thirty years later in Santiago de Chile, both authors came of age during military rule. In their extraordinarily insightful autobiographical narratives, they explore their own schoolday memories marked by military discourses of national security. They reconstruct such memories alongside recollections of collective terror, thereby subverting the myth that militarization stabilized the nation and provided the antidote to social conflict. The juxtaposition is illuminating as both authors draw our attention to a continuum of violence by representing emotionally alienating spaces where religious and military figures instil fear in children through militaristic language and the constant threat of punishment for transgressing the rules and regulations of the state.

Although some critics have examined the perceptive ways in which Giménez and Fernández engage the complexities of memory in the wake of dictatorial violence, I argue that militarized masculinity is missing in the discussion. These texts respond to the gender formations that the Franco and Pinochet regimes imposed through intersecting institutions (education, religion, government, military, media). The authors prompt readers to think critically about how such institutions sought to shape boys and girls into disciplined members of a hierarchical and heteronormative state.

Giménez and Fernández expose the institutions that fomented militarized masculinity within the larger construction of an anti-liberal, ultra-Catholic, misogynist, and homophobic national identity. The ideal of manhood required discipline, the capacity for violence, commitment to the patriarchal family, and a religious zeal for the militarized nation. The indoctrinatory apparatus that instituted this ideal extended from childhood to adulthood as men were summoned for compulsory military service in both Spain and Chile. Young women, however, were expected to serve the state through biological reproduction and domestic management. These gender formations had powerful implications for the state. They served the greater political goal of reinstating the hegemony of the military, the Catholic Church, and the economic elites. Men's education was to produce patriotic professionals, while their military service (viewed as men's national duty) reinforced the imperative of "national unity," a euphemism for the unmitigated elimination of internal political opposition.

A comparative examination of the post-war graphic novels of Carlos Giménez and the novel *Space Invaders* by Nona Fernández through the lens of feminist theory and masculinity studies invites fresh reflection on the complex nature of traumatic memory and its intersections with gender, age, class, sexuality, and politics. In question is the process of children's socialization and identity formation and its impact on remembrance against the post-dictatorial backdrop. Discussing the difference between these works is also valuable. Giménez subverts the discourse of the Auxilio Social by illustrating an institutional breeding ground for a culture of aggression and competition in which boys were forced to suppress emotional needs and suffer degradation for the so-called political transgressions of their parents. Fernández also unmasks the human cost of embracing militarized masculinity through an interrelated story of femicide against the backdrop of the regime.

Militaristic Indoctrination in Carlos Giménez's Graphic Novels

Through masterful black-line drawings and unadorned dialogue, *Paracuellos* (a six-book series) and *Barrio* (a four-book series) confront readers with the constructed nature of boys' behaviour and its relation to privilege and oppression. Giménez allows us to imagine militarized masculinity not as a fixed feature of contemporary Spanish society but as a shifting construction whose meaning is contested and continuously shaped by historical conditions, namely the Spanish Civil War, the extended conflict between the "two Spains," and the democratic transition marked by a sense of traumatic loss and angst over the past and the future.

Giménez's autobiographical comic, first released during the transition to democracy and republished thirty years later during Spain's memory boom, was inspired by the author's lived experience in the Auxilio Social. Originally established in 1936 by Mercedez Sanz Bachiller with the political patronage of the Spanish fascist party (La Falange Española), the Auxilio Social quickly became a site of political and religious indoctrination for those destitute children abandoned, ironically, as a consequence of the right-wing military coup and the egregious class inequalities at the heart of the conflict. The series begins in the 1940s and spans the 1950s by following a group of interned boys from ages six to adolescence within a microcosm of the National Catholic regime. As Carmen Moreno-Nuño correctly observes, the Auxilio Social emulated the Nazi social-assistance system in its totalitarian methods, but unlike the German model, the Auxilio joined forces with the Catholic Church

(194). Giménez represents the orphanage as a hostile detention centre characterized by the arbitrary power of the personnel intent on carrying out a program of moral purification. In that emotionally alienating space, religious and military officials humiliate the children under their guardianship and instil in them fear through aggressive posturing, militaristic language, and draconian forms of discipline and punishment (physical and psychological chastisement, forced positions, excessive physical activity and drills, hunger and thirst, exposure to extreme temperatures, and forced isolation).[2]

In my analysis I situate militarized masculinity within the historical context of the Cold War as well as within Spain's colonial loss and the massive effort by right-wing groups to recover an imperial identity. Within the war and post-war contexts, visual culture in general, and the comic book (*el tebeo*) in particular, became effective media for political propaganda aimed at children. Fascist comics such as *Flechas y Pelayos* and *Chicos* conveyed extremely gendered, colonial, and ultra-right-wing Catholic discourses that in turn played the role of legitimizing certain acts of aggression and violence. While these influenced boys' socialization, feminine comic strips like *Mis Chicas* (a counterpart to *Chicos*) and *Florita* reinforced "feminine stereotypes and the luxurious world of the upper class" (Moreno-Nuño 195).

Censorship meant that these state-approved comics permeated the lives of boys like Carlos Giménez. In the years after Franco's death Giménez inserted the comic genre into the still-ongoing process of collective memorial reconstruction. His graphic novels challenge the superhero archetype of hegemonic masculinity and instead depict physically and emotionally vulnerable boys who are struggling to navigate the limited terrain of militarized masculinity. His artistic style and explicit emphasis on Spain's recent dictatorial past were unique within the 1970s media landscape. Many of his contemporaries rendered erotic or mythical stories of vampires and space odysseys, while he depicted the lived traumas of post-war children.[3] Unsurprisingly his thematic focus was influenced by the 1950s social realism literary movement, particularly works such as Arturo Barea's *La forja de un rebelde* and Ramón

---

2 A similar list of abuses is also offered by Carmen Moreno-Nuño in the essay "The Comic-Strip of Historical Memory."

3 One salient exception is Felipe Hernández Cava (b. 1953), whose work critically engages the effects of war and dictatorship.

J. Sender's *Réquiem por un campesino español,* which Giménez adapted to the graphic novel. In discussing his rationale behind the project, he states in the introduction to *Todo Paracuellos*: "I've made these stories with the intention of leaving a truthful document of how life was lived in the Social Aid orphanages [...] The Spain of those years as we see and know was a very hard and violent society. Built into it were factors such as the proximity of the recent civil war, the disposition of the victors and widespread fear and poverty. In that hotbed, only monsters could develop. And those schools, those 'homes,' were the logical monster that bred a monstrous society" (18, 22). It is precisely the representation of this microcosm of violence that this chapter will address.

In the book *El Franquismo,* historians Giuliana Di Febo and Santos Juliá examine the educational apparatus constructed and sustained by the National Catholic regime. Citing key publications by the clergy, they remind us that during the war the "re-Christianization" of society had become central in the military insurgents' campaign for national regeneration. The condemnation of the Second Republic and its numerous reforms (women's enfranchisement, secularization of education, and agrarian reform) was thus bound up with notions of moral bankruptcy and disorder. For instance, in *La cuaresma de España: Carta pastoral sobre el sentido cristiano-español de la guerra,* Cardinal Isidro Gomá associated "republican secularism" with "public immorality" and interpreted the war as a form of punishment for the disintegration of the traditional family (qtd. in Di Febo and Juliá 71). Reclaiming Catholic influence in the classroom and strictly defining gender and class relations, therefore, became inseparable from the larger ongoing anti-modern discourse communicated in the language of recovery and tradition.

Several years before the establishment of the new National Catholic State, José Pemartín Sanjuán, head of higher and secondary education during the war, defended unbending gender boundaries. His book *Qué es "lo nuevo": Consideraciones sobre el momento español presente* contributed greatly to the regime's educational machine and shows the continuities between the formulation of a political and gender ideology and its translation into law (qtd. in Di Febo and Juliá 72). Drawing from Italian and German fascism, as well as Spanish imperialism of the fifteenth and sixteenth centuries, Pemartín Sanjuán envisioned a uniquely Spanish ideological configuration uniting Catholicism and fascism with an emphasis on the education of youth. For young men Pemartín Sanjuán proposed a model of military asceticism within traditional Catholic structures. The Secondary Education Reform Act (Ley de reforma de la enseñanza media, 1938) promoted an education system designed to disseminate "the virtues of the great captains and politicians of the Golden Age," as opposed to "foreign mimicry, the Russophilia and effeminacy" of the Second Republic

(Di Febo and Juliá 72). The intersecting imperial and gender discourses underpinning the reform act can hardly be ignored. The Falange was to be responsible for instilling patriotism, the sense of hierarchy, and discipline, all illustrated in the textbook series *Formación del espíritu nacional* (Formation of the national spirit), which were used until the 1960s (72). The party name itself, La Falange (phalanx), is a homage to the ancient Greek conception of a mass military formation.

The imperial and gendered myth of the Spanish Christian warrior (*el caballero cristiano y español*) became central to the organizing structure of the state-run orphanage, the Auxilio Social. Once the Sección Femenina de la Falange had come under the direction of Pilar Primo de Rivera, the Auxilio Social emerged as a response to the ravages of war and its particular impact on children. Previously, "state welfare was non-existent and, for ideological reasons, religious organizations provided little succour for the children of the despised 'Reds,'" notes historian Paul Preston in *Doves of War: Four Women of Spain* (236). The Auxilio Social was initially envisioned as a provisional patriotic and religious mission to save the war's innocent victims; however, it later became part of the Francoist re-educational operation.

Preston underscores the paradoxes of the social welfare program and its use of charity as a method of indoctrination: "If the repression was the stick of 'redemption,' Auxilio Social was the carrot, a crucial source of food and shelter for those left hungry and homeless by the war" (*Doves of War* 266). He goes on to concur with Sheelagh Ellwood, who has noted "the bitter irony in such aid being given by an organization that was part of the very forces responsible for the devastation and bloodshed" (qtd. in Preston 266). Indeed, it was the founder's husband, Onésimo Redondo, who advocated a radical anti-Semitic, ultra-Catholic, Spanish fascism characterized by militarized masculinity and performed through unrestrained violent revolt against the democratic republic. In 1934 he wrote a battle cry inciting members and supporters of the Juntas de Ofensiva Nacional-Sindicalista (JONS, Councils of National Syndicalist Offensive) to rebellion: "Get your weapons ready. Learn to love the metallic clunk of the pistol. Caress your dagger. Never be parted from your vengeful cudgel! Wherever there is an anti-Marxist group with cudgel, fist and pistol or with greater instruments, there is a JONS. Youth should be trained in physical struggle, must love violence as a way of life, must arm himself with whatever he can and finish off by any means the few dozen Marxist swindlers who don't let us live" (qtd. in Preston, *Doves of War* 71–2, 82–4).

Redondo's pre-war rhetoric exemplifies the relationship between race, class, gender, sexuality, and nation in the fascist identity. Concurring with Paul Preston, Soledad Fox argues that by claiming that

Marxism was a Jewish invention that would herald the "re-Africaniza-tion" of Spain, Redondo identified Spain's fifteenth-century "others" with the progressive left (Fox 32–3). Redondo also glorified the image of an ultra-virile heteronormative male impassioned by imperial myths. For proponents of such myths, acts of violence only facilitated the nationalists' quest for renewal and moral righteousness. Such aggression then further solidified the notion of masculine superiority and dominance. It is precisely this form of militarized masculinity that war orphans were expected to embrace under the auspices of the Auxilio Social, along with the uniform of the triumphant rebel forces, the fascist salute, a gratitude for the Nationalist "saviours" of the fatherland, and a hyper-idealized view of Generalíssimo Franco and José Antonio Primo de Rivera, whose portraits were enshrined and routinely venerated.

The implications of the regime's indoctrinating practices are effectively illustrated in Carlos Giménez's graphic novels in images that are redo-lent of the profound trauma that he endured in the Auxilio Social over a period of eight years (ages six to fourteen) after his widowed mother had been diagnosed with tuberculosis. "Trauma affects not only the brain, but the body too, its musculature, joints, and posture," writes Ocean Vuong (19). Giménez captures the internalization of trauma in the bent backs of young boys, in their large fearful eyes, and their bony, callused knuckles. The space in which most of the scenes take place is within the orphan-age: inside the sleeping and eating quarters and in the yard. The "homes" (*hogares*) are separated by gender following the National Catholic ideol-ogy, and readers only have access to the boys' residence.

The title, *Paracuellos*, recalls the site of the wartime execution of 2,300 prisoners, mostly Nationalist officers, by Republicans outside of Madrid in 1936. While the author recognizes the controversial impli-cations of the title, he emphasizes its reflection of historical accuracy because Hogar Paracuellos del Jarama was the actual site of one of the orphanages in which the stories take place. The construction of the fascist orphanage at the site of previous Republican control reads as an attempt by the consolidators of the regime to regain territory and colonize the passive "red" victims in need of redemption. Giménez's subsequent "adoption" of Paracuellos as the site for his visual archive translates as yet another inscription on a palimpsest, poignantly reused but still bearing evocative traces of numerous bloodstained conflicts.

The fashion, cars, and furniture are also designed to convey the historical detail of the 1940s and 1950s. Military and clerical style pre-dominate in the orphanage. Young interned boys wear homogeniz-ing uniforms and are often drawn with shaved heads, reminiscent of the dehumanizing practices of the Holocaust. Superior nuns wear close-fitting, high-collar, black dress uniforms with black cloaks, while lower-ranking women wear black dresses with white aprons. Priests are attired in their clerical habits. The navy-blue shirts (rendered in black in the re-edition) of the fascist headmasters are an important symbol of masculine power. As Carmen Moreno-Nuño notes, "The hierarchic relation between the sexes that existed in Franco's society also existed in the Auxilio, with men capturing all power and managerial positions" (194). Their uniforms are brandished with the gold-embroidered symbol of the Falange – the yoke and arrows. This emblem originally served as the shield of the monarchy of Ferdinand and Isabella and was later reappropriated by the Falange to signify the value of obedience (the yoke) and military action (the arrows). The garments of the national delegates of the Falange (men and women who would frequently visit and review the orphanage) are also steeped in a context of social hierarchy. The women delegates are overweight and lavishly dressed, unabashedly displaying their status and power with jewels and furs.

The setting is a hostile atmosphere of militaristic discipline. The entrance, typically appearing at the beginning of each story, represents a strict set of boundaries not to be crossed. The opening drawing varies from story to story, at times displaying the entry doors and at others the gate. The initial image is always preceded by another frame that recalls the year and name of the orphanage. In each story Falangist symbols abound, featuring the fist and dragon or the yoke and arrows.

These drawings conjure images of the prison panopticon characterized by constant surveillance and threat of punishment. Tall towers standing sentinel over the patios and courtyards are constant reminders of the watchful gaze that controls behaviours. In many ways these sites resemble not only the adult prison system as described by Foucault in *Discipline and Punish* but also the military barracks as described by Muñoz Molina. In these orphanages physical punishment for missteps was a public spectacle that performed a key role in "maintaining the arbitrary and despotic power of the State, and of attaining a re-education of minds through the segregation of bodies" (Moreno-Nuño qtd. Mullaney 127). Children, like recruits, were afforded scant privacy as caretakers could always observe them, even in their sleeping quarters, through architectural design elements and strategic staffing. This "enclosed, segmented space," to use Foucault's words, is a model of the disciplinary mechanism "in which individuals are inserted in a fixed place, in which the slightest movements are supervised" (*Discipline* 197). The fear of punishment for even the smallest transgressions, as well as the compulsory self-monitoring and paranoia that fear produces, is captured throughout the series.

The first instalment, "1953, Carretera de Aragón" ("Aragón Highway"), illustrates the daily dehumanization of the interned boys and

OW!
SSHHHH!
¡NOW!
1953
ARAGON HIGHWAY
14 KM FROM MADRID
THERE ARE SOME ORANGE RINDS IN HERE, BUT THEY'RE ALL GREASY!
THERE'S NOTHING IN HERE.

Figure 1. "1953 Aragón Highway" (Giménez and Marsé, *Paracuellos* 16).

the hierarchies formed among them based on age and the capacity for violence. The storyboard shows two boys as they briefly escape through the window to search the dumpsters for scraps of food. As they devour dirty orange peels, another, older boy approaches them. A low angle makes his figure look powerful and larger than life. He towers over the boys and intentionally intimidates them through a tough guise. A close-up of the boys' faces reveals their youthful appearance, innocence, and fear. By the combination of the high-angle shot looking down at the boys and the close-up, the effect is intensified. The dominant boy denounces the weaker ones to the chief fascist official (identified by the emblem on his belt), and together they punish the two boys by pressuring one to strike the other, thereby breaking the bond between them and fomenting a culture of acrimony.

The story culminates with an unsettling critique of the socializing practices that encourage boys to internalize a role of combative masculinity to promote competition and reward domination. One of the boys says to the other, "Just you wait and see. I will split your mouth open." That frame is set by an image of the building's exterior with the fascist hymn "Pregones de imperio" (Proclamations of empire) in the comic balloon: "Vuelan al viento pregones, de gesta imperial, son cadetes de falange" (Flying in the wind, proclaiming imperial feats, are the Falangist cadets). The author effectively uses juxtaposition and irony to critique the regime's version of masculinity and to undermine the tenets of imperialism and National Catholicism.

Throughout the series well-established military terms and routines characterize the behaviours and monologues of the keepers. In "Hombrecitos" (Little men) five frames illustrate the intersecting discourses of the regime and their relation to boys' socio-political formation, including the construction of an imperial, Catholic, and militaristic identity. The first guardian recycles the discourse of the imperial past: "Nadie es pequeño para servir la patria. Plenitud histórica, por el imperio de Dios" (Nobody is too small to serve the fatherland. Historical plenitude, on behalf of God's empire). The following three frames foreground the Catholic rhetoric of fear as a means of ideological control: "El demonio, el demonio a la oreja te está diciendo 'no reces el rosario'" (The devil, the devil whispers in your ear, "Do not pray the rosary"). The final guardian mimics the militaristic language of José Antonio Primo de Rivera: "¡He dicho a formar! ¡Firmes! ¡Los hombres no lloran! Mitad monje y mitad soldado. ¡Una grande y libre! ¡Disciplina! ¡Disciplina! ¡Disciplina! ¡Diezmaré las filas!" (Line up, I said! Firm! Men don't cry! "Half monk, half soldier." Great and free! Discipline! Discipline! Discipline! I will decimate the ranks!).

Figure 2. "Little Men" (Giménez and Marsé, *Paracuellos* 122)

Strategically placed at the end of the strip, this final figure, suggestively named Antonio, becomes a symbol of National Catholic hegemony. For this figure, the ideal form of masculinity is embodied in the Spanish fascist, seen as part warrior, part prophet. Taken together, these frames critically illustrate boys' indoctrination, shaped by the glorification of the colonial Catholic past and the veneration of the heroic fallen Nationalist soldier. Working jointly, the narrative and graphic images link Spanish imperialism, the erasure of secular Republican identity, and militaristic boys' socialization.

Giménez brings further depth to this intersectional critique by connecting religious dogma and militarism with heteronormativity. In "Los impuros" (The sinners) the author exposes the pervasiveness of homophobia and its close relation to dominant forms of masculinity. In this way Giménez's vignettes precede the arguably groundbreaking work of R.W. Connell, who alerted us to the intimate ties between hegemonic masculinity and homophobic ideology (*Masculinities* 40). Giménez shows the systemic policing of the boundaries of acceptable behaviour and the campaign of fear that aims to maintain the masculine script. The backdrop of the story is Christmas, when interned boys with surviving family members would return home temporarily. Two orphan boys without relatives sit together in a largely empty building when they decide to spend time together and support each other. When one of the keepers encounters them sleeping in the same bed, she urgently summons the headmaster and implores the boys to confess their immorality. Calling to mind Kafka's *The Trial*, these children are absurdly persecuted for unspecified charges, thereby showing the extent to which the repressive rule of the National Catholic state coexisted with a profound homophobia. Under these conditions all men were policed, but particularly those men who deviated even slightly from the hypermasculine norm. Not unlike in other heteronormative societies, gay men in Spain were subordinated by straight men with a range of negative attitudes and practices, including imprisonment under sodomy statutes that were intact until 1979, intimidation, murder, and economic discrimination.

Giménez also testifies to the tenaciously honed ability of these children to survive and even the potential of the subordinate staff to assert sovereignty. As Carmen Moreno-Nuño and Ángela Cenarro Lagunas point out, within the orphanages the resistance against disciplinary policies involved escape, the decision by poor families not to return their children, the expression of criticism in letters to political figures or family members, and humour (Cenarro Lagunas 170–4). Giménez further defines stories of survival and struggle against Francoist hegemony in the subsequent comic series *Barrio*, which follows the autobiographical character (Carlines) as he moves out of the orphanage and into the streets of Madrid and Barcelona. Occasionally the stories are set in the protagonist's home, where he lives with his widowed mother, who was previously too ill, impoverished, and emotionally traumatized to care for her son.

One story that reflects the parallels between the reproduction of ideologies and identities, and the resistance to them in both the orphanage and the broader Francoist society, is "Bernardo." Readers see how the intersections of sexism, classism, militarism, religious fanaticism, and imperial notions of the state remained widely internalized in the late 1950s, decades after the war, and served to maintain negative identities like the "gendered other," the "political other," and the "atheist or non-Catholic other."[4] Giménez demonstrates how within that context the most victimized figures were arguably leftist, proletarian, and middle-class women for challenging the oppressive political and class structures of the regime as well as its patriarchal underpinnings.

"Bernardo" begins as the teenage protagonist, Carlines, unexpectedly encounters his friend and co-worker Bernardo Serrat. This male character is a Catalan intellectual and a role model for Carlines, whose own father had died when he was only an infant. Bernardo interrupts the youth's reading of the serial drama (*folletín*) *Madrecita* and recommends to him "real" literature by Russian authors including Tolstoy, Chekhov, and Dostoevsky. Readers would recognize the political implications of such authors within Franco's Spain and come to see Bernardo as a key figure in the autobiographical character's political education. This education is at the same time gendered. In a series of flashbacks Bernardo recalls developing critical consciousness through his relationship with a former co-worker and underground syndicalist named Marga. A close-up depicts her with a defiant gaze while the comic balloon emphasizes her solidarity with factory workers and her dangerous commitment to the production of a clandestine newspaper calling for organization. Whereas in *Paracuellos* we only see images of women who have internalized the hierarchical structures of patriarchal society, in *Barrio* we see alternative forms of both femininity and masculinity.

Bernardo's flashback goes on to show that the regime's agents stormed the meeting's headquarters of the clandestine newspaper and punished the four men (one of whom was a leftist priest) with warnings and intimidation, while they sentenced the woman figure (Marga)

---

4 See DiGiovanni, "Masculinity."

THE SINNERS
PARACUELLOS DEL JARAMA
1948
OVER CHRISTMAS, MANY BOYS LEAVE TO SPEND THE HOLIDAYS AWAY FROM THE SCHOOL.
GIMÉNEZ.—
THE ONES THAT HAVE NO FAMILY OR FRIENDS STAY AT THE "HOME."
DO YOU REMEMBER YOUR FATHER?
NO, I WAS ABANDONED AS A BABY AND I NEVER MET HIM.
ELIAS AND MORTALLA SPEND CHRISTMAS EVE TOGETHER.
MINE DIED WHEN I WAS SIXTEEN MONTHS OLD, FROM AN EAR AILMENT. WHEN HE WAS ABOUT TO DIE, HE LOOKED AT ME AND SAID, "COME HERE, MY BUNNY."
YOU REMEMBER THAT?
NO, BUT THEY TOLD ME ABOUT IT.
SHALL WE EAT OUR BREAD NOW?
OKAY. THEN LET'S TELL STORIES.
HOW HARD IT IS! IT'S LIKE ROCKS! IT'S EASY TO TELL THAT WE'VE BEEN SAVING IT FOR A LONG TIME!
IT'S BETTER THIS WAY 'CAUSE IT'LL LAST US LONGER!
WE'VE GOT FOUR FIGS AND TWO PIECES OF MARZIPAN TOO.
WHAT A FEAST!
WE'RE NOT HAVING SUCH A BAD TIME, ARE WE?
NOT AT ALL! IF ONLY IT COULD BE CHRISTMAS EVE EVERY DAY!
TONIGHT'S CHRISTMAS EVE AND TOMORROW...

Figure 3. "The Sinners" (Giménez and Marsé, *Paracuellos 36*)

to twelve years in prison. Giménez brings out the gendered experience of leftist women under the regime and shows the profound continuity of right-wing civil-war discourses, which depicted Republican women as "prostitutes" whose sin had caused the breakdown of traditional Spanish values. The telling of this traumatic story takes place as the protagonist walks with his mentor (Bernardo) to pick up the promised censored Russian literature. Suddenly, after Bernardo has the clandestine literature in hand, the two men are apprehended by the police and interrogated.

Part 2 begins in the police headquarters where Carlines, only slightly removed by a separating wall, bears witness to the systematic masculinized posturing and physical force upholding political repression. A significant leitmotif is the crucifix hanging on the wall between photographs of Franco and José Primo de Rivera. This recurrent image powerfully evokes a twofold reflection on the struggle of the earthly Jesus as well as the complicity of the Catholic Church in the regime's repression of oppositional voices. One frame features only the crucifix and a narrative balloon showing death threats coming from within the interrogation room. The following medium shot spotlights a callous police officer leaving the interrogation room while Bernardo, only partially pictured, is lying in a pool of blood. At that point Giménez once again uses the flashback as a rhetorical strategy to underscore the significance of memory and the continuity of masculine violence. Framed as a disruption in time, Carlines suddenly imagines a fearful boy in the hands of an intimidating older bully. It is the same image pictured in "1953, Carretera de Aragón." The two scenarios become one. As the chief militarized male denounces Bernardo to the fascist keeper Antonio for possessing "subversive" literature, readers come to see him as inextricably linked to the oppressor of the day. Drawing a jarring parallel between different temporal periods and locations, Giménez depicts the continuity of patterns of privilege and oppression (i.e., militarization, conformity, and incarceration). The flashback imbues the autobiographical protagonist's tears with special poignancy. Readers witness the production of militarized socialization and the cycle of violence and trauma that it generates.

Militarizing Children in *Space Invaders* by Nona Fernández

One interpretive reflex would lead us to compare Carlos Giménez's graphic memoir with examples of Chilean visual culture that revolve around the Allende government and the military dictatorship. Over the last ten years Chile, like Spain, has witnessed a boom in the genre.

Noteworthy titles include *Historias clandestinas* by Sol Rojas Lizana and Ariel Rojas, and *Los años de Allende* by Carlos Reyes and Rodrigo Elgueta. A comparison of these graphic narratives with *Paracuellos* would no doubt produce valuable insights into parallels between the Spanish and Chilean dictatorships as portrayed through the drawn image.

Another interpretive instinct would lead us to explore connections between institutions such as the Sección Feminina of the Falange in Spain and the Secretaría Nacional de la Mujer and the Fundación CEMA (Centro de Madres) in Chile to trace the similarities and differences in the ways women played a role in producing militarized masculinity. A comparison of the Spanish Auxilio Social and the Chilean Servicio Nacional de Menores (SENAME) would also be insightful in understanding how these institutions (supported by the military regimes) contributed to the maintenance of militarized masculinity. The short documentary *Canada 5351* by Catalina Brügmann and the feature film *Volantín cortao* by Aníbal Jofré and Diego Ayala capture on screen the gendered abuse in the SENAME and reveal that the conditions portrayed in *Paracuellos* are not unique to Spain.

Although these comparisons are omitted in this book, that does not signal their irrelevance. As indicated earlier, I will direct my attention instead to the unique short non-fiction novel *Space Invaders* by the multi-talented Nona Fernández. The visual form that characterizes Giménez's graphic narrative contrasts with Fernández's prose in terms of genre, but the comparison is eye opening in the way that both authors conjure childhood vignettes in short chapters that expose the institutions and narratives that fomented militarized masculinity and violence during and after dictatorial rule.

Fernández's *Space Invaders* ends in 2013 when the author-narrator remembers her childhood friend Estrella González Jepsen, who was murdered in 1991 by Lieutenant Félix Sazo. The twenty-one-year-old woman worked at Avis Rent a Car. Just before the murder witnesses saw her arguing with the lieutenant (22), with whom she had a four-month-old son. He threatened her with death if she did not marry him or if she dared to leave him. He returned, in full military uniform, and shot her four times before shooting himself in the head. One witness snapped a photograph of her in a fetal position just before she died. The perpetrator, Felix Sazo Sepúlveda, had entered the military in 1987 and remained in that institution until his death on the day of the crime in 1991 when he was close to graduating as an officer.

Nona Fernández met Estrella González in 1980 at the Avenida Matta School in Santiago de Chile when they were both about ten years old. Fernández and her classmates recall González and her father (Guillermo

González Betancourt) who, they later found out, was a carabineros officer working in the DINA. In 1994, three years after his daughter's murder, he was sentenced to life in prison for his direct participation in the 1985 assassination of José Manuel Parada, Manuel Guerrero, and Santiago Nattino. That crime became known as the Slit-Throat Case (el Caso Degollados), the same case that Nona Fernández explored in depth in her subsequent 2016 non-fiction novel *The Twilight Zone*, analysed in chapter 3 of this book.

By exploring childhood recollections of political repression alongside memories of a woman who was murdered *after* the dictatorship by her ex-boyfriend, the author connects the dots between different forms of killing and stretches our understanding of the ties between violence and militaristic culture. Fernández's approach in *Space Invaders* looks at the problem of violence in terms of social institutions and gender norms. She recognizes the similarities between the Pinochet regime's use of torture as a method of social control and the positive views voiced more politely around the dinner table and in schools about the need for a "strongman" leader and the inevitability of war. The homicide of Estrella González, in other words, cannot be simply understood as a so-called crime of passion committed in response to heartbreak. The murder represents a continuum of violence shaped by patriarchal militarism tethered to the view that dominance over the "other" is a true sign of masculinity and that violence is the only effective response to conflict.

Space Invaders contains four sections, titled "First Life," "Second Life," "Third Life," and "Game Over," with short chapters that share a narrative structure. Each one defies a neat chronological plot line, featuring different narrators who jump from childhood memories to the present. Through that form, the author makes explicit the ways in which the dictatorial past shapes identity and impinges on the here and now. Fernández writes: "Time isn't straightforward, it mixes everything up, shuffles the dead, merges them, separates them out again, advances backward, retreats in reverse, spins like a merry-go-round, like a tiny wheel in a laboratory cage, and traps us in funerals and marches and detentions, leaving us with no assurance of continuity or escape" (50). *Space Invaders*, like *Paracuellos*, renders visible the political climate of the dictatorship not as disconnected from childhood but rather as intimately connected to it in the past, present, and future. "Whether we were there or not is no longer clear. Whether we took part in it all or not isn't either. But we're left with traces of the dream, like the vestiges of a doomed naval battle" (51).

Fernández asks readers to consider how militarized culture, discourse, and politics influenced children's socialization and how, in turn, that process shaped young people to later uphold an ideology of male military power (or conversely, consciously resist it). To bring nuance to a story reflective of various experiences, Fernández manages to link multiple voices that are reconstructions based on the perspectives of her childhood friends. They are all referred to by their surnames, which pushes against the gendered system of naming. Among them, readers come to identify five boys (Riquelme, Bustamonte, Zuñiga, Donoso, Acosta) and four girls (González, Maldonado, Fuenzalida, Fernández). By weaving these narrative threads into a collective story about childhood during the Pinochet dictatorship, Fernández highlights some of the most influential ideological processes that permeate private and public spaces to perpetuate militarism and justify violence.

Fernández makes these connections at every turn. In "First Life," for instance, one short chapter describes the children carefully dressing in school uniforms in 1980; the next chapter displays the authoritarianism and nationalism taught in class. The militarization of children's lives is recognized in the regulation of bodies and minds. They brushed their hair "into submission" and stood perfectly in line as if in military formation while one student raised the Chilean flag. The depiction summons back to the many days in which schoolchildren sang the regime's version of the national anthem, which included praise of the armed forces: "Vuestros nombres, valientes soldados, que habéis sido de Chile el sostén, nuestros pechos los llevan grabados; los sabrán nuestros hijos también. (Your names, brave soldiers who have been Chile's pillar, are engraved in our chests; our children will know them as well.) The memory of the hymn is also redolent of the image depicted by Carlos Giménez in *Paracuellos* when the boys were forced to sing "Proclamations of Empire" ("Flying in the wind, proclaiming imperial feats, are the Falangist cadets"). Antonio Muñoz Molina's account of military formation also resonates with Fernández's description. "They've arranged us in a long single file down the middle of the schoolyard. Next to us is another long line, and then another, and another. We form a perfect square, a kind of game board. We're pieces in a game, but we don't know what it's called" (Fernández, *Space Invaders* 9). In all three cases these Spanish and Chilean authors render visible notions of military discipline and conformity that shaped wider societal approaches to education.

Fernández recalls nationalist indoctrination and patriotic myths in which wars were idealized in stories of bravery framed as Chile's proud history. In one of the class performances Zuñiga plays the role of Arturo Prat, the naval officer killed in the War of the Pacific. He says: "Year after year I take part in that perpetual disaster that, it seems, will never end. In a moment of déjá vu, it's my turn to die again on the enemy deck for my country and my honour" (21). These acts are part and parcel of a militarized culture that permeates children's lives, normalizes war, and enables the justification of violence. Fernández knows that such beliefs and attitudes are gendered and that notions of masculinity are bound to nationalist discourses of war and bravery. Related to this idea, Carol Cohn argues in her article "War, Wimps, and Women: Talking Gender and Thinking War" that gendered images and words "shape how we experience, understand, and represent ourselves as men and women" (229). But they also do more than that: "they shape many other aspects of our lives and culture. In this symbolic system, human characteristics are dichotomized, divided into pairs of polar opposites that are supposedly mutually exclusive: mind is opposed to body; culture to nature; thought to feeling; logic to intuition; objectivity to subjectivity; aggression to passivity; confrontation to accommodation; abstraction to particularity; public to private; political to personal, ad nauseam. In each case, the first term of the 'opposites' is associated with male, the second with female" (Cohn 229).

In *Space Invaders* Fernández makes visible the challenges of resisting such culturally constructed systems of dichotomies. Zuñiga's inner voice reveals his struggle to perform like a so-called manly man: "I want to ask for help, but it wouldn't look good. I'm a hero, not a coward" (Fernández 22). He has internalized gendered pejoratives and disallows his fear to be spoken. To borrow Cohn's idea, "Equally, if not damagingly, is the way in which this interpretive coding not only limits what is said, but even limits what is thought" (Cohn 235). Zuñiga's dreams reveal the subconscious impact of such patriarchal and militaristic myths. They contained elements of battle narratives, including the story of the War of the Pacific (1879–83). Importantly, in the mid-1970s, that conflict with Peru over control of the resource-rich Atacama Desert was renewed. Border disputes with Argentina and claims over the resource-rich south also resurfaced and nearly boiled over into war in 1978. Inside the classroom under Pinochet the rhetoric of counter-revolutionary war with the so-called internal leftist enemy was intertwined with the contemporary version of Chile's nineteenth-century battles against the external enemies to the north and south. "In the dream, I think about the Battle of Concepcion ... The War of the Pacific, Chile's endless struggle with Peru and Bolivia. Skirmishes under the sun, in the middle of the desert. The idea of an ambush, a trap, and the certainty that there were dead children in this battle. Probably they weren't so little. Probably they were like us, an army of adolescents ... Little tin soldiers splashing in this fake sea, no clue what battle they are fighting" (Fernández 56).

Just as Fernández exposes the relationship between war stories and gender binaries, she reveals the porous boundaries between childhood and adulthood, as well as civilian socialization and militarization. Despite the desire to compartmentalize, the horrors of the military regime cannot be reduced to one single moment in time and space: "coffins and funerals and wreaths were suddenly everywhere and there was no escaping them because it had all become something like a bad dream. Maybe it had always been that way and we were only just realizing it" (Fernández 49). The uneasy attempt to recognize the unfamiliar (coffins, unconcealed dictatorial brutality) within the familiar (enactments of battles, nationalistic school assemblies, discourses of external enemies) recalls Bolaño's "Words from Outer Space." With reference to the recorded tape of military orders on 11 September 1973, Bolaño writes: "The tape rolls and little by little the voices become familiar, as if they had always been there, talking to us, threatening us. The image is redundant" (*Between Parentheses* 85). The resemblance between these reflections is striking. Both authors seem to concur with Enloe that the institution of the armed forces is only a piece, albeit paramount, in the process of cultural militarization. Fernández, Bolaño, and Giménez, among others in the book, substantiate Enloe's worry that militarist culture becomes obfuscated when the actual military is seen as the *only* site for militarized thought and action.

Bound up with the memories of militarism, education, and violence is the recurring image of Estrella González. She is a distant but prominent memory: they cannot seem to put a finger on exact details like her face or hair, but they remember letters and stories involving her. One of Riquelme's foundational memories takes place at Estrella's house where they play the video game *Space Invaders* for hours. When he witnesses her father remove a prosthetic hand, Estrella explains that he lost it in throwing a bomb. The group later discovers that the accident was related to his work as a military officer in the secret police (DINA).

In recollecting these scenes in tandem, Fernández not only brings out the complexities of memory but also correlates the struggle to navigate adolescence against the militarized backdrop of police brutality with the fight to survive in a video game. *Space Invaders* seems to mirror their experience: "They run back and forth, fleeing in terror, but the hand clutches at the first Martian within reach, and at its touch there is an explosion. The body of the little Martian flies apart into coloured lights that vanished from the TV screen" (Fernández 41). Like in *Paracuellos*, the narrators in the book *Space Invaders* recall the anxieties and fears that they did not seem to communicate to adults; however, they were never completely autonomous as children. They always shared with adults the same militarized world of soldiers, secret service agents, and opposition fighters. Just as militarized culture bleeds into civilian society, Fernández shows how childhood and adulthood are not hermetically sealed. The seemingly inescapable, slow, and unconscious process of children's socialization is part of what makes the boundaries between life stages so blurry, and memory so fluid.

Whereas "First Life" focuses on the school memories of 1980 when the group of friends met Estrella González, "Second Life" centres on acts of resistance to violence that take place two years later when the children are around twelve years old. In February of 1982 they discover that the head of the Chilean intelligence agency had shot the union leader Tucapel Jiménez "five times in the head before slitting his throat" (Fernández 27). In 2002 twelve military men were convicted for that crime, but Fernández shows that, at the time of the murder, voicing fear or concern was out of bounds. Taking that risk, Zuniga and Riquelme secretly distribute flyers in front of the school regarding a march against Pinochet. They are subsequently suspended. When students ask their mathematics teacher about the situation, the twelve-year-olds are met with silence: "What does it mean to get into politics? How old do you have to be? Silence. The teacher stares, startled. Silence […] Fuenzalida dreams of him, of the silence that settled over the classroom, which she can hear as clearly as our voices. Silence. No one says a thing, not a seat creaks, not a sheet of paper rustles. Boys and girls, says the math teacher, this is math class and you're here to learn, not to talk nonsense" (38).

Children's education under Pinochet and military training were hardly synonymous; however, insofar as the former required the enforcement of sanctioned beliefs and strictly controlled behaviours, it mirrored some underlying elements of military education. This is something that Passmore finds when looking at the relationship between soldier testimonies and the writing of Diamela Eltit: "The vigilance described by many former recruits recalls the internalized surveillance identified by Diamela Eltit. In her 1994 novel *The Custody of the Eyes*, Eltit dissects the claustrophobia, atomization, self-control, anxiety, and suspicion of life under Chilean authoritarianism. An atmosphere of mistrust and repression hangs over society but also invades intimate spaces, shaping the home lives and personal interactions of characters who police their own thoughts and behaviors" (*Wars* 28).

Similarly, in Fernández's *Space Invaders*, either out of fear or complicity or both, instructors taught students that to learn meant to obey, not to question. When Estrella stops coming to school in 1985, her friends only have her letters and notes for clues as to why she has disappeared.

Writing to Maldonado in 1982, Estrella explains that she can no longer go out alone and that she must stay at home under surveillance by one of her father's co-workers, named "Uncle Claudio." Years later in 1994 Estrella's friends would connect the dots. They would learn from televised news that the 1985 Slit-Throat Case was a brutal triple homicide ordered by Guillermo González Betancourt (Estrella's father) and executed by military corporals including Claudio Alberto Salazar Fuentes. Fernández conveys the dismay that the group of friends later felt when recalling "Uncle Claudio" parked near the school, always watching them with a suspicious smile from his red Chevy Chevette.

When the group of friends leave school to join a large protest through the streets in 1982, they wear their neat uniforms and march through Santiago like "a block that advances in lockstep, a single unit moving on the game board" (Fernández 41). The author's reference to a military-like march against the Pinochet regime alerts us to several important matters related to the links between military and civilian culture. There is a cadence in their march – "One and two, one and two" – and a conformity between them in their verbal expressions: "Someone shouts something, and someone repeats it. Somebody else shouts something, and many others repeat it. We shout what's being shouted. We don't understand what it means, but that's what we do" (42). In the same dream that Zuñiga has about the War of the Pacific, he imagines leading his group of friends, marching in an army of little soldiers.

The repetition of this image is not a trivial detail. Popular protest groups under Pinochet that demanded better housing and better employment, for instance, often challenged the regime from within its own discourse of gender relations. An acknowledgment of those relationships is not meant to conflate the different practices and ideologies of opposing groups, but rather to recognize that militarism cuts across the political spectrum and through Chilean society, like the engrained sexist and homophobic attitudes that pervaded the political right and left. Even many years later, Fernández writes, "We're pieces in a game that we don't know how to stop playing" (69). In their dreams "there are no cars, no buses, no people. Just us and this guerrilla logic that we can't wake up from" (69). Even though they are civilians, they have been educated in the logic of perpetual war. Recognizing the ways in which they participate or disrupt such conditioning is a necessary step in producing change.

"Third Life" digs up a string of violent acts perpetrated by secret agents to forestall the collapse of the military regime at a time of increased social upheaval. The Slit-Throat murders, detentions, and torture were all pieces of the army's defence of a military state in its waning years. Estrella completely withdraws from school, and homes are ransacked. Zúñiga's family members are detained on suspicion of political agitation. "Riquelme's mother was kidnapped. Twelve hours later she was released. Crosses had been cut into her nipples with a razor blade" (Fernández 51). Torture involving rape and the desecration of naked bodies was intimately connected to patriarchal history and to the nature of the militarized state. Fernández prompts readers to consider how those gendered patterns of police brutality affected the children of the victims. Nightmares about the fear of engulfment offer some clues: "Our paper ship begins to take on water. We tumble onto the white sheet and go under. We lie there submerged. Not knowing how to wake up" (61).

The final section describes the murder of Estrella González Jepsen at the hands of a militarized man in the wake of the dictatorship. It is titled "Game Over," partly in reference to the end of Estrella's life, but unlike the video game, the physical and emotional toll of militarization is real and ongoing. Estrella González's death represents a continuum of violence, as the author's description of attack reveals: "Estrella is attending to a customer when Lieutenant Sazo aims his service revolver at her. They've been separated for some time. The Lieutenant has struggled to accept the fact of their separation. That's why he's been following her, harassing her over the phone, threatening her the way you'd threaten an enemy, an alien, a communist teacher" (Fernández 65). Fernández maps out the crime in terms of the engrained militarist belief that the assertion of force is a natural and necessary male behaviour to maintain control and social order. The author makes clear that militarization is at work in this femicide. "Like a little Martian she flies apart into coloured lights [...] Police lieutenant Félix Sazo immediately shoots himself twice in the head with his smoking service revolver and falls to the ground" (65). The repetition of the word *service* as the descriptor for the revolver reminds readers of the killer's role in the armed forces. It also denaturalizes the word defined as the action of helping others. Whereas the term *military service* usually serves to rationalize or legitimize the use of force as the most effective form of conflict resolution, Fernández uses the word to delegitimize that meaning.

Police lieutenant Félix Sazo came from the same militarized environment as did Guillermo González Betancourt, and their crimes were equally as bloody. In the same place where Estrella's classmates found the 1985 headline "Throats Slashed," they learned of Estrella's slaying. The detail urges readers to move beyond a narrow approach to violence: "We read it in the crimes pages of a newspaper found on the fourth shelf of the third aisle in the school library" (Fernández 65). Within these lines the author drives in a searing commentary about a continuum of violence. Similar gendered values and behaviours that shape femicide are repeated if they go unquestioned. The culmination of that critique is set in Santiago de Chile in 2013. Fernández describes one last dream: "A payphone rings on the street, right by the school entrance. We look at each other. Somehow, we've been expecting this call. A woman or a child is breathing nervously at the other end of the line, waiting for a reply" (69). While Fernández does not say so directly, it is a call to action. But it is not a militarist call to duty, rather a call to remember and to acknowledge the interconnection between seemingly different forms of violence. "Standing in the street, uncomfortable in our old uniforms, now too tight and faded, we listen attentively" (70).

With these texts Carlos Giménez and Nona Fernández join a chorus of voices that have denounced the damaging association of children's education with militarization, war, and quotidian violence. Education needs rebuilding, Virginia Woolf famously insisted as a response to the question of fascism in her 1930s *Three Guineas*. Woolf's concerns about the Spanish Civil War, evident in that landmark essay, make her work particularly relevant to this discussion. She argues that forcing children's bodies into unnatural positions, tightly cased in uniforms and symbols, only teaches them to perform like the dictators that oppress them. "For do they not prove that education, the finest education in the world, does not teach people to hate force, but to use it?" (29). Through a rhetorical approach she utilizes a photograph of maimed bodies in war-ravaged Spain, not to incite more hatred but to foster empathy, cultivate a sense of shared humanity, and provoke awareness concerning the horrors of a militaristic ideology that venerates carnage. She advocates for transformative action, an engaged consciousness, and even the metaphorical burning of colleges. Instead of reinforcing divisions, like those seen in rigid gender roles and other categorical thinking, she advocates for the college to be a space for profound exploration (34). Perhaps Woolf anticipates, in her own way, Audre Lorde's later articulation of the productive power of rage.

Fernández, much like Woolf, uses a powerful image – the ringing payphone – to inspire a rejection of conformity and a proactive effort to redefine the figures of tyranny and death. Fernández seems to channel Woolf's conclusion that "we are not passive spectators doomed to unresisting obedience but by our thoughts and actions can ourselves change that figure" (Woolf 142). Overcoming war, dictatorial violence, and the construction of militarized masculinity demands the creation of novel strategies and language, rather than the replication of old ones (Woolf 143). We see a recurrence of the concepts explored in the previous chapter concerning Mendez's "The Language of the Dead" within these arguments. Language is used to shape the meaning of violence, often with euphemisms that celebrate battle and justify suffering. The protagonist of that story, so familiar with the dehumanization of language by his militarized captors, endeavors to discover similarities "between writing and caresses, words and affection" (Méndez 53). The confining language of patriotism was central to the upbringing of Giménez and Fernández, and a target of their critique. The redefinition of patriotism requires its disentanglement from militarized masculinity, a task made necessary by the inherent paternalistic link in the word itself, as seen in the Latin *pater* or *padre*. Similarly, the rigid link between manliness, pride, and dominance requires severance. By exposing the compounded strata of the militarized masculine identity, the authors discussed here (Giménez, Fernández, Méndez, and Woolf) illuminate its dual nature as both absurd and dangerous.

These narratives also present resistant masculinities that reject violent conflict resolution. The resistance manifests through critical inquiry, providing a counter-narrative to the obedient type of soldier figure. Furthermore, an empathetic engagement with the other is evident, notably in the expressive portrayals of boys in Giménez's graphic novels, which challenge the stoic representation of militarized masculinity. Fernández, in a parallel manner, emphasizes that boys, like girls, are vulnerable and have the same fundamental need for love and support. To conclude, empathetic bravery, demonstrated through acts of connection, redefines heroism as rooted in friendship and solidarity, thereby critiquing the militarized paradigm that equates individual bravery with dominance. Focusing solely on the similarities between societies facing the persistent danger of militarized masculinity leaves our work incomplete unless we also recognize acts of resistance, agency, and the ways in which we can actively dismantle these structures.

5 Militarized Masculinity, Misogyny, and Mass in Spain and Chile

In *Down Girl: The Logic of Misogyny*, Kate Manne redefines the term *misogyny* by bringing out the inadequacies of its common usage. "By the lights of the naïve conception, misogyny essentially becomes too psychologistic a notion, on the model of a phobia or a deep-seated aversion. It becomes a matter of psychological ill health, or perhaps irrationality, rather than a systematic facet of social power relations and a predictable manifestation of the ideology that governs them: patriarchy" (49). She draws a distinction between sexism as a set of beliefs and misogyny as an enforcement mechanism of prescribed gender roles that keep women in a subordinate position to men. She explains that as long as women perform their assumed duty as emotional, social, domestic, and sexual caregivers, then they receive validation or a place on a pedestal that gives the appearance that misogyny is absent. However, she states, "this seamless appearance is almost inevitably deceptive, since more or less subtly hostile, threatening, and punitive norm-enforcement mechanisms will be standing ready, or operating in the background, should these 'soft' forms of social power prove insufficient for upholding them [...] These coercive enforcement mechanisms vis-à-vis patriarchal norms and expectations, and the social roles they govern, are the functional essence of misogyny" (46–7).

Reading Manne's recent *Down Girl* alongside Klaus Theweleit's *Male Fantasies*, first published in 1979, deepens our understanding of the multiple facets of misogyny and its relation to violence. Focusing on the German Freikorps, Theweleit makes the case that masculine identity for the proto-fascists in the 1920s hinged upon the rejection of the feminine and played a crucial role in the rise of Nazism. In his analysis of certain German writers who emerged from the First World War (including Ernst Jünger), he finds three key patterns in the representation of women from their diaries, letters, and publications. These include the proletarian monstrous "whore"; the nameless, faceless, absent wife; and the chaste upper-class, caring, white nurse. "Women who don't conform to any of the 'good woman' images are automatically seen as prostitutes, as the vehicles of 'urges' (Theweleit 171). Men, proto-fascist writings suggest, must "take the offensive before these women can put their horrible plans into practice" (171).

Misogyny and militarist socialization underlie and fuel acts of political persecution, subjugation, and religious fanaticism. In this chapter I contextualize twentieth-century misogyny in Spain and Chile and then analyse the novels *Blind Sunflowers* by Alberto Méndez and *By Night in Chile* by Roberto Bolaño. These narratives provide thought-provoking vehicles that heighten awareness of the gendered ideologies underpinning violence in the context of the Franco and Pinochet regimes.

Stealing the Narrative in Spain and Chile

Misogyny's entrenched history in Spain and Chile faced potential uprooting by the reforming agendas of the democratically elected Second Republic in 1931 and the Popular Unity government in 1970, respectively. However, patriarchal and heteronormative views on family and sexuality were deeply rooted across the political spectrum in both contexts. Julie Shayne notes that during Allende's tenure women contributed to revolutionary change in Chile, but they were prevented from reaching their full potential (73). As Gina Herrmann illustrates in "Voices of the Vanquished: Leftist Women and the Spanish Civil War," that was also the case in Spain. Leftist militant groups in both Spain and Chile upheld a far-reaching revolutionary platform that encompassed the emancipation of women, but insofar as they considered the struggle for gender equality as subordinate to the class struggle, their ideologies remained fundamentally patriarchal. Nevertheless, as Herrmann and Shayne agree, women's pro-emancipation movements emerged within these contexts, placing in question the traditional gender norms that excluded women from the public sphere.

By 1933 the new constitution in Spain had extended universal suffrage to women, established freedom of speech and freedom of association, and secured the right to divorce. In Chile women were granted partial voting rights in 1931 and national voting rights in 1949, but divorce was not legalized until 2004. In both contexts the series of social transformations regarding the roles of women in society provoked protest, particularly among conservative Catholic groups and the military, two bastions of masculine power. After the Spanish Civil War the political repression

carried out to solidify the Franco dictatorship had clear gender specific-
ities. As historian Sebastian Balfour contends, Franco's Army of Africa
invaded the peninsula in 1936 with a mission to destroy the atheist
enemy and re-establish the "authentic" Catholic Spain (*Deadly Embrace*
280). The dictatorship that followed was portrayed as the continuation
of that colonial crusade through an intricate web of discourses and
images. Like the previous Spanish colonizers who had sought to justify imperial rule through the lens of religion and civilization, Franco's
multiplex political machine sought to legitimize the civil war by underscoring a fellowship between the military, the Church, and the state and
their shared vision of a cleansed National Catholic state. Similarities
can be detected in Chile where the Pinochet regime sought to seize the
narrative to enforce patriarchal, militarist, and Catholic values. This is
not a mere coincidence. As I stated in the introduction, Weld contends
that the Spanish Civil War – in which the military purged Spain of
communism in a kind of Christian reconquest – was a key component
of the paradigm that some anti–Salvador Allende revanchists used to
understand their world.

Certain notions of Catholic righteousness, the superiority of the
militarized male, and subjugation of leftist political groups shaped the
regimes' discourses and served to sanction social practices of political, gender, and cultural oppression. Taking hold of the narrative, both
military regimes framed men as soldiers, nation builders, and scholars,
while women were cast as wives, bearers of children, and caregivers.
As evinced in school textbooks and media representations, women's
bodies became the terrain on which the tenets of Catholic virtue and
nationalism were written.[1] A network of institutions, customs, and
laws that dictated passive and pious female behaviour became gospel.
This socio-political move backwards towards religious intolerance and
aggressive chauvinism was particularly demoralizing for non-Catholic
women. Identity markers, such as religion, political affiliation, gender,
sexual identity, and class, therefore shaped women's particular experiences of the political and economic consequences of the military coups
in both cases. (Graham 183).

---

1 See Morcillo Gómez, "Shaping True Catholic Womanhood." Also see Martín Gaite,
  Usos amorosos de la postguerra española.

The regimes' seizure of the narrative also had ramifications on masculine gender norms. To quote Ian Winchester, the Francoist military formulated the principles of its normative masculinity through discursive means (books, magazines, manuals, etc.) and enforced them through compulsory military service: "underlying and buttressing the Francoist military's mission of educating the nation's youth, military authors made clear that the recruits could only become true men by learning how to be good soldiers, and vice versa" (235). Gendered military discourse identified secular, non-military, intellectual men as unmanly, which was seen as an abnormal divergence attributable to the republic. The regime's construction of manhood also idealized the solider-religious figure, as Mary Nash explains: "the image of the warrior-monk shaped around a combination of conquistador and the founder of the Jesuits, Saint Ignatius de Loyola, and combining courage, virility, religiosity, and military values, became the prototype of role models for young Spanish males" (qtd. in Winchester 235). Men's sexuality was formally policed through a discourse that framed women with sexual desire as diseased and subsequently a threat to masculine morality (Winchester 240). Outside official discourse, however, the exploitation of the body of a prostitute was normalized. The misogynist policing of women's bodies and the imposition of militarized masculinity were therefore intimately intertwined.

Since the mid-1990s new memorial accounts and novels have emerged in Spain and Chile as a critical response to the Franco and Pinochet regimes' seizure of narrative control. Using the novels *Blind Sunflowers* by Alberto Méndez (1941–2004) and *By Night in Chile* by Roberto Bolaño (1953–2003), I contend that fictional narrative can help us decipher the ways in which the Franco and Pinochet regimes were shaped by militarist and misogynist discourses. Both authors denaturalize the regimes' underlying interdependent ideologies and deepen our understanding of their roles in the repression of oppositional voices. In different ways these texts invite us to imagine how gendered acts of domination contributed to the broader political goal of internal colonization, which meant the restoration of the hegemony of the military, the Catholic Church, and the economic elites in Spain and Chile. Through narrative strategies characteristic of literature, Méndez and Bolaño confront the ways in which violent conflict has been glorified through social constructions of aggressive masculinity. By extension, they render visible the link between violence, gender, and discourse.

For a nuanced understanding of *Blind Sunflowers* and *By Night in Chile*, it is important to consider them in the context of their production, that is, during the first decade of the twenty-first century when memories of state violence re-emerged powerfully in the literary imagination. The urgency to deal with memory involved many factors, including the imminent death of the perpetrators and the victims of dictatorial violence. Against this backdrop Bolaño published *By Night in Chile*, and Méndez published *Blind Sunflowers*. I begin with Méndez, who, before his untimely death in 2004, had devoured old forgotten books and documents written by fascist authors (Intxausti). That meticulous documentation and remarkably perceptive interpretation of the regime's euphemistic language provides invaluable material for the construction of the characters and plot in Méndez's only work of fiction. The author summons pro-Franco voices not to reinforce them but to subvert and denaturalize them. In so doing, he generates a new way of understanding the past.

Blind Sunflowers between Light and Darkness

Blind Sunflowers is a hybrid novel with four interconnected stories of "defeats" that take place in various settings between 1936 and 1942.[2] As Antonio Gómez López-Quiñones indicates, the stories "not only share common motives and themes but also characters and narrative threads" ("El giro" 103). Here I focus on the last story, titled "The Fourth Defeat: 1942 or Blind Sunflowers," which was translated to English in 2008 by Nick Caistor and can be read independently. In 2008 the story was also adapted to film by José Luis Cuerda. From my point of view, the adaptation mischaracterizes the protagonists and fails to fully convey the original version's eye-opening insight into the logic of misogyny, so my focus will be exclusively on the original literary version and the particular ways in which the narrative lends special attention to the alliance between the Church, the military, and the state and to their complicity in the persecution of Republican voices. Méndez calls attention to the ways in which the militarized state sought to shape women's roles and how gender, class, and religion determined the gain or loss of power. These findings bring complexity to the larger argument in *Militarized Masculinity*, which holds that the social construction of gender and militarist socialization underlie and fuel acts of political persecution and subjugation.

Mendéz's narrative is set in Madrid in 1942 and revolves around a family of four: Elena, an urban working-class seamstress and mother of

---

2 The word *Republican* is used by Méndez as a general term for ideological variants of the political left He does not specify between parties, trade unionists, or general supporters of the republic.

two; Elenita, her adolescent daughter who is in hiding with her communist companion; Elena's younger son, Lorenzo; and finally, her husband, Ricardo, an erstwhile Republican intellectual forced to live in a cell-like closet of their apartment out of fear of reprisal for his involvement in left-wing politics during the war. As a result of maintaining the appearance that Ricardo was killed in the war, Lorenzo and Elena live in constant fear and secrecy, virtually cut off from the rest of society. The family faces economic deprivations, the loss of loved ones, repeated raids by Falangist squads, and the general ongoing terror provoked by the Nationalist victors.

The chief Nationalist figure in the story is Lorenzo's Catholic schoolteacher, Salvador, a former fascist soldier and libertine, now a deacon, who believes that Elena is a widow. Méndez renders this character as the embodiment of emotional, psychological, and sexual repression who seeks through the Church a reaffirmation of his triumphant role in the war and guidance to assuage his sexual desire. Yet he fails to embrace doctrinal celibacy and soon pursues Elena. He disguises his desire for her as a benevolent concern for her well-being based on a patriarchal notion of the family, whereby the mother and child are deemed subordinate to the authoritarian father figure. In a climactic final scene he resolves to shed his cassock in order to fulfil his carnal desires and exercise power over her. When she refuses his sexual advances, he explodes into a fit of rage and attempts to rape her. Ricardo then emerges from the closet to defend her, at which time Salvador flees to notify the police. Seeing no real option for survival, Ricardo throws himself from the apartment window, whereby Salvador successfully destroys the family.

By analysing certain character representations I argue that *Blind Sunflowers* highlights the ways in which the Franco regime's discourses created an intersectional system of oppression that played the important role of legitimizing acts of violence such as physical and psychological torture. As Kimberle Crenshaw explains, intersectionality is a useful concept to understand how multiple socially constructed categories of prejudice are inextricably linked and form part of a complex system of social and economic discrimination. *Blind Sunflowers* asks us to consider how the forms of injustice in Francoist society functioned not in isolation but in tandem. In analysing the effects of an ideology imbued with such interdependent imperialist and sexist discourses, I focus in particular on the ways in which these were used to control Republican women and their bodies.

This analysis also goes beyond the initial work of pinpointing the intersections of identity. I highlight how the novel raises questions about the ways in which militarist and misogynist discourses were instruments of power in Franco's Spain as they transformed historical events like war into mythical events. The text denaturalizes a primary Francoist discourse, according to which the militarized male held supreme authority and the family symbolized "natural" power relations (father over son, man over woman). Méndez suggests that those power relations fed into the logic of others (the National "victors" over the Republican "vanquished") as defined through a paternalistic and militarist language. I focus particularly on Salvador's behaviour and confessions. In them we see assumptions about the naturalness of the patriarchal family, a strict division of spheres for women, and men's and women's "true natures" as ordained by God. This character prompts readers to think critically about the way in which militarism, sexism, religious fanaticism, and imperial notions of the state facilitated the creation of negative identities like the "gendered other," the "political other," and the "atheist or non-Catholic other," which were seen as corrupt and had to be redeemed and "cleansed." As these identities were already spoiled, anyone having one or more of these traits was already less than human and consequently without bodily integrity or a legitimate claim to human rights.

Blind Sunflowers is recounted by three different narrators, allowing readers to track various points of view, and by extension increasing our capacity for analysis. The narrators include Salvador, whose narration takes the form of a confession that seeks to justify the events leading to the final violent encounter with Elena; Lorenzo, now in adulthood, reflecting on his own lingering traumatic childhood memories; and a third-person omniscient narrator who tells of the events as they occur. These three storytellers are distinguished by different type styles: Salvador in italics, Lorenzo in bold, and the third-person narrator in regular font. The diversity of the narrative forms and temporal currents is significant. Salvador's obsessive focus on "truth" starkly contrasts with Lorenzo's contemplative interior monologue that questions a range of symbiotic relationships between the past and the present, reality and representation, and history and memory. The past for Lorenzo is elusive, accessible only through imperfect memory, which is inevitably fluid and filtered through a subjective lens. Furthermore, his narrative catalogues the long-term effects of the repression and violence of the post-war years, thus underscoring the presence of the past in the present.

The author juxtaposes these contrasting narrative lenses in order to deconstruct Francoist truth claims and signal the mythical distortions to which history was subjected during the regime. He also points to silences as the reader is denied access to Elena's inner reflections on the violent operations of the military state. We only hear her dialogue with others through the third-person narrator, who observes from above the unfolding family drama. Equally absent are the thoughts of Lorenzo's father, who as a *topo* (mole) is forced underground (in the closet) out of fear of reprisal. As the title suggests, he is one of the blind sunflowers, driven into the darkness by the regime's forces. Through these silences and allusions to darkness and blindness, the novel evokes the regime's sweeping exclusion of oppositional voices from the public sphere and the lack of intellectual diversity and growth as a consequence. There is much to mine in this richly textured and elegantly written story; however, as previously mentioned, I will mostly focus on Salvador's character, which embodies the confluence of the regime's values operating to subordinate and colonize Republican women and their bodies.

The story opens with a confession by Salvador that draws on Catholic iconography to vindicate his role as a crusader in the Spanish Civil War: "Everything began when I took your advice, Father. I enlisted in the Glorious National Army. I fought three years on the front, as part of our Crusade [...] With my blood I helped convert Mount Sinai into a Golgotha" (Méndez, *Blind Sunflowers* 75). This grandiose myth celebrates the war as a meaningful holy battle and the male soldier as a leading light and triumphant liberator in the fight against the secularization of the proletariat that had "invaded" the homeland. Salvador draws a parallel between the crucifixion of Jesus and the civil war, thereby vindicating the military uprising and the bloodshed that it saw as necessary in the trajectory of the nation's redemption. The self-righteous language of Spanish militarism and imperialism that emphasized salvation and moral purification can hardly be ignored. Such rhetoric is found in countless post-war speeches disseminated by the regime, such as the following by Franco, in which he declared: "No es un capricho el sufrimiento de una nación en un punto de su historia; es el castigo espiritual, castigo que Dios impone a una vida torcida, a una historia no limpia" (qtd. in Casanova *La iglesia* 235). (The suffering of a nation at one point in its history is not a whim; it is spiritual punishment, punishment that God imposes on a distorted life, an unclean history.) Franco's language evokes common colonial motifs that associate notions of Catholic virtue with cleanliness, a point of view considered to be a God-given sign of the colonizers' moral superiority.[3]

---

3 Anne McClintock's *Imperial Leather* also examines colonial discourses and representations that connected morality and cleanliness. The chapter "Soft-Soaping Empire" specifically addresses soap advertisements that reinforced colonial stereotypes about British purity and evolutionary superiority.

This obsession with the virtue of the National Catholic identity and its protection through the militarized male soldier reflects the colonial period's fixation with conversion. As Jo Labanyi suggests, this concern was primarily "the expression of an intolerance of cultural difference; belief in the efficacy of conversion supposed that 'others' could and should be made 'the same'" ("Miscegenation" 58). Significantly, as Labanyi contends, Spanish colonial discourse largely articulated miscegenation as a way to improve the race: "in reality, of course, this was the normalization of rape, resemanticized in Spanish colonial discourse as the myth of the white male generously donating his seed to the woman of colour and thereby founding a new hybrid race in which differences were transcended and redeemed" (58). In *Blind Sunflowers* this rhetoric vindicating the redemption of women through sexual conquest and subjugation informs Salvador's understanding of his relationship with Elena and soon determines his aggressive pursuit of power over her. Through the characterization of Salvador and his narrative voice, readers gain insight into the ways that militarism and misogyny come together in a discourse that is used as a tool of power.

Salvador's lexicon also alludes to the writer Ernesto Giménez Caballero, whose most famous work *Genio de España* reveals the convergence of unbending fascist, imperialist, patriarchal, and ultra-conservative Catholic values, which he directly linked to the metaphor of purification (i.e., cleansing in the blood of the lamb, purifying the sin of women, purging the savagery of leftists, etc.). The fascist writer compared Republican Madrid to the Whore of Babylon, symbolizing both sexual sin and the Antichrist mentioned in the Book of Revelation (Labanyi, *Myth and History* 36–7). His overtly sexist and dogmatic use of language likened the hypermasculine founder of the Falange, José Antonio Primo de Rivera, to the Lamb of God that would atone for the sins of Spain. According to Giménez Caballero, Spanish fascists could deliver the nation from evil, as the Spanish conquistadores had previously done during the sixteenth century, by disseminating their regenerative genes.[4] In *Blind Sunflowers* Salvador transmits these eschatological musings, which formed part of a larger gendered, militarist, and imperialist discourse that was enforced under the regime as natural and eternal

---

4 In "Miscegenation, Nation Formation and Cross-Racial Identifications in the Early Francoist Folkloric Film Musical," Jo Labanyi offers an insightful critique of the use of the colonial model of miscegenation in the writings of Giménez Caballero. My analysis also draws from Labanyi's "Women, Asian Hordes and the Threat to the Self in Giménez Caballero's *Genio de España*," which examines the intersections of sexuality, nationalism, and race in Giménez Caballero's text.

through the recycling of biblical myths that held soldiers as the saviours of humanity and women as the source of its decline.

It is also interesting to trace the kind of temporality emphasized in the discourses of the military regime, which Salvador uses to guide his behaviour and justify his actions. A nostalgia for the imperial past, as opposed to the degenerate state of mankind in the present, is a strong current in the deacon's reflections. The imperial past becomes synonymous with the "Golden Age," and modernity with "the Fall." The deacon's nostalgic language emphasizes the notion that Spain's Republican history was an inauthentic divergence from the country's natural origins and that the military regime "saved" Spain by steering it back to its essential Catholic roots. Salvador, whose name significantly means "saviour," compares himself to Bossuet (1627–1704), the court preacher to Louis XIV of France and an advocate of political absolutism: "I felt like a shepherd, I was happy that there were lost sheep in my flock. How little did I realize, Father, that I was the wolf! Like Bossuet, I filled my cup to give them the Lord's secrets to drink" (Méndez, *Blind Sunflowers* 84). Conjuring Bossuet is not a trivial detail. He was an influential politician who argued that government was divine and that kings received their power from God. In a similar vein, Salvador, who sheds his military uniform for the cassock to finally return to his military identity, represents the symbiosis between Church, state, and the armed forces.

As a fascist soldier, Salvador is catholicized and sanctified, and as a deacon he is militarized and bellicose. In reference to the Second Republic he declares: "They wanted to change the course of the world, to alter the Lord's designs. They ignored the fact that *non est potestas nisi Deo*, with the result that we had to set the guilty on the straight and narrow. We had to glorify our Victory" (Méndez, *Blind Sunflowers* 76). The expression *non est potestas nisi a Deo* (government is illegitimate without God) was reinscribed by the Church in order to portray the Second Republic as an unlawful aberration or a divergence from Spain's predestined path. This teleological view of time greatly affected the way in which the consolidators of the militarized nation framed history. It served the crucial function of establishing the rebels as the "martyrs" and helped reshape the sufferings of war into a prelude to martyrdom. The bloodshed of the rebel soldier then was not only legitimized but in fact seen as inevitable in the course of the history of mankind's redemption. According to this profoundly militarized ideology, every time there was deviation, there was bound to be a "crusade" (synonymous with "colonization") to silence the opposition, and its justification would be beyond question.

This religious myth of the past shaping political and military ideology is at the same time deeply misogynist. As we know, the Fall is inevitably tied to the sin of Eve – the undoing of humankind due to the lust of a woman. During the regime this religious dogma fed into patriarchal gender norms that called for the subjugation of women. In *Blind Sunflowers* Salvador's voice suggests that the regime did not impose a silence about women's sexuality per se but rather sustained a misogynist discourse based on religious myths, whereby women were innately dangerous and in need of domination. This interpretation is clearly rendered in Salvador's confession: "I will not deny that in Elena I glimpsed the descendant of Eve. Not that beautiful, pure and gracious Eve created to enchant the heart of man and ascend with him to the presence of God. No, the fallen, naked and repentant Eve, the first instigator of Evil" (Méndez, *Blind Sunflowers* 84).

Méndez highlights the relationship between the misogynist meanings ascribed to women's bodies through Catholic representations and the ramifications of those meanings in Franco's militarized Spain. Salvador uses religious doctrine to suggest that the female body is innately deviant and inferior, while he conceals the male position of privilege by upholding its normativeness. The female body becomes the object of the male gaze and a sexual spectacle. Through the discourse of the protagonist, Méndez prompts thoughts on how this misogynist construction of women served a larger political purpose in militarized Spain. Republican women's bodies became sites of revenge whereby the Nationalist militarized male sought to reaffirm his moral and ideological superiority. In this narrative, while Salvador conflates the Eve/Elena image into one morally corrupt figure, sexuality becomes the site of rule. That is, for Salvador, sexual submission and possession of a Republican woman becomes a metaphor for Nationalist supremacy.

To this point, I have argued that narrative voice, characterization, and plot structure constitute the vehicle through which Méndez explores the links between gender, sexuality, militarism, and religion. The text probes the effects of patriarchal ideology and questions the role of misogynistic violence in the consolidation of a militarized state. To paraphrase Ann Stoler, the possession of women's bodies has always been a theft of power – a strategic move in a male-dominated battlefield, whereby the psychic damage of the raped woman is inevitably extended to her family and community. The social metaphor of colonial supremacy has consistently been sexual domination: "sexuality illustrates the iconography of rule" (635). Similarly in Salvador's masculine domination fantasy, the Republican woman is reduced and objectified. In the following passage he divulges his carnal desire but at the same time asserts his own innate moral purity: "Flesh is like a tiger living inside man, the Amphion who by his art can move all stones, move everyone, shift even the foundations of their souls. As you know from the confessional, Father, flesh can be all-powerful. It can create the pride of sin in us, and even offer the perverse satisfaction of pleasure to a body that seeks only to die, and to draw from it, despite all sense of shame, a cry of life so strong it melts the anvil on which the crusader seeks to forge his steel" (Méndez, *Blind Sunflowers* 76).

Sexual desire, roused by the female body, is an untamed creature (a tiger) that lives underneath the skin of men. Lust is also the Amphion, the delicate musician of Greek mythology who builds the walls of Thebes by charming the stones with a lyre. On the one hand, the female figure (Elena) and the sexual appetite that she provokes suggest profound ambivalence in the male (Salvador). She is the aggressor who weakens male defences in the slow process of attrition. The sexual metaphor of the anvil – a massive block – represents the body of the woman, while steel symbolizes the male instrument of dominance. The deterioration of the anvil in Salvador's fantasy heralds the destruction of Elena. In this way Salvador's steel becomes a symbolic tool not only of male insemination but also of a weapon of cultural and political conquest.

Gender is intimately intertwined with the militarized male's quest for imperial spoils. Elena is imagined as a passive subject whose feminine existence is reliant upon the desires of a man. In what follows Salvador defines the "natural" attributes of womanhood as those of being delicate, emotional, irrational, and childlike, while the innate characteristics of men include rationality and strength: "Man uses his head to reflect, and that thought descends to the heart to gather strength. Woman on the other hand reasons with her heart so that her instinct can find the light of truth [...] The male deals in forceful, major chords; the female is more adept at soft, hidden, minor ones" (Méndez, *Blind Sunflowers* 90).

With this narrative gesture Méndez points out the way in which the National Catholic political apparatus sought to protect the "natural" gendered system of values and identities. This gendered perspective, though vindicated by the regime, has its sources in a long history of Spanish patriarchal discourse. *La dòna mediterrania: Llegendes històriques* by the Catalan positivist Pompeyo Gener (1848–1920) constitutes one example of a text that seeks to confirm the psychological differences between men and women. He described women, and particularly Mediterranean women, as hypersensitive and predestined to act more on impressions than on reason. Gener's argument sought to associate women with nature, thus creating a dichotomy between female sensibility and male rationality (qtd. in Nash, "Un/contested Identities," 27).[5] As Ania Loomba points out, the division between rational European male civilization, on the one hand, and childlike, female primitivism, on the other, is also a recurring theme in colonialist writings (137–8). This constructed dichotomy was disseminated in Spanish post-war textbooks, through which the regime identified Spain with the masculine conquistadores, and the "virginal new world" with Indigenous "primitive" women (Escudero; Morcillo Gómez).[6]

As this book's introduction states, some of the most fervent proponents of militarism and misogyny are in fact civilians, and many are women. Pilar Primo de Rivera defined women entirely in terms of lack. She devalued their creative capacity and their aptitude for discovery. Above all, her discourse described men and women as innately opposite, and women as a group that was subordinate to men, deficient in physical and intellectual aptitude. In *Blind Sunflowers* this construction of women's gender roles and biological distinction shapes Salvador's expectations of Elena. Consequently, when she does not conform to them, his image of her transforms from the mother to the whore (i.e., the source of the sins of the flesh and a territory to be conquered).

In *Imperial Leather*, a book that examines the liaisons between gender, race, and class that shaped British imperialism, Anne McClintock reminds us that the actual colonial map was paramount in imperialist discourse because it served colonial plunder and professed to capture the truth; it was a "technology of possession, promising that those with the capacity to make such perfect representations must also have the right of territorial control" (27–8). Maps, McClintock observes, were also gendered. They demonstrated sexist and racist ideologies: "As European men crossed the dangerous thresholds of their known worlds, they ritualistically feminized borders and boundaries. Female figures were planted like fetishes at the ambiguous points of contact, at the borders and orifices of contest zone" (24). In *Blind Sunflowers* Salvador recycles this imperialist and misogynist logic to describe Elena's body, which symbolizes a primitive land that invites conquest. In a confession he imagines a map representing a territory that he names "Elena."

---

5 See Mary Nash, "Un/contested Identities."

6 See Escudero, "Cortes and Marina" and Morcillo Gómez, "Shaping True Catholic Womanhood:." Morcillo Gómez examines how the Francoist educational discourse built up the notion of "true Catholic womanhood," while Escudero traces how gender codes in school textbooks were used for naturalizing power relationships between men and women in Spain and Latin America.

Conquering that territory-body becomes a symbol of Nationalist victory over defeated Republicans and a fetish that could offer a sense of satisfaction or security in the absence of other fixed guarantees during the consolidation of the Francoist state. "I was naïve, Father, because I believed that everything in this world had already been named, classified [...] Yet there is a no-man's-land, Father, which is not where sin and punishment are to be found, but is not where virtue and its rewards reside either: if I had to draw a map, I would draw a broken dark border which, as is a discoverer's right, I would be so bold as to name Elena [...] Saint Thomas would have been taken aback by the complexities of my map!" (Méndez, *Blind Sunflowers* 82).

This narrative conveys the logic of domination. The Republican woman's body becomes a cryptic map of an uncultivated, obscure territory, while the Nationalist soldier becomes the explorer, the light in spiritual darkness, the "liberator" from barbarism, the colonizer. The image of the map and its association with "unbroken" animals (reminiscent of the previously mentioned tiger) both excites and disturbs the deacon. His attempt to name the no-man's land Elena is a gesture that signals his desire to appropriate the "other's" power to self-identify and, in so doing, to strip the "other" of her subjectivity. The author thus underscores the injustice involved in the act of renaming the other and of robbing a group of the authority to determine its own cultural, gender, and political identity.

The former soldier's determination to conquer a Republican woman's body is complicated by his apparent aspiration to demonstrate the restraint of Catholic "civilization" as opposed to the "savagery" of Republican secular barbarism. He attempts to provide Lorenzo with an ideological re-education and baptism so that he – and, by extension, Elena – might achieve moral redemption. Drawing from McClintock, we find a relationship between Salvador's imperial act of mapping and the Christian act of baptism, insofar as they both are surrogate birthing rituals.

> The imperial act of discovery can be compared with the male act of baptism. In both rituals, western men publicly disavow the creative agency of others (the colonized/women) and arrogate to themselves the power of origins. The male ritual of baptism – with its bowls of holy water, its washing, its male midwives – is a surrogate birthing ritual, during which men collectively compensate themselves for their invisible role in the birth of the child and diminish woman's agency. In Christianity, at least, baptism reenacts childbirth as a male ritual. During baptism, moreover, the child is named after the father, not the mother. The mother's labors and

creative powers (hidden in her "confinement" and denied social recognition) are diminished, and women are publicly declared unfit to inaugurate the human soul into the body of Christ. In the eyes of Christianity, women are incomplete birthers: the child must be born again and named, by men. (McClintock 29)

McClintock's parallel between the Catholic ritual of baptism and the colonial act of mapping serves as an insightful theoretical lens to interpret Méndez's portrayal of the Church during the Franco period. Both baptism and colonial mapping function to reinforce masculine culture by usurping the agency of women and limiting their role in decision making. Méndez dramatizes that dual critique through Salvador's narrative, in which Lorenzo is an unborn child awaiting Christian baptism and the symbolic naming of the father, while Elena is an uninhabited land passively awaiting male (Nationalist) penetration and insemination. Through Salvador's birthing ritual, he gives life to a symbolic trinity: the cultural authority of the Catholic Church, the patriarchal privilege of male hegemony, and the political order of Nationalist rule. This "matrix of domination," to borrow Hill Collins's term, casts Salvador as the champion of post-war Spanish progress and the nucleus of the Nationalist family, a family that exclusively sanctions male authority.

Blind Sunflowers exposes the emergence of violence from ingrained misogynist and militarist myths that endorse the authority and disciplinary practices of militarized men. From the voice of a former fascist soldier and religious leader, readers observe an intersecting vindication of masculinity, militarism, and subjugation. But the author does not merely provide an outlet for Francoist discourse. He employs techniques that effectively challenge the Nationalist narrative. One way in which he accomplishes this is through the narrative structure, specifically, through the juxtaposition of perspectives and voices.

Lorenzo (who is represented in the narrative as an adult remembering childhood memories) destabilizes the myth of the Holy Crusade through reflections such as the following: "At school Franco, José Antonio Primo de Rivera, the Falange, and the Nationalist Movement were things that had appeared as if by magic [...] There were no victims, only heroes [...] There was no war because Victory, with its capital letter, was something more akin to the law of gravity than the result of a conflict between men" (Méndez, *Blind Sunflowers* 92). If the militarized Catholic education system attempted to inculcate youth with the belief in war as manly and inevitable, then the author uses Lorenzo's narrative to vindicate dissenting voices. His anti-hegemonic language also overturns Salvador's imperialist logic. By emphasizing an uncanny fear of being devoured by cannibals, his reflections subvert Salvador's interpretation of the Nationalist Catholic regime as "civilized" and the Republicans as "savage." Lorenzo recalls the horror stories, based on fact and fiction, that one of the neighbourhood boys would tell during the postwar years: "The characters in his stories were always a group of boys of our own age, threatened by an army of lepers who came lurching in our direction as if the only way they could survive was by disemboweling us. Leprosy was not an infectious disease, it was a disease of the soul, dangerous not because we could catch it, but because of its voracious cannibalism" (93).

This description is interrupted by a brief narrative shift back to the deacon, who confesses his lust for Elena. Then the voice of Lorenzo returns to say, "I kept this fear of lepers for many years [...] my mind was filled with images of bloody figures advancing slowly and inexorably towards me" (Méndez, *Blind Sunflowers* 93). The juxtaposition disrupts the regime's official Manichean narrative of good and evil. Lorenzo's fear of being disembowelled and devoured by cannibals connotes a symbolic fear of being placed at the centre of a brutal site on which the Nationalists waged war against the remaining Republicans. Lorenzo's imaginings also evoke the biblical association of Jesus with lepers. However, here we observe an ironic twist: Salvador becomes the leper or the anti-saviour in Lorenzo's imagination. The reference to cannibalism is also reminiscent of the Eucharist ritual associated with the Catholic Church. By ascribing cannibalistic language to the National Catholic state, Méndez inverts the Francoist narrative. The ruthlessness, insatiability, and contagion that the cannibal exemplifies represents the Francoist state, upon which illusory moral structures were linked to notions of Christian civilization.

Lorenzo's image of the man-eating Nationalist (i.e., the colonizer) is a clever reversal of the cannibal trope in imperialist discourse insofar as the "civilized" colonizer feared being consumed by the colonized "savage." McClintock argues: "As in many imperial scenes, the fear of engulfment expresses itself most acutely in the cannibal trope. In this familiar trope, the fear of being engulfed by the unknown is projected onto colonized peoples as *their* determination to devour the intruder whole" (27). This imperialist version of the cannibal trope is manifest in Salvador's paranoid ruminations on the sexual prowess of the tiger and the ambiguity of the map. However, his version is undermined by Lorenzo's counter version, which frames the colonizer as the diseased and predatory body preying on the healthy, young, and innocent.

The conclusion of *Blind Sunflowers* disrupts the Francoist image of the male soldier-hero distinguished by his integrity. The tension behind

Salvador's determination to penetrate Elena's body underscores the hypocrisy inherent in the grandiloquent rhetoric used to justify Francoist rule. Salvador describes his role as that of a shepherd and his treatment of the defeated as part of a benevolent project of "civilization," when in fact he wields power through intimidation, manipulation, and violence. This is similar to the attitude that the Spanish colonizers had towards the colonized in the Americas. As Edward Said suggests, colonialism "is supported and perhaps even impelled by impressive ideological formations that include notions that certain territories and peoples *require* and beseech domination, as well as forms of knowledge affiliated with domination" (9). For Salvador, the defeated Republican woman becomes a dehumanized object, denied subjectivity, and reduced to a metaphorical annex of the larger domain over which the Nationalists claimed authority.

Paradoxically, however, it is this male figure who finds himself victimized and on the verge of insanity. "Elena attracted and repelled me in equal measure. I went mad, and am not sure whether I have as yet regained my senses" (Méndez, *Blind Sunflowers* 104). His madness is described not as a mere individual character flaw but rather as a symptom of the larger societal context in which patterns rooted in heightened nationalism, militarization, and religious fundamentalism provide grounds for misogynist violence that torments victims and victimizers, albeit in very different ways. In Salvador's character, Méndez underscores the way in which gender norms in Spain were riddled with contradictions and inconsistencies. The militarized male was glorified as the symbol of masculine power, representing a return to the conventional gender order and the defeat of the deviant republic. However, the regime also championed the figure of the pious, refined, and chaste Catholic priest as the symbolic father, the spiritual cultivator, and the male surrogate in the birthing ritual. Therein lies the irony of Salvador's authority: he understands that power emanates not only from the end of a weapon but also from the end of the phallus; however, as a deacon he is prohibited to engage in sexual forms of male domination.

The final scene sharpens readers' awareness of how misogynist discourse facilitates the physical subjugation of women and safeguards privilege for the militarized male. Salvador's tension is unleashed as he exchanges his cassock for civilian clothing to confront Elena. It is a symbolic gesture that prefigures his violent attempt to rape her. Yet he legitimizes his actions as the unfolding of a holy, natural decree. He conceives of himself as a religious and military man who is simply trying to cleanse a fallen being: "God had used me as his instrument of justice. That is why I took sides with those who conquered empires [...]

Driven by a force I still find hard to acknowledge as part of me, Father, I launched myself at the temple which that woman was denying me. And the tiniest part of my wrath was sufficient to lure the cause of this Evil from his lair, to flush out the abject schemer who had devised all this web of deceit. Elena's husband was hidden in the flat" (Méndez, *Blind Sunflowers* 108).

This passage renders visible how discourse is a tool of control and a self-masking mechanism. Intertwining misogynist, militarist, and Catholic social scripts provides a means to frame the Republican woman's agency (i.e., her refusal to submit) as an offence serious enough to warrant the brutal enforcement of subjugation. The definition of the defeated as dissenters of God's will is not only fundamental to the self-definition of the Nationalists as victors but also a necessary instrument in the justification of eroticized violence and colonial plunder (i.e., the rape of Elena). In the end Salvador attempts to raid and pillage the physical, psychological, and symbolic Republican territory (i.e., Elena's body), at which time Ricardo emerges from the closet in an act of both defence and resistance. Aware of the consequences of his exposure, he leaps from the apartment window. Salvador believed that God used him as his instrument of justice, as a crusader extending Nationalist empire, and as the guardian of patriarchal family values so defined by the Francoist state. It is thus paradoxical that while Salvador claims to protect Christian family values, he effectively destroys the social fabric of the vanquished. His confession attests to his affliction, yet he explicitly states that he has no remorse (Méndez, *Blind Sunflowers* 93). The story ends with Salvador's confession and his assumed exoneration. With this detail the author suggests that the objectification of women in the clerical and national spheres of influence under the Franco regime not only paved the way for gender-based aggression but also protected perpetrators of misogynist violence.

Roberto Bolaño's Transnational Nightmares

Framing Roberto Bolaño's *Nocturno de Chile* (*By Night in Chile*) as a counterpart to Méndez's *Blind Sunflowers* allows us to bring further nuance to the arguments outlined previously: that formations of misogyny, masculinity, and militarism intersect with dictatorial violence and religious intolerance. Both authors explore the ways in which the normalization of slow and indirect forms of violence contributes to the legitimation of murder. They also grasp how the Church functioned as a key agent in both the dismissal and the justification of violence, whether through explicit deeds or implied endorsements. Bolaño's novel focuses on the connections between the Pinochet regime, the

Opus Dei, and the world of the upper-class literati in Chile and Spain where the exercise of torture went hand-in-hand with societal myopia that permeated poetry and culture. Although the novel is set primarily in Chile, Bolaño makes clear that the power wielded by the Church, the state, and the military did not function in national isolation. *By Night in Chile*, like many of Bolaño's novels, elucidates transatlantic connections that transcend continental boundaries. Bolaño traces the parallels between Pinochet's Chile and Franco's Spain, charting the common ground on which the regimes' followers stood.

Opening against the backdrop of the early post-Pinochet years, the story follows the narrator, a priest named Father Urrutia, as he looks back on his life before, during, and after the military regime. In what can be described as a monologue that recalls Camus's *The Fall*, the narrator reveals that he mingled with secret agents under Pinochet and taught counter-intelligence to military generals. Like the aspiring priest in Méndez's *Blind Sunflowers*, Urrutia envisions himself as a shepherd whose message defended the moral purification of the sinful elements ushered in by a left-wing government. His perspective depends on conventional thought and repetition rather than on reflection. This allows him to accept no conscious responsibility for the defence of human rights so long as those humans have historically been deemed "other." His voice of conscience, the "wizened youth," puts him ill at ease and sometimes even haunts him. But, like Salvador in *Blind Sunflowers*, Urrutia's critical voice within is not enough to change the messianism and abstractions that fuel self-deception and the rationalization of cruelty.

As Jean Franco suggests in *Cruel Modernity*, Urrutia is a thinly veiled stand-in for José Miguel Ibáñez Langlois (Ignacio Valente), an Opus Dei priest who gave Pinochet lessons in Marxism so that he would understand the enemy better (115). Like Ibáñez Langlois (b. 1936), Bolaño's fictional priest is a published poet and literary critic known by a pseudonym. Both characters, real and fictitious, studied in Italy and Spain during the Franco dictatorship, meeting with leading figures of the Opus Dei and following the teachings of Josemaría Escrivá de Balaguer (1902–75), the founder of the Opus Dei. While Escrivá de Balaguer claimed to be apolitical, he was staunchly anti-communist, radically patriarchal, and supportive of the Franco and Pinochet regimes. Shortly after the military coup, he visited Chile in 1974 and wrote a letter praising the members of the junta.

Escrivá de Balaguer used militarized language, emphasizing the need for a crusade of manliness and purity, seeing the supernumerary married members of the Church as the troops, and their large progeny as the foot soldiers for the army of God that must obey and propagate the message of the Opus Dei. Many of Escrivá de Balaguer's followers became Chile's neoliberal technocrats, accumulating extraordinary wealth during the Pinochet regime and beyond. An example is Joaquín Lavín (b. 1953), a Chilean politician of the ultra-right-wing Independent Democratic Union (UDI). He studied economics at the University of Chicago under Milton Friedman and is a supernumerary member of the Opus Dei. As Marcela Said shows in the documentary *Opus Dei: Una cruzada silenciosa*, the organization continues to wield significant power in politics, industry, and finance in Spain and Chile.

What Bolaño's *By Night in Chile* has distinctly in common with Méndez's *Blind Sunflowers* is the narrative voice of a tormented right-wing Catholic collaborator. Both writers use that perspective to explore the justifications of dictatorial violence shaped by religious, military, and patriarchal discourses. The comparison also brings out the multiple faces of misogyny. If misogyny visibly entails hostility towards and contempt for women who challenge male dominance, then the flip side of the coin is the erasure of women. Unlike Méndez's militarized priest for whom the female body becomes an obsession (that attracts and repels in equal measure), women are mostly nameless and absent for Bolaño's protagonist. When they are mentioned, it is with contempt or mistrust. Bolaño puts the priest's voice and actions under a microscope, making it evident whom readers are observing. That is, rather than inadvertently presenting negative images of women, Bolaño carefully constructs male figures who see women as necessarily subordinate to them. The juxtaposition of *By Night in Chile* and *Blind Sunflowers* thus enables a deeper awareness of misogynist logic whereby women are either seen as threatening or are simply unseen.

By Night in Chile opens in around the year 2000 with a confession in which the main character and narrator, Sebastian Urrutia Lacroix, states that he is dying but that he still has many things to say because "slanderous rumors" by a "wizened youth" have damaged his reputation. As mentioned, readers can conjecture that the "wizened youth" is Urrutia's conscience that disallows him from completely ignoring the wrongdoing that he has committed throughout his life. And yet his monologue is not only half-hearted; it attempts to justify actions and motivations rather than acknowledge responsibility in injustice. Like Salvador in *Blind Sunflowers*, Lacroix, whose name means the cross, wants to set the record straight: "I will lift my noble, trembling head, and rummage through my memories to turn up the deeds that shall vindicate me" (*By Night* 1). Matching Salvador, he shows little or no capacity for self-reflection.

On his deathbed the priest recalls four major moments in his life that loosely follow a chronological order. Through those moments Bolaño raises questions about intersecting discourses that have perpetuated militarism, misogyny, and violence in Franco's Spain and Pinochet's Chile. They include the development of the priest's identity in relation to the Chilean literary critic named Farewell, which began in the late 1950s; his trip to Italy, France, and Spain to help save European churches from decay in the late 1960s; the lessons in Marxism that he gave to General Pinochet, General Leigh, Admiral Merino, and General Mendoza just after the coup; and the soirees at María Canales's house in the 1970s and 1980s.

An analysis of the first section serves to emphasize the discrete faces of misogyny and militarism, as well as the continuities between them. The Opus Dei priest reveals an obvious disregard and, at times, revulsion for women, in contrast to his undue attentiveness to men. As a literary critic he makes frequent references to the Western canon, never mentioning women writers. In one of his emblematic memories he travels to the home of Farewell (a reference to Hernán Díaz Arrieta, known by his pen name Alone) where the conversations mostly revolve around literature. If women were present at the gathering, they apparently did not deserve the attention of the narrator. Women are not seen as writers or readers. However, Farewell is perceived by the priest as a brilliant intellectual whose mere presence is a blessing. He is also a wealthy landowner and a political conservative. For Urrutia, Farewell had a "Homeric silhouette" and "the face of an aging Greek god" (Bolaño, *By Night* 14). Not unlike Salvador in *Blind Sunflowers*, the Chilean priest's references are often marked by a nostalgia for a glorious yesteryear as opposed to the degenerate state of mankind in the ungodly twentieth century. His comments regarding Farewell also have a homoerotic aspect. Urrutia thinks of Farewell in loving terms and makes little effort to separate himself from him; however, he wants to give the impression that he himself remains "pure," which he associates with a detachment from sexual desire.

As Judith Lorber suggests, religious doctrine attempts to secure the boundaries between genders and ensure that what is demanded, what is permitted, and what is taboo are well known and followed (67). However, in the case of the Catholic clergy, notions of masculinity and their corresponding gender performances differ from those of their non-clerical male counterparts. In contrasting ways Salvador in *Blind Sunflowers* and Urrutia Lacroix in *By Night in Chile* convey the tense relationship between these different masculinities in Franco's Spain and Pinochet's Chile. Readers are prompted to reflect on the negative role of gendered narratives, even for those in positions of power who gained social dominance from such narratives.

The positive image of the male Greek god contrasts sharply with the Opus Dei priest's disdainful view of the Indigenous women whom he meets on Farewell's estate. The encounter happens by chance when he wanders around the property in search of solace. First, he sees a boy and a girl who, in his words, were naked like Adam and Eve. Bolaño's narrator alludes to the misogynist religious myth of the Fall, akin once again to the case of *Blind Sunflowers*. After comparing the children to Adam and Eve, he describes them in a state of filth that nauseates him. He regards them as unclean and avoids contact, disgusted by the idea of contamination. As Theweleit suggests, "Dirt is first and foremost, anything that impinges on the tidy insularity of a person, on a person's anxiously guarded autonomy" (385). The priest averts his gaze and moves on, only to imagine the site populated by rats, wild boars, and vultures (Bolaño, *By Night* 18–19). He associates them with the animal kingdom and uses whiteness as an index of civilization. He upholds the familiar stereotype, which Méndez also brings out in *Blind Sunflowers*, based on a racist link between animals and Indigenous people that sanctioned abuse on the grounds that they were less than human.

Bolaño understands that communication cannot be separated from the interpretive lens by which it is understood. The faces of the farm workers were severe, mysterious, and blank, while their expressions were "tense with mute questions or opening in wordless exclamations" (*By Night* 21). The priest's perception of the workers' speech arises from a sense of superiority, rooted in colonialism and patriarchal dominance. When he is approached by two women, he concludes that they had come on foot from another estate just to see him. As he flouts his own self-worth, he describes them with dehumanizing language: "Rings under their eyes. Parted lips. Shiny skin stretched over cheekbones. A patience that I feared was not Christian resignation. A patience native to some faraway place" (20). They were not Chilean or European, he thinks, but rather from a place beyond the human world. Abhorrence of a population that he sees as monstrous is no doubt related to an obsession with the virtue of Catholic European identity and the colonialist belief in the superiority of the white male over the savage brown female.

Both Bolaño and Méndez use narrative voice, characterization, and the monologue structure as a vehicle to explore the links between gender, sexuality, misogyny, militarism, and religion. There are also differences, however, in the way that they make those links visible. In *By Night in Chile* the Opus Dei priest is repulsed at the appearance, dress, and language of the farm workers. Specifically, in relation to the peasant women, Bolaño's protagonist says, they "were ugly and their words were incoherent" (*By Night* 21). The women are unclean because they are not white, and they are beastly in their perceived inability to produce intelligible words. When one woman offers to "escort" him back to the lodge, he finds the verb *escort* incongruous in her mouth. It sends a wave of hilarity all through his body, and he shakes with suppressed laughter (22). As we saw earlier in "Words from Outer Space," Bolaño's protagonist appears even more deplorable because of his sense of amusement at a time of insult. Readers imagine the priest's disdainful repressed laughter at the expense of the other that only increases his sense of detachment. His cruel laughter is a mechanism of power.

When he turns his back and walks away, he does so with a "vaguely *military* rhythm" (Bolaño, *By Night* 22; italics mine). This striking comment alerts readers to the extent to which militarized masculinity pervades non-military men. Like Méndez, Bolaño points to the intersecting cultures and institutions, namely the military and the Church, and their long history of violence, racism, and misogyny. These connections are further developed in *By Night in Chile* through the main character's fascination with Ernst Jünger (1895–1998). In the 1920s Jünger became a recognized writer who expressed some of the key tendencies of the Freikorps, the former First World War combatants who, as Emilio Willems explains, found a sense of joy in conflict and destruction. Although Jünger was later considered a critic of Nazism, he shared with the Freikorps a zeal for what he saw as comradeship in battle and self-sacrifice for a common cause; it was a storm-trooper mentality bound to militarized masculinity. Jünger regarded fighting, as Willems observes, "as something that constitutes a value in itself, independent of any political cause" (118).

The war novels of Jünger, as Theweleit indicates, are key to understanding "the construction of a male type who finds life without war and weapons unimaginable" (24). Jünger writes in the preface to the English translation of *Storm of Steel* that time only strengthens his conviction that "the war, for all its destructiveness, was an incomparable schooling of the heart. The front-line soldier whose foot came down on the earth so grimly and harshly may claim this at least, that it came down cleanly" (xii). At the end of *Storm of Steel* he concludes, "the nation was no longer for me an empty thought veiled in symbols," and he asks, "how could it have been otherwise when I had seen so many die for its sake, and been schooled myself to stake my life for its credit every minute, day and night, without a thought?" (316). Salient words like *fantastic* and *enlivening* are used to describe material warfare as an exalting experience. For Jünger a "calendar full of hardships and privation, divided by the red-letter days of battles" distills the idea of the "Fatherland" in a "clearer and brighter essence" (*Storm of Steel* 316).

Jünger is only a peripheral character in *By Night in Chile*; however, Bolaño's decision to include him is revealing, just as it is in several of his other novels including *2666*, *Nazi Literature in the Americas*, and *The Third Reich*. For instance, in *Nazi Literature in the Americas* Jünger appears as an inspiration for Franz Zwickau (1946–71), a fictious Venezuelan poet and son of German immigrants. Through Zwickau, Bolaño creates a militarized male character who began publishing poetry about the "will to purity" and ended writing "The War Criminal's Son," in which he bemoans being born twenty-five years too late, feeling cheated out of the war experience (*Nazi Literature* 90). Notably, Zwickau recited Jünger. Readers may also perceive echoes of *Mein Kampf*, particularly Hitler's youthful pre–World War I fear of missing the glory of battle: "Why couldn't I have been born a hundred years earlier? Say at a time of the Wars of Liberation" (Hitler 157). Hitler viewed the early 1900s era of "law and order" as an "undeserved trick of fate" (158). In Bolaño's *Nazi Literature*, the fictional Arizona-based poet-preacher Rory Long (1952–2017) also found inspiration in the warmongering Jünger, penning a poem where Leni Riefenstahl makes love with Jünger. Long imagines "Old Ernst" "riding her hard" while "the German whore" begs for more (145). If Walter Benjamin praised Chaplin for lampooning Hitler, he'd likely applaud Bolaño's takedown of Jünger. Across Bolaño's writings, allusions to Jünger undermine the notion that engaging in battle is a heroic way to tap into the universe's mythical core.

In *By Night in Chile* Jünger comes into the narrative through another character, the real Chilean author and diplomat Salvador Reyes (1899–1970), whom Jünger mentions in his Paris diaries during the Nazi occupation (1940–4). Don Salvador Reyes tells Urrutia that he was introduced to the German writer at an embassy gathering during the Second World War. The setting of the encounter, Reyes explains, was occupied Paris around 1941 when he served as consul for Chile, and Jünger worked as an intelligence officer for Germany. Jünger's real diaries describe his thoughts on literature, his conversations with intellectuals, and his experiences in bookshops and cafes. In one fragment, Jünger writes, "Current reading: *Night Shift* by Salvador Reyes, the Chilean consul, whom the Doctorese introduced me to." Reyes's work, Jünger states, could be described as romantic, puritanical, global (*A German Officer* 290). Reyes was the only Chilean whom Jünger included in his chronicle (Bolaño, *By Night* 37).

Through these characters Bolaño challenges readers to consider collaboration and coexistence during the Nazi occupation and prompts us to reflect on how militarized men have shaped war narratives, and how these in turn have had an impact on the wider society. Bolaño's Opus Dei priest admires Jünger, seeing him firmly positioned in the world of men and in a virtuous male social order. He speaks of "purity" and male bonding to introduce the character in his monologue: "while I'm on the subject of purity, one evening, when I was at the house of Don Salvador Reyes, with five or six other guests, Farewell among them, Don Salvador said that one of the purest men he had ever met in Europe was the German writer Ernst Jünger" (Bolaño, *By Night* 26). So begins Bolaño's thirteen-page story of Jünger, who the Opus Dei priest concludes was not only a man of culture but a man who epitomized the "immaculate body of the hero" (38).

The novel's shifting settings, coupled with the careful arrangement of male characters, enable Bolaño to dissect the spectrum of masculine identities. Reyes's account of meeting Jünger and a Guatemalan painter in besieged Paris during the Second World War reveals a transnational network of intellectual figures, highlighting their interconnected influence as well as their varying political stances and ethical frameworks. As a military man but also an intellectual and a patron of the arts, Jünger was captivated by the avant-garde Guatemalan artist, who seems to be loosely based on Carlos Mérida (1891–1985). Like Mérida, Bolaño's character lived in Mexico City around 1920 and in Paris in the early 1940s to study art and work as an artist and diplomat. He was of mixed Spanish-Maya-Quiché heritage, which he reflected in his art through a combination of European modern painting styles and Latin American images. Bolaño imagines more than a hint of estrangement between the painter and the other two men. The distance between them involves not only the prejudice that shapes Jünger's and Reyes's view of the Guatemalan but also the painter's rejection of them. He obstinately turns his back, ignoring their attention, staring out the window at the occupied city. Jünger (always dressed in military uniform) and Reyes expect to be treated deferentially by the Guatemalan, and when he denies them that treatment, they ignore him. They enjoy "a free-ranging conversation, touching on the human and the divine, war and peace, Italian painting and Nordic painting, the source of evil, and the effects of evil that sometimes seem to be triggered by chance" (Bolaño, *By Night* 33). When they leave, Jünger callously comments that the Guatemalan probably would not live through the year, which Reyes thought was an odd remark because "many thousands of people were not going to live until the following winter" (36).

In Bolaño's tale about Jünger, Reyes, the Guatemalan painter, and the Opus Dei priest, gender and race intersect in complicated ways. The priest's vision of ideal masculinity is presented as a fantasy based on the figure of the German soldier and intellectual. He imagines himself writing a poem about Jünger's "immaculate body" in a spaceship among wreckage. The poem, together with the writings of other heroes like Jünger, "would compose a hymn to the glory of God and civilization" (Bolaño, *By Night* 38). Bolaño's use of satire through exaggeration to expose the absurdity of the priest's discourse contrasts with Méndez's more serious tone. However, Bolaño shares with Mendéz a perception of the bond between militarist and imperialist logic. While the Guatemalan painter views with horror the human carnage and the high cost of war against the land, Jünger, Reyes, and Urrutia celebrate the meaning of battle and the strength of the soldier at the centre.

Nowhere in the conversations between Jünger and Reyes do they speak of women. Women are absent and insignificant. As for Urrutia, he sees himself, alongside his war heroes, within a higher male order that is capable of producing culture and enlightenment through bloodshed. In Jünger's real war diaries, as Bolaño was likely aware, women occasionally appear. Commenting specifically on Reyes's novel, Jünger notes: "Among his sentences I find, 'It is the love of women that forms a man's character.' Correct, yet they shape us as the sculptor his marble: by removing parts of us" (*A German Officer* 290). Jünger conjures an image of dismemberment and fear of emasculation along the same lines as Salvador does in Méndez's text.

Unlike *Blind Sunflowers*, *By Night in Chile* has no counter-narrative. There is no corrective to these intersecting ideologies. Gendered stereotypes, recycled through war stories, are pervasive. Farewell's final words about the priest's lionization of Jünger speaks volumes about the transversality of militarized masculinity. As he listens to Urrutia's praise of Jünger, Farewell says, "The literature of heroism is vast. So vast that two people with diametrically opposed tastes and ideas could dip into it at random without any likelihood of hitting on the same thing" (Bolaño, *By Night* 38). Bolaño takes a long view, providing a cogent critique of any narrow approach to militarism and violence.

Like Salvador in *Blind Sunflowers*, the narrator-priest in *By Night in Chile* considers the ushering in of a leftist government to be a divergence from the nation's predestined path. Both characters have a teleological view of time, in which the military takeover was not only legitimized but seen as inevitable. "My country was not in a healthy state," Urrutia recalls saying to himself. "I must be a patriot"

(Bolaño, *By Night* 79). On the night of Allende's victory he remembers praying, "Let God's will be done" (82). Amidst the strikes and political upheaval he finds refuge in the Greek classics and compares "the long wars of Thucydides" to what he was witnessing in Chile (82). Then came the 1973 coup, and he thinks, "Peace at last" (82). He returns to writing poetry, which he admits veered to the "demonic": "I wrote about women, hatefully, cruelly, I wrote about homosexuals and children lost in derelict railway stations" (84). The misogyny underlying these comments must be understood in relation to the abundance of war narratives that have shaped the priest's perspective, as well as the myth of the Fall of Man due to the lust of a woman. This is another powerful example of the parallels between *Blind Sunflowers* and *By Night in Chile.* Méndez and Bolaño trace the links between philosophy, theology, and misogyny and the ways in which these influenced world views and served to justify the military's seizure of power.

Bolaño embeds important symbolism in the events that just precede the victory of the Popular Unity. At a time of revolutionary change the Opus Dei priest is summoned to travel to Europe to find a way to stop the deterioration of churches (Bolaño, *By Night* 65). Two businessmen, Mr Raef and Mr Etah (names that spell *fear* and *hate* backwards), fund his mission to Spain, Italy, and France. Once there, he finds that pigeons (birds associated with contamination and the multitude) posed a major threat to the cathedrals. In Italy he meets Father Pietro who uses a falcon as a "radical" weapon against the pigeons. As Susana Draper observes, "the war on communist-Marxist-liberationist 'subversion' is framed in the narrative by the imagery of architecture and hunting" (*Afterlives* 136).

When Urrutia travels to France and Spain, he learns that they are also using falcons to control the pigeons. His reaction to the hunt, a highly masculinized sport, is revealing. Urrutia revels at the sight of bloodshed and finds beauty in the birds' suffering. The figure who raises questions about the practice is Father Antonio, a Spanish priest who has become reflective and doubtful: "Maybe this business with the falcons is not such a good idea; it's true they protect churches from corrosive and, in the long term, destructive effects of pigeon shit, but one mustn't forget that pigeons or doves are the earthly symbol of the Holy Spirit, are they not?" (74). The dying priest decides to free his falcon, but it returns only to deposit a dead pigeon at Urrutia's feet, a powerful symbol that marks a step closer to complicity. It foreshadows his subsequent move to kill by proxy in assisting the military regime.

In *By Night* the protagonist's transformation into a complicit subject begins with his trip to Europe and continues upon his return to Chile, where he is approached again by Mr Raef and Mr Etah. This time, shortly after the coup, the priest is tasked with the job of giving lessons in Marxism to General Pinochet, General Leigh, Admiral Merino, and General Mendoza. When he is escorted on this paid mission to teach members of the junta about "Chile's enemies," he realizes that he has changed out of his suit and into his cassock: "Was it that I wanted to be in uniform too, so to speak, when facing my illustrious pupils for the first time? Was I afraid of something? Did I feel the cassock would ward off some indefinable, undeniable danger?" (Bolaño, *By Night* 89–90). Both Bolaño and Méndez recognize the significance of uniforms and their role in upholding hierarchies of power and shared interests. Whereas Méndez's priest in *Blind Sunflowers* sheds his cassock to embrace militarized masculinity as a means to "conquer" the female threat, Bolaño's priest uses the cassock as a sign of religious authority and membership in a fraternity of men in uniform who impose their vision of the nation by force. He walks into a militarized brotherhood of killers as an accomplice by choice.

As to be expected from this group of militarized men, a revolutionary woman becomes the target of vitriol. Marta Harnecker, one of the most important disseminators of Marxist thought, occupies the centre of attention for the generals in the priest's classroom. "Is she good-looking?" Admiral Merino asks Urrutia (Bolaño, *By Night* 93). General Leigh later remarks on her sexuality, admonishing her for being "intimately acquainted with a pair of Cubans" (94). Pinochet retorts, "Are we talking about a woman or a bitch?" (94). As Kate Manne suggests, misogyny "functions to enforce and police women's subordination and to uphold male dominance, against the backdrop of other intersecting systems of oppression" (19). The generals' sexist comments about Harnecker kindle the priest's imagination: "Suddenly I had an idea for a poem about a degenerate woman" (Bolaño, *By Night* 94). Bolaño makes clear the shared misogyny in the room. By becoming a Marxist intellectual and leader, Harnecker has violated gender norms. To quote Manne, "These reactions may not, and typically do not, reveal their causal triggers – that is, her being a woman who is deviating, or aspiring, in ways historically verboten" (xx). This perception "stems from an illicit sense of entitlement that is the legacy of patriarchal norms and values. But because they are entrenched, indeed deeply internalized by both men and women, they often go unnoticed" (Manne 230). Therein lies the insightful value of *By Night in Chile*. Bolaño, like Méndez, renders visible the ties between masculinity, militarism, and misogyny.

There are two forms in which women appear in *By Night in Chile*: one is repulsive and threatening, and the second is mysterious. Both of these are part of the misogynist's repertoire of female images. When the priest encounters the peasant women on Farewell's estate, he is seized with utter revulsion. In them he sees foul beasts devoid of language and feeling. The other female type, the uncanny one, can be identified in the figure of María Canales, a stand-in for the real-life Mariana Callejas. She was the co-perpetrator of the murder of General Prats and an agent of the DINA, along with her husband, Michael Townley, who appears in the novel as James Thompson. Their house became the grounds for the planning and execution of transatlantic operations that included the torture and murder of the Spanish-Chilean diplomat Carmelo Soria. Nona Fernández, also studied in this book, focused her first theatrical work on Callejas, titled *El taller*.

In *By Night in Chile* the image of María Canales eerily takes shape. The first reference to her reads: "There was a woman. Her name was María Canales. She was a writer, she was pretty, she was young. In my opinion she was not without talent […] Her talent was, how can I put it? Inward, sheathed, withdrawn" (Bolaño 106). Bolaño's portrayal enables an understanding of the "diverse range of ways misogyny works on girls and women given their intersectional identities, in terms of the quality, quantity, intensity, experience, and impact of the hostility" (Manne 21). As a middle-class, white, right-wing woman collaborator, Canales enjoyed certain privileges among men like Urrutia who would attend her weekly soirees for poets and painters. Yet she was never to be trusted.

Bolaño frames María Canales as a complicit subject and also a scape-goat for men like Urrutia. When the priest learns that her house, with its long corridors and dark basement, was used by the couple as a centre for the interrogation of prisoners, he tries to look away. While he defends his decision to remain silent about the violence, claiming that he saw nothing, he remains unsettled, returning to the house years later during the transition to democracy. He notes that Canales has the same look that he had described earlier: "There was, undeniably, a native cunning in that face of hers" (Bolaño, *By Night* 113). In her laughter he detects a "note of defiance" that makes him shudder. He tries to claim moral authority over her, but she challenges him, asking if he would like to *see* the basement. Torture, of which he only has theoretical knowledge to this point, is suddenly stripped of its abstraction. The comment infuriates him: "I could have slapped her face" (125). He refuses to allow himself to imagine torture, and he resents her for prompting him to do so. "She burst out laughing uncontrollably. Or maybe I just imagined that" (126). He wants to imagine her laughter as it would represent her lack of empathy and her ability to live among atrocity without shrinking or turning away. The priest wants to envision her, unlike himself, as deserving to be despised.

By conjuring the ghosts of the basement, she tears him from his peaceful, willed blindness. She reminds him what is hiding in the darkness of his silence. By the end of his monologue his fear of a reckoning is palpable: "Is that the true, the supreme terror, to discover that I am the wizened youth whose cries no one can hear?" (Bolaño, *By Night* 129). The faces of those whom he had attacked and protected suddenly flash before his eyes at a vertiginous speed, "the faces I hardened myself against and those I sought in vain. And then the storm of shit begins" (130). He cowers in the face of memory in a way comparable to Salvador in *Blind Sunflowers*. The Spanish priest never resolves his anguish nor recognizes his responsibility for violence. He concludes, "From now on I will be nothing more than another blind sunflower among the multitude" (Méndez 110). Both priests would rather accept a murderous world than consciously and bravely reflect on their own culpability.

"Himpathy" and Mirrors

Manne's *Down Girl* offers insight for an additional interpretation of the dominant male figures' distress in *Blind Sunflowers* and *By Night in Chile*. She coins the term *himpathy* to describe the "mirror image of misogyny" with its key structures in reverse (197). To paraphrase Manne, women's humanity is held to be *owed* to others, and her value contingent on her giving moral goods to them: life, love, pleasure, nurture, sustenance, and comfort. She is punished in brutal and inhumane ways when her mind appears to be oriented to the wrong thing and to the wrong people, including herself (22–3). When the male figure in *Blind Sunflowers* acts violently to punish the female figure for such a perceived offence, his hyper-privilege yields "himpathy" from others and exonerates him. The figure of Salvador provides a revealing example of this process. From his perspective his faith, vocation, victory, and integrity had all been stolen from him by a woman who refused to offer what he believed he deserved. His words are unambiguous: "She was refusing it out of her sense of failure, her lack of piety, her defeat – and I admit it now, her beauty. How could a woman buffeted by so many failures remain unmoved by all the proof of my devotion? I had to have an answer" (Méndez, *Blind Sunflowers* 106).

The protagonist's behaviour resonates with Virginia Woolf's depiction of men in *A Room of One's Own*. Woolf employs the metaphor of the mirror to illustrate the dynamic in which men expect women to reflect an unchallenged, magnified image of themselves. When a woman's writing contains criticism of a man, the resulting defensiveness often stems not just from bruised ego but from a deeper need to safeguard his own self-perception of superiority (Woolf, *A Room* 51). Women, she argues, have historically functioned as "looking-glasses possessing the magic and delicious power of reflecting the figure of man at twice its natural size" (51). Writing with incredible foresight in 1928, Woolf uses Mussolini to exemplify this, noting his insistence on "the inferiority of women, for if they were not inferior, they would cease to enlarge" (52) the male ego. With biting sarcasm she asks, "How is he to go on giving judgement, civilizing natives, making laws, writing books, dressing up, speechifying at banquets unless he can see himself at breakfast and at dinner at least twice the size he really is?" (52). This highlights men's dependence on unchallenged affirmation to maintain their perceived authority.

In *By Night in Chile* the priest-protagonist rejects women but also feels a sense of entitlement so great that he feels victimized and, by extension, deserving of self-"himpathy." This is an example of how power "works through reversal," as Sara Ahmed argues (25). "Those who are more represented in the public domain tend to represent themselves as more censored" (25). It is a "performative contradiction" and "a mechanism of power" (26). When acts of violence are retold in the distorting light of these myths, figures like Salvador and Urrutia become the champions of religious and moral righteousness. The acts then end up further solidifying the myths of masculine and Catholic superiority and dominance. This relates to what Rita Segato calls in her book *The War against Women* a "pedagogy of cruelty" through which the repetition of violence produces a normalizing effect (21). Extrapolating these ideas, *Blind Sunflowers* and *By Night in Chile* offer important insights into the ways in which state violence has been marked by the intersections of patriarchy, religion, and the military. Through a feminist analysis of these narratives, centring on militarized masculinity, we can understand why this violence has frequently been made invisible and why we must shine a bright light on such violence to make it visible.

6 Cinematic Scenes of Gendered Torture and Resistance in Spain

In the essay "Doing Torture in Film" Marnia Lazreg writes: "Apologies for torture, whether in print or speech, follow a familiar pattern whereby the practice is acknowledged as being extreme and unusual, even evil, before hailed as necessary and mandatory under exceptional circumstances. Written defenses of torture usually rest on its effectiveness and are generally based on fictitious, hypothetical emergency situations such as the ticking time-bomb scenario" (257). Lazreg worries that the centrality of torture in official government policies that involve politically motivated persecution and its lasting impact on the victims often goes unseen in cinematic representations. These observations coincide with the perspectives of Michael Flynn and Fabiola Salek, the editors of the volume *Screening Torture* in which Lazreg's essay appears. They share the concern that on-screen displays of graphic inflictions of pain frequently turn torture into a banal and even tantalizing act (11).

Global in scope but showing particular interest in post-9/11 Hollywood cinema, Flynn and Salek's book probes the problems of films and television series that legitimize physical and psychological torment as a necessary evil and endow it "with an effectiveness it does not possess" (12). They also critique how certain portrayals make the tortured body a spectacle that appeals to the voyeuristic gaze. Nowhere is that more evident than in Nazisploitation films, a subgenre that mixes historical shock value with sexploitation. Naomi Holwill's documentary *Fascism on a Thread: The Strange Story of Nazisploitation Cinema* explores the catalogue of these lurid films, mostly produced in 1970s Italy and the United States. The graphic depiction of fascist brutality and experimentation in concentration camps through long sequences of rape, mutilation, and other dehumanizing cruelties, makes these films unwatchable. While such depictions show a link between militarized masculinity and torture, the focus on gore and suffering is meant to entertain rather than critique.

How, then, can films represent the sexualized torture of political prisoners at the hands of militarized men without relying on sexploitation that may appeal to the morbid fascination of viewers? This chapter examines three narrative films from Spain that push viewers to reflect critically on why, when, and how torture was exercised in Franco's prisons. They accomplish this without resorting to gratuitous violence. By exploring cinematic choices like historical contextualization, characterization, and presentation of explicit scenes (length, framing, sequencing), we can identify the ways in which cinema can denaturalize violence, expose its pervasiveness in military dictatorships, and uproot its gendered nature.

Crime in Cuenca (Pilar Miró) takes place more than a decade before the Spanish Civil War, but it reflects gendered torture techniques similar to those used by the civil guard to eliminate Republican resistance and consolidate power. The film conveys Cockburn's assertion that the mutilation of men's genitalia "is no less gendered: it is their masculinity that enemy men are deriding" (Cockburn, "The Continuum" 36). Whereas *Crime in Cuenca* deals with the torture of men, the other two films in this chapter explore the torture of women. *The Sleeping Voice* (Benito Zambrano) and *The Endless Trench* (Jon Garaño, Aitor Arregi, and José Mari Goenaga) are both set during the Franco dictatorship. The perpetrators of torture in these films are agents of the civil guard (i.e., the law enforcement agency organized as a military force charged with police duties). The victims are mostly leftist political prisoners, or their family members, who were controlled and punished for posing a threat to the regime's authority. Based on oral and written testimonies as well as other historical sources, these film-makers recreate via cinematographic imagery the forms of corporeal subjugation that were systematically used as a means to a political end.

Torture in these films is graphic and often explicitly sexual in nature, but in no way entertaining. It is an indefensible act that is difficult to watch, yet it is also eye opening and thought provoking. In examining these films, I argue that the cinematic treatment of torture has the potential to deepen our understanding of the ways in which gender and militarism shape violence. The film-makers represent forced nudity, electric shock, sexual humiliation, and rape. These and other gendered inflictions of pain are framed as demonstrations of military authority and masculine domination. Their depictions of the misogynist and homophobic language and practices of the Spanish civil guard highlight the mutually constitutive relationship between militarism, misogyny, and homophobia. They raise key questions about the way in which intersecting belief systems have contributed to gendered torture as a systematic method to punish, instil fear, and impose military power. This chapter also foregrounds the transmission of contradictory meanings by discussing how *The Endless Trench* paradoxically, and perhaps inadvertently, reinserts some of the ideologies that it simultaneously challenges.

The larger questions that have guided my film selection and interpretation revolve around how cinema might present disruptive ways of seeing torture. How does the film-maker sequence torture scenes, and what does that sequence convey? In the depiction of interrogation what is revealed and what is concealed? How does the film-maker present the victims and victimizers, as well as the gendered power dynamics between them? How does the film present the perpetrator's motivations? How does dialogue contribute to the characterization, and how does language function particularly in the torture sequences? What purpose does the soundtrack serve, and how is the image of torture transformed by sound? How is the setting of the torture world recreated? What do the camera angles and lighting seek to impress on the viewer? By grappling with these questions, I aim to explore how the representation of torture in these films serves not as a spectacle of suffering but as a critical examination of the intertwined militarist and misogynist ideologies that fuelled state violence in Franco's Spain.

Torture of Men in *Crime in Cuenca*

Crime in Cuenca by Pilar Miró (1940–97) centres on the systematic torture of two tenant farmers who have been accused of a crime that never happened. While the motives of the accusations varied from the personal to the political, it is significant that the farmers were suspected of anarchist ties. With that detail, viewers are reminded of the well-known story of Sacco and Vanzetti, two Italian migrant anarchists in the United States who were falsely convicted of a crime and executed in 1920. The film by Miró is set at around the same time and is based on a true story that was first documented in 1932 by Alicio Garcitoral, Cuenca's civil governor at the time of the events. The story was subsequently fictionalized by Ramón Sender in the novel *El lugar de un hombre* (The place of a man).

The alleged crime took place in Osa de la Vega in the province of Cuenca and involved the disappearance of the twenty-eight-year-old shepherd named José María Grimaldos (nicknamed El Cepa, or the Stump). On 20 August 1910 Grimaldos sold his sheep and then went missing without a trace. Several weeks later his mother arrived at the unfounded conclusion that two farmers, León Sánchez and Gregorio Valero, who had mocked her son, had stolen his money and then murdered him to cover up the crime. Due to the lack of evidence the case was initially dismissed in 1911. Nevertheless, in 1913 it was reopened at the request of the Grimaldos family, as well as the town's powerful oligarch (Francisco Antonio Ruiz), the local deputy and right-wing strongman (Francisco Martínez de Contreras), and the parish priest (Pedro Rufo Martínez Enciso). The newly appointed conservative judge (Emilio Isasa Echenique), influenced by Contreras, ordered the civil guard to detain and interrogate Valero and Sánchez.

During their detainment in 1913 they were brutally tortured by the sergeant of the civil guard, Juan Taboada, until they confessed to a crime they had never committed. In 1925 they were released from prison after serving over twelve years in total. To the shock and horror of the villagers, Grimaldos (declared deceased) reappeared in 1926 after having spent the previous fifteen years living in another town. The Supreme Court reversed the guilty verdicts, and the confession was considered an outcome of exceptional continuous violence. Criminal proceedings were opened against those involved in the false conviction, but all of the men implicated were ultimately exonerated. The power of the political elites, the judiciary, the Church, and the military remained entirely intact.

In 1979, four years after the death of Franco, Pilar Miró worked with Lola Salvador and producer José Vicuña to reconstruct and film the story. In her own words, Miró wanted to explore "how two people can be destroyed, how they can be turned into animals, physically and psychologically, through the application of savage procedures" (qtd. in Triana-Toribio, "In Memoriam"). The film-maker depicts the extraction of teeth, nails, and facial hair, and, perhaps most significantly, she captures an image of one of the prisoners hanging from the ceiling with his naked genitals tied to a metal conduit. As Federico Bonaddio notes, "This aspect of the film unnerved Spain's then-ruling party, the Union of the Democratic Center, which allowed the film to be confiscated by the military authorities and its director to become subject to investigation by a military tribunal" (qtd. in Jimenez Murguía and Pinar, *Encyclopedia* 111).

Crime in Cuenca was denied an exhibition licence in 1979, and, as Peter Besas explains, "military authorities started legal and criminal proceeding against Miró for defamation of the Benemérita, as the Civil Guard is respectfully called in Spain" (198). In this fragile period for the new democracy, civilians who were accused of any affront against the military authorities came under the jurisdiction of military tribunals according to the military code of justice (Besas 199–202). Miró was interrogated and threatened with a six-year prison sentence, which was ultimately dropped. The film remained in limbo until its uneasy release in July 1981 just after Congress had changed the law. "The case dragged on for a year and a half and might have continued much longer had it not been for the political changes in Spain. Adolfo Suárez resigned as president of the government in January 1981" (Besas 198). The film was finally released against the backdrop of the failed military coup in February of that same year headed by Antonio Tejero, a former lieutenant colonel of the civil guard.

Given that the events in Cuenca had taken place over sixty years earlier, the outrage that the film produced in the immediate post-dictatorship is telling. The Ministry of Culture called for censorship on the grounds of explicit violence; however, many other films containing gruesome depictions of assault were being circulated at the time. Barbara Zecchi argues that the film's censorship hinged upon questions of gender and the discriminatory treatment of women in the male-dominated world of cinema. She observes that Miró shattered expectations and scandalized the public by projecting a frontal display of the limp penis of a tortured man (311). The film-maker's critical portrayal of militarized masculinity is also central to the film's disruptive power. The crime to which the film's title refers is undoubtedly the crime of gendered torture committed by the civil guard to serve the greater political goal of maintaining the hegemony of economic and military elites and the Catholic Church.

The film-maker's presentation of civilian victims and militarized perpetrators, as well as the gendered power dynamics between them, prompts viewers to see violence differently. Recounted in chronological order, the film begins with Grimaldos's disappearance and the collusion between the family, local political authorities, and law enforcement to convict Sánchez and Valero. The leading figure representing the civil guard follows the orders of the conservative judge to attain a confession at any cost. As Bonaddio observes, "The depiction of torture is realistically brutal and stark. In scenes where the accused are at the total mercy of the sadistic 'Sergeant Toboada' (Francisco Casares) of the civil guard, close-ups are employed to a horrific effect" (*Encyclopedia* 111).

If gratuitous scenes of violence serve to entertain the viewing public by glorifying dominant views of aggressive masculinity, then Miró's non-gratuitous depiction of torture creates a sense of revulsion and reflection. Unlike many action films that frame violence in fast and stylized sequences full of visual effects, Miró's camera captures unbearable physical distress in long arrangements of shots that elicit emotion and critical thought. Some shots allow viewers to take in the space and focus on the disfigured male body and the militarized perpetrators. Sequences with close-ups of blows to the groin or the violent removal of facial hair (beards and mustaches) with pliers not only provoke unease in viewers but also raise questions about the gendered nature of torture since the targets of abuse are all emblematic symbols of masculinity.

The film implores us to regard the imposition of militarized masculine authority over civilian men that explicitly involved sexualized brutality. The most disturbing image, as I previously stated, involves the graphic assault on one of the prisoner's genitals. In the low light of the torture chamber a camera slowly pans over his half-naked body as he struggles to cling to a ceiling pipe. An extreme close-up of his torso fragments the body, forcing the viewer to zoom in on the violation of the prisoner's most intimate space. The shot reveals that he is bound to the pipe only by a string knotted to his penis. His masculinity is literally on the line. One slip or weakening of his grip would result in dismemberment. That specific kind of mutilation has a symbolic nature, as Joshua Goldstein emphasizes in his book *War and Gender: How Gender Shapes the War System and Vice Versa*. Castrating men before or after killing them was a "way to feminize conquered enemies" (357). Cutting off the testicles or penis "left no doubt that the ultimate symbolic meaning of the act was to take away their manhood and thus their power" (356).

As viewers witness the prisoner's extreme suffering and fear of mutilation through tight framing, we also observe a long shot of the civil guard on duty in the background, somewhat out of focus. Slouched in his chair, he appears entirely unmoved by the enormity of the prisoner's desperation, pain, and humiliation. Miró's framing of subjugation against the civil guard's indifference conveys a powerful message. The scene suggests that sexualized torture was a normalized feature of detention and interrogation. This is perhaps the most prominent example of how the film-maker interprets bodily domination as both gendered and part and parcel of social control.

It is significant that the film-maker does not place all culpability on the rank-and-file perpetrators but instead emphasizes the complicity between powerful patriarchal institutions. In this way the film dramatizes Lazreg's contention that "torture partakes in the work of the civilization in whose name it is practiced, and in which it finds its justification against the alleged barbarity of the enemy" (*Torture and the Twilight* 5). In *Crime in Cuenca* the civil guard is depicted as an organization at the service of the powerful upper-class elite, the Catholic Church, and the armed forces. When Sergeant Toboada is instructed to carry out the order and extract a confession, he obeys without question or hesitation. The arguably unnuanced characterization of Toboada does not suggest that he faces any moral dilemma, and several close-up reaction shots even lead viewers to believe that he takes pleasure in asserting his authority over the civilian men. However, in no way does the film-maker reduce the responsibility to the military police force alone. Instead she sharpens our awareness of how torture and militarism work. Together they provided the means for authoritarian regimes, including those of Miguel Primo de Rivera (1923–30) and Francisco Franco (1939–75), to rise to power and preserve the interests of economic and military elites, while further entrenching patriarchy.

It is also important to examine how the film reveals the long-lasting effects of torture. In *Crime in Cuenca* the sexualized infliction of pain, in combination with solitary confinement, destroys the world of men who experience it. What is more, the suffering of the victims is not limited to the male prisoners but extends to their spouses and children from whom they become alienated. In one scene the film-maker brings viewers into the dark domain of a prisoner who has been deprived of water for so long that when his wife visits him with their baby in arms, he aggressively holds her down to drink the milk from her breasts. If one of Miró's goals was to explore the process and cumulative effects of dehumanization, then she achieves that goal in this scene. It is an unsanitized view of the impact of state violence that stings our gaze. The film also emphasizes how friendships are torn asunder. In desperation Sánchez and Valero end up placing the blame on the other, thereby destroying the fraternal bond between them. The film thus exposes the enormous dilemmas facing victims of torture. Suffering becomes not a source of power but the cause of debilitation and irreversible devastation. That is the silenced and gendered tale of torture conveyed by the film-maker.

Although the film is set in the pre-Franco past and was produced shortly after the transition to democracy, it is unsurprising that Miró's explicit depiction of interrogation enraged military officials, who threatened the film-maker with a court martial for insulting the civil guard (Besas 197–9). Her critical portrayal publicly threatened its monopoly over the meaning of its role in society and system of control. Such a bold act contributed to the larger push against the persistent authority of the pro-Franco establishment that sought to transform itself superficially during the transition while maintaining the intersecting structures of economic and military power that had engendered the dictatorship four decades earlier.

Miró's cinematic recounting of torture constitutes a forerunner of other films that have destabilized the Francoist narrative that extols the benefits of military rule and dismisses its injustice. The inclusion of *Crime in Cuenca* allows us to trace a longer trajectory of torture and its legitimization in the regime's wake. Miró's depiction illustrates the central notion in this book, namely that militarized masculinity was not casual but *causal* in acts of torture. Only when we probe the normalization of violent masculinity and its link to militarism and the powerful institutions that it safeguards can we identify a unifying factor in the making of authoritarian architects, rank-and-file perpetrators, and civilian bystanders.

Torture of Women in *The Sleeping Voice*

In the early 1900s, torture was not unusual at the hands of the Spanish civil guard, who used techniques of torment on the men and women accused of communist or anarchist activities. The use of torture, however, was not routinized in twentieth-century Spain until the installation of the National Catholic military regime in 1939. Within the hypermasculine and heteronormative regime the infliction of physical and psychological pain involved not only beatings, body hangings, forced positions, and asphyxia but also abuse to the testicles to prove the dominance of the regime over Republican men. For women political prisoners the demonstration of authority carried out by the civil guard routinely involved the assault of sexualized organs including the breasts, uterus, and vagina. The gendered and sexual dimensions of torture were evident in particular acts including forced nudity, head shaving, electric shock, groping, and rape. Though accounts of such sadism were prohibited from publication under Franco, oral histories and letters circulated clandestinely within Spain and in exile communities. For many survivors, however, the experience of imprisonment and torture produced such terror that the result was a self-imposed censorship as a means to protect themselves from further incrimination and abuse.

Since the death of Franco in 1975, historians have advanced in the investigation and documentation of the wartime reprisals and Francoist repression; however, as Gina Herrmann notes, up until the mid-1980s the experiences of imprisoned leftist women were overlooked in Spanish Civil War historiography and frequently neglected even by progressive historians ("Voices" 12). Even at the turn of the twenty-first century when memories of the Spanish Civil War and post-war became a central focus of an enormous body of cultural production, publications dedicated to women's prison memories were still uncommon. In the 2008 essay titled "Mujeres en guerra: Repensar la historia" Mary Nash characterizes the ongoing subordinate position of women in the historical record of the civil war by emphasizing their place in footnotes, appendixes, or single bibliographic references (62). Given that a disproportionate amount of attention has focused on men's experiences of war and political persecution, some historians, survivors, film-makers, and novelists have been anxious to explore women's stories.

One trailblazing figure, who partly inspired the novel *La voz dormida* (*The Sleeping Voice*) by Dulce Chacón (1954–2003) and a subsequent film adaptation by Benito Zambrano (b. 1965), was Tomasa Cuevas (1917–2007), a former political prisoner from 1939 to 1945 who recognized the importance of women's prison experiences decades before others did. Amid the backdrop of the early transition to democracy Cuevas gathered oral testimonies from her former prison companions. In 1985 Cuevas published *Prison of Women* to record Republican women's accounts, particularly during the years leading up to the civil war and in its aftermath. Cuevas's pioneering collection of prison testimonies, along with a compilation of oral interviews conducted by Dulce Chacón, inform *The Sleeping Voice*. The novel establishes a counter-narrative that bears witness to gendered repression; however, unlike the film adaptation, the book only obliquely refers to particular forms of sexualized torture. That elision in the written text reflects silences around the topic in testimonies, which can denote the limits of language and representation to describe torture, or the survivor's lasting trauma compounded by the stigmatization of rape that debases victims.

In the adaptation of *The Sleeping Voice* Benito Zambrano confronts that elision. My analysis of the film focuses specifically on two torture sequences. I argue that the film provides a rare example in Spain of a visual representation of a tortured woman's body at the hands of militarized men, while avoiding exploitive cinematic choices that capitalize on suffering. Combining interviews, extensive historical research, and insights from survivors like Carmen Arroyo and Concha Carretero, who were on set for the filming, Zambrano attempts to interpret the gaps in the historical record and render visible the exact ways in which the military regime used torture to maintain totalitarian control. It is a powerful model of how cinema has the potential to challenge the ways in which the state restrains, punishes, and aims to transfigure the politicized body. As Mark de Valk states in *Screening the Tortured Body*, "cinema's calling attention to authoritarian state practices of bodily repression allows for a reclaiming of power from the patriarchal sovereign" (3). In Zambrano's hands the victim's bodily pain is never represented as essential for the restoration of order but rather for the reinsertion of patriarchal and military dominance. This film brings into sharp relief the gendered dimensions of bodily torment and its relation to militarism and discourse.

Spanning the years 1939–63, *The Sleeping Voice* tells the story of a group of communist women who were incarcerated in Madrid's Ventas prison for their support of the Republican side in the Spanish Civil War. The lives of the imprisoned women and guerrilla fighters are intertwined with those of other victims of the regime who are not incarcerated but suffer pressure from state agents as a result of their familial relationships with prisoners. The film revolves primarily around two characters whose point of view is central. Hortensia is a Cordoban communist prisoner sentenced to death for her involvement with the guerrillas after the Republican defeat. Pepita is Hortensia's sister, who operates as a messenger between the prisoners and guerrilla members. The portrayal of these characters offers readers insight not only into the daily struggles of Republican women in 1940s Madrid as related to hunger, poverty, and fear but also into the use of torture as part of a larger process of political disenfranchisement, religious indoctrination, and patriarchal conquest of leftist women who had worked to promote social and economic change during the Second Republic.

The film-maker depicts the torture of women by militarized perpetrators both indirectly through shots of its after-effects (i.e., bloodied faces, wounded bodies) and directly through graphic interrogation sequences. The first of the latter takes place midway through the film when Pepita is detained after the regime's agents discover that she has aided the resistance. In the interrogation room there are four perpetrators of violence including the police commissioner. Pepita is tied to a chair with her wrists cuffed behind her back when the interrogation begins. As she refuses to give the commissioner the information that he seeks, he brings into the room her shackled brother-in-law named Felipe and her boyfriend named Paulino, both of whom have been operating clandestinely in the anti-fascist underground. Their blood-soaked clothing and badly injured faces implicitly display the torture to which they have been subjected. Now they are forced to witness the police commissioner's gruesome torture of Pepita. A medium shot that frames her figure from the waist up captures the commissioner as he tears open her shirt and applies electrical current with metal pincers to her areolae. The camera cuts to a full high-angle shot that shows her body in torment as well as the men in the room who witness it. The language of torture is central as the repeated use of the word *whore* arrests our attention and renders visible the way in which misogyny shapes the act of torture, functioning to encourage and justify the torturer's degradation of a woman's body. In the following scene a long shot captures Pepita in a half-lit prison cell, curled up in the fetal position, completely naked and badly bruised. The image suggests that the torture session had continued and involved rape and other sexual atrocities.

This scene prompts thought on why and how torture was exercised: the use of violence against the individual body was a method of creating fear and political consent. This scene also asks us to grapple with the gendered nature of torture, that is, how torture was performed. The use of the whore-virgin binary served to goad perpetrators to rape women prisoners and then justify it in the aftermath. The portrayal of explicit torture is not gratuitous but rather a rejection of violence and those who perpetrated it. It is important that Zambrano's presentation refuses to transform the injured woman's body into a mere spectacle or a visual display that capitalizes on suffering. The brief duration of the scene is significant as it makes visible the dimensions of subjugation without becoming sexually exploitative. Shots of the police commissioner are meant to invoke the protagonist's point of view, prompting a rejection of militarized masculinity and a reflection on its centrality in an ideology of power.

The film also counteracts the notion of women as mere objects at the hands of militarized men by moving their diverse experiences from the margin to the centre and by developing their characters in scenes that lead to the torture sequence and that follow it. Images of shackling, stripping, and electric shock situate the intersections of misogyny and torture at the film's core; however, equally important is the principled resistance of the women detainees, their sisters, their daughters, and their mothers. If the torture sequence featuring Pepita exposes the practice of sexualized violence, then the subsequent scenes present her as a survivor and political actor. The film further impresses that notion upon the audience through the figure of Hortensia, who demonstrates that her task is not only to survive but to hold onto her humanity and her political convictions. Rather than reinscribe the reductive perception of women as exclusively targets of male hostility, Zambrano characterizes them as politically engaged subjects struggling against fascist forms of government and culture.

Up to now I have argued that *The Sleeping Voice* pushes us to think anew about the way in which torture works when women are interrogated for their connection to revolutionary political activism. The film also heightens our awareness of the sexualized nature of the torture of men. In the film's second torture sequence the two detained guerrilla fighters, Felipe and Paulino, are subject to a range of atrocities including electrocution, repeated assault to the abdomen and groin, forced nudity, and hanging. In one shot the film-maker uses backlighting in the torture room to transform the image of Felipe's naked figure, dangling in the darkness, into a silhouette. Unlike Miró in *Crime in Cuenca*, Zambrano evades a frontal image of the violated genitals; still, his cinematic choices underscore the sexuality inherent in the torture of men. The perpetrators seek to prove their masculinity by exerting total dominance over them. The parallels between Franco's Spain and Pinochet's Chile are striking, as I will show in the following chapter. In both cases, torture targeting men's sexual organs constituted a practice of heightened hegemonic heteronormative masculinity. The goal of such sexualized torture and gendered mutilation was not only to produce extreme pain but to traumatize and shame the victims by causing permanent damage to their reproductive organs, thereby asserting long-term power over their bodies.

Torture is defined as the action or practice of inflicting severe pain on someone as a punishment or in order to force them to do or say something. When the film-maker explores the experience of pregnant political prisoners and the particular forms of violence to which they were subject in Franco's Spain, viewers are prompted to expand that basic definition of torture. The protagonist, Hortensia, is sentenced to death after the birth of her child. Before she faces the death squad, she is pressured to repent in the penitentiary chapel and consent to the baptism of her daughter. When she refuses to submit to their authority, the prison guards and priest separate her from her newborn, disallowing her to nurse the hungry infant. The sound of the crying baby emphasizes the traumatic effect of the punishment. It is an act of psychological torture against a woman who has challenged the social order. Through this scene the film compels viewers to consider the brutal consequences of an unbending patriarchal ideology of womanhood. If motherhood became a cultural battleground during the civil war, the fascist victory facilitated the unbridled enforcement of misogynist gender norms. The role of mother was reserved exclusively for women who embraced traditional roles and, by extension, abnegation and submission to male authority. Those who did not conform to that model were dehumanized and violently stripped of any claim to motherhood.

In her discussion of the sexual politics of war Enloe explains that "militarization relies on distinct notions about masculinity, notions that have staying power only if they are legitimized by women as well as men" (*The Morning After* 3). In *The Sleeping Voice* Zambrano depicts the militarization of women through the characterization of female prison guards and nuns at the service of the regime. Their standardized uniforms, intended for the display of power and distinction from the prisoners, have a militarized appearance that is emphasized in long shots of the women marching in unison through the prison corridors. Their violent actions and words reveal a belief system entailing the adherence to hierarchical order and forcible suppression of the opposition. They are present at the executions, keep the prisoners under surveillance, order solitary confinement, and exert physical abuse on the women prisoners when they do not obey orders. Similar to militarized masculinity, militarized femininity not only catalyzes aggression but also hinges upon it and is emboldened by it. The film's characterization of militarized women as fervent enforcers of discipline and allegiance to the patriarchal national family reveals that just as antimilitarism and resistance to toxic masculinity are not inherently female endeavours, militarism is not an entirely male domain. The dialogues and behaviours of militarized women in the film also reveal that the justifications of torture, as Lazreg explains, play a crucial role in its routinization (*Torture and the Twilight* 5). *The Sleeping Voice* conveys important insights about what Lazreg describes as "the management of conscience by torturers and observers of torture, and the moral justifications proffered by the Church, individual chaplains, and rightwing Catholics" (8).

To conclude my analysis of the representation of torture in *The Sleeping Voice*, I return to *Crime in Cuenca*. When we analyse Zambrano's film alongside Miró's, we gain a perspective of the longer history of militarism and torture as a method of control in Spain. Violence in Franco's prisons was consistent with the sort of techniques that the civil guard had used to suppress dissent long before the 1940s. Both films uncover the nature and function of militarized masculinity within the civil guard, and they render visible that this aggressive gender construct has been at the centre of the enactment of violence in interrogation rooms.

Gendered Violence in *The Endless Trench*

Torture in twentieth-century Spain was a strategic weapon with which patriarchal institutions reinforced militarized culture and safeguarded hierarchical economic and social structures of power. Placing *Crime in Cuenca* alongside *The Sleeping Voice* brings out a continuum of violence that I would like to examine further in this section on the film *The Endless Trench* by Jon Garaño, Aitor Arregi, and José Mari Goenaga. Most of the work, similar to *The Sleeping Voice*, takes place in the 1940s. Whereas

The Sleeping Voice explicitly engages the topic of state-sanctioned torture of women in the early post-war years, *The Endless Trench* represents torture and other forms of gendered violence implicitly through the stories of non-military Republican men who were driven into hiding for fear of Nationalist reprisals. As I explained in my analysis of *The Blind Sunflowers*, many dissidents were forced to live underground as *topos* (moles) for decades during the Franco dictatorship. Inspired by the biography of Manuel Cortés Quero (1906–91), *The Endless Trench* portrays the lived experience of the former Republican mayor of Mijas (Málaga) who spent thirty years holed up in his home to avoid torture and execution. The idea for the film came, as the directors have stated, after they saw the animated documentary film *30 Years of Darkness* directed by Manuel Martín and based on *In Hiding: The Life of Manuel Cortés* by Ronald Fraser. While Cortés's story influenced *The Endless Trench*, the directors also drew from other testimonies, like those collected in the book *The Moles* by Jesús Torbado and Manuel Leguineche.

The Endless Trench provides thought-provoking perspectives on how sexualized violence and enforced heteronormativity have been at the core of militaristic culture. The film also sheds light on competing masculinities, revealing the immense pressure to conform to the militarized masculine ideal. An unsettling feature of the film is its depictions of masculinity that tend to merge with and reproduce the very Francoist logic that it purports to challenge. To evaluate its import and paradoxes, I highlight three key aspects of the film that frame a continuum of violence inherently linked to the uneven balance of power between the militarized male and all other identities. These aspects include gendered acts of control and impunity like the rape and head shaving of women accused of aiding anti-Franco resisters. The repression of gay men under the military regime also figures prominently in the film. The attitudes and behaviours of gay characters reveal the difficulty of subverting the gendered conditioning that perpetuates patterns of violence and the acceptance of militarism. Finally, an analysis of the representation of the protagonist as conscience stricken and ashamed for not physically fighting allows me to explore how militaristic culture functioned to gaslight non-military Republican men, influencing them to question their own reality, memory, and perceptions.

The film is structured in chapters, each with a title referring to the main themes. The first section, called "Campeada" (The run), sets the film's tone and dramatizes one of its central conflicts, namely the power struggle between militarized men and civilians. Set in Andalucía in 1936 at the beginning of the civil war, the invading Nationalist side aggressively polices the streets, instils fear, and rounds up Republican loyalists for imprisonment or execution. The protagonist, Higinio Blanco, and his wife, Rosa, wake to the sound of Falangist soldiers pounding at their door. As the socialist councilman, he becomes the target of abuse. A subjective, hand-held, shaky camera follows Higinio as he escapes to the sierra. The sequence shows the atrocity of political persecution through both image and sound as the gunfire produces abrupt silences that replicate the deafening sensation experienced by Higinio, whose perspective is the consistent focus of the film. When he encounters a fellow Republican who is also struggling to hide, Higinio adheres to non-violence, which is emphasized as he rebukes the other's violent response to the war's outbreak. The opening chapter offers a suffocating cinematic experience that expresses a climate of terror. Higinio returns secretly at night and takes cover in a trench dug under the kitchen. The next section, titled "Esconder" (To hide), marks the beginning of the protagonist's journey into a state of hiding that would last for thirty years.

The film-makers prompt a reflection on official discourse, double meanings, euphemisms, and the power to define ideas, with each chapter title, which consists of one word and an accompanying dictionary entry. *Detainment* is defined as a "provisional deprivation of liberty, ordered by a competent authority." That description contrasts sharply with the ruthless raiding, pillaging, imprisonment, and torture in the sequence that follows. From Higinio's perspective, the camera captures the civil guard harassing and arresting Rosa, aggressively removing her from her home against her will. As Higinio watches and listens in horror from his subterranean hiding place, the audience is given a window into the psychological torment of witnessing another's pain. The camera angle emphasizes his position underground and evokes his lack of power. This scene presses viewers to see how detainment has gendered dimensions and how reprisals meant different things for men and women.

In visualizing the atrocity of interrogation and torture at the hands of the civil guard, the film-makers render visible its sexual dimensions without directly dramatizing the acts. Rosa returns from the military headquarters on the next night with her head shaven, her dress torn, and her face and body badly swollen and bloodied. She never says exactly what happened to her, but the sexualized nature of the torture is implicit in her appearance. The violence against her does not end with that incident; it also includes constant surveillance and daily reporting to the military headquarters where she was assaulted and traumatized. The film-makers' allusion to rape, and the constant threat of it, conveys that sexualized violence was not only a byproduct of the civil war but also a strategic form of abuse meant to punish, shame, and control women for their so-called transgressions. This sequence also depicts Catherine MacKinnon's claim that the rape of female civilians is often "a humiliation rite for the men on the other side who cannot (in masculinity's terms) 'protect' their women. Many of these acts make women's bodies into a medium of men's expression, the means through which one group of men says what it wants to say to another" (*Are Women Human?* 223).[1] As I discuss later, Rita Segato also complicates simple notions of rape by framing it as a language between men in their competition for dominance.

The sequence also draws attention to particular gendered abuses that often occurred along with rape, like head shaving, which as Laia Quílez Esteve observes, was one of the most widespread forms of Francoist violence against Republican women. With this humiliating punitive act, the repressers tried to objectify Republican women, expelling them from any model of femininity and humanity: "The collective exhibition of their sheared heads, as well as the immortalization of such humiliation in photographs that were later hung on the premises and walls of the towns, turned the image of the shaving into a paradigmatic symbol of victory for the rebels and the oppression they exerted on the body – physical and social – of their opponents. The shame, trauma, and fear that followed these sexual acts of repression long silenced most victims" (Quílez Esteve 488). The film sheds light on this dehumanizing form of gendered torture through the character of Rosa, but at the same time it frames her as a survivor and underscores her enormous strength as she never betrays her husband's location.

If the war context enabled the civil guard to use gendered terror tactics like rape and head shaving to conquer gendered and political "others," then the post-war context solidified that power and facilitated the long-term normalization of the civil guard's unfettered control. The film dramatizes the constant threat of militarized men to civilian women and the continuum of sexualized violence that is perpetrated beyond the interrogation room. This is achieved through a key plot line that involves a civil guard named Rodrigo who hires Rosa as a seamstress and attempts to rape her in her home. After the first attempt at sexual coercion, which the camera captures from Higinio's perspective underground, Rosa manages to fend him off, but the threat is unsettling. When

---

1 See "Feminist Perspectives on Rape," *The Stanford Encyclopedia of Philosophy*, https://plato.stanford.edu/entries/feminism-rape.

she chastises her husband for his inability to use force to defend her, we are prompted to consider how vulnerability and the fear of rape are influenced by societal expectations of masculinity and femininity. Her humiliation becomes frustration and anger directed not towards the male aggressor but towards the man who is unable to protect her. This in turn causes the non-violent man to question his own masculinity.

Rape must be interpreted not only as a pillar of war but also as an act of control that enforces the power of patriarchy.[2] It is a violation that hinges upon misogynistic notions of dominant masculinity and submissive femininity. In *The Endless Trench* viewers witness instances of rape or attempted rape as a form of power that confirms the physical authority of men and their entitlement to treat women's bodies as objects. After Rosa refuses the sexual advances of Rodrigo, he returns, determined to conquer her. Unlike the violation of Rosa at police headquarters, the goal here is not to obtain information or to police her per se; it is to enforce her subordination. Rodrigo's behaviours suggest that it is a calculated and unrestrained response to Rosa's rejection of him. The sound of the military parade taking place outside the home during the attempted rape is evocative. The act is part of a larger patriarchal social order to uphold the sovereignty of militarized men over women. When Higinio hears Rosa's muffled cries for help, he emerges from his hiding place to stop the rape. The unstable camera reveals the severity of the act from his perspective. The scene recalls the conclusion of *The Blind Sunflowers* by Alberto Méndez, discussed elsewhere, but it differs to the extent that here the male protagonist chokes the militarized aggressor while the female victim fatally stabs Rodrigo to escape from his grip. After his dead body has been buried under the house, the multiple traumas produced by sexualized violence linger, long after the act itself.

The process through which non-military men come to doubt their masculinity under the pervasive pressure of militaristic culture is a theme threaded throughout the film. It is transmitted powerfully in one sequence that takes place before Rodrigo's rape of Rosa. It features Higinio reading the only book that Rosa has managed to get for him without alarming the authorities. It is the adventure novel *Sandokan's Revenge* by Emilio Salgari, which tells the story of a man who must recover his throne and avenge the death of his family at the hands of the usurper. The camera captures a contemplative protagonist who closes the book and then attempts to affirm his masculinity, or take out his frustration,

---

2 See Hampton, "Defining Wrong and Defining Rape."

by coercing Rosa sexually without her consent. It is a disturbing scene that forces us to pay attention to the kinds of destructive pressures and transformations that the militarization of masculinity precipitates. Viewers see Higinio's building sense of shame as he later dreams of the return of his dead father. His ghost appears to be admonishing his son for his demonstration of masculinity. This is all part of a longer process of gaslighting whereby societal gender norms in Franco's Spain drive the protagonist to mistrust his own memory, perceptions of others, and view of himself.

As a film that renders visible the complexities and contentions between various masculinities within the context of militarization, *The Endless Trench* provides plot lines that reveal continuities between anti-gay hate and the dehumanization of non-military Republican men because both are deemed unmanly. This is accomplished in the section that is, significantly, titled "Aliado" (Ally) and defined on screen as "description of a state, a country, an army, etc.: that is linked with another for common purposes." The militarized and nationalist framework of the definition is subverted in the film as the allies are not states, countries, or armies but marginalized men. The chapter opens with Rosa's decision to have a baby. The plan is for her to leave the house apparently empty for nine months while she is with her cousins in Granada and, in so doing, avoid questions regarding the identity of the father. At that point, two gay men start to use the home to evade the watchful eye of the townspeople. One day Higinio reveals himself to them, knowing that their clandestine sexual identity is a secret as dangerous as his own. The policing of sexuality had a long history in Spain, and although punishments like castration, head shaving, lashing, and stoning were no longer official methods of sexual control in the twentieth century, under Franco homosexuality was criminalized and gay men were sent to prisons called *galerías de invertidos* (deviants' row).

If the protagonist finds himself living literally closeted, the gay characters in the film figuratively live hidden from view. In this way the chapter titled "Encerrar" (To shut in) takes on a double meaning. Defined as "the action of putting a person or animal in a place from which they cannot get out," the verb describes not only Higinio but also Enrique, an apolitical gay postman who is terrified of being outed. When Higinio befriends him, viewers witness the commonalities in their experiences of repression, but we also distinguish differences as Enrique reminds Higinio of the anti-gay hate that cuts across political affiliations. His comments suggest that with or without Franco, in 1945 any sexuality other than heterosexuality was considered deviant. Their friendship is cut short with the return of Rosa, to whom Enrique cannot reveal his sexual orientation. Later Higinio discovers that Enrique has married a woman and thus passes as heterosexual. With this detail, the film suggests no possibility of sexual diversity in Franco's Spain, only conformity. The loosely forged alliance between marginalized characters unbraids and ultimately fails to exert any political opposition to violence.

With pessimism, the film charts various masculinities and the transformation of political and sexual "others" under the pressure of militarization. The representation of gay men in the film allows the audience to observe the enforcement of heterosexuality. The depiction of the main character demonstrates how men's understanding of their own manliness is constantly negotiated in relation to other men. It occasions viewers to consider how Republican men in hiding were framed as weak (i.e., feminine) and shamed for not physically (i.e., violently) fighting. This is further stressed in the chapters titled "Apartado" (Withdrawn, distant, remote) and "Cambiar" (To change appearance, condition or behaviour). Higino watches his son come of age in the 1950s at a time that the United States becomes an ally of the Francoist state, thereby undermining the resistance and legitimizing repression. By the early 1960s his son is questioning his father's decision to hide and dismisses his struggle as cowardly. Higino's diminished sense of self, which causes him to renounce politics entirely, is produced in relation to his son. This characterization of the second generation raises issues surrounding boys' socialization, the learned performance of combative manhood, and its broader impact on historical conceptions of the civil war. Insofar as the son doubts his father's masculinity as well as his claim to innocence, the film suggests that the regime's political messaging through education and media was largely effective. Soldiering becomes the ideal form of masculinity, and blame for the family's struggles shifts from the Francoist perpetrators of violence to non-combative men. Their decision to hide becomes a source of shame.

On the one hand, the relationship between these characters problematizes the assumption that such gendered shaming would only come from the regime's militarized supporters. The way in which the father is diminished by his son points to the pervasiveness of militarized indoctrination and the extent to which some of the regime's opponents came to view hiding as unheroic and therefore "un-masculine." On the other hand, it could be argued that the film's portrayal *reinserts* some of the attitudes that militarism entails. When we focus on the representation of the main character's reconciliation with the past, the question of whether the film de-normalizes or reinforces dominant views of masculinity becomes particularly salient and disconcerting. If we recall the rape scene, in no way do the film-makers sympathize cinematographically and narratively with the militarized perpetrator. Towards the end of the film, however, Rodrigo returns from the grave in full military uniform in a dream to assuage the protagonist's conscience in an imagined final encounter. In close-up shots the camera captures the two men sharing a cigarette and a reconciliatory conversation in which the perpetrator of violence forgives the victim and confirms his worth. It is a problematic turn in which the perpetrator shows no remorse while the injured civilian man is framed as regretful. The scene suggests total acquiescence to dominant militarized culture.

It is paradoxical that the film nears its end with a positive image of the militarized figure representing the version of masculinity and strength that the Francoists had envisioned, while the Republican in hiding possesses traits including vulnerability and sensitivity that are belittled by the other characters as weak and unmanly, i.e., feminine. Following the encounter in the dream, the 1969 amnesty decree that proposed to pardon crimes committed prior to 1939 is declared, and Higinio leaves his hiding place. The film ends with a long shot of him looking with enormous grief through the window of the home where his experience of persecution and social exclusion had begun. His struggle is framed as futile.

The Endless Trench is a film that finds its strength in its elucidation of the links between political repression and militarized masculinity, but it runs the risk of normalizing rather than subverting the hegemonic discourse that it apparently seeks to overturn. In emphasizing survival only – and not conscious resistance to militarized forms of government and culture – the film gives a two-dimensional image of defeat that must be considered in light of the story of the real man on which the film is loosely based. Manuel Cortés Quero left his hiding place after thirty years of darkness to later become the founder of the local Socialist Party (PSOE) in Mijas and preside over it until his death in 1991. Cortés created strong multigenerational bonds with his granddaughter, who vindicates his memory in the documentary *30 Years of Darkness*. In erasing these final chapters of principled perseverance and bonding, and instead depicting political failure, the film-makers arguably buttress the authority of the arguments repeated ad nauseam by the military regime.

An examination of *The Endless Trench*, alongside *Crime in Cuenca* and *The Sleeping Voice*, inspires a necessary discussion on how rape and the violent repression of political and sexual "others" functioned to fulfil societal norms in Spain to the extent that such acts maintain the symbol of the militarized man as synonymous with power. These films translate into imagery the links between torture and misogyny, which Manne correctly defines as a predictable manifestation of patriarchy (49). When implicit forms of social power prove insufficient, Manne notes, "hostile, threatening, and punitive norm-enforcement mechanisms will be standing at the ready" (47). By bringing together these films and interpreting them through a feminist lens, we gain insight into the tightly woven relationship between attitudes about masculinity, sexuality, and aggression before and during Franco's military regime, and also how hegemonic conceptions of manliness are difficult to dismantle even in the post-dictatorship.

7 Torture and the Language of Subjugation in Chilean Documentary

Gendered torture is a challenging term, not only for the dark images of cruelty that it conjures but also for the uncertainty regarding its meaning and causes.[1] It encompasses a wide spectrum of psychological and physical abuse, from forced nudity and humiliating sexualized positions to rape, genital mutilation, penetration with objects, forced intercourse with animals, provoked abortion, and involuntary sterilization. An understanding of the gendered dimensions of torture requires a general grasp of the social construction of masculinity and femininity, as well as contextual knowledge of the particular socio-political power relations from which they stem. When we turn to the case of Chile, torture under the Pinochet regime (1973–90) was systematized to eliminate leftist political resistance. Unbending convictions about the necessity of the patriarchal family and the absolute authority of the militarized male shaped the regime's policies and facilitated the dehumanization of oppositional identities, including pro-Allende women and non-militarized men who supported cultural transformation and economic reform. In light of the regime's ideology, the gendered abuse of political prisoners constituted not only a predictable display of power but also a fundamental mechanism to enforce male dominance and the supremacy of the armed forces.

The ubiquity of sexualized violence in the military junta's clandestine torture centres is one of the major findings in the official Valech Report (2004). It exposed the extent to which sexual violation was systematically exercised by the regime to elicit a confession, to punish, and to

---

1 Sections of this chapter were previously published in "Modes of Silence and Resistance: Chilean Documentary and Gendered Torture," and "Torture, Masculinity, and Resistance in Chilean Documentary Film."

extinguish dissent (Stern, *Reckoning* 290–2).[2] The rape of blindfolded women detainees at one particular site was so routine from 1974 to 1977 that the perpetrators brazenly named it *la venda sexy* (the sexy blindfold). Stern points out that the data-collection forms and interviews conducted by the Valech Commission "did not seek information about sexual violence. Nonetheless, almost all the women brought up the topic without prompting" (*Reckoning* 296). The pervasiveness of such accounts makes evident that sexualized abuse by the regime's agents cannot be considered sporadic but rather, as Jean Franco states, "an extreme assertion of authority" (79).

Although the Valech Report broke new ground by officially recording gendered torture, the absence of an explicit question regarding sexual abuse both in oral and in written interviews raises questions. It is debatable whether the absence indicates a blind spot, a silence, an attentiveness to trauma, or something else. As the introduction to this book explains, several historians, sociologists, and cultural critics including Elizabeth Jelin, Jean Franco, Diana Taylor, Alice Nelson, Bernardita Llanos, and Ximena Bunster have provided insights into the scope of sexualized abuse committed by state agents. Yet, even as the scope of research widens, there is more to learn about the roots, effects, and meanings of gendered torture and its relation to militarized masculinity. How might documentary film creatively respond to histories of state violence and contribute to our understanding of the relationship between gender and torture? How might documentary provoke thought on the infliction of sexualized injury on male political prisoners in addition to female detainees? And finally, how might the denaturalization of the engrained patriarchal norms that inform and justify subjugation constitute a necessary form of social and political resistance to the logic and legacy of dictatorial violence?

This chapter juxtaposes the documentaries of Chilean film-makers Patricio Guzmán, Marcela Said, and Lissete Orozco to shed light on the gendered dimensions of state violence in relation to the discourses and institutions that create and sustain torture as a form of social control. By examining *The Pinochet Case*, *My Imaginary Country*, *I Love Pinochet*, and *Adriana's Pact* through a feminist theoretical lens, I expose the links between militarism, masculinity, and torture, as well as the relationship

---

2 The National Commission on Political Imprisonment and Torture established that the military, the police, and the intelligence service under the regime were responsible for over 30,000 cases of torture, a figure that was later revised in 2011 to include nearly 10,000 additional victims (Collins 65).

between resistance and documentary film. These non-fiction works give rise to a deeper reflection that expands the fundamental premise that state violence is gendered (Jacobs et al.). If dominant narratives concentrate on micro-level explanations (i.e., isolated stories of individual men and women), then these films constitute anti-hegemonic productions that unmask the large-scale belief systems that generate gendered violence. They demonstrate how sexualized violence has been at the core of patriarchal and militaristic culture in which masculinity is defined in terms of dominance and aggression. Viewers are faced with stories of degradation and trauma experienced by both men and women, but we also witness stories of survival, resilience, and ongoing struggle against militaristic patriarchal power.

First, I analyse *The Pinochet Case* by Patricio Guzmán, which subverts dominant narratives by featuring stories that testify to the gendered nature of torture and simultaneously portray active survivors reclaiming agency. The documentary also complicates the common perception that exclusively equates gendered abuse with female victimhood. Guzmán accomplishes this by rendering visible men's accounts of sexualized torture. Men's vastly under-examined testimonies of assault reveal that acts of torture have hinged upon the assertion of aggressive masculinity as the quintessential demonstration of power. Humiliation and harm to the genitals played a key role in the dehumanization of non-military male political prisoners as they were deemed "unmanly." While *The Pinochet Case* confirms that perpetrators sought to destroy male detainees through gendered torture, the film also combines cinematographic techniques that convey nuanced information about the assertion of agency.

In relation to that film I examine how the documentaries *I Love Pinochet* and *Adriana's Pact* problematize dominant narratives of gender and violence. With a focus on the pro-Pinochet establishment, both films highlight the veneration of authoritarian masculinity that makes sexualized violations possible. Said and Orozco offer a window through which to identify the discourse of militarized masculinity and the specific institutions that have upheld it (the military, Church, media, and state) in the name of patriotism and capitalist modernization. Interviews, archival footage, and voice-over narration prompt us to look beyond short-sighted perspectives that only distract from the extensive social sources of gendered torture. The films uncover the emergence of violence from ingrained misogynist ideologies that glorify male domination and sanction the authority and disciplinary practices of the armed forces. From the voices of Pinochet's supporters, viewers observe an intersecting vindication of masculinity, militarism, and subjugation.

These films do not merely provide an outlet for militaristic discourse. They effectively demonstrate how militarized patriarchal authoritarianism infiltrates and shapes civilian women's lives, enabling and legitimizing the use of violence. Every element – the film-makers' questions, the story's progression, and the captured facial expressions – serves to convey the directors' critical stance. Furthermore, they succeed in capturing pro-dictatorship individuals who expose themselves as willing bystanders or complicit actors in violent acts.

Militarized Masculinity and Torture in Chile

As stated in this book's introduction, the concept of militarized masculinity was originally developed by Cynthia Enloe in response to US militarization and neo-imperialism. In the books *Bananas, Beaches and Bases*, *Maneuvers*, and *Globalization and Militarism*, Enloe explains how the more that militarization transforms society, the more that society sees militaristic imperatives as necessary to ensure security against presumed enemies (*Maneuvers* 4). Militaristic euphemisms play an important role in disguising acts of terror, naturalizing totalitarian rule, and dehumanizing the opposition. The larger purpose is to justify the military intervention and the subjugation of the opposition. Women's roles were also influenced by militarized discourses and institutions. Yet, unlike their male counterparts, they were expected to fulfil their service to the nation within the home, instilling in their children an unbending veneration of the armed forces and their male commanders. This homogenizing framework permeated all sectors of society, but it sought to unmake men and women of the leftist opposition through torture, which was gendered and sexualized.

Guzmán's *The Pinochet Case*, Said's *I Love Pinochet*, and Orozco's *Adriana's Pact* testify to the nature and impact of this militarized masculinity. The first two documentaries were produced in the year 2001, a turning point because Pinochet had been charged with human rights violations while he was in Britain in 1998. The productions also took place three years *before* the official Valech Report was released in 2004. A decade earlier, the public focus had been on cases of murder or disappearance at the hands of security forces. By 2000, human rights organizations, victims' groups, and former political prisoners had made significant progress in exposing the regime's torture tactics. In a watershed moment Felipe Agüero (a professor of political science) denounced Emilio Meneses (a professor of military studies) as one of the perpetrators at the National Stadium where Agüero, among 12,000 others, had been held captive. Meneses denied the charges, claiming that he was merely part of a navy team that had questioned the arriving prisoners. The confrontation is examined in the 2004 edited volume *De la tortura no se habla*. As Stern writes, "By 2000–2001, the political-electoral foundations of memory impasse had eroded" (*Reckoning* 260). Guzmán's timely film features the stories of men and women survivors, while Said's film focuses almost exclusively on Pinochet's supporters. As previously stated, rather than condone the viewpoints of the former dictator's champions, Said spotlights the institutions and discourses that facilitated torture and rationalized it in the aftermath.

I Love Pinochet and *Adriana's Pact* make evident Marina Lazreg's contention that "torture partakes in the work of the civilization in whose name it is practiced, and in which it finds its justification against the alleged barbarity of the enemy" (5). Expanding on Lazreg's premise: torture and terror feed one another. Systematic torture is "not just an instance of violence committed by uncontrolled soldiers" but rather "part and parcel of an ideology of subjugation" (Lazreg 3). Militarized masculinity is at the core of this equation. While this form of aggressive masculinity may be enacted by civilians in the absence of torture (outside the barracks and detention centres), torture *depends* on combative posturing associated with the militarized male. The defence of torture as a method of control also depends on civilians whose support of militarized masculinity goes unquestioned.

Patricio Guzmán's *The Pinochet Case*

Patricio Guzmán is considered to be the most influential documentarian of the Pinochet regime's debasement of human rights. He is known particularly for the films *The Battle of Chile, Chile, Obstinate Memory, The Pinochet Case, Salvador Allende, Nostalgia for the Light, The Pearl Button, The Cordillera of Dreams*, and *My Imaginary Country*. Although many critics have mined Guzmán's films to understand the complexities of political struggles and memory from the right-wing backlash of the 1970s to the post-dictatorial present, insufficient attention has been paid to the ways in which his films cast light on the relationship between masculinity and torture. In *The Pinochet Case* Guzmán elucidates the process through which women's and men's bodies became territories upon which militarized men sought to prove their masculinity and authority over women and non-military oppositional men. Twenty years later in *My Imaginary Country* Guzmán highlights the role of women in resisting militarized masculinity and shaping Chile's future.

In *The Pinochet Case* Guzmán raises stirring questions about violence through narrative voice-over, interviews, and the juxtaposition of images, all skilfully selected, edited, and pieced together. Setting the stage for what becomes a series of survivor interviews, Joan Garcés, a Spanish attorney who worked with Allende, describes the process of listening to accounts of the torture that took place during the Pinochet regime. His statements constitute a narrative bridge that joins three sequential shots: an extreme close-up of a magnifying glass held over black-and-white photographs of the military coup; a panning shot across an empty courtroom in Spain; and a long shot of twenty-three plaintiffs – eighteen women and five men – standing together in silence looking directly at the camera. The frame then shifts from a panoramic shot of the courthouse in Spain to a close-up of a female witness compiling notes. These scenes cast the filmic project as an attempt to investigate the complexity of the multilayered legalistic undertaking and to amplify what Elizabeth Jelin calls the "labors of memory" that are necessary in the process (5).

Every first-person narrative of torture in the film generates a reflection on memory and trauma and their ongoing relation to identity. Yet, an ex-political prisoner named Gabriela tells the only account that details the experience of rape. Her narrative is unique for its blunt illustration of the process through which women's bodies in detainment systematically became sites of sexual assault and control. Foucault described the body as "directly involved in a political field; power relations have an immediate hold upon it; they invest it, mark it, train it, torture it, force it to carry out tasks, to perform ceremonies, to emit signs" (*Discipline and Punish* 25). Gabriela's narrative illustrates Foucault's claim but also his argument that "power is not exercised simply as an obligation or prohibition on those who 'do not have it'; it invests them, is transmitted by and through them; it exerts pressure upon them, just as they themselves, in their struggle against it, resist the grip it has on them," (27). Gabriela states: "When one has received electric shock for a long, long time, you're left unable to move. As if your arms and legs don't work. It's as if you're a rag. It must also be the terror you feel […] so, this guy, not to get information from me, but a case of pure rape […] he started to rape me, and then I had the strength to say I am a political prisoner. I am not for you to abuse" (*The Pinochet Case*).

Gabriela's testimony urges viewers to consider the blurred boundary between institutionalized state control and individual acts of violence. It elucidates the gendered nature of torture and its foundation in larger systems of patriarchal power that equate the sexual domination of women with normative masculinity. This description also brings new depth to Elaine Scarry's claim in *The Body in Pain* that torture strips the victim of language and agency. This survivor's narrative appears both straightforward and fragmentary, denouncing and disseminating the story of state-sponsored violence while struggling to convey the humiliation and psychological damage of the experience. As Jean Franco observes, rape "performs expulsion from the human by first reducing subjects to a state of abjection when the 'I' no longer is sovereign" (77–8).

This testimony, however, also emphasizes a refusal of the military's demand to become a transformed Foucauldian "docile body." It bespeaks Foucault's claim that "power is exercised rather than possessed; it is not the 'privilege,' acquired or preserved, of the dominant class, but the overall effect of its strategic positions" (*Discipline and Punish* 26). The testimony shows that in all power relations there is some possibility of resistance, and it invites viewers to seek out those moments where agency can be encountered. Yet it also warns against an individualized interpretation of survivors' suffering and responsibility. Gabriela foregrounds the first-person plural *we* and states that rape "was part of something else, of the notion that we weren't people" (*The Pinochet Case*). This story thus requires viewers to consider the gendered dimensions of political terror within the historical context of neoliberal capitalism that was upheld by a discourse of patriarchal nationalism. The film goes beyond a critique of individualized private acts of sexualized torture and towards a broader analysis of an ideology and its accompanying network of military and civilian structures that have warranted the assertion of male authority over female dissidents.

Gabriela breaks down precisely when she turns to the ongoing justification by the perpetrators and bystanders of the torture and execution of the opposition in defence of capitalist ideals. This scene underscores the long-term effects of trauma and disrupts any simplistic discourse of reconciliation and closure. It also raises questions about the lasting misogynist and classist ideologies that have informed the present-day rationalization of torture by Pinochet's supporters. For the regime's champions, capitalist modernization warranted the violent assertion of patriarchal authority. Guzmán cuts from the interview to an image of a shower in the former clandestine torture centre called Casa de José Domingo Cañas. Through this rhetorical device Guzmán visually communicates the conditions of dehumanization and challenges viewers to wrestle with the intersecting histories of political persecution, sexual violation, and misogyny. The dilapidated shower also records the passage of time, the lingering vestiges of torture, and the layers of traumatic memory. The shower image finally cuts back to the interview with Gabriela, who concludes her testimony with a recognition of the indelible scars of personal and collective repression, and a critique of the discourse of national consensus that requires reconciliation without redress.

Rather than merely framing Gabriela as a victim, Guzmán presents her, and she presents herself, as an active subject in the process of reclaiming agency. The medium close-up shot and the straight-on angle strategically place the subject at eye level with the viewer. Guzmán's camera angles, combined with the intercutting of shots at torture sites, depict the obstinate memory of violence but also the resilience and courage with which such traumas are faced. Gabriela lucidly explains that the lasting affliction is exacerbated by civilians who uphold the ideals of the military regime. Her final statement leaves viewers thinking about the ability to live with the past while maintaining a principled refusal to simply reconcile without widespread recognition of wrongdoing.

Gabriela's final statement is cleverly connected to the next close-up of a cloudy glass window shot through with a bullet hole. The broken glass evokes irreparable destruction; it also brings to mind the image of an eye within a surveillance society. Considered alongside the interview, however, it communicates what bell hooks called the *oppositional gaze*, which looks back. Guzmán creates a moment of rupture, wherein "the power of the dominated to assert agency by claiming and cultivating awareness politicizes looking relations" (hooks 308). The film-maker reclaims the degrading image of the peeping hole to combine it with an oppositional discourse and, in doing so, works alongside survivors to restore agency. This allusive image also evokes an aperture that is at once fragmentary and limited. Read within the context of the entire interview, this shot can be regarded as the film-maker's attempt to position the spectator not as a voyeur of a sexualized object but rather as an interpreter of a political subject whose traumatic memories of gendered violence are fractured and only partially representational. Guzmán offers a model of how to draw attention to the sexualized dimensions of torture without fetishizing rape or capitalizing on victimhood.[3]

Gabriela transmits a narrative of resistance that encourages the public to consider the moral authority of the opposition and the latter's

---

3 Here I take a cue from Elissa Helms, who asks in her book *Innocence and Victimhood*: "How to honor the undeniable suffering of war victims and condemn brutal violence without fetishizing victimhood? How to point to the intensely gendered nature of war suffering without fetishizing sexualized violence and rape?" (6).

ongoing quest to subvert the military regime's mechanisms of control that persist in unequal power relations and cultural norms even after the dictatorship. In her words, if all the perpetrators are not brought to trial, collective memory will serve as "a historical trial of those responsible. Not just Pinochet, but all of the torturers, as well as the civilians who supported them and continue to defend them today" (*The Pinochet Case*). The camera zooms in on her hands, held together against her chest. The searing image of her clenched fists alongside the final long shot of the group of witnesses who are looking straight at the camera becomes a visual metaphor that asserts the cornerstone belief in the strength of survivors to create counter-narratives in the interest of transfiguring society and unmaking military culture.

Guzmán's film also moves beyond the representation of heterosexual women as the sole victims of male domination. It features an on-screen testimony that exemplifies how militarized masculinity has shaped acts of torture meted out not only on women but also on men. In doing so, it effectively breaks away from what the editors of the book *Gender-Based Violence in Latin American and Iberian Cinemas* call the heteronormative framework that informs canonical modes of representation according to which heterosexual women are placed as the usual victims who are devoid of agency before a male aggressor (Gámez Fuentes et al. 1–6). To frame my discussion I would like to emphasize the general lack of research related to the gendered torture of men. In the essay "Wartime Rape and Its Shunned Victims" Oliviera Simic reminds us that research on sexualized violence in war and genocide has focused on women "while male experiences of sexual assault have, for the most part, been ignored and silenced" (238). According to Adam Jones, male-on-male sexual violence in wartime is human rights' last taboo: "The notion that men and boys are also gendered beings with specifically gendered vulnerabilities has barely begun to be articulated" ("Masculinities and Vulnerabilities" 63). To address such invisibility, Simic argues for increased attention to sexual violence against men and boys and the ways in which it has been used for strategic purposes during armed conflict (240–1).

In the case of Chile, like many other countries, women's experiences of sexualized torture have frequently been suppressed due to rape stigma. However, men's experiences of sexual abuse are arguably invisible. The male survivor's trauma is compounded by shame entrenched in homophobia and the assumption that the *feminization* of men constitutes the ultimate form of humiliation. The limited number of recorded men's testimonies of sexual humiliation requires our attention and our careful recognition of the complexity that shapes them. By listening to men's testimonies of torture, we might not only acknowledge the mere existence of various forms of gendered abuse on men but also interpret the misogynist and homophobic notions in their development.

The Pinochet Case features a former political prisoner named Santiago. He was detained and interrogated in Villa Grimaldi, the concentration camp situated on the outskirts of Santiago de Chile. The parallel between the survivor's name and the name of the capital is striking. Santiago's body, like the city, became the grounds upon which the military exerted its control. His first-person account suggests that the bodies of male detainees were conquered like a territory and exploited by militarized men who sought to prove their masculinity to other men. Torture targeting men's sexual organs constituted an affirming practice of heightened hegemonic, heteronormative masculinity. The goal of such sexualized torture and gendered mutilation was not only to produce extreme pain but also to traumatize and shame the victims by causing damage to their reproductive organs and undermining their identities as men. The perpetrators' use of such tactics therefore points to an acknowledgment of their victims' manliness and their goal to undermine it.

Santiago narrates the process through which militarized masculinity was taught. The executioners placed an electrical current on his genitals and practised karate on his spine. With this gendered gesture the militarized male aimed to attack and deconstruct his adversary's sense of self and masculinity. Santiago reveals key forms of sexualized assault, including the mutilation of genitals, but he also alerts us to his own silences: "That was more or less life in Villa Grimaldi and what I went through, what I had to live, or at least that is what I remember now." The film-maker combines this interview with visual rhetorical strategies to provoke thought on the sexualized violence perpetrated against men. Santiago's interview is intercut with shots of a shower, which is a recurrent image that must be understood in relation to the other contexts in which it appears. This very image followed Gabriela's testimony of rape. Here the image reappears and colours the following clip of Santiago, notably looking down. His silent downward gaze prompts viewers to consider the gendered experience of male victims.

Adeptly conceptualized and edited, this sequence creates a tension between what is voiced and what remains unspoken. Santiago's gaze records the many strata of repression – the pain and humiliation of gendered torture committed by state agents, and the silence surrounding it. Simic argues that in patriarchal culture an "unwillingness to recognize male survivors as victims of sexual torture means there are no ongoing and long-term programs or assistance for this category of victim" (239). Such a lack of recognition is part of a larger narrative that reduces men exclusively to the role of perpetrator and conversely relegates women to the role of sexual victim. By featuring the testimony of Santiago, Guzmán pushes against this hegemonic narrative and calls into question the overlooked legacy of trauma in relation to male survivors of torture.

If we consider the testimonies of Gabriela and Santiago together, we find certain parallels. The rape of women in the context of political interrogation is part of a continuum within patriarchal culture that normalizes sexualized aggression and social policing. The control over women is viewed as a true demonstration of masculinity. The assault of men in detainment, and the fixation on their reproductive and sexual anatomy, is also part of a continuum. It seeks to emasculate men who are opposed to militarized authoritarianism. In accord with hegemonic gender norms, to feminize is to humiliate, subordinate, and defeat. In considering these stories together, it is also instructive to read the details of the survivors' testimonies and their filmic framing as they reveal acts of resistance. In one sequence Santiago is sitting by a window, reading. Using a shallow depth of field, Guzmán features Santiago's figure from the chest to head. Viewers enter his world with measured distance as the camera pans right over metal bars that evoke the prison setting within an apparently domestic space. His half-lit face bespeaks a split, or the coexistence of past and present. Viewers witness the ongoing effects of traumatic memory as well as the power of narrative to transform experiences of suffering into experiences of survival.

The interview closes with a full shot of Santiago looking out from an illuminated balcony, which then cuts to a point-of-view shot of Santiago's belongings: a book, glasses, a magnifying glass, and a photo-booth picture of a younger Santiago smiling with a child. Viewers see these symbols of identity from his point of view, as if we are looking over his shoulder. The final image features Santiago's small bed with a large poster of Salvador Allende towering above it, symbolizing an unbroken belief in non-violent resistance. These symbols contrast with the image of the militarized male. Guzmán's low-angle shot elongates Allende's figure, intensifying the effect. If violence is part and parcel of a collective militarized identity, then non-violent resistance affirms an anti-militaristic collective selfhood. This critically conscious scene is a disruptive act that brings complexity to our understanding of gender and violence. Joshua Goldstein argues that men learn as children to cultivate aggressive behaviour, that misogyny is normalized in that process, and that war is the pinnacle of that socialization. Yet, as Jean Franco brings out, "All men do not participate in atrocities and torture, and all women are not innocent spectators" (94). Guzmán's portrait of Santiago illustrates Franco's first point regarding the complexity of men's experiences.

Patricio Guzmán Then and Now: *My Imaginary Country*

Twenty years after the making of *The Pinochet Case*, the Chilean protest movement known as the *estallido social* emerged and prompted renewed calls for deeper forms of equality. It also intensified tensions between the armed forces and the civilian population. On 18 October 2019 Piñera announced a fifteen-day state of emergency, which permitted the military, alongside the carabineros (Chile's militarized police), to gain control over the protesters. As a response Chileans filled the streets in Santiago, demanding Piñera's resignation. With the official sanction of subjugation, soldiers were unrestrained and subsequently captured on camera as severely injuring demonstrators en masse for the first time since the return to democracy. The excessive use of force, involving the mutilation of eyes with plastic bullets, was widely documented. For some groups, that brutality only increased calls for dramatic social change.

In his most recent documentary, *My Imaginary Country*, Guzmán captures this moment of political protest while exploring female leadership in its unfolding. Through archival footage the film goes back in time to illustrate the revolutionary fervour of the Allende years and the ferocity of the military backlash. Guzmán links the past to the post-dictatorial present by cleverly juxtaposing archival images with present-day scenes of women paramedics, first responders, and activists. In this way the film isolates glimmers of hope that alternative systems are possible, systems built not on hierarchy and competition but on mutual caring and concern.

The first interview centres on a woman wearing protective protest gear: a gas mask, ski goggles, and a black hoodie with bright yellow-and-fuchsia-coloured cloth roses stitched on it. She later removes the goggles to show her bright green eyes that look into the camera. As with Gabriela in *The Pinochet Case*, her oppositional gaze disrupts looking relations and projects agency. The flowers say something about her identity, which Guzmán notices and incorporates in his interview questions. She explains that they match her tattoos, which represent her process of blossoming through the uprising. Partly protection, partly symbolic, this quasi-uniform takes the place of military-style camouflage. Rather than protest with a particular political party, she identifies with a larger collective that is working to influence social structures through non-violent resistance.

The feminist collective LasTesis is also captured at the front lines, playing a powerful role in the resistance to militaristic violence. The title of the collective's performance, *Un violador en tu camino* (A rapist in your path) subverts the Chilean national police force's slogan *Un amigo en tu camino* (A friend in your path). Performed in a public space the piece consists of a choreographed dance accompanied by song lyrics that are vocalized in unison by women wearing black blindfolds. Videos of the performance went viral, inspiring feminists around the world to come together and denounce publicly rape culture, victim blaming, and the complicity of patriarchal institutions.

> The patriarchy is a judge,
> that judges us for being born,
> and our punishment is the violence you don't see.
> [*repeat*]
> It's femicide.
> Impunity for my killer.
> It's disappearances.
> It's rape.
> And it wasn't my fault,
> Not where I was nor how I was dressed.

The feminist collective addresses the intersections of social constructs of gender, class, race, and sexuality. They offer a multidimensional perspective in which gender is key but not the only component of a critical inquiry into militarized oppression. From an intersectional perspective disseminated through texts, performances and visual arts, LasTesis critiques how men have exercised power over women *and* how domination rises from neoliberal capitalism. In *Quemar el miedo* (*Set Fear on Fire*), a written manifesto that came out in 2021 at around the same time as the film did, the collective makes clear that both economic and gender constructs demand revision. The collective shares with Judith Butler an emphasis on how bodies display and perform genders and sexualities and how they can resist the driving power of oppressive patriarchal norms (*Gender Trouble*). LasTesis, as Guzmán's film demonstrates, represents a micro-turned-macro community of support in which resistance to militarized masculinity can find expression in the still patriarchal but shifting current moment.

By focusing on the experiences and perspectives of women, *My Imaginary Country* challenges the traditional portrayal of political movements as driven by men. The film gives a platform to a diverse group of Chilean women who gather in solidarity to share their stories of suffering in the post-dictatorship and their roles in resisting militarized masculinity. Beyond LasTesis, Guzmán features figures like Valentina Miranda, a student activist, and Elisa Loncón, a Mapuche scholar who became president of the body tasked with rewriting Chile's constitution. He combines the voices of anti-Pinochet women who resisted militaristic forms of government and culture in the 1970s and 1980s with the voices of a new generation of female leaders who are redefining what it means to have power. Spotlighting multiple generations of progressive women fighting for deeper forms of equality and justice offers viewers insight into the gendered dynamics of militarization in 1970s Chile and also provides a historical through line to the present.

Militarized Civilians in *I Love Pinochet* by Marcela Said

I Love Pinochet is the first in a thought-provoking series of films that delve into the culture of Pinochetism. It was followed by *Opus Dei: A Silent Crusade*, a documentary that probes the links between religion, authoritarianism, and neoliberal capitalism. More on that documentary is found in the conclusion. In *El mocito* Said explores the question of complicity through the story of Jorgelino Vergara, a man who worked as a young boy in a torture centre during the military regime. More recently, Said produced a feature fiction film titled *Los perros*, which digs deeply both into the recent history of the perpetration of state violence and also into civilian complicity. Although Said's recent films have attained international exposure, *I Love Pinochet* was a small-budget film that failed to reach any mainstream circuit. As Michael Lazzara observes, while Chilean documentary film about memory has captured the experience of the victims of human rights violations, Said has boldly dedicated her films to the examination of Pinochetism in all of its complexity. Lazzara notes that the originality of her themes and the tension and creativity of her sequences, in addition to the ethical-political dilemmas that she puts forth, make her films invaluable in the canon of Chilean memory ("Radiografía" 249).

I Love Pinochet shows how the language of militarized masculinity has propagated gendered hierarchies that have subjected women and men to torture and have served to justify dictatorial violence in the aftermath. It also illustrates how military discourse has projected the regime's leader, General Augusto Pinochet, as the epitome of patriarchal masculinity. On-screen conversations among the pro-Pinochet population suggest a continuum, rather than a break, of misogynist and militaristic ideologies in the post-dictatorial present. By listening to the voices of the regime's supporters, we gain analytical tools to cut through any naive notion or disingenuous claim that torture is an anomaly, an aberration perpetrated by rogues outside the system. We might see torture as both gendered and generated by patriarchal authoritarian culture.

The promotional artwork of *I Love Pinochet* notably features a bird's-eye view of a figurine of Pinochet that is casting a long, dark, phallic-shaped shadow in the background, visually suggesting the unabated spectre of the military regime. The film is set immediately after the negotiations undertaken by the administration of Eduardo Frei Ruiz-Tagle had allowed Pinochet to return to Chile in 2000 and thus escape international justice. In the first voice-over the film-maker states: "In my country a high percentage of citizens support the former general despite being aware of the abuse and violation of human rights. Who are the Pinochet supporters and what do they think? Many of them still control important aspects of national public opinion" (*I Love Pinochet*). This voice-over positions the film-maker as a critical investigator, rather than an apologist for the regime.

The opening sequence powerfully displays the discourse of militarized masculinity that naturalizes the use of force as the only response to political division. It is set in a country club where Pinochet supporters celebrate the former general's release and return from Britain after he had spent a year and a half under house arrest (1998–2000). The militaristic vocabulary that celebrates the nation and the patriarch is explicit. Women raise their champagne glasses to toast "Mission accomplished!" Another woman, alongside her adult son, shouts, "The homeland is whole again because our grandfather is back!" This language offers a concrete example of the internalization of militaristic and patriarchal ideology. It is precisely this discourse that framed the military coup as an act of liberation driven and secured by the military leadership.

This scene illustrates Enloe's observation that militarized masculinity requires both men's and women's acceptance, but it privileges masculinity (*Maneuvers* 4). This is one of many segments in the documentary that challenge the notion of militarism and war as exclusively male arenas. One scene in particular shows women as "complicit in the construction of gendered war identities" (Goldstein 48). Whereas Gabriela's testimony in *The Pinochet Case* describes the punishment faced by detained women for their having challenged male dominance, the women in *I Love Pinochet* by Said show how misogyny rewards women who reinforce the status quo. One interview with Mónica Salinas, a former Miss Chile, showcases this point. The settings in which she is filmed (a luxury SUV and a gated residence) evince her upper-class status, while the photographs she flaunts spotlight her close rapport with the ex-dictator. The film-maker zooms in on a particularly relevant photograph of the former Miss Chile dressed in a Chilean flag of Lycra fabric with the general by her side. The large white star of the national flag fits tightly over her breast; the feminine body and the nation become one. The film-maker effectively projects an image of a woman protecting the culture of militarism and defending state violence as a means to an end. From this perspective, opponents of the regime were internal enemies outside the boundaries of state protection and thus vulnerable and deserving of interrogation, punishment, and extermination (Franco 99).

Combined with another scene, the image of militarized civilian womanhood gains depth. The subsequent sequence takes place within a gated community where women supporters of Pinochet express a celebratory rhetoric of dominant masculinity. Patriarchal assumptions about male superiority are evident in their statements, vehemently expressed by one woman who insists: "One has to be ruled with a firm hand […] This country worked perfectly when we had the general on top of us." The thinly veiled sexual imagery cannot be dismissed. Again, the feminine body and the nation become one. They are both sexualized and dependent on the male body, which is seen as naturally assertive and superior. Societal fervour surrounding male aggression depends on the devaluation of women and the categorization of their bodies as sites of conquest. The epitome of the masculine leader is the nation's preordained authoritarian patriarch, Augusto Pinochet. The feminine becomes synonymous with the nation that must be ruled by force.

The internalization of such norms has become so entrenched that Chilean women have mobilized against their own reproductive rights, which continue to be highly restricted in the country today. The state-ments transmitted in this scene also substantiate Enloe's aforemen-tioned argument that the more that militarization transforms society, the more that society sees militaristic imperatives as necessary (*Maneuvers* 3). In an emphatic defence of the regime one woman insists, "Chileans function under pressure," while another states, "Maybe there was some excess, but most of them [those persecuted] were not innocent doves and they know perfectly well why they died and how they died." This scene draws our attention to the intersection of gender and class as we witness how socially constructed views of masculinity and the patriarchal nation have fuelled the validation of neoliberal-capitalist authoritarianism and its bloody defence.

This film is instructive not for an explicit examination of gender and violence but rather for its representation of the construction of a national identity that enabled the silencing, sexualized torture, and disappear-ance of the opposition. In the aforementioned scene the term *excess* is used as a euphemism for the abhorrent human rights abuses that were already well known at the time of filming. In the same breath Said's subject unabashedly states that the regime's opponents got what they deserved. Instead of reinforcing the otherness of violence, this film asks viewers to consider the discourses and institutions in which violence emerges, by showing its quotidian nature and how it is cultivated by both men and women (Wunker 62). Torture is not only gendered but also shaped by a patriarchal culture that praises male domination and permits militarized methods of social control.

The director strategically shows that not all the regime's supporters live in gated communities. By filming her passage through the wealth gap that divides one side of Santiago from the other, Said brings out the similarities in pro-Pinochet testimonials while showing the drastically different socio-economic conditions of the interviewees. This move effectively raises questions about what unites them. In one scene, shot in the low light of a humble home, Israel Arcos, the father of the family, states: "Pinochet's revolution, the military government's revolution, triumphed and in only seventeen years. And that is what hurts Communism. Like Father Hasbún said: Parasites. Parasites don't think on their own. Father Hasbún said 'parasite,' Admiral Merino [spokesperson for the military] said 'humanoid.' That is what they are. They are traitors to the fatherland" (*I Love Pinochet*).

The glorification of patriarchal authoritarianism and the dehumanization of dissenting voices are expressed through the language of two key institutions: the Church and the armed forces. Although the Catholic Church had a fragmented base – with a progressive wing that created the Committee for Peace and the Vicaría de la Solidaridad to defend human rights, and an ultra-conservative faction in Opus Dei – the public discourse of Catholicism was manipulated by the military state. As one film segment shows, human rights abuses were normalized through religious and nationalist discourse. The priest Raúl Hasbún, who had been the unwavering mouthpiece of the conservative vein of the Catholic Church in Chile, and Admiral Merino, a spokesperson for the military, both used a lexicon that explicitly justified the use of violence as a method of control.

By intercutting archival footage, Said shows the immense role of the media and the Church in the normalization of these intersecting discourses, which are at the same time gendered. Chilean television continuously portrayed Pinochet as a father figure and a national saviour. Significantly, television programs like the one starring Raúl Hasbún continued after the dictatorship. The massively popular newspaper *El Mercurio* also continues to be the voice of the conservative right and a well-known apologist of the regime's human rights violations, a point that the film-maker highlights through on-site interviews with the newspaper's leading figures. In its attention to the bonds between the military, the media, and the state, as well as their use of a Catholic discourse to mask state terror, the film counters dominant narratives that conveniently frame violence as incomprehensible and entirely disconnected from societal norms.

Media plays a key role in the perpetuation of militaristic ideologies, but what enshrines the inseparable relationship between the armed forces and the state is the constitution of 1980, which allows the declaration of a state of exception and the transfer of authority to the military. The continuity between the dictatorship and the post-dictatorship is exemplified in the interview with Cristián Labbé, the military government's last secretary general. As the voice-over narration indicates, Labbé was a colonel in the armed forces for over thirty years. During the regime he played a role in the DINA, which was responsible for massive human rights violations. He later became the mayor of Providencia, Santiago, one of the country's wealthiest communities. In 2003, two years after *I Love Pinochet* had been produced, Labbé was investigated for his involvement in Tejas Verdes, a clandestine detention and torture centre. From 2014 to 2018 he was arrested on several occasions until he was finally prosecuted in October 2018. Despite those legal actions he has managed to avoid imprisonment by paying bail. In the following statement, filmed in 2001 when he was still in power, Labbé makes evident the relationship between the military, Church, and state:

> Societies are made up of institutions that change over time. They appear, grow, develop, and die. But two institutions are permanent: the Church and the armed forces. The armed forces in Chile have walked hand in hand with the country throughout its history. In Chile people are proud of them, and nothing and no one will stain the honour and respect that Chileans feel for their armed forces. At the same time, the armed forces are committed to an institutional order, a juridical order, a social order, and an economic order. The merit of these four functions stepped in to save a people that were drowning. (*I Love Pinochet*)

With this interview, shot in the mayor's office, the film-maker foregrounds the adherence to male power and the view of the military as permanent and vital to the health of the nation. As Joane Nagel writes, "terms like honour, patriotism, cowardice, bravery and duty are hard to distinguish as either nationalistic or masculinist, since they seem so thoroughly tied both to the nation and to manliness" (119). Militarism and nationalism are not one, but not entirely two either.

Given the close association between masculinity, militarism, and nationalism – and the dominance of men who have upheld these associations through violent repression and institutional control – it is not surprising that Labbé has transitioned from the armed forces to the intelligence agency and finally to the political sphere in the post-dictatorship. Said prompts us to ask crucial questions about the transition to democracy and the issue of redress in the wake of state violence. How can meaningful societal transformation take shape alongside the unwavering attachment to the belief in military solutions to conflict and the wide range of patriarchal norms that support them?

The director selected a pre-military institute for the penultimate scene, which is a choice that brings to mind the spectre of militarized violence. Viewers are invited into a space in which young men are taught conformity and obedience. At the front of the class is Capitan Bernardo Acuña, who lights a candle and states that it represents the presence of God among them. He then begins the lesson: "The philosopher says that the greatest expression of freedom is obedience. From that perspective no one has as much freedom as a soldier." Like the characters in Orwell's *Nineteen Eighty-Four*, he practices "doublethink" ("War is Peace," "Freedom is Slavery") to maintain contradictory beliefs (5). He continues, "Some people don't like us because they haven't realized that everything that is good was left by the military government" (*I Love Pinochet*). This discourse establishes the regime's consolidators as "saviors" and symbols of patriotism and righteousness. The persecution of political opponents is not only warranted but also framed as inevitable and even holy. Viewed as such, the documentary warns of the multiple steps that lead to mass atrocity and illuminates the centrality of intersecting masculinist institutions (the military, Church, and state) in facilitating the process.

The juxtaposition of opposing viewpoints is an important cinematic strategy that undercuts the discourse of the military regime and brings insight to the historical context. The film-maker features the historian Alfredo Jocelyn-Holt immediately after an interview with the powerful lawyer Fernando Barros, who founded the civilian movement in favour of Pinochet while the dictator was held under house arrest in London. Said spotlights the pro-Pinochet figure at his mansion where he describes the violence under Pinochet not as state terrorism but as an inescapable civil war provoked by the left. Then he offers an even more provocative statement: "Delivery pains gave rise to a new country" (*I Love Pinochet*). He equates the Chilean nation to a woman's body and her act of childbirth to the submission to military control. She is a thing to be sacrificed in the name of nationalism. In this evocative gendered euphemism Barros seeks to justify the suffering experienced by marginalized groups that were subjected to mass atrocities, including murder and rape, as part of a natural and necessary process. By intercutting Barros's interview with the more critical perspective of Jocelyn-Holt, the film-maker denaturalizes the violent discourses underpinning the human rights abuses perpetrated by the regime and defended in the post-dictatorial present. Jocelyn-Holt looks beyond the late twentieth century, arguing that the coup was part of a longer history of violence. When we analyse this filmic juxtaposition through a feminist lens, we gain insight into the inseparability of the recent past and its many roots in authoritarianism, militarism, colonization, war, and occupation of lands and peoples.

Militarized Pacts in Orozco's *Adriana's Pact*

R.W. Connell (*The Men and the Boys*) reminds us that almost all soldiers and perpetrators of violence around the globe are men. How, then, can we understand the development of women collaborators or active participants in torture? How does the process of making male and female perpetrators differ in the context of state violence, and how can documentary film shed light on such difficult questions? Let's recall the text "Gendering the Perpetrator" where Clare Bielby observes that the perpetration of violence is "a dynamic process, a form of doing (perpetrating) rather than being (the perpetrator) and a form of doing intimately bound up with many others, not least the doing of one's gender" (163). Under certain circumstances the behaviours characteristic of aggressive masculinity can be adopted by women, showcasing the fluidity of gendered expressions of dominance. Militarized masculinity, understood as a learned display of power – a set of beliefs and actions – opens the door for women to enact it. However, the film demonstrates that the forces of militarization and inequality intersected with pre-existing gender disparities, resulting in unique experiences for female perpetrators compared to their male counterparts.

The book *Luz Arce and Pinochet's Chile: Testimony in the Aftermath of State Violence* (edited by Michael Lazzara) examines the experiences of one woman who started as a leftist militant and then became a collaborator under torture. Arce was not the only woman who worked with Pinochet's secret police. Viewing her story, and its multiple interpretations, alongside other accounts like Orozco's, sheds light on the broader issue of women's roles in perpetrating violence during the Pinochet regime. Orozco's *Adriana's Pact* is by and about women. Propelled by a family question, Orozco explores the complexities of women's involvement in acts of violence. Raised entirely by two generations of strong women (grandmother, mother, aunts), the film-maker hardly includes male voices; however, the patriarchy, and the place of Orozco's aunt Adriana within it, loom large. "When I was a girl, I had a strong role model in my life: my aunt Adriana," recounts Orozco. "In 2007 she was detained, and I found out she worked as an agent in the DINA in Pinochet's secret police, which has often been compared to the Gestapo of Nazi Germany. My aunt claims to have never seen or participated in any instances of torture, but nevertheless she fled to Australia to avoid trial." In April 2010, three years after Adriana Rivas (nicknamed "Chany") had been arrested, Orozco interviewed her about her four years in the DINA (1974–8).

Orozco interweaves family video footage, photographs, and interviews of her aunt that had taken place over several years. These cinematic strategies function together to present a complex portrait of a female collaborator in the context of militarized masculinity. When Adriana reflects on her youth, viewers witness how she struggled in the 1970s to define herself and to reflect, reject, or revise prescribed notions of women's roles and rights. Moving beyond a black-and-white portrait of working-class women, the film-maker brings out issues like internalized oppression, negotiations of power, and the struggle for economic self-determination. The case of Adriana shows how some women worked within an oppressive patriarchal militarized system to carve out an identity and economic security at the expense of other women. In this way the film demystifies the false idea that women are a homogeneous group.

Her story raises questions about the ways in which women exercised their power as women in the realm of militarized men. Claiming herself to be innocent, Adriana begins by explaining that she worked for the Ministry of Defence. First, she became a secretary and translator of classified documents in English for Alejandro Burgos, who was the assistant to Manuel Contreras, the notorious Chilean army officer and head of the DINA. When the film-maker brings into focus a photograph of the young Adriana, she uses an aesthetic strategy that complicates her aunt's testimonial. Adriana is smiling alongside Contreras, which raises questions about her involvement in the collection of information, arrests, interrogations, electric shock, rape, murder, and disappearance of the bodies of the detainees. At the time of filming, these were crimes of which Contreras had already been found guilty. Adriana recalls working in "security" with Juan Morales Salgado, another DINA agent and a military colonel found guilty of human rights abuses, and affirms that those were the best years of her life. Salgado, who was also featured in Marcela Said's *El mocito*, was the director of the Lautaro Extermination Brigade, which systematically eliminated the leadership of the Communist Party in Chile and in exile.

Adriana's nostalgic reminiscence about her decision to become a functionary of the Lautaro brigade gives away her unbroken deference to those military men in power and her aspiration to be among them. It is a reverence that we also observe in Jorgelino Vergara's narrative, as I previously stated. Adriana's unreflective recollections suggest that she used her femininity and sexuality in the negotiation of power, but at the same time she wanted to be one of the boys: "Since I was pretty, I had a pretty body, I was friendly, I had good diction. That meant I had a good status. I knew how to behave, how to act, so I could go anywhere. And I would be treated like one of them" (*El pacto de Adriana*). While militarization and economic inequality contributed to the making of both male and female perpetrators in Chile, the film reveals that with each of these contexts women were already marginalized, holding less power in relation to men. To recognize this is not to offer an apology for female violence workers but rather to gain a better understanding of how militarism, with its dominant narratives of gender, becomes instrumental in the making of perpetrators. Orozco positions herself, and the viewer, as an interrogator of such intersecting ideologies, probing how patriarchal militarism has been embraced by both soldiers and civilians, men and women.

Orozco also uses silence to undercut the pro-Pinochet narrative. For example, she lets silences hang after statements, thereby allowing the audience to fill the void with their own suspicions. In one salient scene she observes in silence a forty-year commemoration of the military coup outside the Caupolicán Theatre in Santiago, where she is captured on camera wearing an expression of dismay on her face. The militant defence of the regime involves many vociferous men and women. One holds a sign with a photograph of Pinochet and the words "Good Father, Good Grandfather." Inside they raise their arms in a fascist salute as they shout: "General Francisco Franco. ¡Presente! General Augusto Pinochet. ¡Presente! ¡Arriba España! ¡Viva Chile! ¡Viva la América española!" As Orozco leaves the theatre, they chant: "Comunistas, maricones, les mataron a sus parientes por huevones" (Communists, faggots, they killed your relatives for being losers). This sequence exposes a gendered discourse of militarism that defends state violence and invites viewers to share in the film-maker's critical reflection through silence.

Similar to the other documentaries in this study, the film unpacks the historical context through voice-over narration and by intercutting pro-Pinochet voices with detractors. Orozco interviews leading Chilean journalist Javier Rebolledo, who broke the story on Jorgelino Vergara "El mocito." Vergara also makes an appearance in Orozco's film and claims that Adriana proved her equal capacity for violence and loyalty to the militarized men above her. According to his testimony, she would beat the detainees and apply electrical shocks during interrogations, all actions that Adriana vehemently denies. Viewers are left thinking about the values associated with men such as the aggressive drive for domination, and how this female figure fit into that equation. The film therefore prompts reflection on women's roles in state violence and the imbalance of power in the making of female violence workers, which occurred under the watchful eye of militarized men. The transformational effects of fear, militaristic language, and a system of rewards and punishments are all gendered and constitute cornerstones in the creation of perpetrators and, more broadly, controlled members of a hierarchical, patriarchal military state.

The film, which follows the case until around 2017, has an open-ended conclusion. In that year the attorney general in Australia agreed to the extradition of Adriana Rivas. In November 2021 Rivas lost her second extradition appeal in Australia and will be forced to return to Chile. As I write in 2024, the case is still unresolved, Adriana remains in Australia, and the film-maker is no longer in contact with her aunt. Making the film became a sacrifice that ended in a broken relationship; however, it also resulted in a well-constructed and valuable exploration of militarized masculinity's effects on women and how they contribute to the making of female perpetrators.

Chile, Twenty Years Later

Since the documentaries in this chapter were produced, militarized masculinity has been challenged by multiple groups. In an interview conducted by Lazzara a decade after *I Love Pinochet* was made, Said observed that although Pinochet still had a following and many former agents continued to hold positions of power, post-dictatorial memory production had played a role in cultural transformation. Young people, in particular, are far more open to dialogue and less likely to support Pinochet (Lazzara, "Radiografía" 251). In light of developments since the release of *I Love Pinochet* and *The Pinochet Case*, it is worth pointing out that Guzmán's cinematic choices for the final sequences anticipated the then-galvanizing grassroots movements that would continue to build over the following two decades. Strategically situated in the conclusion of the film, Guzmán's penultimate interview with a woman named Nelly conveys a discourse of transgenerational reclamation of an identity in opposition to the military regime. As she explains earlier in the film, her partner was "disappeared" in 1974 while other family members were detained and tortured. When confronted with the arrogance of the military, she finds solace in a vision of the future in which she and her children, unlike the children of perpetrators, will be proud of their past. Viewed twenty years later, her comment stands out for its foresight.

Despite these examples it would be naive to assume that intergenerational conflict is entirely the norm. In a 2018 article Passmore drew attention to groups that have emerged in defence of the perpetrators and that have tried to appropriate the language of human rights. A milestone, he indicated, came in 2006 when convicted officers began serving prison sentences. "From that moment on, the narrative of the military family became a narrative of martyrdom." A vocal figure in the debate has been José Antonio Kast, the ultra-conservative politician. In his bid for the presidency in 2021 he claimed that he would consider pardoning inmates of Punta Peuco Prison, the special facility built for those convicted of human rights abuses under the regime, insisting that he would protect the fundamental human rights of current and former members of the military. As many critics have suggested, this narrative has established a facile moral equivalence between perpetrators and victims.

In closing, a brief, final example will further illuminate these conflicting intergenerational political perspectives. Lorena Manríquez, in her 2014 documentary *La odisea de Ulises*, delves into these political divides by documenting her personal journey to reconcile the contrasting views of her retired military father and her exiled uncle. This personal exploration becomes a powerful microcosm, revealing the nation's broader struggle to bridge ideological gaps. Ultimately her efforts to resolve the family's rift fail as her father reinforces Pinochet's war narrative. He emphasizes the violence of the years prior to the coup and recycles the regime's lexicon of military patriotism. These films show a gamut of reactions including apathy, disenchantment, regret, shame, and willed ignorance, which are some of the topics that I will discuss in the following chapter.

Examining the reactions together, we find striking patterns that allow us to trace the role of ingrained militaristic and misogynist ideologies in the defence of torture in the aftermath. We are occasioned to confront the extensive social and political sources of torture. The culture of militarism, social policing, and rape precedes, foments, and rationalizes dictatorial violence. In that form of culture, adherence to the militarized patriarchal figure has played a crucial role in the construction of systematic gendered torture of oppositional women and men. Such adherence serves to secure and legitimize the hegemony of historically dominant groups.

Ultimately an analysis of these documentaries catalyses a necessary debate about the often-ignored gendered causes and consequences of torture and mass atrocity crimes, and contributes to the ongoing process of redress and societal transformation. In innovative ways Guzmán,

Said, and Orozco intervene in the struggle against violence by unmasking the ideology of subjugation that informs militarized masculinity and underpins authoritarian regimes. They pose a challenge to the militaristic and misogynist logic of genocidal practices by making that logic visible and denaturalizing it.

8 Unmasking Civilian Complicity in Chilean and Spanish Film

Complicity can be described as the participation with others in an unlawful act or in the encouragement or enabling of perpetrators of criminal activity. What it means exactly to *participate* in, *encourage*, or *facilitate* an unethical or unlawful act is open to debate. In Chile the concept of complicity in dictatorial violence has become increasingly clear over the past decade with the publication or release of historical studies, novels, biographies, and documentary films. The theoretical groundwork for understanding bystander complicity and memory was laid by influential writers including Diamela Eltit and Nelly Richard, and developed by scholars such as Michael Lazzara, Ana Ros, Valentina Ripa, Fernando Canet, and Antonio Traverso. In *Civil Obedience: Complicity and Complacency in Chile since Pinochet*, Lazzara sheds light on the role of civilians in the military coup and the subsequent creation of a neoliberal militarized state. He points out that the torture, deportations, and disappearances of tens of thousands of people in Chile under Pinochet were not carried out by the military alone. Lazzara positions individuals' complicity on a spectrum, arguing that while some Chileans vocally championed the regime and even willingly participated in human rights violations, others conformed silently. This spectrum "now ceases to include only those who bore some direct or active relationship to the machinery of state terror and comes to include all those who tacitly supported the regime and its violent uprooting of Allende's Socialist project – perhaps by turning a blind eye to the violence either out of fear or because of the benefits to be gained from doing so, or both" (14).

In Spain twentieth-century historiography is, Paul Preston observes, "overwhelming, and perhaps inevitably, obsessed with the examination of the causes, course and consequences of the Civil War" (*Politics of Revenge* xiii). But, he notes, "most of those who have written about, or have been sympathetic to, the Left have little or nothing to say about the right" (xiii). Since the publication of Preston's *The Politics of Revenge* (1990), critical perspectives of the ideologies and practices of the right have emerged in greater numbers. The bibliography is now extensive; some salient examples include authors Julián Casanova, Mary Nash, Ángela Cenarro, and Michael Richards. Even so, the theorization of complicity has not received as much attention, and there has been even less on the relationship between gender and complicity.

In the article "Singling Out Victims" Peter Anderson explores the role of denunciation and collusion in driving the post–civil war judicial repression in Spain between 1939 and 1945. Like Preston, Anderson argues that in recent years historians have advanced our understanding of the Franco regime's killing and incarceration of political opponents long after the formal end of the war, but he insists that the role of mass complicity behind the violence remains to be explored. With a focus on the widespread practice of denunciation, Anderson looks at how community members often conspired with government officials and the civil guard to round up and punish their shared enemies.

This chapter explores how complicity is another point of comparison between the Franco and Pinochet regimes. Neither regime simply imposed itself without receiving significant support from below. Some critics who have written about complicity, including Lazzara and Diamela Eltit, have advocated for post-dictatorial measures that go beyond truth telling to include "the mitigation of neoliberal structures and the search for ways to combat racism, sexual discrimination, gender bias, and profound socioeconomic inequities" (Lazzara, *Civil Obedience* 97). The possibilities of addressing complicity and reshaping exclusionary social structures in the post-dictatorial present will remain distant if the construction of militarized masculinity is not given sustained attention. Fear, revenge, and economic gain certainly figured prominently in decisions to support the authoritarian regimes of Franco and Pinochet publicly or privately. Nevertheless, the links between the views of sexuality and those of masculinity that enabled the collusion of civilians and military authorities must be addressed. Complicity must be understood in light of the widespread support of patriarchal power and militaristic culture. It is too often overlooked that authoritarianism is gendered, with gendered origins and consequences. If we acknowledge the gendered nature of military dictatorships, we must also point out the gendered dimensions of complicity.

To listen and think anew about militaristic culture and complicity, I return to the Chilean film-maker Marcela Said and compare her work to Agustí Villaronga's *Black Bread*. Both film-makers stand apart from their peers for situating their camera as much on the direct victims of the regime's brutality as on the regime's supporters. While this is arguably more the case in Said's films, Villaronga also highlights the wider structures of violence, misogyny, and anti-gay hate that pervade the right and the left. Both directors also focus our attention on hegemonic masculinities and femininities, never isolating one from the other. They dramatize their interplay in the larger construction of inequality and violence.

Said's fiction film *The Dogs* and Villaronga's *Black Bread* confront the topic of civilian complicity in the crimes of the Pinochet and Franco regimes and also explore the features and effects of violent masculinity. In *The Dogs* one character in the film puts it bluntly in saying that Chile's real problem is that the country "is full of passive accomplices." The comment seems to reference the then outgoing president Sebastián Piñera's 2013 remarks about "passive accomplices" (Passmore, *Wars* 11). The right-wing politician acknowledged that the support for the yes campaign to continue the Pinochet dictatorship was an error and that many turned a blind eye to human rights violations. The 2013 statement sparked debate, but it seems that factional politics and competition within the right had a greater influence on Piñera's statement than on a commitment to address bystander behaviour in relation to past atrocities. Later Piñera was re-elected for a second term, from 2018 to 2021. In Said's film the theme of complicity is made explicit, but the complexity with which she treats it in relation to societal views of gender makes the film compelling.

Both *The Dogs* and *Black Bread* are feature-length dramas that unmask the normalization of the violent masculinity undergirding human rights abuses. Said and Villaronga unearth the ways in which patriarchy constitutes the bedrock of brutality. In so doing, they mount a meaningful challenge to the regimes' logic, albeit without any alternative. In addition to problematizing the narrative that violence was an aberration (merely an "excess"), they explore the profound tensions that such violence produces not only for the regimes' opponents but also for its followers. Thought-provoking and unsettling, *The Dogs* and *Black Bread* boldly expose the emergence of torture from widespread and ingrained gendered ideologies. They also raise questions about the links with the domination of women, children, animals, and the environment, as well as the role of violent masculinity in these intersecting forms of domination.

Gendered Complicity in *The Dogs*

The plot of *The Dogs* revolves around the world of Mariana, an upper-class, forty-two-year-old woman whose family benefited from the economic, political, and social injustices brutally upheld by the Pinochet regime. Mariana wilfully turns a blind eye to the human rights violations perpetrated by the military junta under which she was raised and from which her family profited. She lives a life of privilege, but, while her class status affords her a certain level of power, her gender plays a role in her subordinate position both within and beyond the home. She is confined and bored in a passive role as wife and daughter, called upon only to sign unexplained business documents. She is expected to obediently follow without question the duties prescribed to her. Her husband, a businessman, shares her father's belief that a woman's role should be limited to the domestic sphere, servicing her husband and children. His primary interaction with her centres on the topic of in vitro fertilization, which constitutes a process that she unenthusiastically undergoes.

Her servility is internalized, but she understands that her conventional role is entirely unfulfilling. The dramatic tension arises after she begins an extramarital sexual relationship with her riding instructor, Juan, who she discovers is an unapologetic former secret agent under investigation for Pinochet-era human rights violations. This key fictional character is interpreted by Alfredo Castro and is based on the real Juan Morales Salgado, an ex-operative of the DINA. The ethical issues of the plot pivot upon the way in which the film-maker represents Mariana's struggle to understand the agent's crimes and to negotiate her own complicity within the post-dictatorial context of ongoing foundational inequalities.

By creating a plot around perpetrators, collaborators, and bystanders, the director emphasizes that the military coup constituted a civilian-supported backlash to the reforming projects of the Popular Unity government (1970–3). Through the fictionalization of Morales Salgado, she also raises awareness about one of the regime's strategic agents. The tale of the way in which Said learned of his story is not a mere anecdote; it is crucial to the conceptualization of *The Dogs*. Said originally contacted the real Morales Salgado for her documentary *El mocito* (*The Young Butler*), another cinematic exploration of the theme of complicity. As previously mentioned, the focus in that film is the life story of Jorgelino Vergara, an orphan boy who became the young butler to the regime's secret agents and later became a hired operative and an accomplice to torture and murder. To corroborate Vergara's account, Said requested an interview with Morales Salgado, which he originally refused. As a strategy, she became his riding student and effectively secured the interview. As the director revealed in an interview, *The Dogs* had its genesis in that experience and the uncomfortable conversations around it. She recalled the hypocrisy of acquaintances who responded with shock at her decision to take classes from an ex-DINA agent. Their blindness to their own complicity in the regime's work to protect the economic elites was just as significant as her interactions with Morales Salgado in the conception of *The Dogs*.[1]

At the time of filming *The Young Butler* Morales Salgado was under investigation for his role in the kidnapping, torture, and execution of political prisoners. The investigation revealed that, as the director of the Lautaro Extermination Brigade (organized by Manuel Contreras and based at the clandestine quarters of Calle Simón Bolívar), he had worked to eliminate systematically the leadership of the Communist Party, as well as key political dissidents in exile. The brigade operated with a cohort of more than seventy members, of which its operatives carried out the collection of information, arrests, interrogations, electric shock, rape, murder, and the disappearance of the bodies of the detainees. Importantly, the members of the brigade came from the four branches of the armed forces and also depended on civilian agents like Mariana Callejas and Michael Townley, who attended the Simón Bolívar barracks to experiment with toxic gas on the detainees.

Placing the investigation of torture at the centre of *The Dogs* and telling the story from the post-dictatorial present is a strategic cinematic move. Rather than setting the film in the past, and by extension placing the regime's human rights violations at a comfortable distance, the director situates the plot in 2010, just prior to the film's making (2014–18). In so doing, Said underscores a continuum of violence and the imperfect process of transitional justice that is bound up with the unequal power structures and belief systems that sustain them. The film-maker grapples with stories of the complicit and contradictory figures of the economic elite who populated the lavish hierarchical world that Salgado protected through torture and extermination. As the fictional character in the film implies, Salgado's power remained intact long after the dictatorship had ended, and in 1991, with the rank of colonel, he served in the army's personnel directorate.[2] Investigations into his actions began in 2001 and culminated in 2010 when he was finally sentenced to fifteen years in prison by Chile's supreme court. Along with eight other

---

1 See the *Los perros* interview with Marcela Said, https://www.youtube.com/watch?v =7H-lbDAUwJ8.

2 See reports on Memoria Viva, an archive of human rights abuses committed during the dictatorship: https://www.memoriaviva.com/criminales/criminales_m/morales _salgado.htm.

military officers and civilian agents he was found guilty for his role in the assassination of Sofía Cuthbert and Carlos Pratts, the commander-in-chief who defended Salvador Allende.

Unlike the real case that concluded with a prison sentence, in *The Dogs* the ex-DINA agent writes a letter implicating the civilians in the story and then commits suicide only after reaffirming his identity as a stoic military man: "I know no fear," he tells Mariana. When he says goodbye, he salutes her in military fashion. Viewers never know exactly what the letter contains, but it is clear that the information incriminates her father and his business partners. She grapples with the question of responsibility and suffers from a lack of clarity, yet in the final sequence she decides to remain silent. She resumes fertility treatments and her routine life of complacency. Sitting near a bonfire, she burns the letter in a symbolic act of self-deception. The film culminates with a dystopian panorama of the Pinochet aftermath. In a potent final shot Mariana comes to find her Dalmatian, murdered in the forest near her estate. The young dog, like a previous one that had also been shot by neighbours, was a symbol of both loyalty and defiance, a duality that reflected Mariana's own divided self. She had insisted on leaving the dogs unchained even after her neighbours had threatened to kill them for trespassing. The grotesque image of the dead dog implies the eventual subjugation of women and animals and a warning against rebellion. Likewise, the image frames the protagonist's silent acquiescence to masculinist domination as a source of death and decay. The film offers no defence against violence, only a dark image of its grave consequences.

Whereas the trial of the real Morales Salgado ended in a conviction, the film points to unresolved conflicts and unacknowledged complicities. The figure of Mariana and her family present viewers with the persistent consent of civilian accomplices who defended the regime's violent actions. The figure of the colonel underscores a belief system that not only permitted the military's unbridled use of force but also celebrated it as heroic patriotism. The film thus challenges the attempt by the regime's supporters and the Chilean army to distance themselves from all those involved in the case. As Lazzara points out, the armed forces' repudiation of the case was a move that "reflected the army's by then well-established 'modernizing' politics, which sought to whitewash its public image and delink it from past human rights abuses" (*Civil Obedience* 104). Released in 2018, but set around 2010, the film-maker captures the unfolding of this process and prompts us to consider how acquiescence is gendered.

Through a cast of complicit characters the film renders visible Lazreg's contention that torture is "a political practice that unfolds in a social *situation* from which it is inseparable" (*Torture and the Twilight* 7; italics in the original). By exploring the story of state violence from the perspective of a civilian upper-class woman, the film allows us to consider how the social situation in which torture emerged in Chile was characterized by unequal power relations between men and women of different classes and races. The portrait of Mariana and the story that she confronts reveal that torture was never merely about gaining intelligence but about the maintenance of class privilege and the enforcement of military authority. The narrative opens a window to imagine the extent to which the armed forces shored up patriarchal power and buttressed the dominance of economic elites.

While the consequences of the military coup had an impact on all women, such effects cannot be described in the singular because class, race, and sexuality played a role in the gain or loss of power. With Mariana's story of complicity, the film-maker shines a light on the workings of women's marginalization and privilege while illustrating how these cannot be isolated from the social situation in which torture was perpetrated and justified in militarized Chile. As a wealthy, white, heterosexual, conservative, cisgender woman, Mariana stands at the intersection of identity positions of power (class, race, sexuality) and marginalization (gender) within patriarchal neoliberalism. The film-maker brings us into Mariana's world where she defends her class privilege while posing a twofold challenge to the gendered political order. She questions the regime's history of torture and simultaneously pushes against the misogynistic control that pervades her own reality and keeps her in a subordinate position in relation to men. Viewers might imagine some transformation, but Said ultimately conveys dark pessimism. The protagonist protects her economic status and acquiesces to male dominance, a reality to which she apparently cannot visualize a corrective.

Marcela Said's Taxonomy of Male Types

The Dogs portrays the various intersecting hegemonic masculinities that R.W. Connell describes in detail. These include "the masculinity of the business executives who operate in global markets, and the political executives and military leaderships who constantly deal with them" ("Masculinities" 37). *The Dogs* makes visible the way in which power dwells primarily within male-dominated institutions that function in a mutually beneficial relationship. In Chile male entrepreneurs required the backing of military leaders to uphold by force their unregulated moneymaking world. Meanwhile the military leaders used the profitable resources of the economic elites to carry out the militarization of society that remunerated the armed forces with power, not only to control bodies but also with a narrative that framed colonels and generals as national saviours.

The complicit figure that subtly monopolizes the most prominent position of power in the film is a business entrepreneur and patriarch. He is Mariana's father, and he dominates power hierarchies both inside and outside the home. With his soft guise he illustrates Connell's contention that "the relationship of masculinity to violence is more complex than appears at first sight […] some patterns of masculinity are not personally violent, but their ascendancy creates conditions for violence" ("Masculinities" 39). As the owner of a massive forestry company, he is part of a powerful industrialist elite that has accumulated wealth through the exploitation of land and labour, a process facilitated by deregulation and the repression of the opposition. As ecofeminist theorists would contend, this is an example of the links between the domination of nature and the domination of marginalized groups, including women. Said's attention to the association between corporate extractivism and patriarchal social and state forms is also evident in her film *El verano de los peces voladores*.

In *The Dogs* the patriarch's reverence for the military regime is explicit, while his business and personal entanglements with it are implicit. In one scene he receives from a friend the gift of an inactive land mine from Kabul for his collection of weapons that is displayed in a glass case in the background. When he sets the gift on his desk near a black-and-white portrait of himself shaking hands with Pinochet, we grasp the film-maker's larger message. Later he is publicly accused of collaboration, and his assets become the object of scrutiny. When Mariana confronts him, he acknowledges his contribution of transport trucks to the regime that served to transfer political prisoners, yet he suggests that he was simply following orders.

The film thus points to the normalization of military culture and shows the way in which the deference to the armed forces has served to justify human rights abuses while protecting the economic elites. Mariana's attempt to address such violence is met with hostility and intimidation by her father's male colleagues and lawyers who populate the masculinized culture of his organization. Such brazen hostility is intended to redirect any deviation from the patriarchal ideology that governs the social and class relations in this microcosm of Chile. The misogynist aggression serves a twofold purpose: keeping the leading female figure in a subordinate role and silencing her questions regarding the regime's crimes and her family's involvement. Ultimately Mariana's failure to confront the past and her role in covering for her father brings us back into conversation with the reckoning predicted at the end of *The Pinochet Case* by Patricio Guzmán.

If these figures symbolize active complicity, then Mariana's husband, Pedro, embodies the image of hypocrisy. His behaviours reveal ideological conformity even as his statements suggest an attempt to create distance from the military regime. In an indirect way he claims to have moral standards or beliefs above those of the ex-DINA agent under investigation; his actions reveal otherwise. His relationship with his father-in-law is entirely deferential, even when he becomes aware of the patriarch's collaboration with the regime's death squads. As an Argentinean business type, he performs a transnational neoliberal masculinity, which contrasts to a degree with militarized masculinity but depends on it to safeguard class privilege. While he is not soldier-like, and even disparages the military men in his own family, his vested interest in maintaining the status quo has clear class and gendered dimensions. As he practises martial arts in one scene, he reprimands Mariana for not informing him of her whereabouts. As a contemplative camera captures him wielding a Japanese sword, a symbol of manly self-expression, viewers are prompted to think about the multiple forms of masculinity and violence, from the subtle to the blatant. He upholds notions of aggressive masculinity even as a non-military man. Through this character the film-maker denaturalizes understated forms of gender-norm-enforcement strategies that determine unequal power relations inside the home and beyond.

In tracing the relationship between neoliberal corporate masculinity, complicit femininity, and militarized masculinity, it is necessary to examine the portrayal of the former colonel and his entanglements with Mariana and her family. He is a complex character who mostly expresses no regrets and makes no attempt to recognize wrongdoing. In several scenes he rationalizes his involvement in the repression of political opponents as duty to the nation. That unwavering narrative, however, becomes more nuanced towards the end of the film when he states plainly: "I wish I had been someone else. I'm not a good person" (*The Dogs*). The comment, muttered under the influence of alcohol, is not a public recognition of wrongdoing, because it is spoken privately to Mariana. Although it is a far cry from an apology, it projects a sense of torment and a degree of shame. The unexpected disclosure does not excuse Juan's past or erase his attempts to vindicate it, but it brings some depth to the character's inner world and the complex and uneven process of reckoning. It is also revealing that while the colonel is forced to face a court of law, the complicity of the upper-class business executives who profited from the bloodletting remains unexamined.

If we look at the behaviours and discourse of this character, we gain insight into the features of militarized masculinity and the ways in which it is perceived by civilians in the post-dictatorship era. Our perspective of the power dynamic between Mariana and the colonel is coloured by the scene in which they meet. As Mariana mounts the horse for her first riding lesson, the colonel grabs her thighs and compares them to the muscular legs of the horse. A close-up then captures his hand as he puts it on her lower abdomen and instructs her to breath calmly. It is a gesture that bespeaks male entitlement. Like the horse, her body is not entirely her own, but she submits fawningly to his act of dominance. In this and subsequent scenes his military stoicism captures her interest and gains her respect. Even when he strikes her thigh with a leather horsewhip for her incorrect mounting of the horse, she accepts the aggression without protest. It is a brief but crucial act that reveals the colonel's capacity for violence. It also shows the civilian woman's acceptance of it.

The power play between the militarized man and the civilian woman becomes nuanced as she initiates a sexual relationship with him. The film thereby complicates any view of women as mere victims. Her character shows the profound tensions between the inertia to conform to and the desire to challenge the patriarchal paradigm that devalues women's subjectivity. In the end, however, she relinquishes her agency as she accepts the male authority personified by her father, her husband, and the colonel. In a revealing scene Juan lashes a horse repeatedly and forcefully after the animal throws two of his students. When Mariana calls the act into question, he explains that he was not hitting the horse but *educating* her. The comment speaks volumes to the political and social creed guiding his decisions and offers another example of how domination over women, animals, and the environment are connected. It harkens back to the regime's lexicon that framed a range of abuses as forms of re-education. The colonel then goes on to say that "some horses like to test their riders" (*The Dogs*). There is a thinly veiled measure of ideological influence behind the comment. The rebellious horse (like Mariana) must be dominated into submission by the male rider. These remarks may appear only vaguely hostile and threatening, yet they reflect a whole belief system that is held not only by the militarized figure but also by the civilian men in the film. The scene effectively prompts viewers to consider the regime's human rights violations within a post-dictatorial, militarized patriarchy. Morales Salgado is both the product and the producer of a militaristic discourse, which shapes knowledge, meaning, and power.

Taken together, these scenes raise important questions about a broader ideology of subjugation, which holds that society requires the assertion of hypermasculine power to maintain the gender order, as well as the racial and class hierarchies. The film does not merely provide an outlet for militaristic rationale or a sentimental humanizing portrait of the perpetrators. Viewers observe numerous masculinities and a complexity of interests with a shared goal of maintaining the gender and class order through language, intimidation, and force. The anxiety that emerges from such ideologies is also central to the film and is conveyed not only through Mariana's performance but also through the musical score. The audio-visual system suggests that her unease surges not from a sudden loss of a fulfilling life but rather from the recognition of manifold injustices and complicities that have both shaped her life of privilege and maintained her subordination.

Rape and Continuum of Violence

In "Territory, Sovereignty, and Crimes of the Second State," an essay in the book *Terrorizing Women: Feminicide in the Americas*, Rita Segato theorizes rape not as a moment but as a language. In a heteropatriarchal system, dominance over women and non-hegemonic men is seen as a true sign of masculinity that is communicated through the language of rape and other forms of violence: "He competes with his peers, showing that because of his aggressiveness and power of death, he deserves to be part of the virile brotherhood and even to acquire a distinguished position in a fraternity that recognizes only a hierarchical language and a pyramidal organization" (Segato, "Territory" 76). The male aggressor controls the female body by force in the domestic space to affirm existing domination. In a public space the act aims to prove dominance and exhibit territorial control. As Segato holds, it is all a performance of power.

The Dogs renders visible the performance of patriarchal power in a jarring representation of rape perpetrated by a criminal investigator who paradoxically purports to defend transitional justice and human rights. Given that the film is set in 2010, he is in fact a police investigator working under the government of Michele Bachelet, who was in the final year of her first presidential term. What is striking is that this character is portrayed not as someone against the authoritarian, patriarchal model but as one firmly within it, thereby challenging neat ideological divisions. With this character the film-maker points to the intersections between masculinities in the military and police forces and to a continuum of violence spanning the dictatorial past and persisting in the post-dictatorial present.

This particularly disturbing feature of the film takes place in a bar where Mariana meets with the investigator to discuss Juan's confidential case. Her inquiries about the former colonel at once irritate the investigator and rouse his curiosity about the pair's relationship. The tenor of the meeting intensifies when the investigator tells Mariana that her father collaborated with the regime: "Men like your father paid the colonel to do their dirty work" (*The Dogs*). Dodging the implications of the comment, she takes the reins of the conversation, trying to subvert the power dynamic. To justify her class privilege and to undermine his moral and male authority, she calls him a *resentido social* (ingrate), a well-known insult with clear class connotations. As if to call out his contradictions, she poses questions with gendered implications: "Did you have a nanny as a child? "Who does things for you at home?" Mariana's remarks signal a defence of the power that her economic class affords her, as well as an understanding of the gendered limitations of that power. As she underscores the entitlement that men sense in relation to women, the investigator grows more irritated and attempts to deny his male privilege.

This key dialogue sequence precedes the most violent scene in the entire film and therefore must be understood within the context of this dialogue about gender roles. After Mariana becomes visibly intoxicated, she exits the bar with the investigator. In the low light of the parking lot he forces himself on her from behind in a demonstration of masculine power. Then he rapes her. Pressed up against her vehicle, Mariana's limp body once again becomes a sexualized object at the service of men. The implications of this act are significant. While the police investigator stands in opposition to the colonel's perpetration of violence, his assertion of aggressive masculinity reveals what they share. His behaviour is at odds with the discourse of human rights that he ostensibly defends. The film thus brings out profound incongruities, shaped by unequal power relations, which inhibit the potential for societal transformation in the post-dictatorship era.

The film-maker's larger denouncement of patriarchy as the bedrock of violence is at the core of what is represented by the police investigator. When male domination is not only normalized but celebrated, and sex is viewed as a source of power, then sexualized violence is not a departure from the norm but its realization. In this way the film prompts viewers to trace the links between instances of sexualized torture in the dictatorial past and rape culture in the aftermath. It is significant that after the attack Mariana retreats, taking the path of least resistance, silently moving back to her societal role in the domestic sphere. Such a move suggests that gender norms have become so entrenched that they create a situation in which bodily autonomy is not defended. Mariana's world, as represented through her relationships with her father, her husband, the colonel, and the police investigator, constitutes a microcosm of post-dictatorial Chile. Male control over women's bodies – their sexuality and their reproductive choices – goes beyond the context of the military dictatorship.

The film's representation offers insight into the broader societal norms that uphold torture and rape culture and which shift blame to the victims in the aftermath. Such gender hierarchies effectively underpinned sexualized violence during the regime. Let us recall that from the perspective of the regime's supporters, politically active women who departed from the established model of respectable Chilean womanhood relinquished societal protection. As Enloe maintains, "A woman who strayed from this model, who participated in all-women anti-Pinochet rallies, who organized soup kitchens in the urban shanty towns, thereby surrendered her protective shield of respectability. She deserved to be raped, to be treated by the government's men as a 'whore.' By choosing to discard her cloak of feminized respectability, she was asking for it" (*Maneuvers* 130). Misogynist discourses that glorified patriarchal constructions of gender and sexuality laid the foundation for the perpetration of sexualized violence within the regime's clandestine torture centres. Ximena Bunster's research demonstrates that military torturers believed "that if they could take from the woman all sense that she could control her sexuality [...] she would be reduced in her own eyes to a non-person. As a non-person, she would do as she was told" (qtd. in *Maneuvers* 130). What is striking about *The Dogs* is not any direct rendering of this process but rather the continuum of violence. Deeply rooted societal inequalities and masculinist conventions continue to shape the structures of violence perpetrated against women and, as the film suggests, not just against leftist women framed by the regime's champions as the ultimate transgressors of societal norms.

The film makes evident the pervasiveness of misogynist ideology and sexual injury even among the regime's proponents and prompts thought on how they are rooted in a long history of violence. The idea conveyed in the police-investigator plot line is illuminating, though given the entrenched nature of patriarchal ideology, it should be unsurprising that men and women across the political spectrum continue to view social and political passivity as the ideal model of respectable womanhood and view defiance of this model as punishable. As Enloe explains, the simultaneous mobilization of conservative women and the punishment of those deemed transgressive were intended to be two mutually reinforcing cogs in the same militarizing system (*Maneuvers* 131).

Since the end of the dictatorship Chile has undergone social and political change; however, as Said reveals, there are strong continuities that remain unrecognized. *The Dogs* powerfully dramatizes Cockburn and Žarkov's contention that "a failure to understand the politics of masculinity and femininity in causing and sustaining violence" makes peacekeeping efforts less effective than they could be (11). In *The Dogs* Said imagines a scenario in which those responsible for redressing violence feed the existing gender order by acting out predatory behaviours.

Masks and Dogs

One of the most haunting cinematic strategies that Said uses to mobilize new ways of seeing complicity in violence involves the image of the mask. Masks have long been used for many purposes: to instil fear, heal, disguise, tell a story, mock, mourn, remember, and communicate with spirits or drive them away. Significantly the mask comes starkly into view in the film's first sequence when Mariana, a patron of the arts, attends a photo shoot featuring masks. What we see is also manipulated by what we hear. The soundtrack of a deep and slow cello overlays the image and sets an ominous tone. The mask fills the frame in a close-up and provokes viewers to consider its design and symbolic meaning. As an anthropomorphic mask, it has human features, though they seem mutilated, scarred, and pieced together out of fragments.

Its appearance as both human and non-human is what makes it so frightening. The yellowish mask is a creative abstraction that combines materials (possibly leather, wax, or plaster) and has black markings that delineate different sections of the face, including the eye sockets, which look like dark, empty holes. It is a disturbing *false face* that evokes an identity riddled with schisms. The frame-filling mask motif becomes a tool to foreground a socially and sexually divided self, suffocating under the pressures of the mask. The protagonist experiences a crisis of identity against the backdrop of a post-dictatorial, patriarchal society that is still deeply wounded by political conflict and social injustice.

With its monstrous and broken aesthetic, the mask is suggestive of a malformed body politic in which the fundamental divisions that led to the coup, as well as the militarized culture that shaped and justified it, remain largely intact. The economic and militarized violence that fuelled the dictatorship is rendered in the film as ever present, affecting the still-fraught power relations between men and women of different classes and races. Metaphorically Mariana is a key wearer of the mask, revealing a direct association with the symbol of fracture. As she contemplates her position at the intersection of class privilege and gender marginalization, she understands the social exclusion that questioning entails. Cracking open the façade and publicly recognizing wrongdoing would mean estrangement from the economic and political establishment to which she belongs but feels no clear sense of belonging. Therein lies a dilemma that is never resolved.

The mask motif is evocative of injured and traumatized identities; it also signifies concealment and deceit. The object returns in a subsequent scene set in an art gallery where large photographs of grotesque false faces, like a human-pig face and a human-dog face, hang side by side on white walls. Masks keep identities, behaviours, and intentions cloaked and out of sight. They therefore constitute a very appropriate trope in the exploration of complicity in violence. The false face is suggestive not only of the main female character's façade but also of the guise of the male characters in the film. The police investigator postures as an upholder of justice while using his power to sexually abuse the main character. The film-maker exposes such incongruence while making its invisibility evident. The view that dominance over women constitutes a true sign of masculinity is so engrained that it simply coexists with hegemonic behaviour. When acts of violence like rape are so normalized, the aggressive command of men over women's bodies not only goes unrecognized but also becomes expected. Under these circumstances it is the woman who is framed as transgressive for even thinking about stepping out of bounds.

The mask trope combines with another haunting motif that plays an essential role in the film, which is indicated in the title. It is the symbol of the dog, which ranges in meaning from fidelity, affection, and guardianship to defiance and menace. As previously mentioned, Mariana identifies strongly with her dogs and insists on leaving them unleashed. That futile act of resistance bespeaks her own desire to live unshackled. When she goes to an art show featuring a sculptor whose work centres on the image of the dog, the film-maker heightens our awareness of the animal's significance. The exhibition includes wild dogs preserved in formaldehyde, as well as sculpted domesticated ones. The public display highlights startling deaths of animals and their attempt to escape out of enclosures. Long shots of preserved specimens behind glass and close-up shots of lifeless bodies with dead black eyes arrest our attention. Mariana's interest in the show, like her interest in masks, is twofold: fascination and also revulsion at the stories behind them. The dog trope brings up larger questions about the impact of the dominant (humans/men) on the dominated (animals/women/children).

She buys one of the sculptures for her own gallery, then takes it to the former colonel's home where they engage in sex. While she holds some agency in the act, he remains fully clothed as she lies naked, exposed, and vulnerable. Such a detail connotes an imbalance of power. Like the dog, Mariana is imagined as a subject whose existence is always reliant upon her relation to men.

The dog trope figures prominently in another artwork in the film, a large oil painting titled *Laura and the Dogs* by the Chilean painter Guillermo Lorca García (b. 1984). The highly conceptual piece appears in the story as a gift to Mariana from her husband. Said also used the painting as the poster image to promote and advertise the film. The Caravaggesque style of the painter engages an aesthetic of realism, but, like the film-maker's, his baroque approach unsettles the illusory appearance of transparency by portraying a cover-up. The subject at the centre is a beautiful young girl whose blue-hued hair alludes to defiance. She is pictured in bourgeois decadence surrounded by a pile of greyhounds, some at ease and others rummaging around her.

The dogs are depicted in the painting, as they are in the film, as domesticated and faithful on the one hand and curious, obstinate, and threatening on the other. The ambiguous expression on the girl's face, combined with the suggestive crimson drapery upon which they stand, speaks to viewers of the theme of concealment and complicity. Something hidden under the blood-red rug is just beyond sight. The greyhound in the front reveals the possibility of exposing it while the young girl stares provocatively at the viewer. When the painting is analysed in the context of the film, it is hard to ignore the association between Mariana and the young Laura portrayed on canvas. The worlds of both characters are marked by latent horror.

The strategic placement of Lorca García's painting in the film speaks evocatively to legacies of the Pinochet regime. *The Dogs* portrays the after-effects of a bloody dictatorship that integrated the enforcement of ideological conformity with a gendered discourse of "tradition." Rigid militaristic and patriarchal language defined the "natural" attributes of womanhood as those of being emotional, childlike, and weak, while the "innate" characteristics of men included rationality, stoicism, and strength. These constructions of gender roles and biological distinction moulded expectations of men and women and continue to shape present power dynamics in the post-dictatorship era. By exploring these norms and the weight they carry, the film-maker chips away at the façade of a peaceful post-Pinochet democratic moment. She unearths signs of entrenched economic and gender-based violence that bring with them multiple forms of torment and despair.

Recurrent tropes like the mask and the dog function with the script, performances, and intercutting to explore unexamined issues and taboos involving false appearances, moral ambiguity, and ideological conformity. The film inspires viewers to move beyond narrow perspectives of state violence that mistakenly shift our attention away from its extensive social sources. *The Dogs* conveys the belief that the quotidian histories within domestic spaces shed light on the way in which oppression reaches beyond authoritarian figures, pervading entire networks of cultural practices, thoughts, and institutions.

Intersecting Forms of Post-War Violence in Spain

As an adaptation of a novel by Emili Teixidor i Viladecàs (1932–2012), a Catalan writer and journalist, *Black Bread* recreates the context of the early post-war years through the perspective of a boy whose family suffers humiliation, the loss of loved ones, and acute economic deprivations that result in inhumane living conditions. The title refers to the shortage of wheat to make white bread, which was considered a delicacy. Black bread, made with rye flour, was rationed to the poor in Spain during *los años de hambre* (the hunger years). Situated during the first four years of the Franco dictatorship, the film renders visible the massive effort made by the victors to destroy not only the surviving Republican leaders but also the sympathizers and their families through soft and hard forms of repression. The regime executed around 200,000 and incarcerated more than 400,000, but the number of those suffering from hunger and disease is hard to estimate. As Gina Herrmann puts it, "even those most ideologically inclined to support the guerrilla hesitated to further imperil their own precarious situations" ("Franco in the Docket").

Black Bread reflects Cockburn and Žarkov's questioning of the notion of a post-conflict peace by emphasizing the omnipresence of militarism, homophobia, torture, and misogyny as tools of repression beyond the civil war. "A continuum of violence runs through the social sphere, and the economic and political spheres" (Cockburn and Žarkov 10). *Black Bread* is a film that stresses this continuum by probing in equal measure the human rights violations against the defeated Republicans at the hands of the military regime and the broader subjugation of women, gay men, and children over time. Villaronga also leaves us with no other option than to consider how leftist women and men not only suffered from violence but also participated in it as complicit actors or through acceptance of it as an unavoidable given.

Providing a bridge between repression and complicity in post-war Spain is, as historian Peter Anderson argues, a topic at the cutting edge of historical research about the civil war and its aftermath. Anderson probes local Francoists' accusations whereby Republican loyalists and sympathizers were selected for prosecution in military courts. He shows how insubstantial and hostile testimony formed the bedrock of investigations, secured convictions, shaped harsh sentencing, and continued to form the foundation of harassment for years after the Republicans had emerged from prison. Like Lazzara's *Civil Obedience*, Anderson's research on terror and complicity challenges the narrow view that the Franco regime imposed a police state upon a passive Spanish society.[3] Pushing further, my analysis of *Black Bread* considers the hypermasculine culture of the defeated Republicans whose livelihood was threatened by the regime's support base and whose capacity for violence contributed to a powerful repressive system in which they waged war on each other.

Many scholars have analysed *Black Bread*, but I place the film in a comparative framework with *The Dogs* to reveal how both directors complicate the simplistic victim-perpetrator binary and render visible the attitudes about gender and sexuality that enabled complicity in the violent subjugation of political and sexual "others." The Catalan film could be analysed based on the theme of socialization alongside *Space Invaders* and *Paracuellos*, but I place it here to discuss how Villaronga and Said uncover the discourses and institutions that perpetuate inequality and aggressive masculinity and how such normalization creates the circumstances for torture and sexualized violence.

Villaronga uses characterization, plot, and symbolism to illustrate that the war and the post-war period were far more complex than a battle between two perfectly split sides. There is no doubt that the Francoist victors are depicted in the film as possessors of power who brazenly use that power to uphold an economically divided heteronormative, patriarchal, authoritarian, military state. In no way is that portrayal sympathetic; however, the film refuses to depict the capacity for violence as something only possible within the limited frame of the Nationalist side. The film is a damning portrait of war and the Franco regime, but more broadly it goes to the centre of the cycle of violence. It shows how that cyclical pattern is associated with militarized masculinity, compulsory heterosexuality (to borrow Adrienne Rich's term), and the doctrine of retribution.

---

3 Ángel Alcalde also situates the topic of collaboration at the cutting edge of historical research, specifically exploring how Francoist veterans of the Spanish Civil War became either active or passive collaborators and eventually transformed into members of the fascist party. James Matthews has also contributed to the debate by examining how the Nationalist Army managed its left-wing conscripts in the Spanish Civil War (*Journal of Contemporary History*, vol. 45, no. 2, 2010, pp. 344–63).

Through a child's point of view, Villaronga builds a multilayered plot, containing unpredictable turns that break down glorified mythologies of war up until the final frame. The way in which the events unfold and are reconstructed in an unchronological order constitutes a cinematic strategy that creates a puzzling narrative that in turn reflects a confusing real dystopia. The story revolves around several crimes set in a Catalan town near Vic between 1941 and 1944. One of the central crimes is perpetrated against a gay young man named Marcel Sauri (nicknamed Pitorliua). Pitorliua was the gay lover of Pere Manubens, a man who belonged to the wealthiest and most powerful family in the area. Under Franco, that family's wealth only increased as it benefited from the economic, political, and social injustices upheld by the regime. When Mrs Manubens discovers her brother's gay relationship, she hires two men, Dionís and Farriol, to scare Pitorliua out of town. As supporters of the republic, they are at the mercy of the regime's proponents like Mrs Manubens. Living in poverty and desperate to maintain their families, they accept payment from Mrs Manubens to terrorize Pitorliua.

The two leftist men become complicit characters when they set out to scare Pitorliua and shame him for his sexuality. Out of rage or shared homophobia, the act goes further than they had planned. In a brutal torture scene the young man is dragged into a cave, tied down, and stripped naked. His genitals are attacked as the gang wraps his testicles with a pig-castrating tool. The castration cord destroys his testicles, and he bleeds to death. The episode is the most horrific among other violent scenes in *Black Bread*. The castration, however, was not carried out directly by the Francoist victors, as many viewers might expect.

That gruesome homophobic act is the fulcrum of the plot and reveals the relationship between political violence, poverty, anti-gay hate, and aggressive masculinity. The crime becomes shrouded in mystery. Pitorliua becomes a ghost-like figure that haunts the cave, according to local legend. Farriol's son, Andreu, must piece together the homophobic atrocity, which becomes increasingly harrowing for the eleven-year-old boy as he begins to understand his father's role in the violence, as well as his own homoerotic desires. He comes to understand that he is not only on the side of the defeated but also queer and poor in a world that detests both. This character gives voice to an experience of intersecting forms of marginalization that Dorothy Allison so brilliantly captures in her own story about growing up queer in poverty: "By the time I understood that I was queer, that habit of hiding was deeply set in me, so deeply that it was not a choice but an instinct" (13). Andreu comes to fear his desire for a teenage boy (nicknamed Tísic for his illness) who is confined to a tuberculosis sanatorium, where Andreu visits him. Their dreams of flying away together are thwarted by the fear of there being no escape from their dystopian reality.

Like the case of *The Dogs*, the characters that populate the protagonist's life wear masks. Farriol lives a double life: by day he speaks of the honourable social goals of the Second Republic and by night he is a hired killer. When the story emerges more clearly, Andreu has a nightmare that allows viewers to imagine the violence that transpired in the cave. The brutality reaches a fever pitch as the gang enthusiastically encourages more violence by screaming homophobic slurs. The raging men appear to revel in the absolute power over the supine, naked, and terrified young man. As the face of the victim transforms in a flash just before Andreu wakes from his nightmare, he envisions the young man whom he desires reflected in the figure of Pitorliua. The image in the nightmare reveals Andreu's fear and his subsequent motivation to hide behind his own mask and conform to the norms of dominant masculinity. Through this character the film-maker probes the conflict between the need to question the workings of power and the underlying fear of retribution, a theme that connects back to Said's *The Dogs*.

Piecing the murder together is a process that begins in around 1944, several years after Pitorliua's death. It is at this point that Dionís tries to blackmail Mrs Manubens for her schemes, which also include the attempt to steal her brother's fortune. Since Dionís has too much information, she hires Farriol to eliminate him. This is where the film begins. A hooded Farriol attacks his former friend from behind, smashes his head with a boulder, and pushes his horse-driven cart off a cliff. Andreu hears the crash and discovers the remains of the fallen cart and Dionís, along with his now-moribund son, Colet, who was riding in the coach. The young boy is still alive when Andreu arrives, but he only manages to say one word: Pitorliua. The suspense of *what will happen* and the mystery surrounding the *who* and the *why* behind the three murders is sustained by a steady stream of unsettling signs throughout the film. In the end Farriol is found guilty of the crimes, but viewers know that he was already an easy target due to his political past.

Villaronga's depiction reflects Anderson's claim that local officials and conservative civilians often "shared a deep ideological loathing for supporters of the Republic and worked easily and effectively together to pummel and destroy neighbors that they detested" (Anderson 23). What makes the conclusion to *Black Bread* so jarring, though, involves the way in which, in some instances, those who practised denunciation secured not only the execution of former Republicans but also the usurpation of their progeny. Mrs Manubens buys Farriol's complicity and silence, concealing her own role in all three murders in exchange for providing an education for his son. When Farriol is ultimately put to death, Mrs Manubens adopts Andreu. Viewers are left with a devastating shell of a boy who rejects his mother and represses his sexuality. The final images of both Andreu in *Black Bread* and Mariana in *The Dogs* contrast in some ways, but the similarities are striking to the extent that both characters bespeak an anaesthetized state, a silent acquiescence to the demands of a context that requires conformity and rewards cruel behaviour.

Black Bread requires viewers to look at the misogynistic and homophobic views of gender and sexuality that enable complicity. Like *The Dogs*, the Catalan film explores these intersections through the perspective of a son or daughter of a father who was complicit in violence; however, *Black Bread* has a logic and form all its own. Unlike *The Dogs*, *Black Bread* is told from the vantage point of the military regime's opponents. Turning a critique of the Franco dictatorship into something much larger, Villaronga dares to scrutinize not only the dehumanization of the political "other" but also the dehumanization of the sexual "other." The film shows both the political right and the political left to be guilty of homophobia, and that such gendered dehumanization disfigured the broader society, including not only the direct victims but also the perpetrators and bystanders. These characters make visible Connell's argument that while "gender dynamics are by no means the whole story," they play a crucial role in the shaping of violence ("Masculinities" 38). The characters also stage Connell's point that different masculinities exist in definite relations with each other – often relations of hierarchy and competition (35). The film-maker reveals the intersections between the heteronormative masculinity of the Republican side and the militarized masculinity of the Francoist victors.

Situating sexualized torture at the film's centre is a strategic cinematic decision in both *The Dogs* and *Black Bread*. As Marsha Kinder observes in *Blood Cinema*, film-makers like Villaronga "expose the legacy of brutality and torture that lay hidden behind the surface beauty of the Fascist and neo-Catholic aesthetics" (138). Villaronga's cinema is characterized by an interest in the experience of minors in authoritarian contexts, as well as their repressed sexuality and post-war traumas. His first full-length feature film, *Tras el cristal*, explores the torture and abuse of children by a Nazi doctor in concentration camps. One of his victims finds him years later and submits him to humiliation like what he had suffered during his childhood. In *El mar*, based on a novel by Blai Bonet, three childhood friends from Republican families are reunited as young adults in a sanatorium for tuberculosis patients during the early Franco years. Having witnessed murder and suicide during the civil war, they are not only traumatized but also unable to break the cycle of violence. The representation of cruelty is almost as immoderate as in his first film.

Villaronga creates both a world of political repression that the young protagonist must negotiate and a world of inescapable homophobia. We should recall that adult, consensual, same-sex activity was illegal until 1979. The dictatorship was responsible for arrests and imprisonment of gay men under the Ley de peligrosidad y rehabilitación social (Law on danger and social rehabilitation). Even before the Franco regime, the disciplining of sexual "others" was implemented under the Ley de vagos y maleantes (Law on vagrants and common delinquents). In *Black Bread*, telling the story from the child's point of view demonstrates that homophobia was transversal and learned. Virility, heterosexuality, and domination, these too were transversally viewed as normal male traits.

Humiliation of non-conforming men and women functioned as a norm-enforcement mechanism to protect male heterosexual privilege. That is a key piece of the story that the film-maker tells by conjuring the mind of a young queer boy from a Republican family who ends up conceding to the logic of male violence and National Catholic control. Andreu's mother, Florència, seems to be the only proponent of different forms of masculinity. Although Pitorliua was Florència's dearest childhood friend, Andreu's relatives who help raise him speak pejoratively of the gay young man's "difference." Cumulative heterosexist comments are part of the films' commentary on how even leftist families participated in the patriarchal system of subjugation. The comments also contribute to the account of boys' socialization: the way in which they react to the roles forced on them. The overwhelming weight of such comments push Andreu into a limited masculine framework. The system of gender conditioning is so ubiquitous in fear-producing stories that it barely requires violent coercion.

Villaronga explores how the dominance of one group over another is often obtained through sexual subjugation and how that process is learned. In this way he illustrates Kate Millet's idea of the sexualization of power (Millet 43). Using Andreu's point of view allows Villaronga to probe the ways in which children come to understand that rape and other forms of sexual assault are not anomalies that depart from heteronormative patriarchy but behaviours that maintain its sweeping power. The sexualization of power is transparent in the torture of Pitorliua; it is also evident in Andreu's relationships with his mother, father, cousins, and the local authorities. The leading fascist male figure is the mayor, with whom Farriol fought for Florència's love. After she marries Farriol instead and has a child with him, the Falangist mayor ends up resenting the entire family and wielding his power over them in the post-war period. The mayor sexually uses Florència in exchange for leniency towards her husband. In *The Dogs* and *Black Bread*, the potential of the leading female figures to disobey the norms that keep them in subservience to men is curtailed by fear of reprisal. They slip back into the reductive and cruel patriarchal world that prescribes feminine and masculine behaviours, upholds economic inequalities, and turns a blind eye to violence. Complicity, as these films so brilliantly illustrate, is gendered.

Andreu learns about several forms of sexual coercion of women by powerful men within heteronormative patriarchy. He observes the abuse of his mother, as well as his orphan cousin Núria, a maimed adolescent girl who lost a hand while playing with a grenade. Andreu fends off her propositions to play sex games and listens to her stories of implicit and explicit forms of violence. Some of them involve sexual relations between her and the local teacher, Mr Madern, who is at least thirty years her senior. The characterization of Núria and Florència drives the point that the consent by girls and women to subordinate status is attained by different kinds of force including conditioning, fear, and manipulation. Through the beliefs and actions of these characters, the film explores how power hierarchies are based, too, on sexuality, not only gender and class. The subjugation of women, girls, boys, and subordinate men everywhere, from the home to the school and the police station to the local and national government, is the bedrock of patriarchal society. However, Villaronga's *Black Bread*, like Lorca's *La casa de Bernarda Alba*, complicates the notion that all women are passive victims and men innate perpetrators. Mrs Manubens and the chief civil guard have the monopoly on power and must be consistently assured of their superiority over sexual and political "others."

Birds, Vulnerability, and the Manipulation of Rage

Whereas Marcela Said uses the dog as a symbol of the tension between submission or obedience and dissent or freedom, Villaronga uses the bird to convey similar conflicts. This common trope in literature and film is threaded throughout Villaronga's entire film as noted by many scholars (Enjuto Rangel, Alvarez Sancho, Dean Allbritton, Erin Hogan). When Andreu learns that his father (a bird dealer) has killed Colet, he takes an axe and destroys his father's birdcages, killing all the feathered creatures he can.[4] When Andreu must decide about his future, Mrs Manubens condescendingly praises him for not yet having his wings clipped. Tísic, the teenage boy with tuberculosis at a nearby monastery, imagines that he has wings like a bird that will set him free. The one photographic image of Pitorliua features the young man dressed as a winged angel. In these disquieting references to birds in relation to children and repression, there are allusions to Carlos Saura's 1975 classic, *Cría cuervos*, whose title cites the Spanish proverb "Raise ravens and they'll peck out your eyes."

Burying sparrows alive, comparing Andreu to a dead bird, and conveying the desire to set a bird on fire are all acts that signal Núria's obsession with the symbolic animal. She tries to convince Andreu to escape with her, and for a moment their combined rage seems to have the potential to drive change and allow them to move beyond the patriarchal norms that cage them. However, in the end Andreu's vulnerability, fear, and rage become exploited by those in power. Mrs Manubens manipulates Andreu's anger by shifting the blame for his anguish to the marginalized "others." As a result, the "uses of anger," to use Audre Lorde's term, are diminished. The film makes evident that when shame and fear fuel rage, it loses its productive potential and becomes destructive. Rage keeps Andreu captive instead of setting him free. After his father has been executed, his mother is left destitute. As mentioned earlier, Mrs Manubens adopts him by the end of the film and begins the forced erasure of his past. In denying his roots out of fear and rage, Andreu reconstructs himself in the image of those behind his pain. In this scenario the powerful manipulate the vulnerable and devour their integrity, making them collaborators in their own destruction and that of others. The film depicts a world of political repression, economic inequality, and anti-gay hate in which children learn that violence is not an anomaly but a tool.

Andreu's rage ends up reinforcing patriarchal norms when he accepts that adherence to both the fascist state and the dominant definition of ideal masculinity (heterosexual, upper-class) will provide him with the most societal benefits, like status and respect, in a world of cruel competition. The prescription of that model of masculinity leads Andreu to minimize his need for the support of others. For the protagonists in *Black Bread* and *The Dogs* there is no exit from the masculinity hierarchy, no reprieve from the social situation of gendered and sexualized

---

4 Also see Enjuto Rangel's "Spectrality in Pa negre's Queer Aesthetics and Its Politics of Memory."

violence. There is also neither a return to some better past nor the possibility of a peaceful acceptance of themselves within the patriarchy around them.

If, broadly speaking, militarization is a *process* and militarism is an *ideology* based on the core beliefs that force is the only solution to conflict and that men are naturally violent, then the protagonists in both cases find themselves trapped in a militarized culture that they must accept. That is evident in the last scene of *Black Bread*, which takes place at an elite boarding school where Andreu (now Andrés) is dressed like all the other boys. He listens to the instructor speak of Polyphemus, the Cyclops described in Homer's *Odyssey*. His expression of discomfort suggests that he sees his own reflection in the monsters, like Mariana sees herself in the deformed mask. In Andreu's final encounter with his mother, he fights back tears, following the masculine directive to be invulnerable, inexpressive, "hard," that is, non-feminine. The pain of his solitude is evident, but he seems to conclude that it is better to be angry than to address his feelings and embrace vulnerability. The difference between his ability to feel empathy for his mother and for himself at the beginning of the film and his feelings at the end is vast.

There are many reasons to look to Said's and Villaronga's films for valuable insight about the belief systems that shaped violence under Pinochet and Franco. In both cases the unsettling endings save the films from the Manichaean tone of simple heroes and villains that is evident in some narratives about these periods. However, it is also important to reflect upon what these films do *not* do. While they offer a taxonomy of male types and probe the complexity of violence, complicity, and rage, they offer no cinematic vision of a remedy to cruelty or a productive use of rage. The lack of models of resistance gives pause. What does it mean when an exploration of the gendered processes of conflict does not combine with a vision for social change? Might the absence of a meaningful challenge to militarism, misogyny, and homophobia end up signalling a form of reluctant acceptance of the authority of the arguments produced by the military regimes? If, as some feminists including Gloria Steinem have argued, hope is a form of planning, then how can we look to the future with a vision entirely lacking in hope?

The Dogs and *Black Bread* suggest that representing violent masculinity and complicity in violence is enough. The films suggest a shared familiarity with these realities, resulting in a more cynical than optimistic outlook. As Said has hinted in interviews, the world of unquestionable hierarchies and closed castes is the world in which she was raised and which she came to question. Occupying a position of privilege, she has been permitted into spaces that were prohibited to others. She has become a witness, observing the dark underbelly and concealed violence of the upper echelons of Chilean society that her peers would have wanted her to conceal. Her repudiation of the business-government alliance, and specifically the forestry companies that have usurped and exploited the land to enrich the few, is never hopeful.

Said and Villaronga depict a grim vision of an unequal and individualistic world dependent on the violent suppression of protest to exist. Said, on the one hand, not only emphasizes the futility of resistance but also offers a dismal field of characters who cannot go against the grain in a conscious or persistent way. Villaronga, on the other hand, follows Andreu as he encounters and reflects upon exclusionary paradigms, but any development of resistance is thwarted. In both cases there is no cinematic vision of an answer to the social contract that has established cruel gendered rules of behaviour.

Whereas *Black Bread* won thirteen Gaudí and nine Goya awards in Spain, critical reception of *The Dogs* was divided in Chile. Carolina Urrutia's review is particularly salient: she notices an ideological ambiguity that is difficult to decipher. To paraphrase Urrutia, what seems to be denounced in the film is never clearly articulated. It arises from the place of the camera's focal point, which is the narrative of those upholding the status quo. That is not the case in *Black Bread*. As Enjuto Rangel argues, *Black Bread* is not neutral, even-handed, or reconciliatory. In the case of *The Dogs*, Urrutia suggests that Said's point of view becomes diluted.[5] Although I agree with that assessment to a degree, I would critique Said's film for arguably becoming monotone through its lack of contrasting political perspectives. For instance, the film makes no reference to the struggles of leftist women to dismantle the regime and their perseverance in the fight for justice in the aftermath. At the same time I see the film as valuable for the way that it complicates violence and complicity by showing how they are gendered and how they are produced.

In different ways *The Dogs* and *Black Bread* allow us to understand better how the creation of the hierarchical militarized states that quelled opposition through torture emerged from societies already steeped in military culture and shaped by deeply rooted social and economic inequalities. These films also illustrate Enloe's claim that violent masculinity has as its conforming complement a passive femininity that must accept exclusion from full and assertive participation in public life

---

5 See the article "*Los perros:* Naturaleza muerta" by Carolina Urrutia, http://lafuga.cl /los-perros/919.

("Demilitarization" 23). The taxonomy of toxic male types in both films also reveals rivalries between civilian and militarized masculinities as well as their shared presumptions about gender and sexuality.

These films allow us to move beyond gender-neutral conceptualizations of violence and ask more questions about the social significance of gender socialization and militarization. As such, these depictions contribute to larger efforts to account more adequately for the factors that produce authoritarian regimes and for the repression that such regimes generate. The failure to probe these gender norms and their link to militarism and complicity not only produces short-sighted historical understanding but also perpetuates the ongoing post-dictatorial gender politics that make violence against women and non-normative men and boys an ordinary occurrence.

Conclusion: Reimagining Masculinity to Disrupt Violence

The framework of this book centres on the connection between masculinity and violent social control in twentieth-century Spain and Chile, but militarism and torture have a long history that cuts across continents and epochs. In her poem "Tortures," Polish poet Wisława Szymborska underscores the enduring nature of this atrocity, observing that the fundamental reactions to it remain constant throughout history: "The gesture of hands shielding the head is the same. The body writhes, pulls and struggles, knocked down it falls, doubles up, turns blue, swells, salivates and bleeds. Nothing has changed" (258). Torture (from Latin *tortus*, "to twist, to torment") was not only codified during the Spanish Inquisition (spanning the fifteenth and nineteenth centuries) but also normalized. The catalogue of sexualized devices in torture museums, like the one in Toledo, Spain, reveals some commonalities between the role of gendered ideologies in acts of subjugation in a distant past and their roles in the twentieth century.

As Foucault describes in "The Spectacle of the Scaffold" (in *Discipline and Punish*), torture often took place in both underground prison cells and public squares where passersby would witness attacks on the bodies of religious heretics or sexual dissidents. By the nineteenth century, however, punishment had mostly moved away from the public eye throughout Western Europe. The Museum of Torture in Toledo attempts to recreate some of those spaces from a more distant past and attests to the effort that was put into creating contraptions of grotesque sexualized cruelty as a method of punishment and political control. One such device, the Oral Pear, was used in the mouth, anus, and vagina. As the description at the museum explains, "In opening the cavity the spikes at the end would irreversibly rip the walls of the mouth, the intestines or the inside of the vagina." Another overtly sexualized torture tool was the Breast Stripper, which was "applied to women accused of witchcraft, blasphemy, adultery, provoked abortion or any other crime." The Mask of Shame also stands out for its misogynist character. The masks were designed to punish women for challenging the ruling male powers (civil or ecclesiastical). They often contained mouthpieces with nails that pierced the tongue and mutilated the palate, forcing the mouth to remain closed. The men who created the device clearly envisioned the mask's multiple functions as a tool to discipline, silence, and starve the women who were shackled by them.

These torture instruments reveal that the infliction of severe physical and psychological suffering was intentionally tied to gender identity, sexual humiliation, and the destruction of reproductive organs. The Toledo Museum of Torture is not unique; there are comparable examples in cities throughout Europe (in Siena, San Gimignano, Amsterdam, Bruges, Prague, and Zagreb, among others). These museums often share a problematic presentation of the artefacts and historical documentation to cater to the morbid curiosity of tourists. They may even be categorized as pain tourism. Indeed, the gory details run the risk of capitalizing on suffering. They also mostly place torture in a comfortably distant medieval past, thereby blocking any unsettling reflection on the widespread use of torture throughout the twentieth century and into the twenty-first. By thinking through the sexualized nature of the instruments in the exhibits in relation to the gendered violence perpetrated recently by military regimes, we might move beyond the superficial narratives typical in torture museums.

The modern delivery of pain is mechanized, but the cause and effect of the weapon are the same. As I explained earlier, Pilar Miró's *Crimen de Cuenca* dramatizes historical documentation concerning the ruthless interrogations of men falsely implicated in a criminal case that spanned 1910–25. Graphic scenes of the civil guard's brutal procedures to produce a confession, including tearing off fingernails and crushing teeth, are reminiscent of the procedures carried out in the sixteenth century. Significantly, Miró's sickening portrait was filmed on the grounds where torture had taken place for centuries. As the documentary *Regresa el Cepa* (dir. Víctor Matellano García, 2019) points out, Miró's filming location was the original spot where the Spanish civil guard had tortured León Sánchez and Gregorio Valero. It was also an interrogation site during the Inquisition. Between 1520 and 1600, Muslims and Jews were tortured within those walls with some of the same methods. The palimpsestic nature of the setting is uncanny. We are urged to consider how militarism and violence were normalized long before the Franco regime and how such roots facilitated the practice of sexualized torture as an instrument of social control during the dictatorship.

The severity and sexualized character of the civil guard's methods of interrogation in militarized Spain are also the main themes in Benito Zambrano's adaptation of the novel *La voz dormida* by Dulce Chacón, this time in the context of the post-war period. Based on accounts by former political prisoners, the film illustrates that torture functioned as a methodical means to consolidate the power of the Franco regime. Explicit interrogation scenes explore the way in which militarized men punished leftist women not only for defying class hierarchies but also for challenging patriarchy. Such punishment invariably took the form of sexualized acts of torture including stripping, groping, and electro-shock to the breasts with tools that recall the horrific Breast Stripper of the Toledo Museum of Torture. Zambrano's film offers new avenues to generate discussion not only on the gendered nature of violence but also on the organized practices of torture that were perpetrated by groups of militarized men who habitually used sexist language to goad more violence and to justify their acts.

Whereas the perpetration of torture in Spain was not officially addressed during the course of democratic transition, in Chile the Ricardo Lagos administration (2000–6) established the Comisión Nacional sobre Prisión Política y Tortura (National Commission on Political Imprisonment and Torture). Through the testimonies of victims, as well as witnesses and accomplices to violent acts who were offered incentives like immunity, the commission's report confirmed that military, police, and intelligence agents of the Pinochet regime were responsible for over 30,000 cases of torture. The testimonies of sexualized torture in Guzmán's *The Pinochet Case* illustrate how militarized masculinity became the fulcrum of armed intervention in political conflict and a key factor in the government's draconian reprisals of dissidents.

One interview, not yet mentioned, involves a survivor named Ofelia. She was detained in Villa Grimaldi (1974–7), the previously mentioned clandestine concentration camp in Santiago where approximately 4,500 prisoners were tortured. In the film a close-up of Ofelia's hand-drawn illustration of the site cuts to a long shot of the gated entrance, now gutted after a strategic cover-up between 1989 and 1990. The camera then brings to the fore the interviewee's position in relation to her adult daughter seated alongside her. Guzmán poses questions that generate reflection upon the gendered dimensions of torture and the stigmatization of rape that prohibits communication and bonding. Ofelia's daughter states that she never dared ask her mother about the torture for fear of what she might learn: "Above all the sexual aspect made me back off … I didn't want to know" (*The Pinochet Case*). The scene closes with an image of Ofelia looking down in silence, next to her daughter. Her gaze records the many shades of repression – the ongoing subjugation of histories and the humiliation of rape inflicted by the military regime and sustained in the aftermath.

In *Discipline and Punish* Foucault explains how individuals within a surveillance society internalize the codes of their own subjection and become "docile bodies" (138). Foucault links the notion of docility to "a policy of coercions that act upon the body, a calculated manipulation of its elements, its gestures, its behavior" (138). Ofelia's testimony brings out the role of sexual injury in the process of discipline and the asymmetry of gendered power relations in its development. Rape not only dehumanizes women in confinement but also degrades them in the aftermath by rape stigma that places blame on the victims (Herrmann, "They Didn't Rape Me" 77). As a method of control performed by militarized men, rape extends beyond the act itself, thereby threatening continual subjugation and heightened self-surveillance of the body.

Grasping the magnitude of how gender and power interact, and the pivotal function of rape in the imposition of patriarchal, misogynist, and militarist values, holds significant ramifications. Many critics, including Foucault, have paid scant attention to the particular means by which female "docile bodies" are created and the extent to which women come to view themselves as vulnerable to sexual danger and guilty for enabling it if they test normative behaviour (Cahill 43–63). Sandra Lee Bartky has specifically critiqued Foucault for his treatment of the body "as if it were one, as if the bodily experiences of men and women did not differ and as if men and women bore the same relationship to the characteristic institutions of modern life" (132). Ofelia's testimony exemplifies internalized beliefs about the limited capacity of the woman's body and her guilt for failing to limit her movements sufficiently. Guzmán's documentary foregrounds "the forms of subjugation that engender the feminine body" and therefore addresses the blind spots that "perpetuate the silence and powerlessness of those upon whom these disciplines have been imposed" (Bartky 132).

Under Pinochet and Franco, misogynist discourse served to sanction the dehumanization of non-Catholic, proletarian, and middle-class leftist women whose "transgressions" were framed as the source of societal decay. Some of the most radical religious defenders of the regimes came from the Opus Dei. If we fast-forward to the early 2000s when, through literature and film, Roberto Bolaño and Marcela Said confronted the Opus Dei's complicity in dictatorial violence, we find the ongoing secrecy and justifications of the Opus Dei linked to religious, military, and patriarchal discourses. The majority of the organization's members are supernumerary, married, have at least eight children, and are expected to bring the ultra-conservative teachings of the Church into the everyday world. Since the Opus Dei conceals membership statistics, the exact percentage of the population is difficult to pinpoint, but the power of its members in business, banking, politics, and private education is disproportionately high.

In *Opus Dei: A Silent Crusade*, Marcela Said explores the institution's role in shaping the economic and political agendas of the Pinochet and Franco regimes. The ideological pillars included unbending patriarchal views of men's and women's separate spheres, classist beliefs of natural hierarchies, and militarist notions of the necessity of military power to maintain order. They require obedience, discipline, and confidentiality. By filling its ranks with elite lawyers and politicians, Opus Dei controls dissent with the threat of defamation. One numerary (celibate member), Gonzalo Rojas Sánchez, uses his position of power as a historian, lawyer, and associate of the Jaime Guzmán and Pinochet Foundations to defend the legacy of the dictatorship. The conservative newspaper *El Mercurio* has given Rojas a major outlet for his brazen support of the military officials who were involved in heinous human rights violations, like Miguel Krassnoff Martchenko.

When we rewatch *Opus Dei: A Silent Crusade* in 2024, nearly two decades after its release, one interview stands out. It is with the law student and Opus Dei numerary Luis Alejandro Silva Irarrázaval (b. 1978). At the time of filming he was in his twenties. Like an automaton speaking from a script, he explains on screen his ambition to advocate for conservative social policies. Using militarized language, he emphasizes the need for a "crusade" to change the minds of Chileans who depend on the state. When asked about the institution's restrictions on literature and film, he freezes, dumbfounded, and declines to respond. Today the forty-six-year-old holds a position of power as a lawyer, university professor, and politician elected to serve as one of the 155 members of the Chilean Constitutional Convention. The Opus Dei no longer has the military regime to enforce social control through purges, executions, and widespread surveillance, but they continue to wield massive economic and political influence on social and cultural issues like abortion, divorce, and same-sex marriage. As civilians, the religious "soldiers" of the Opus Dei perform a different kind of militarized masculinity, but they function together and serve as the defenders of power, as their antecedents did during the Inquisition.

This should remind us that while secret agents and executioners carried out barbaric forms of punishment under the Pinochet and Franco regimes, they were instruments in the service of the militarized state that benefited the economic elites. Basilio Martín Patino's documentary *Queridísimos verdugos* makes this point clear. The secretly recorded film focuses on three executioners under Franco who were all versed in the use of the garrotte, an iron collar tightened from behind by a handle, both choking the prisoner and snapping their neck. Antonio López Sierra was the official killer in Madrid, while Vicente López Copete and Bernardo Sánchez Bascuñana were in charge in Barcelona, Aragón, Navarra, Sevilla, and Granada. By giving them a platform, the film does not exculpate the executioners, but it raises necessary questions about the longer chain of command and the social and military conditioning that creates official killers.

One of the executioners, López Sierra (1913–86), was a poor conscript from Extremadura who fought in Franco's army in the civil war and later with the Nazi-aligned Blue Division in the Second World War. As an unemployed war veteran, he was targeted as an ideal candidate for the job of executioner. The other two had backgrounds in the Falange and the civil guard. After his first execution in 1949, López Sierra went on to kill at least sixteen people including Salvador Puig Antich, a Catalan anarchist found guilty of murdering a civil guard. The execution took place in Barcelona's Modelo prison in March 1974 and involved the use of the garrotte vil for the last time. The film contrasts the socioeconomic situations of López Sierra, who came from abject poverty, and Sánchez Bascuñana, who had the means to pursue a different profession.

The film deserves an in-depth analysis, but a commentary by the director himself sums it up well: "After getting to know the executioners in depth, it is very difficult to tolerate the hypocrisy of a society that considers them appalling. That same society uses them as an alibi to wash their hands of their own shit. Some are forced to spend all their energy on surviving and defending themselves, becoming entirely indifferent in the process, atrophied and insensitive to the value of life. The least of it is that they submissively accept the role of executing their own brothers in misery under superior orders. Unhappy, poor executioners, dear executioners" (Martín Patino 47). The hierarchies of militarism, which target the poor and disenfranchised, not only harm the direct victims of violence but also the perpetrators. Nona Fernández's depiction in *The Twilight Zone* shares a similar critical perspective with Martín Patino's.

Recycling Militarized Violence beyond Spain and Chile

To canvass the way in which the concept of militarized masculinity serves as a tool in other contexts, we can briefly turn to several conflict sites that have experienced democratic backsliding and increased human rights violations. In the essay "El cadáver es el mensaje" (The cadaver is the message) published in *La metamorfosis del sabueso* (*The Metamorphosis of the Hound*), Salvadoran writer Horacio Castellanos Moya discusses what he sees as one of the fundamental problems of the democratic transition in El Salvador: "el reciclamiento de la violencia" (34; the recycling of violence). To elaborate, he recalls his first novel, written in 1988, called *La diáspora*. One of the characters, identified as a former sergeant of a counter-insurgency battalion, dedicates himself to crime after being demobilized at the end of the civil war. He survives on the street thanks to his ability to kill. This story urges us to consider the conversion of past political violence into present-day criminal acts.

In her rigorous study of the disarmament, demobilization, and reintegration (DDR) of former paramilitary combatants in Colombia, anthropologist Kimberly Theidon insists on the dire need of a gender perspective at each level of transition. Through extensive interviews with ex-combatants, community members, representatives of state entities, and NGOs, she builds an indisputable case for a feminist lens. Her conclusion is clear: "Successful reintegration requires not only fusing the processes and goals of DDR programs with transitional justice measures, but also that both DDR and transitional justice require a gendered analysis that includes an examination of the salient links between weapons, masculinities, and violence in specific historical contexts" (3). To achieve meaningful social reconstruction and coexistence, rather than just demobilizing combatants, post-conflict strategies and Waller's "downstream efforts" must prioritize gender-sensitive re-education. Learning new forms of communication, rethinking stereotypes, and gaining depth of self-awareness are part of the equation. Ex-combatants need a new script of possibilities that go beyond what Alyson Cole calls a "triangulated gendered logic in which two masculine types – the dominator and the savior – act upon the feminized victim" (Cole 120). What is constructed can only be transformed if it is identified and explored. Emotions, as Theidon reminds us, are "gendered, and gaining access to a wider range of emotions is also a component of demilitarizing these men" (27).

The recycling of violence that Theidon and Castellanos Moya describe is a latent theme in the Spanish film *La caza* (*The Hunt*) directed by Carlos Saura. Briefly turning back to Spain, the 1966 psychological thriller depicts the link between Spanish Civil War violence and post-war homicide. Set outside Madrid during the Franco dictatorship, the film follows three middle-aged Falangists who reunite for a rabbit-hunting trip on the former battlefield where they had once hunted Republican soldiers.

The wealthiest of the three veterans recruits his adolescent nephew, who witnesses the unravelling of the camaraderie between them as the hierarchy of power and the competition for dominance become all consuming. The themes of violent masculinity and the lingering traumatic effects of the civil war are evident, but it is also interesting to trace the trajectory of war mobilization, demobilization, and return. Just as boot camp begins with soldiers' separation from women and children, the characters experience a physical, emotional, and psychological change when they enter the hunting ground. In a step-by-step process they detach from society, feed their fascination with weapons, visualize killing through target practice, become desensitized, find pleasure in shooting animals, turn disempowerment into power lust, and finally undergo a breakdown. The film ends in a triple murder. The last scene is a wide-angle, bird's-eye view of the young man as he climbs out from the slope to escape the cult of masculinity and death.

In Saura's film, economic factors contribute to the culture of violence because the inequality among the characters drives a wedge between them. Castellanos Moya also identifies the link between violence and the enormous concentration of income and the corresponding growth of poverty due to neoliberal policies of deregulation and privatization of public services and security. Most striking, however, is his emphasis on the psychological and emotional trauma to which young men were subjected during Central American political violence and mass atrocities and the lack of policies and incentives for their reintegration into civilian society. If they are educated as ferocious war machines, he asks, how can they rejoin civilian life? No wonder that the ranks of organized crime are filled with ex-combatants. Castellanos Moya laments, "What I never imagined when I wrote my book was that the character's violent behavior that some readers considered exaggerated, within a few years, would be dwarfed by the grotesque levels of violence that affect several Latin American countries today" (*La metamorfosis* 35).

Other societies that have emerged from intense armed conflicts, such as Guatemala and Nicaragua, have also experienced this phenomenon. The official report of the Recovery of Historical Memory Project (REMHI) addresses the impact of militarization before, during, and after the Guatemalan genocide (1970s–1990s): "The army's strategy was to militarize the social fabric. This was accomplished through widespread forced recruitment and the establishment of Civilian Self-Defence Patrols and military commissioners responsible for maintaining control over the population and fighting the guerrillas [...] This strategy dragged the civilian population into the war. Militarized structures dominated the daily life of every village and neighborhood, trampling local values and culture. Civil patrols and military commissioners implicated neighbors and community leaders by making them directly responsible for numerous murders and massacres. People's lives were transformed into a battleground" (Proyecto Interdiocesano, xxxiii). Even in the absence of official military structures, militarized violence can occur where internalized militarism exists. The REMHI report also found: "From fear of aggression or death to the normalization of violence as a way of life, children were influenced by the warlike socialization patterns of life in a militarized environment" (36). Today rates of crime in Guatemala are very high, like those of its neighbours to the north (Mexico) and south (Honduras and El Salvador).

The links between militarism and extreme civilian violence are represented in Colombian, Mexican, and Brazilian literature and film. Plots often revolve around common tropes like the former combatant turned drug-trafficking gunman, the dual identity of the police officer–hitman, and the relationship between organized crime and powerful political and business groups. In his final novel, *2666*, Roberto Bolaño paints a brutal portrait of the systematic sexual assault and mutilation of hundreds of women and girls since the early 1990s in Ciudad Juárez, Mexico. The magnum opus ends Bolaño's jarring investigation of misogyny that had been initiated decades earlier in works like *Estrella distante*. That novel tells the story of a Pinochet-era hitman and intellectual who photographed the tortured and dismembered bodies of anti-fascist women.

These narratives signal a continuum of violence in which the murder of a female body is considered the ultimate form of possession, and the possession of a woman's body is viewed as the ultimate form of power. Such misogyny, combined with the concealed complicity of wealthy landowners, corrupt politicians, and former Franco-era policemen, is brilliantly characterized in the Spanish film *La isla mínima* directed by Alberto Rodríguez. The film takes place in 1980s rural Spain where the murder of young women constitutes both a backlash against the advancement of women's rights and a language of territorial control communicated by men to other men and women who might challenge the status quo. As synthesized in the subtitle of Rita Segato's essay "Territory, Sovereignty, and Crimes of the Second State: The Writing on the Body of Murdered Women," feminicide is a communication system. It is "a sinister war code, an argot made up entirely of 'acting out' behavior" (Segato, "Territory" 71). Segato urges us to understand the murders of women not as "crimes of passion" or social anomalies committed by deviant or mentally ill individuals. As Segato insists, reporting them as such only sends the public down the wrong path. We must look at the social construction of masculinity and femininity to decode "femicidal" crimes that are otherwise unproductively deemed enigmatic.

Any perception that the current culture of militarized masculinity plagues only Latin American nations is sorely mistaken. "The

Psychology of Putin and the Dangers of 'Militarized Masculinity'" is the title of a *USA Today* article for which I was interviewed by Alia Dastagir, along with Ruth Ben Ghiat and Jackson Katz, author of *Man Enough? Donald Trump, Hillary Clinton, and the Politics of Presidential Masculinity*. The interview took place at the outbreak of Russia's full-scale invasion of Ukraine. We concurred that ignoring Putin's performance of aggressive masculinity was dangerously short sighted.

Likewise, it is foolish to take lightly the strong presence of former combatants and paramilitaries at the insurrection of 6 January in the United States. Militarized bravado fuels right-wing militia organizations like the Proud Boys and the Oath Keepers, two prominent groups leading the attacks on the Capitol. Enrique Tarrio, the former chairman of the Proud Boys and now a convicted seditionist, emerged in the Florida Latinos for Trump movement. Although Tarrio has more of a criminal background than a military one, his appearance suggests otherwise as he dresses in camouflage, wears dark sunglasses, brandishes firearms, and wears a bulletproof vest, with a gas mask on his hip. He was sentenced to twenty-two years in prison but was later granted a presidential pardon by Donald Trump. A month after the pardon he was arrested again for assault.

Trump's re-election in November 2024 highlighted the dogged prominence of militarized masculinity in US politics and culture. Trump never served in the military, but his military academy experience was formative, and it comes across loud and clear to his supporters. Filmmaker Michael Kirk emphasized this detail in a Frontline documentary: "Trump would emerge from military school with a blueprint for leadership by force and ridicule" (Taddonio). The weaponization of masculinity was at the heart of his campaign, as evident in his constant emphasis on strength, aggression, and the willingness to engage in violence. His references to the use of the military to control the so-called internal enemy have the most dour implications.

Just as in the 1930s, the threat of political myth-making, and its militarized instigators, must be taken seriously. When conservatives in the United States nostalgically conjure the memory of Franco or when libertarians create memes of Pinochet, we cannot take them lightly. Before the 2021 Capitol riots, members of a pro-Trump student group at Portland State University held up signs of a snake offering "free helicopter rides" to leftists. The image consisted of a coiled serpent wearing Pinochet's military cap. In a similar alt-right meme, the Pinochet snake asks, "I'm evil for throwing people out of helicopters?" To which he responds, "False. Commies aren't people" (Ketcham). This pro-Trump-Pinochet meme brings together the Patriot movement's Gadsden flag featuring a coiled snake sitting on the words "Don't Tread on Me" with the libertarian "Hoppean Snake" that celebrates the German-American economist Hans-Hermann Hoppe. Whereas Michela Murgia's satirical manual *How to Be a Fascist* presents readers with an unreliable narrator to critique current populist movements, Hoppe's voice in *Democracy: The God That Failed* is dead serious. His anti-democratic opposition to universal suffrage and his comments on the expulsions of democrats and homosexuals have earned Hoppe a following of US white nationalists, neo-Nazis, and paramilitaries.

The Argentine far-right populist economist and politician, Javier Milei, has also turned to Hoppean ideology (Callison). By bringing a chainsaw as a prop to his rallies in 2023, Milei sold the neoliberal pledge to slash the welfare state, while selling himself as a hypermasculine iconoclast aligned with Brazil's Jair Bolsonaro, Spain's Santiago Abascal, and of course Donald Trump. His hyped background as a soccer player and a rock-band singer also bolstered his macho televised image. The strong voter turnout among socially frustrated male youth in the 2023 presidential elections demonstrates the effectiveness of that gendered campaign strategy. Since taking office, Milei has villainized Argentina's powerful feminist movement, minimized the effects of climate change, downplayed the atrocities of the former military regime, and discussed the pardoning of dictatorship-era military officials who are currently in jail for human rights abuses. His vice-president, Victoria Villarruel, hails from a military family and has spent part of her legal career defending such officers. The implementation of his radical economic "shock therapy" à la Pinochet has already caused collective pain and given rise to protests (Callison). Many observers, including political scientist William Callison, fear that Milei will mobilize the military to control them.

These current events sharply outline the centrality of militarized masculinity in present authoritarian groups worldwide. Using the term *militarized masculinity* helps us to de-normalize the discourse and values integral to their political agendas that aim to strip communities and environments of protection from exploitation. When we look beyond Latin America, we can map the trends in the political landscape that depend on militarized masculinity for their survival. As I write, wars are raging in Gaza and Ukraine, where the death toll will have certainly increased by the time this book is published. There have been seven military coups in African countries in the last three years: in Mali, Guinea, Sudan, Chad, Burkina Faso, Niger, and Gabon. Others have witnessed failed military putsch attempts to overthrow fragile democratic governments. Sudan tops the list for the most since 1950, and those coups have not restrained violence but rather fuelled waves of genocides, massive human rights violations, and displacement.

A pessimistic view of the military's role in political conflict argues that military action can only escalate tensions and lead to wider conflicts. If we were to take the most optimistic view of the armed forces as a possible peacekeeping institution in contexts of extreme instability, "boots on the ground" may only temporarily produce a ceasefire. In either case, they will never achieve lasting peace so long as societies do not take on the complex fractures that divide them through democratic structures and socio-economic development. Maintaining authentic peace and legality in Spain and Chile did not arise from the draconian forms of Francoist or "Pinochetist" repression, as some right-wing nostalgists might suggest. Instead, violence was sanctioned by the state. Long-term security in those countries has emerged out of the solid democratic structures that have been made to ensure the non-violent conflict resolution developed by civil society in the wake of those dictatorial regimes.

The current surge in military takeovers has been called an epidemic, but the phenomenon never arises enigmatically. These contexts are speaking to each other, and, if we listen carefully, we will understand that there is more work to be done to break down the false notion that a military response to social and political upheaval is the most effective one. That view takes shape in the book *Servants of War* by Rolf Uesseler. The German journalist brings the complexity of modern militarism to our attention by unearthing the hidden deals between American arms manufacturers, the Pentagon, and private military corporations (PMCs). The book exposes the dangerous global presence of PMCs and mercenary contractors commissioned by governments, intelligence agencies, and industries to protect their economic interests without visibly deploying their official military forces. His sober analysis of the matter gives weight to Idelber Avelar's observation that "the line that separates law enforcement from military action has become increasingly blurred, with strong states repeatedly waging acts of war in the name of law enforcement" (10). It is the "methodological waging of international aggression without the acknowledgement of such acts as war" (10). This also happens on the domestic front, where publicly funded police forces use militarized methods of control in the name of peacekeeping and fail to invest in alternatives.

Hollywood representations of militarized police or soldiers for hire, like *Rambo*, often conceal how such figures put national and international peace and stability at risk.[1] Uesseler emphasizes how PMCs operate in places where they are forbidden and avoid public scrutiny by going under the radar. The last chapter of his book focuses on violence prevention, by juxtaposing two opposing models of intervention in

---

1 *First Blood* (the original Rambo story) critiques war by portraying a troubled veteran suffering from post-traumatic stress disorder, but the later *Rambo* films glorify violence.

crisis zones: "Option one is to make peace by imposing security and stability from above, using legitimated military or police force. PMCs play a significant, indeed integral, role in this idea. Conflict resolution, long-term development, and lasting peace are secondary aims. Option two, by contrast, aims at fostering peace, building up security structures, and stabilizing societies from below" (218). Advocating for the second option, he cites the importance of civilian-led medium- and long-term measures including investments in education, health care, women's rights, and the reintegration of soldiers into society. These actions are crucial, but socio-economic development will stay patchy if we pay no attention to the ways in which gender (together with race, class, sexuality, ethnicity, and ability) affects our lives. Using the term *militarized masculinity* as a cultural construct provokes an ideological shift and generates a deeper conception of various forms of violence – past, present, and future.

Resisting Militarized Masculinity

In discussions of militarized masculinity and demilitarization in a global context, it would be remiss of me to ignore the case of Costa Rica (although an analysis of that context far exceeds the scope of this conclusion). As Enloe points out, "despite the radical demilitarization of Costa Rican society ever since the adoption of its 1948 constitution eliminated its national army, notions of masculinity are still etched sharply enough in the culture to have sustained patriarchal privileges for men and to have provoked one of Latin America's liveliest feminist movements" (*The Morning After* 53). Costa Rica experienced a period of extreme polarization in the 1930s and 1940s, followed by a civil war and later the dissolution of the armed forces. Under the leadership of José Figueres Ferrer an alternative security framework was established, involving a police force and the channelling of military funds into education, health care, and social programs, which fostered stability and reduced inequality. While demilitarization has not meant the elimination of all forms of violent masculinity or a panacea for the country's ills, it has contributed to the development of a strong democracy that is capable of averting dictatorial violence and genocide, unlike its highly militarized neighbours throughout the north and the south.

How realistic is demilitarization on a larger scale? In *Regarding the Pain of Others*, Susan Sontag asks: "Who believes today that war can be abolished? No one, not even pacifists. We hope only (so far in vain) to stop genocide and to bring to justice those who commit gross violations of the laws of war." (5). If war cannot be abolished, then demilitarization may also be a chimera. Yet Sontag's statement in no way signals indifference. She uses Virginia Woolf's *Three Guineas* as a starting point to explore how war is waged, how depictions of violence desensitize viewers, and how photography has the capacity to unsettle us and expand our empathic response. She commends the German conscientious objector Ernst Friedrich who published *War against War!*, a book of photographs featuring the hard-to-look-at mutilated faces of young men sacrificed to militarism between 1914 and 1918. In 2025, over one hundred years later, Friedrich's anti-war book along with Sontag's reflections are relevant today. She asks, How should we respond to the steady stream of information about the agonies of war, especially those of us who cannot imagine how dreadful war really is? She emphasizes this point: "Can't understand. Can't imagine. That's what every soldier, and every journalist and aid worker and independent observer who has put in time under fire, and has had the luck to elude the death that struck down others nearby, stubbornly feels. And they are right" (Sontag 126). Even so, she strives to answer the question "What does it mean to protest suffering, as distinct from acknowledging it?" (40).

Most feminists around the globe would agree on the importance of institutions dedicated to peacekeeping, protecting human rights, and serving in humanitarian or disaster relief. How those institutions have functioned and what those institutions should look like are points of disagreement. Finding common ground, we might first recognize that militaries are not monolithic. In Spain and Chile, military forces have transformed over time in many ways, a catalogue and analysis of which would also exceed the scope of this conclusion; however, of note is the change involving the inclusivity of women and the acceptance of openly non-heterosexual service members. That does not inherently mean, though, that such evolution includes a concerted effort to address the effects of militarized masculinity. Serious inquiry into the problems related to militarized masculinity is an important factor not only in adequately explaining past dictatorial atrocities but also in changing the social conditions that contribute to the continuum of violence today both within the military and beyond.

Over the last two decades in Chile, training in human rights and international humanitarian law has been part of the curricula at military academies and other institutions related to the armed forces and the Chilean national police force (*carabineros de Chile*) (Henckaerts et al.). Nevertheless, human rights training often passes over questions of gender and therefore produces uneven results. As evinced in the 2019–20 student protests against inequality, these institutions have not managed to prevent the use of brutal force as a method of social control. The disconnect between training in human rights and the ongoing knee-jerk reaction of violence has been recognized by the Instituto Nacional de Derechos Humanos. The INDH is a government human-rights body originally created under Ricardo Lagos but independently operated.

In 2018, one year before the excessive use of force by state agents during the *estallido social*, the INDH produced an executive summary that reported instances of both torture by law enforcement officers during detention of student protesters and abuse of minors under the state's care (Servicio Nacional de Menores, SENAME), including physical, mental, psychological, and sexual abuse. The report also found police abuse against Indigenous populations, torture during criminal arrests, and torture at prisons.[2] At the SENAME the degrading treatment of minors as a form of punishment has occurred despite the creation of an early-warning system of monitoring, assessment, and preparedness activities. In *Canadá 5351*, director Catalina Brügmann Urzúa shows that the same physical space, in San Joaquín, where torture was committed under Pinochet is today a SENAME centre in which human rights violations are repeated. The short film alerts us to the reality that torture is not a thing of the past.

Law enforcement authorities have also been responsible for the arbitrary arrest, verbal discrimination, and physical violence against lesbian, gay, bisexual, transgender, and intersex (LGBTI) individuals in Chile. They were reluctant to use the 2012 anti-discrimination law, including charging attackers of LGBTI victims with a hate crime, which would have elevated criminal penalties.[3] That was the backdrop of the unleashing of a whole spectrum of corporeal and psychological abuse on unarmed student protesters in 2019. In the following year the ultra-conservative politician José Antonio Kast gained support with a "firm hand" law-and-order message and won 45 per cent of the presidential vote in 2021. This suggests that while the cultural landscape in Chile is visibly in flux and human rights organizations are trying to address the excessive use of force, the model of masculinity in the armed forces under Pinochet is, at least to some degree, intact today.

In the case of Spain the link between masculinity, militarism, and violence has been undermined to a large extent since the death of Franco; however, like the case of Chile, in 2019 Amnesty International and the non-governmental organization Rights International Spain reported

---

2 See https://www.state.gov/wp-content/uploads/2019/03/CHILE-2018.pdf.

3 See https://www.state.gov/wp-content/uploads/2019/03/CHILE-2018.pdf. Here I also draw from some unpublished and personal correspondence with Leith Passmore.

cases of law enforcement's excessive use of force. The UN Subcommittee on Prevention of Torture reported that authorities in prison and detention centres frequently resorted to undue violence. The Council of Europe's Committee for the Prevention of Torture also noted that admission procedures in prisons failed to consider gender-specific needs, including detection of sexual abuse or other gender-based violence inflicted prior to admission.[4]

These recent reports in Spain and Chile illustrate Enloe's contention that "there are serious implications" for leaving "militarized dynamics unnamed and unchallenged" ("Demilitarization" 25). Enloe concurs with Cockburn and Žarkov who suggest that the "failure to understand the politics of masculinity and femininity in causing and sustaining violence" renders efforts to redress and stem violence largely ineffective (Cockburn and Žarkov 11). In the article "There Is a Crack in Everything: Problematising Masculinities, Peacebuilding and Transitional Justice,"Brandon Hamber shares similar concerns about the lack of focus on masculinity in the study of mass atrocity crimes. He explains that for societies emerging from conflict, many priorities (i.e., truth commissions, constitutional change, the implementation of justice strategies) take precedence over the analysis of violent masculinities and hidden systems of power. It is alarmingly misguided, he suggests, to treat as inessential an analysis of masculine power within and between the structures aimed at building peace (11). Steps towards the prevention of mass atrocities, as well as everyday forms of violence, must include widespread and robust educational efforts to transform fundamentally the dominant perceptions of masculinity, to rethink the role of the armed forces and national police forces, and to demilitarize notions of security.

The study of gender and torture through feminist theory, literature, and film can play a role in such educational efforts by opening a window to visualize the relationship between violence and militarized masculinity. That is not to say that we should expect gender studies to offer an antidote that will cure all forms of violence. It is important to imagine, however, some of the concrete outcomes. If human rights training prioritized the critical study of masculinity, such education could help break the cruel hazing culture in combat training that seeks to eliminate "the girl" in the soldier. Such a shift could change the tactics used to transfigure civilians into obedient killers, decrease military

---

4 See https://www.state.gov/reports/2020-country-reports-on-human-rights-practices /spain/.

brutality, and, by extension, reduce the mental trauma that many soldiers report. If the study of gender played a central role in the education of officers before they officially assumed their position at a higher rank, the management of soldiers and the planning of missions would yield different results. If college-educated commissioned officers had a solid foundation in gender studies before taking command of entire battalions of enlisted men (privates, corporals, sergeants, and sub-officers), then they could have the potential to change military culture.

Journalist Philippe Labreveux had foresight when he reported in *Le Monde* in 1974 that "the only hope of putting a halt to the all-destroying machinery of the military must lie within the military itself" (MacEóin 25). Such a reshaping would require violence-prevention strategies informed by theories of gender and sexuality. For instance, sexualized violence against a targeted group must be considered to be a tool of militarized and masculinized violence and an early warning sign of genocide. As Enloe insists in *Twelve Feminist Lessons of War*, the investigation and documentation of sexual abuse must become routine in the effort to map patterns and hold abusers and their enablers accountable (*Twelve Feminist Lessons* 93–5). In the aftermath of violence, spending must be shifted towards universal access to necessary resources, including support for traumatized survivors of genocidal and wartime rape. Likewise, militarization must be understood as both an accelerant of and a trigger for mass atrocity crimes. De-escalation and demilitarization go hand in hand. By concentrating on militarized masculinity, we are more likely to deconstruct the logic of militarization that fuels the dehumanization of the "other" and serves to justify armed domination rather than the use of political debate and non-violent intervention.

When we pay attention to gender and sexuality, we recognize the nuanced ways militarized violence affects both soldiers and civilians – including men, women, children, and non-binary individuals – differently. With feminist tools we can understand better the dynamics at play when women soldiers or perpetrators appropriate masculinist roles and force "enemy men" into feminized roles. Instead of challenging gender norms, they perpetuate the binary misogynist thinking and gender performance that subordinate women to an inferior status. Only when we break down the positive images of the warrior as the quintessential male and of war as a meaningful and effective solution to political conflict will we chip away at the global problem of violence.

It is not merely aspirational to think that an understanding of the links between patriarchal power and militarism would contribute to the curbing of the rising authoritarianism and nationalism that is stoking mass atrocity crimes around the globe. Militaristic patriarchy has and continues to form the bedrock of fascism, right-wing populism, and soviet-style communism even when women play central roles in their formation. If violent masculinity contributes to the fabrication of national myths and heroes, then feminist theory can be instrumental in their deconstruction. In their manifesto *Set Fear on Fire* the collective LasTesis teaches us that "feminism can educate and guide people, especially starting in childhood. Feminism must create tension in order to demolish violent practices inherited through institutions, social relations, and patriarchy" (16). It would be a radical change, but radical change is needed to confront democratic backsliding, economic exploitation, and territorial expansionism, which is only compounded by environmental destruction and resource scarcity.

Given the difficulty of changing deeply ingrained views of masculinity and femininity in adulthood, a broader proposal would suggest that the commitment to the critical study of gender must start earlier. Whereas officers are commonly required to have a four-year degree or equivalent and have special officer training from a military academy or officer training school, enlisted service members usually need only a high school diploma or equivalent. As Muñoz Molina describes in his memoir, *Ardor guerrero*, the drill sergeants (usually soldiers who were non-commissioned and had been recently promoted through the lowest enlisted ranks) were some of the most unsparing and competitive service members in his experience. Since enlisted service members constitute the backbone of most militaries, the critical study of gender must inform high school curricula and involve an intersectional approach that examines how masculinity interacts with race, nationality, class, ability, sexuality, and other identity positions.

The impact on enlisted soldiers, however, is not the only reason to support the critical study of militarized masculinity, and gender more broadly, in secondary education. As Hamber states, exclusively centring on soldiers as the custodians of violence risks both stereotyping them and ignoring more everyday forms of violence perpetrated by non-military men. "Violence is considerably more endemic in the society than that which is simply linked narrowly to past political conflict" (Hamber, "There Is a Crack" 19). That is why it is so important to enact widespread educational efforts to understand the larger influence of militarized masculinity in war and peace. Although this book revolves around that specific form of masculinity, it is important to reiterate the notion of a continuum in which militarized culture and the learned warrior performance interact and affect other masculinities in civilian society. Put differently, militarized masculinity is not embraced only by active-duty soldiers, and the difficult task of confronting militarized masculinity is not simply about combat. We need to focus our attention on the larger story of violence and the interactions between rape and other displays of force in extreme situations like war and genocide and in quotidian spaces.

In *The Patriarchs*, Angela Saini reminds us that "at least as long ago as antiquity, military leaders learned that one of the most effective ways to secure power over people was to use a strategy of 'divide and rule'" (203). Feminists know that. Concerted efforts to change ground-in views of masculinity have been most visible and effective in Spain and Chile through large feminist protests and performances, including the massive annual march on International Women's Day (8 March) and the previously mentioned public performance *Un violador en tu camino*. In another performance piece, called *Hoy, hundimos el miedo*, LasTesis made a clear call for collective action. If division gives patriarchy power, unity is part of the response. As members of the collective tossed the Pinochet-era constitution into a boat in the Valparaíso harbour, they shouted the following message in unison:[5]

JUNTAS, ahuyentamos el miedo [TOGETHER, we drive away fear].
JUNTAS, nos sostenemos [TOGETHER, we sustain each other].
JUNTAS, hundimos la opresión [TOGETHER, we defeat oppression].
JUNTAS, atravesaremos [TOGETHER, we will get through].

The Men's Story Project demonstrates how men (regardless of sexual orientation, gender identity, race, class, ability, etc.) must also play a role in this global public forum to reshape notions of masculinity. Founded in San Francisco by Chilean-American Jocelyn Lehrer, MSP made two documentaries in California and Chile that feature men sharing reflections on masculinity through personal stories in front of live audiences. Such actions are valuable not only for emphasizing the effects of endemic masculine violence but also for building spaces for alternative masculinities to be explored. As Hamber reminds us, transformation "requires pointing to the ruptures between masculinities as they change and emerge" ("There Is a Crack" 26).

In this moment of increased conservative backlash against progressive views of gender and sexuality, it is not a platitude to suggest that we need unsettling forms of literature and film to serve as vehicles for nuanced stories that present multiple models of masculinity. The range

---

5 Colectivo LasTesis, *Hoy, hundimos el miedo*, https://www.youtube.com/watch?v=bq8Wbxx5NHQ.

of compelling examples provided in this book accounts for not only how gendered power relations operate but also how forms of resistance to the militarized ideal either develop or die. In his memoir Antonio Muñoz Molina explains that literature became his safe haven during his basic training as a conscript. It nourished his critical consciousness, allowing him to reflect upon his own responses to male brutality. Reading and writing allowed him to gain an evaluative distance, to question binary thinking, and to remember the existence of his own agency. Such acts effectively worked against the erasure of his civilian identity. In turn, he was able to resist conformity in the military and reassess previously learned actions of obedience that "were revived by the discipline and claustrophobia of the army" (*Ardor guerrero* 93). These reflections underline the relationship between narrative, consciousness, and power and offer a model of how men might oppose the harmful myths of militarized manhood. Muñoz Molina foregrounds the disempowerment of the conscript experience, but he also evokes memories of agency and their life-giving and knowledge-producing meaning.

Listening to difficult stories of conscription and war that go beyond superficial narratives is also a way to reintegrate traumatized soldiers and victims into civilian society. Goldstein concludes that "to think into the future beyond the war system requires breaking out of psychological denial regarding the traumatic effects of war on human society" (403). The Spanish Civil War poet Miguel Hernández (1910–42) understood this when he wrote about war's assault on the senses and corruption of one's inner beauty: "A lust for murder possesses the secret places of the lily" (347). Expressions of fear, shame, regret, doubt, and despair demystify war stories of manly courage and contribute to the de-normalization of militarized masculinity. The poem "Nanas de Cebolla," written by Hernández from a Francoist prison, reveals a vulnerable father warning his young son of the human cost of war: "Lark of my house, laugh freely. I woke from childhood: don't you ever" (353). As Goldstein suggests, "Confronting war in this way may, in turn, reshape gender relationships" (403).

Literature (poetry and memoirs like these) could be leveraged along with feminist theory and collective action in the larger attempt to transform the way we see violence. Each of these three pieces matter, and they function best together. The arts, and the apparatus we use to analyse them, help us recognize and confront militarized masculinity. Without feminist tools of interpretation the insights gained from cultural production often remain underdeveloped. Equipped with those tools, we may learn something from viewing the sexualized torture devices at the Toledo Museum of Torture in Spain, rather than from distancing them or from viewing them as morbid artefacts of some backward time and place. Even when the presentation of violence is *not* for entertainment, and the critique of injustice is clear, feminist concepts help us go beyond the surface. We can identify how Carlos Giménez's graphic novels reveal the reproduction of militarized masculinity through discourses and institutions. Through the lens of engaged theory we see how Giménez complicates notions of a homogeneous or static masculine identity. Engaged theory helps us trace how authors like Nona Fernández present the various degrees to which men and women open themselves up to change and resist the pressures to conform to militarization. We can detect how film-makers and writers like Roberto Bolaño, Agustí Villaronga, Patricio Guzmán, and Marcela Said treat torture, rape, anti-gay hate, misogyny, and war as *related* problems. At a time that these problems continue to make headlines, but their core remains unseen, we must look for pathways to recognize patterns and to conceive of a continuum of violence in order to disrupt it.

As Ruth Ben-Ghiat writes, "We carry with us the stories of those who lived and died over a century of democracy's destruction and resurrection. They are precious counsel for us today" (261). The normalization of militarized masculinity is an enduring problem rooted in myths about male supremacy that *must* be remade in our attempt to learn from the past and create a different future. If war continues to be narrated through the myopic lens of heroic bravery, then militarized masculinity will continue to shape people's lives and perpetuate the notion that dominance over others is a true sign of masculinity. Until we tune into patterns of gender socialization and imagine alternative notions of bravery, our understanding of the continuum of violence will remain incomplete.

Afterword: There Is Nothing Natural about Militarized Masculinity

Ximena went shopping for Reebok shoes. Her mother and her aunt were fashionable, elderly, Chilean women. If they were going to attend anti-Pinochet rallies and be equipped to run from soldiers' tear gas, they were going to run in stylish sneakers. Ximena Bunster features in Lisa DiGiovanni's provocative exploration of militarized masculinities. Ximena was one of Chile's most prominent anthropologists, employing her feminist ethnographic methods to expose the beliefs and practices underpinning the actions of both the junta officials and their civilian supporters. Her mother, whom we fondly called the Señora, was the first woman to hold a Chilean cabinet post, serving as Minister of Education under an earlier, democratic administration. Ximena's sister, a successful fashion designer, was tortured by the junta's jailers. So too was her niece, though years later, in the post-Pinochet era, she broke her silence to reveal her horrific ordeal.

Lisa DiGiovanni shows us that it can take years to expose fully the gendered workings and the impacts of any regime fuelled by militarized masculinity. Ximena bravely wrote and published her articles while Pinochet was still in power, but many of the revealing explorations of the gendered dynamics fuelling the Chilean and Spanish autocratic regimes have been crafted, published, read, and viewed in the post-war or post-junta decades. As DiGiovanni demonstrates, a post-war period is a risky time. We should not turn our attention elsewhere when an autocratic regime falls. It is during the years following the end of a militarized autocracy that women and men develop their beliefs about what happened and why and whether it matters. It can take a generation for those who collaborated with the regime to muster the courage to examine their own complicity. During those salient post-regime years historical accounts will be circulated, and school textbooks will be adopted. During those precarious years memoirs will be drafted, novels will be crafted, and films will be produced.

Even creators of critically informed works will not agree on the whys and wherefores and the consequential "So what?" Moreover, not everyone will read or view these exploratory works. Hence, we need to remain curious. It is up to us to exercise our feminist curiosities as we continue to investigate the gender dynamics determining who will read or view any critical accounts and which lessons the readers or viewers will internalize – lessons about the rewards and the pitfalls of adopting or admiring militarized manliness.

Readers and viewers matter. The first, second, and third generations of readers and viewers matter. Young Augusto Pinochet was a post-Franco viewer of Francisco Franco's brand of masculinity, developing an admiration for that distinctively militarized mode of manliness. DiGiovanni shows us that he not only adopted it for himself but also became convinced that in militarized manliness and feminized admiration of militarized manliness lay the salvation of the entire Chilean nation. In Spain today voters for the right-wing party Vox appear nostalgic for what they imagine to be the fascist patriarchal ideal of the family. The family – or, as many social conservatives think of it, the Family – remains an object of fierce debate in societies as disparate as contemporary Italy, Turkey, Hungary, China, Poland, the United States, and India precisely because it calls into public and private question the possible relations between women and men. That is, contests over the sorts of masculinity that guarantee the security of the state are always simultaneously debates over the power dynamics within families. And who are better equipped to track the undercurrents of family life than novelists, memoirists, and film-makers?

Yet, as everyone who has ever joined a book group knows, novelists, memoirists and film-makers are not the final arbiters of their works. Readers and viewers are. DiGiovanni is calling on us here to join the conversation, not only for the sake of art but also to ensure that contests over rewarded masculinities and respectable femininities are seen for what they are: contests over the character of civic life.

Reading DiGiovanni's chapters, I was struck afresh by the power of fiction to expose how, in reality, boys and men develop their notions of what it means to be manly. Proponents of patriarchy want us – lazily – to imagine that boys and men adopt their narrow patriarchal understandings of masculinity quite "naturally." These patriarchs claim that the road to approved manliness is straight and narrow, that the rewards are obvious and forthcoming, and that the risks of deviation are clear and persuasive. Lisa DiGiovanni uses these critical, post-autocracy, Spanish and Chilean writers and film-makers to shed a bright light on a more complicated, tenuous gender reality: for most boys and men – even those growing up under autocratic regimes – the routes to their own sense of masculinity are twisting, perilous, and muddy.

Patriarchal militarizers hide the strenuous, violent decisions they take to achieve their gender objectives. If coming to embrace patriarchal masculinity were as "natural" as they contend, Franco, Pinochet, and their contemporary Syrian, Belorussian, Egyptian, Russian, Myanma, and Turkish autocratic ilk would not have to train their officials in the dark arts of torture. Moreover, if manliness were so easily militarized – that is, shaped in ways that serve the needs of the state's uniformed military and those parties and industries organized to bolster the military – surveillance and disciplinary regimens would be redundant; there would be no need for army recruiters or drill sergeants.

DiGiovanni urges us to absorb a crucial caveat: we should not slide into imagining that we can explain the militarization of masculinity anywhere in the world by paying attention only to boys and men. We need to take seriously the actions and beliefs of diverse women and girls. If sculpting boys into patriarchally militarized men were easy, patriarchal autocrats would not work so assiduously to persuade women as mothers, wives, and girlfriends that they should eschew the wide assortment of masculinities that fall outside the preferred patriarchal moulds. After all, as feminists have shown, the turning of boys into militarized men depends in significant part on keeping women in line, not because women have power but because the politics of femininities are so entwined with the politics of masculinities – in the processes of shaming, frightening, enticing, encouraging, dissuading, and nurturing.

That is, as DiGiovanni so graphically reminds us, to squeeze most boys or men into the straitjacket of militarized masculinity takes patriarchal strategizing; it takes resources, it takes attentiveness, and it takes heavy doses of brutality. No wonder the Franco and Pinochet regimes were riddled with anxiety. They knew – and today their admirers nervously are aware – that there was nothing natural about their violence-dependent, misogyny-fomenting political projects.

That is the good news.

Cynthia Enloe
January 2024

Bibliography

Abrahamyan, Milena. "Tough Obedience: How Is Militarized Masculinity Linked with Violence in the Army?" *Gender Discrimination*, 2017, http://feminism-boell.org/en/2017/02/08/.

Adams, Carol J. *The Sexual Politics of Meat: A Feminist-Vegetarian Critical Theory*. Twentieth anniversary edition, Bloomsbury Academic, 2020.

Agüero, Felipe. *Soldiers, Civilians, and Democracy: Post-Franco Spain in Comparative Perspective*. Johns Hopkins UP, 1995.

Ahmed, Sara. *The Feminist Killjoy Handbook: The Radical Potential of Getting in the Way*. 1st. ed., Seal Press, Hachette Book Group, 2023.

Alcalde, Ángel. "Francoist Veterans and the 'New State': Social Benefits and the Consolidation of the Franco Regime (Spain, 1938–1945)." *New Political Ideas in the Aftermath of the Great War*, edited by Alessandro Salvador, Anders Granas Kjøstvedt, Palgrave Macmillan, 2017, pp. 219–40.

Allison, Dorothy. "A Question of Class." *Skin: Talking about Sex, Class and Literature*, by Allison, Firebrand, 1994, pp. 13–36.

Amnesia. Directed by Gonzalo Justiniano, Arca, 1994.

Anderson, Peter. "Singling Out Victims: Denunciation and Collusion in the Post–Civil War Francoist Repression in Spain, 1939–1945." *European History Quarterly*, vol. 39, no. 1, Jan. 2009, pp. 7–26.

Animales extintos. Directed by Lucas Quintana, Luminaria (CL), 2018.

Los archivos del cardenal. Chilean TV series, CNTV, TVN, 2011–.

Arendt, Hannah, and Amos Elon. *Eichmann in Jerusalem : A Report on the Banality of Evil*. Penguin Books, 1963.

Aresti, Nerea. "The Battle to Define Spanish Manhood." *Memory and Cultural History of the Spanish Civil War: Realms of Oblivion*, edited by Aurora Morcillo, Brill, 2014, pp. 147–78.

Avelar, Idelber. *The Letter of Violence: Essays on Narrative, Ethics, and Politics*. Palgrave Macmillan, 2011.

Balfour, Sebastian. *Deadly Embrace: Morocco and the Road to the Spanish Civil War*. Oxford UP, 2002.

Barea, Arturo. *La forja de un rebelde*. 2nd. ed., Editorial Losada, 1954.

Bartky, Sandra Lee. "Foucault, Femininity, and the Modernization of Patriarchal Power." *Writing on the Body: Female Embodiment and Feminist Theory*, edited by Katie Conboy et al., Columbia UP, 1997.

Bawden, John R. *The Pinochet Generation: The Chilean Military in the Twentieth Century*. U of Alabama P, 2016.

Ben-Ghiat, Ruth. *Strongmen: How They Rise, Why They Succeed, How They Fall*. Profile Books, 2020.

Benjamin, Walter. "The Cultural History of Toys." *Walter Benjamin: Selected Writings, Volume 2, Part 1, 1927–1930*, edited by Michael W. Jennings, Howard Eiland, and Gary Smith, Belknap, 1999, pp. 113–16.

– "Hitler's Diminished Masculinity." *Walter Benjamin: Selected Writings, Volume 2, Part 2, 1931–1934*, edited by Michael W. Jennings, Howard Eiland, and Gary Smith, Belknap, 1999, pp. 792–3.

– "Theories of German Fascism." *Walter Benjamin: Selected Writings, Volume 2, Part 1, 1927–1930*, edited by Michael W. Jennings, Howard Eiland, and Gary Smith, Belknap, 1999, pp. 313–21.

– "Toys and Play." *Walter Benjamin: Selected Writings, Volume 2, Part 1, 1927–1930*, edited by Michael W. Jennings, Howard Eiland, and Gary Smith, Belknap, 1999, pp. 117–21.

Berglar, Peter. *Opus Dei: The Life and Work of Its Founder, Josemaría Escrivá de Balaguer*. Scepter Publishers, 1994.

Besas, Peter. *Behind the Spanish Lens: Spanish Cinema under Fascism and Democracy*. Arden Press, 1985.

Bielby, Clare. "Gendering the Perpetrator – Gendering Perpetrator Studies." *The Routledge International Handbook of Perpetrator Studies*, edited by S. Knittel and Z. Goldberg, Routledge, 2021, pp. 155–68.

Bird, Sharon R. "Welcome to the Men's Club: Homosociality and the Maintenance of Hegemonic Masculinity." *Gender and Society*, 1996, pp. 120–32.

Bolaño, Roberto. *Antwerp*. Translated by Natasha Wimmer, New Directions, 2012.

– *Between Parentheses*. Translated by Natasha Wimmer, New Directions, 2011.

– *By Night in Chile*. Translated by Chris Andrews, New Directions Books, 2003.

– *Distant Star*. Farrar, Straus and Giroux, 2004.

– *Estrella Distante*. 1st. ed., Debolsillo, 1996.

– *Last Evenings on Earth*. Translated by Chris Andrews, New Directions, 2006.

– *Nazi Literature in the Americas*. Translated by Chris Andrews, New Directions, 2008.

– *Nocturno de Chile*. Vintage Español, 2000.

– *The Secret of Evil*. Translated by Chris Andrews and Natasha Wimmer, New Directions, 2012.

– *The Third Reich: A Novel*. Translated by Natasha Wimmer, 1st American ed., Farrar, Straus and Giroux, 2011.

– *2666*. Translated by Natasha Wimmer, 1st. American ed., Farrar, Straus and Giroux, 2008.

Bonaddio, Frederico. *The Encyclopedia of Contemporary Spanish Films*, edited by S. Murguia and A. Pinar. Rowman & Littlefield, 2018.

Borges Jorge Luis. *El Aleph*. Penguin, 1996.

Borges, Jorge Luis, and André Maurois. "Deutsches Requiem." *Labyrinths: Selected Stories & Other Writings*. Edited by Donald A. Yates and James East Irby, translated by Sherry Mangan, New Directions, 1964, pp. 141–7.

Browning, Christopher. *Ordinary Men*. Rev. ed., Harper Collins, 2017.

Bunster, Ximena. "Surviving beyond Fear: Women and Torture in Latin America." *Surviving Beyond Fear: Women Children and Human Rights in Latin America*, edited by Marjorie Agosín et al., White Pine Press, 1993, pp. 98–125.

– "Watch Out for the Little Nazi Man That All of Us Have Inside: The Mobilization and Demobilization of Women in Militarized Chile." *Women's Studies International Forum*, vol. 11, no. 5, 1988, pp. 485–91.

Butler, Judith. *Frames of War: When Is Life Grievable?* Verso, 2016.

– *Gender Trouble: Feminism and the Subversion of Identity*. Routledge, 2015.

– "Melancholy gender / refused identification." *Constructing Masculinity*, edited by Maurice Berger, Brian Wallis, and Simon Watson, Routledge, 1995, pp. 21–36.

– *Who's Afraid of Gender?* 1st. ed., Farrar, Straus and Giroux, 2024.

Cahill, Ann J. "Foucault, Rape and the Construction of the Feminine Body." *Hypatia*, vol. 15, no. 1, winter 2000, pp. 43–63.

Callison, William. "Milei's Chainsaw." *New Left Review Sidecar*, 5 October 2023 – Politics, https://newleftreview.org/sidecar/posts/mileis-chainsaw.

Camus, Albert. *Neither Victims Nor Executioners: An Ethic Superior to Murder*. Wifp & Stock Publishers, 2008.

Casanova, Julián. *La iglesia de Franco*. Ediciones Temas de Hoy, 2001.

Castellanos Moya, Horacio. *La diáspora*. Literatura Random House, 2018.

– *La metamorfosis del sabueso: Ensayos personales y otros textos*. 1st. ed., Penguin Random House Grupo Editorial, 2023.

La caza [*The Hunt*]. Directed by Carlos Saura, Video Mercury Films: Divisa Home Video, 2015.

Cenarro Lagunas, Ángela. *La sonrisa de Falange: Auxilio social en la guerra civil y en la posguerra*. Crítica, 2006.

Cercas, Javier. *The Anatomy of a Moment*. Bloomsbury Publishing, 2012.

Chacón, Dulce. *The Sleeping Voice*. Translated by Nick Caistor, Harvill Secker, 2006.

– *La voz dormida*. Alfaguara, 2002.

Cockburn, Cynthia. "The Continuum of Violence: A Gender Perspective on War and Peace." *Sites of Violence: Gender and Conflict Zones*, edited by Wenona Giles and Jennifer Hyndman, U of California P, 2004, pp. 24–44.

– "Don't Talk to Me about War. My Life's a Battlefield." *50.50*, Open Democracy, 25 Nov. 2012, https://www.opendemocracy.net/en/5050/dont-talk-to-me-about-war-my-lifes-battlefield/.

– Keynote video address. Gender and Peace Conference. 5–7 May 2017, Sabanci University, Istanbul, https://www.youtube.com/watch?v=NiOH5qWS-50.

Cockburn, Cynthia, and Dubravka Žarkov, editors. *The Postwar Moment: Militaries, Masculinities and International Peacekeeping*. Lawrence & Wishart, 2002.

Cohn, Carol. "War, Wimps, and Women: Talking Gender and Thinking War." *Gendering War Talk*, edited by Miriam G. Cookie and Angela Woollacot, Princeton UP, 2014, pp. 227–48.

Cole, Alyson M. "The Other V-Word: The Politics of Victimhood Fueling George W. Bush's War Machine." *Feminism and War: Confronting U.S. Imperialism*, edited by Chandra T. Mohanty et al., Zed Books, 2008, pp. 117–30.

Collins, Cath. "Truth-Justice-Reparations Interaction Effects in Transitional Justice Practice: The Case of the 'Valech Commission' in Chile." *Journal of Latin American Studies*, vol. 49, no. 1, Feb. 2017, pp. 55–82.

El color del camaleón [*The Color of the Chameleon*]. Directed by Andres Lübbert, 3boxmedia, 2017.

Connell, R.W. *Gender and Power: Society, the Person and Sexual Politics*. Stanford UP, 1987.

– *Masculinities*. Polity Press, 1995.

– "Masculinities, the Reduction of Violence and the Pursuit of Peace." *The Postwar Moment: Militaries, Masculinities and International Peacekeeping*. edited by Cynthia Cockburn and Dubravka Žarkov, Lawrence & Wishart, 2002, pp. 33–40.

– *The Men and the Boys*. Allen & Unwin, 2000.

Connell, R.W., and Rebecca Pearse. *Gender: In World Perspective*. Polity, 2021.

Crenshaw, Kimberle. "Mapping the Margins: Intersectionality, Identity Politics, and Violence against Women of Color." *Stanford Law Review*, vol. 43, no. 6, 1991, pp. 1241–99.

Cría cuervos. Directed by Carlos Saura, Criterion Collection, 1976.

El crimen de Cuenca [*Crime in Cuenca*]. Directed by Pilar Miró, 1980.

Cuevas, Tomasa. *Prison of Women: Testimonies of War and Resistance in Spain, 1939–1975*. Edited and translated by Mary E. Giles, State U of New York P, 1998.

Dastagir, Alia. "The Psychology of Putin and the Dangers of 'Militarized Masculinity.'" USA Today, 9 Mar. 2022, https://www.usatoday.com/story/life/health-wellness/2022/03/09/putinukraine-invasion-militarized-masculinity-psychology/9426237002/?gnt-cfr=1.

Davis, Angela. "A Vocabulary for Feminist Praxis: On War and Radical Critique." *Feminism and War: Confronting U.S. Imperialism*, edited by Chandra T. Mohanty et al., Zed Books, 2008, pp. 19–26.

Dawes, James. *Evil Men*. Harvard UP, 2014.

– "MacTalks with Jim Dawes." Video presentation. Macalester College, Saint Paul, Minnesota, https://www.macalester.edu/english/facultystaff /jamesdawes/

De Valk, Mark, editor. *Screening the Tortured Body: The Cinema as Scaffold*. Palgrave Macmillan, 2016.

Dickinson, Emily. "Flags Vex a Dying Face." *Women on War: Essential Voices for the Nuclear Age*, edited by Daniela Gioseffi, Simon & Schuster, 1988, p. 199.

Di Febo, Giuliana, and Santos Juliá. *El Franquismo*. Paidós, 2005.

DiGiovanni, Lisa. "Masculinity, Misogyny and Mass in *Los girasoles ciegos* by Alberto Méndez." *Anales de la literatura española contemporánea*, vol. 37, no. 1, 2012, pp. 39–61.

– "Militarized Masculinity: Boys' Socialization and the Postwar Graphic Novel of Carlos Giménez." *The Dynamics of Masculinity in Contemporary Spanish Culture*, edited by Lorraine Ryan and Ana Corbalán, Routledge, 2017, pp. 63–79.

– "Modes of Silence and Resistance: Chilean Documentary and Gendered Torture." *Cinema and the State-Tortured Body*, edited by M. de Valk, Palgrave Macmillan, 2017, pp. 177–206.

– "Return to Galicia: Nostalgia, Nation and Gender in Manuel Rivas's Spain." *Memory-Nostalgia-Melancholy: Re-imagining Home in a Time of Mobility*, edited by Maja Mikula, Cambridge Scholars, 2017, pp. 15–34.

– "Torture, Masculinity, and Resistance in Chilean Documentary Film: Patricio Guzmán and Marcela Said." *Gender-Based Violence in Latin American and Iberian Cinemas*, edited by M.J. Gámez Fuentes et al. Routledge, 2020, pp. 109–25.

– *Unsettling Nostalgia in Spain and Chile: Longing for Resistance in Literature and Film*. Lexington Books, 2019.

Draper, Susana. *Afterlives of Confinement: Spatial Transitions in Postdictadorship Latin America*. U of Pittsburgh P, 2012.

Eichler, Maya. *Militarizing Men: Gender, Conscription, and War in Post-Soviet Russia*. Stanford UP, 2012.

Enders, Victoria Lorée, and Pamela Beth Radcliff. *Constructing Spanish Womanhood: Female Identity in Modern Spain*. State U of New York P, 1999.

Enjuto Rangel, Cecilia. "Spectrality in Pa Negre/Black Bread (Villaronga 2010): Queer Aesthetics and Its Politics of Memory." *Studies in Spanish & Latin American Cinemas*, vol. 18, no. 3, 2021, pp. 317–33, https://doi .org/10.1386/slac_00058_1.

Enjuto Rangel, Cecilia, et al. *The Iberian and Latin American Transatlantic Studies Reader*. Liverpool UP, 2019.

Enloe, Cynthia. *Bananas, Beaches and Bases: Making Feminist Sense of International Politics*. U of California P, 1990.

– *The Big Push: Exposing and Challenging Sustainable Patriarchy*. U of California P, 2017.

– "Demilitarization – or More of the Same? Feminist Questions to Ask in the Postwar Moment." *The Postwar Moment: Militaries, Masculinities and International Peacekeeping*, edited by Cynthia Cockburn and Dubravka Žarkov, Lawrence & Wishart, 2002, pp. 22–32.

– *Globalization and Militarism: Feminists Make the Link*. Rowman & Littlefield, 2007.

– *Maneuvers: The International Politics of Militarizing Women's Lives*. U of California P, 2000.

– *The Morning After: Sexual Politics and the End of the Cold War*. U of California P, 1993.

– *Twelve Feminist Lessons of War*. U of California P, 2023.

Ensalaco, Mark. *Chile under Pinochet: Recovering the Truth*. U of Pennsylvania P, 2000.

Escudero, María. "Cortes and Marina: Gender and the Reconquest of America under the Franco Regime." *Constructing Spanish Womanhood: Female Identity in Modern Spain*, edited by Victoria Lorée Enders and Pamela Beth Radcliff, State U of New York P, 1999, pp. 71–94.

El espinazo del diablo: The Devil's Backbone. Directed by Guillermo del Toro, Columbia TriStar Home Entertainment, 2004.

Fascism on a Thread: The Strange Story of Nazisploitation Cinema. Directed by Naomi Holwill, Severin Films, 2019.

Fasteau, Marc F. *The Male Machine*. Dell Publishing, 1974.

Feitlowitz, Marguerite. *A Lexicon of Terror: Argentina and the Legacies of Torture*. Oxford UP, 2011.

Fernández, Nona. *La dimensión desconocida* [*The Twilight Zone*]. Literatura Random House, 2017.

– *Space Invaders*. Alquimia Ediciones, 2013.

Fernández, Nona, and Natasha Wimmer. *Space Invaders: A Novel*. Graywolf Press, 2019.

Ferrante, Elena. *My Brilliant Friend*. Translated by Ann Goldstein, Europa Editions, 2012.

Finchelstein, Federico. *A Brief History of Fascist Lies*. U of California P, 2020.

– *Fascist Mythologies: The History and Politics of Unreason in Borges, Freud, and Schmitt*. Columbia UP, 2022.

Fischer, Carl. *Queering the Chilean Way: Cultures of Exceptionalism and Sexual Dissidence*. Palgrave Macmillan, 2016.

Flynn, Michael, and Fabiola F. Salek. *Screening Torture: Media Representations of State Terror and Political Domination*. Columbia UP, 2012.

Folkart, J.A. "On Pencils, Places, and the Pursuit of Desire: Manuel Rivas's *El lápiz del Carpintero*." *Revista de Estudios Hispanicos*, vol. 40, no. 2, May 2006, pp. 296–315.

Foucault, Michel. *Discipline and Punish*. Vintage. 1995.

Fox, Soledad. "Violence and Silence: The Repressed History of the Franco Regime." *Mass Graves and the Recovery of Historical Memory in Spain: Unearthing*

Franco's Legacy, edited by Carlos Farrán Jerez and Samuel Amago, U of Notre Dame P, 2010, pp. 30–41.

Franco, Jean. *Cruel Modernity*. Duke UP, 2013.

Fraser, Erica L. *Military Masculinity and Postwar Recovery in the Soviet Union*. U of Toronto P, 2019.

Frazier, Lessie J. *Salt in the Sand: Memory, Violence, and the Nation-State in Chile, 1890 to the Present*. Duke UP, 2007.

Full Metal Jacket. Directed by Stanley Kubrick, Warner Bros. Pictures, 1987.

Gámez Fuentes, María José, Rebecca Maseda García, and Barbara Zecchi, editors. *Gender-Based Violence in Latin American and Iberian Cinemas*. Routledge, 2020.

Gättens, Marie-Luise. "Three Guineas, Fascism, and the Construction of Gender." *Virginia Woolf and Fascism*, edited by Merry M. Pawlowski, Palgrave Macmillan, 2001, pp. 21–38.

Gener, Pompeyo. *La dòna mediterrania: Llegendes històriques*. Societat Catalana Edicions, 1916.

Giménez, Carlos. *Paracuellos: Children of the Defeated in Franco's Fascist Spain*. Edited by Dean Mullaney, translated by Sonya Jones, illustrated by Carlos Giménez and William Stout, EuroComics, an imprint of IDW Publishing, 2016.

– *Todo Barrio*. Debolsillo, 2011.

– *Todo Paracuellos*. Random House Mondadori, 2007.

Giménez Caballero, Ernesto. *Genio de España: Exaltaciones a una resurrección nacional y del mundo*. La Gaceta literaria, 1934.

Goldman, Emma. "Patriotism as a Cause of War." *Women on War: Essential Voices for the Nuclear Age*, edited by Daniela Gioseffi, Simon & Schuster, 1988, pp. 119–20.

Goldstein, Joshua S. *War and Gender: How Gender Shapes the War System and Vice Versa*. Cambridge UP, 2009.

Gómez López-Quiñones, Antonio. "El giro irónico de la violencia: La posutopía de la Guerra Civil española en 'Los girasoles ciegos' y 'Capital de la Gloria.'" *Revista canadiense de estudios hispánicos*, vol. 34, no. 1, 2009, pp. 99–113.

González Cangas, Yanko. *Los más ordenaditos: Fascismo y juventud en la dictadura de Pinochet*. Hueders, 2020.

Graham, Helen. "Gender and the State: Women in the 1940s." *Spanish Cultural Studies: An Introduction; The Struggle for Modernity*, edited by Helen Graham and Jo Labanyi. Oxford UP, 1995, pp. 182–95.

Grandes, Almudena. *Episodios de una guerra interminable*. Tusquets Editores, 2010–20. 6 vols.

Guillermo del Toro's Pinocchio. Directed by Guillermo del Toro, Netflix, 2022.

Hamber, Brandon. "There Is a Crack in Everything: Problematising Masculinities, Peacebuilding and Transitional Justice." *Human Rights Review*, vol. 17, no. 1, 2016, pp. 9–34.

Hampton, Jean. "Defining Wrong and Defining Rape." *A Most Detestable Crime: New Philosophical Essays on Rape*, edited by K. Burgess-Jackson, Oxford UP, 1999, pp. 118–56.

Hatty Suzanne. *Masculinities, Violence, and Culture*. Sage Publications, 2000.

Haynes, Stephen R. "Ordinary Masculinity: Gender Analysis and Holocaust Scholarship." *Genocide and Gender in the Twentieth Century: A Comparative Survey*, edited by Amy Randall, Bloomsbury, 2015, pp. 165–88.

Helms, Elissa. *Innocence and Victimhood: Gender, Nation, and Women's Activism in Postwar Bosnia-Herzegovina*. U of Wisconsin P, 2013.

Henckaerts, Jean-Marie, et al. *Customary International Humanitarian Law*. Cambridge UP, 2010.

Hernández, Miguel. *The Selected Poems of Miguel Hernández*. Edited by Ted Genoways, U of Chicago P, 2001.

Herrmann, Gina. "Franco in the Docket: CM Hardt's Memory Movie." Modern Languages Association conference paper, 2006.

– "They Didn't Rape Me: Traces of Gendered Violence and Sexual Injury in the Testimonies of Spanish Republican Women Survivors of the Franco Dictatorship." *Tapestry of Memory: Evidence and Testimony in Life-Story Narratives*, edited by Nanci Adler and Selma Leydesdorff, Transaction Publishers, 2013, pp. 77–95.

– "Voices of the Vanquished: Leftist Women and the Spanish Civil War." *Journal of Spanish Cultural Studies*, vol. 4, no. 1, 2003, pp. 11–29.

Hill Collins, Patricia. *Black Feminist Thought: Knowledge, Consciousness, and the Politics of Empowerment*. Routledge, 2000.

Hiner, Hillary, and Daniela Castro. "Women, Torture, & Spectacle on Chilean Television." *Popular Communication*, vol. 16, no. 2, 2018, pp. 106–18.

Hirsch, Marianne, and Nancy K. Miller, editors. *Rites of Return: Diaspora Poetics and the Politics of Memory*. Columbia UP, 2011.

Historias del Kronen. Directed by Montxo Armendáriz. Manga Films, 1995.Hite, Katherine, and Paola Cesarini. *Authoritarian Legacies and Democracy in Latin America and Southern Europe*. U of Notre Dame P, 2004.

Hitler, Adolf, and Ralph Manheim. *Mein Kampf*. Houghton Mifflin Company, 1971.

Holland, Jack. *A Brief History of Misogyny: The World's Oldest Prejudice*. Robinson, 2006.

hooks, bell. "The Oppositional Gaze: Black Female Spectators." *Feminist Film Theory: A Reader*, edited by Sue Thornham, New York UP, 1999, pp. 307–20.

Hoppe, Hans-Hermann. *Democracy – The God That Failed: The Economics and Politics of Monarchy, Democracy and Natural Order*. Transaction Publishers, 2001.

I Love Pinochet. Directed by Marcela Said, Imago, 2001.

Intxausti, Aurora. "La cruda mirada de Alberto Méndez sobre la posguerra gana el Nacional de Narrativa," *El País*, electronic version, 7 Oct. 2005, https://elpais.com/diario/2005/10/07/cultura/1128636003_850215.html. Accessed 20 April 2018.

La isla mínima. Directed by Alberto Rodriguez et al., Atípica Films, Sacromonte Films, Antena 3 Films, 2014.

Jacobs, Susie, et al. *States of Conflict: Gender, Violence and Resistance*. Palgrave Macmillan, 2000.

Jarhead. Directed by Sam Mendes, Paramount Pictures, 2005.

Jelin, Elizabeth. *State Repression and the Labors of Memory*. U of Minnesota P, 2003.

Jimenez Murguía, Salvador, and Alex Pinar, editors. *The Encyclopedia of Contemporary Spanish Films*. Rowan & Littlefield, 2018.

Jocelyn-Holt Letelier, Alfredo. *El peso de la noche: Nuestra frágil fortaleza histórica*. Ariel, 1997.

Joeden-Forgey, Elisa. "Gender and the Future of Genocide Studies and Prevention." *Genocide and Gender in the Twentieth Century: A Comparative Survey*, vol. 7, no. 1, 2015, pp. 298–320.

Johnson, Rebecca. "Anti-Militarist Stance of Feminism." Sisterhood and After: An Oral History of the Women's Liberation Movement, British Library. https://blogs.bl.uk/socialscience/2013/03/sisterhood-after-the-womens -liberation-oral-history-project.html.

Jones, Adam. *Genocide: A Comprehensive Introduction*. Routledge, 2017.

– "Masculinities and Vulnerabilities in the Rwandan and Congolese Genocides." *Genocide and Gender in the Twentieth Century: A Comparative Survey*, edited by Amy Randall, Bloomsbury, 2015, pp. 62–84.

Juguetes. Directed by María Luisa Bemberg, 1978. Retrieved in December 2023. https://www.youtube.com/watch?v=N5AjjBv_2bo.

Jünger, Ernst. *A German Officer in Occupied Paris: The War Journals, 1941–1945*. Columbia UP, 2020.

– *Storm of Steel*. Obelisco, 2021.

Katz, Jackson, and Sut Jhally. *Tough Guise: Violence, Media, and the Crisis in Masculinity*. Media Education Foundation, 1999.

Kelly, Liz. "Wars against Women: Sexual Violence, Sexual Politics and the Militarised State." *States of Conflict: Gender, Violence and Resistance*, edited by Susie Jacobs et al., Zed Books, 2000, pp. 45–65.

Ketcham, Christopher. What the Far-Right Fascination with Pinochet's Death Squads Should Tell Us." 4 Feb. 2021, https://theintercept.com/2021/02/04 /pinochet-far-right-hoppean-snake/.

Ketz, Victoria. "ReinFORCEment of Masculinity through Violence." *The Dynamics of Masculinity in Contemporary Spanish Culture*, edited by Lorraine Ryan and Ana Corbalán, Routledge, 2017, pp. 139–56.

Kimmel, Michael. "Masculinity as Homophobia: Fear, Shame, and Silence in the Construction of Gender Identity." *Sex, Gender, and Sexuality: The New Basics*, edited by A.L. Ferber et al., Oxford UP, 2009, pp. 58–70.

Kinder, Marsha. *Blood Cinema: The Reconstruction of National Identity in Spain*. U of California P, 1993.

Kirk, Gwyn, and Margo Okazawa-Rey. *Women's Lives: Multicultural Perspectives*. McGraw-Hill, 2010.

Kirkwood, Julieta. *Ser política en Chile: Las feministas y los partidos*. LOM Ediciones, 2010.

Labanyi, Jo. "Memory and Modernity in Democratic Spain: The Difficulty of Coming to Terms with the Spanish Civil War." *Poetics Today*, March 2007, pp. 89–116.

– "Miscegenation, Nation Formation and Cross-Racial Identifications in the Early Francoist Folkloric Film Musical." *Hybridity and Its Discontents: Politics, Science, Culture*, edited by Avtar Brah and Annie E. Coombes, Routledge, 2000, pp. 56–71.

– *Myth and History in the Contemporary Spanish Novel*. Cambridge UP, 1989.

– "Women, Asian Hordes and the Threat to the Self in Giménez Caballero's *Genio de España*." *Bulletin of Hispanic Studies*, vol. 73, 1996, pp. 377–87.

El laberinto del fauno [*Pan's Labyrinth*]. Directed by Guillermo del Toro, Hopscotch Entertainment, 2007.

LasTesis, and Alejandra Carmona López. *Quemar el miedo: Un manifiesto*. 1st. ed., Editorial Planeta Chilena S.A., 2021.

– *Set Fear on Fire: The Feminist Call That Set the Americas Ablaze*. Translated by Camila Valle, Verso, 2023.

Lazreg, Marnia. "Doing Torture in Film: Confronting Ambiguity and Ambivalence." *Screening Torture: Media Representations of State Terror and Political Domination*, edited by Michael Flynn and Fabiola F. Salek. Columbia UP, 2012, pp. 257–72.

– *Torture and the Twilight of Empire: From Algiers to Baghdad*. Princeton UP, 2008.

Lazzara, Michael J. *Civil Obedience: Complicity and Complacency in Chile since Pinochet*. U of Wisconsin P, 2018.

– "Familiares de colaboradores y perpetradores en el cine documental chileno: Memoria y sujeto implicado." *Atenea*, no. 521, 2020, pp. 231–48.

– editor. *Luz Arce and Pinochet's Chile: Testimony in the Aftermath of State Violence*. Palgrave Macmillan, 2011.

– "Radiografía del pinochetismo: Una conversación con la documentalista Marcela Said." *Chasqui: Revista de Literatura Latinoamericana*, vol. 42, no.1, 2013, pp. 247–56.

– "Uncovering Complicit Narratives." Presentation at Truth, Memory, and Justice Colloquium, Bowdoin, Brunswick, Maine, published online 8 May 2019, https://www.bowdoin.edu/romance-languages/news/2019/uncovering-complicit-narratives.html.

Leatherman, Janie. *Sexual Violence and Armed Conflict*. Polity Press, 2011.

Lemebel, Pedro. *My Tender Matador*. Translated by Katherine Silve, Grove Press, 2003.

Levi, Primo. *The Voice of Memory: Interviews, 1961–1987*. Edited by Marco Belpoliti and Robert Gordon. New Press, 2001.

Littell, Jonathan. *The Kindly Ones: A Novel*. 1st ed., Harper Collins, 2009.

Llanos, Bernardita. "Género, violencia sexual y delito en *Carne de perra* de Fátima Sime." *Cuadernos de Literatura*, vol. 21, no. 42, 2017, pp. 219–37.

Lodge, David. *The Art of Fiction Illustrated from Classic and Modern Texts.* Penguin Books, 1994.

Loomba, Ania. *Colonialism/Postcolonialism (The New Critical Idiom)*. Routledge, 1998.

Lorber, Judith. "The Social Construction of Gender." *Women's Lives: Multicultural Perspectives*, edited by Gwyn Kirk and Margo Okazawa-Rey, McGraw-Hill, 2009, pp. 64–7.

Lorde, Audre. "The Uses of Anger." *Women's Studies Quarterly*, vol. 9, no. 3, 1981, pp. 7–10.

Loveman, Brian. *The Politics of Antipolitics: The Military in Latin America.* Scholarly Resources, 1997.

Luxemburg, Rosa. "Militarism Is a Province of Accumulation." *Women on War: Essential Voices for the Nuclear Age*, edited by Daniela Gioseffi, Simon & Schuster, 1988, pp. 129–30.

MacEóin, Gary. *Chile, under Military Rule: A Dossier of Documents and Analyses.* IDOC/North America, 1974.

Machuca. Directed by Andrés Wood, Menemsha Films, 2004.

MacKinnon, Catherine. *Are Women Human? And Other International Dialogues.* Harvard UP, 2006.

Mama, Amina. "Challenging Militarized Masculinities." *50.50*, Open Democracy, 29 May 2013, https://www.opendemocracy.net/en/5050/challenging-militarized -masculinities/.

Manne, Kate. *Down Girl: The Logic of Misogyny.* Oxford UP, 2018.

Mansfield, Nick. *Subjectivity: Theories of the Self from Freud to Haraway.* New York UP, 2000.

El mar. Directed by Agustí Villaronga, Cameo D.L., 2000.

Marsé, Juan. *Si Te Dicen Que Caí.* 1st. ed., Biblioteca breve, Seix Barral, 1976.

Martín Cabrera, Luis. *Radical Justice: Spain and the Southern Cone beyond Market and State.* Bucknell UP. 2011.

Martín-Estudillo, Luis, and Roberto Ampuero. *Post-Authoritarian Cultures: Spain and Latin America's Southern Cone.* Vanderbilt UP, 2008.

Martín Gaite, Carmen. *Courtship Customs in Postwar Spain.* Bucknell UP / Associated University Presses, 2004.

– *Usos amorosos de la postguerra española.* Anagrama, 1994.

Martín Patino, Basilio. "No lo repetiría. Así fue el rodaje de Queridísimos verdugos." *Cuadernos para el Diálogo*, no. 206, 1977, pp. 44–7.

Matthews, James. *Reluctant Warriors: Republican Popular Army and Nationalist Army Conscripts in the Spanish Civil War, 1936–1939.* Oxford UP, 2012.

Matute, Ana María. *Doce historias de la Artámila.* Edited by Manuel Durán and Gloria Durán, Harcourt, Brace & World, 1965.

McClintock, Anne. *Imperial Leather: Race, Gender, and Sexuality in the Colonial Contest.* Routledge, 1995.

Méndez, Alberto. *Blind Sunflowers*. Translated by Nick Caistor, Arcadia Books, 2008.

– *Los girasoles ciegos*. Anagrama, 2004.

Millet, Kate. *Sexual Politics*. Columbia UP, 2016.

Mi país imaginario [*My Imaginary Country*]. Directed by Patricio Guzmán, Icarus Films Home Video, 2022.

Miralda, Antoni. "Soldats Soldés (1965–1973)." *Cowboy's Dream*, 29 May–17 Sept. 2023, Circulo de Bellas Artes, Madrid, Spain.

El mocito [*The Young Butler*]. Directed by Marcela Said and Jean de Certeau, Icalmafilms, 2011 (DVD).

Mohanty, Chandra T. *Feminism without Borders: Decolonizing Theory, Practicing Solidarity*. Duke UP, 2003.

Moon, Seungsook. *Militarized Modernity and Gendered Citizenship in South Korea*. Duke UP, 2005.

Morcillo Gómez, Aurora. "Shaping True Catholic Womanhood: Francoist Educational Discourse on Women." *Constructing Spanish Womanhood: Female Identity in Modern Spain*, edited by Victoria Lorée Enders and Pamela Beth Radcliff, State U of New York P, 1999, pp. 51–70.

Moreiras-Menor, Cristina. "War, Postwar, and the Fascist Fabrication of Identity." *Teaching Representations of the Spanish Civil War*, edited by Noël Valis, Modern Language Association of America, 2007, pp. 117–29.

Moreno-Nuño, Carmen. "The Comic-Strip of Historical Memory: An Analysis of *Paracuellos* by Carlos Giménez, in the Light of *Persépolis* by Marjane Satrapi and *Maus* by Art Spiegelman." *Vanderbilt Journal of Luso-Hispanic Studies*, vol. 5, 2009, pp. 177–95.

Mullaney, Dean, editor. *Paracuellos: Children of the Defeated in Franco's Fascist Spain*. Translated by Sonya Jones, illustrated by Carlos Giménez and William Stout, EuroComics, an imprint of IDW Publishing, 2016.

Muñoz, Molina A. "Antonio Muñoz Molina revela la violencia de la transición al relatar su mili en el País Vasco." *El País*, electronic version. 21 Mar. 1995, https://elpais.com/diario/ 1995/03/22/cultura/795826814 _850215.html.

– *Ardor guerrero: Una memoria militar*. Booket, 2016.

Murgia, Michela. *How to Be a Fascist: A Manual*. Penguin Books, 2020.

Murguía, Salvador J., and Alex Pinar. *The Encyclopedia of Contemporary Spanish Films*. Rowman & Littlefield, 2018.

Nagel, Joane. "Masculinity and Nationalism: Gender and Sexuality in the Making of Nations." *Nations and Nationalism: A Reader*, edited by P. Spencer and H. Wollman, Rutgers UP, 2005, pp. 110–31.

Nash, Mary. "Mujeres en guerra: Repensar la historia." *La guerra civil española*, edited by Julián Casanova and Paul Preston, Editorial Pablo Iglesias, 2008, pp. 61–83.

– "Un/contested Identities: Motherhood, Sex Reform and the Modernization of Gender Identity in Early Twentieth-Century Spain." *Constructing Spanish Womanhood: Female Identity in Modern Spain*, edited by Victoria Lorée Enders and Pamela Beth Radcliff, State U of New York P, 1999, pp. 25–49.

Nelson, Alice A. *Political Bodies: Gender, History, and the Struggle for Narrative Power in Recent Chilean Literature*. Bucknell UP, 2002.

Ocampo, Hilda. "Los cuentos son muy viejos." *Composición: Proceso Y Síntesis*, 5th ed., edited by Valdés Guadalupe et al. McGraw-Hill, 2008, pp. 184–5.

Opus Dei: Una cruzada silenciosa. Directed by Marcela Said Cares, Valparaiso Productions, 2007.

Orwell, George. *Nineteen Eighty-Four*. Secker & Warburg, 1949.

Orwell, George. *The Road to Wigan Pier*. Oxford UP, 2021.

El pacto de Adriana [*Adriana's Pact*]. Directed by Lissette Orozco, Meikincine, 2017.

Pa negre [*Black Bread*]. Directed by Agustí Villaronga, Massa d'Or Produccions, 2010.

Passmore, Leith. *The Wars inside Chile's Barracks: Remembering Military Service under Pinochet*. U of Wisconsin P, 2017.

Pawlowski, Merry M. *Virginia Woolf and Fascism: Resisting the Dictators' Seduction*. Palgrave, 2001.

Payne, Leigh A. *Unsettling Accounts: Neither Truth Nor Reconciliation in Confessions of State Violence*. Duke UP, 2008.

Pensky, Max. "War and Critical Theory." *War and Literary Studies*, edited by Anders Engberg-Pedersen and Neil Ramsey, Cambridge UP, 2023, pp. 67–84.

Los perros [*The Dogs*]. Directed by Marcela Said, Karma Films, 2018.

The Pinochet Case. 2001. Directed by Patrico Guzmán, First Run/Icarus Films, 2002.

Platero, Raquel, et al., editors. *Barbarismos queer y otras esdrújulas*. Edicions Bellaterra, 2017.

Power, Margaret. *Right-Wing Women in Chile: Feminine Power and the Struggle against Allende, 1964–1973*. Pennsylvania State UP, 2002.

Preston, Paul. *Doves of War: Four Women of Spain*. Northeastern UP, 2003.

– *The Politics of Revenge: Fascism and the Military in Twentieth-Century Spain*. Routledge, 1990.

Proyecto Interdiocesano Recuperación de la Memoria Histórica (Guatemala), et al. *Guatemala, Never Again!* Orbis Books, 1999.

Queridísimos verdugos. Directed by Basilio Martín Patino, Linterna Mágica-Suevia, 1977.

Quílez Esteve, Laia. "Pelonas' y rapadas: Imágenes-trofeo e imágenes-denuncia de la Represión de género ejercida durante la Guerra Civil Española." *Hispanic Review*, vol. 86, no. 4, 2018, pp. 487–509.

Radio Ambulante. "El helicóptero, el silencio, el balazo, la huida," season 4, episode 28, 3 Mar. 2020. https://www.npr.org/2020/03/30/823957014/el-helic-ptero-el-silencio-el-balazo-la-huida\.

Randall, Amy E., editor. *Genocide and Gender in the Twentieth Century: A Comparative Survey*. Bloomsbury Academic, 2015.

Rebolledo, Javier. *A la sombra de los cuervos: Los cómplices civiles de la dictadura*. 1st. ed., Ceibo Ediciones, 2015.

Regresa el Cepa. Directed by Víctor Matellano García, 39 Escalones Film, 2019.

Reyes, Carlos. *Los años de Allende: Novela Gráfica*. Illustrated by Rodrigo Elgueta, 1st. ed., Editorial Hueders, 2015.

Richard, Nelly. *Cultural Residues: Chile in Transition*. U of Minnesota P, 2004.

Rivas, Manuel. *El lápiz del carpintero* [*The Carpenter's Pencil*]. Punto de Lectura, 1998.

Rodríguez de Arce, Ignacio. "'Estrella distante' de Roberto Bolaño: La tematización de una poética teratológica." *Hipertexto*, vol. 12, 2010, pp. 179–88.

Rogers, Gayle, "Virginia Woolf and the Spanish Civil War: *Three Guineas*, Victoria Ocampo, and International Feminism." *Modernism and the New Spain: Britain, Cosmopolitan Europe, and Literary History* by Rogers, Modernist Literature and Culture, 2012, pp. 125–62.

Rojas Lizana, Sol, and Ariel Rojas Lizana. *Historias Clandestinas*. 2nd. ed., LOM Ediciones, 2023.

Ros, Ana L. "*El Mocito*: A Study of Cruelty at the Intersection of Chile's Military and Civil Society." *Genocide Studies and Prevention*, vol. 12, no. 2, 2018, pp. 107–24.

Said, Edward W. *Culture and Imperialism*. Vintage Books, 1994.

Saini, Angela. *The Patriarchs: The Origins of Inequality*. Beacon Press, 2023.

Scarry, Elaine. *The Body in Pain: The Making and Unmaking of the World*. Oxford UP, 1985.

Sedgwick, Eve Kosofsky. *Between Men: English Literature and Male Homosocial Desire*. 30th anniversary ed., Columbia UP, 2016.

– "Between Men: English Literature and Male Homosocial Desire." *The Norton Anthology of Theory and Criticism*. 1st ed, W.W. Norton, 2001, pp. 2432–8.

Segato, Rita Laura. *La guerra contra las mujeres* [The war against women]. Traficantes de sueños, 2016.

– "Territory, Sovereignty, and Crimes of the Second State." *Terrorizing Women: Feminicide in the Américas*, edited by Rosa Fregoso and Cynthia Bejarano, Duke UP, 2010, pp. 70–91.

Sender, Ramón José. *Réquiem por un campesino español*. 2nd. ed., Ediciones Destino, 1975.

The Shape of Water. Directed by Guillermo del Toro, Twentieth Century Fox, 2017.Sharp, Gene. *From Dictatorship to Democracy: A Conceptual Framework for Liberation*. New Press, 2012.

Shayne, Julie D. *The Revolution Question: Feminisms in El Salvador, Chile, and Cuba*. Rutgers UP, 2004.

Simic, Oliviera. "Wartime Rape and Its Shunned Victims." *Genocide and Gender in the Twentieth Century: A Comparative Survey*, edited by A. Randall, Bloomsbury, 2015, pp. 237–57.

Smaill, Belinda. *The Documentary: Politics, Emotion, Culture*. Palgrave Macmillan, 2010.

The Smell of Burning Ants. Directed by Jay Rosenblatt et al., Jay Rosenblatt Film, 2007.

Snyder, Timothy. "Hitler's World." *New York Review of Books*. 24 Sept. 2015. https://www.nybooks.com/articles/2015/09/24/hitlers-world/?srsltid=A fmBOoqlykKosXgHsSqnv0_51D7vI2KeEgEGqnuo8de0Em3aY5lh1nyU.

– *On Tyranny: Twenty Lessons from the Twentieth Century*. Tim Duggan Books, 2017.

Sontag, Susan. *Regarding the Pain of Others*. Picador, 2003.

Stern, Steve J. *Reckoning with Pinochet: The Memory Question in Democratic Chile, 1989–2006*. Duke UP, 2010.

– *Remembering Pinochet's Chile: On the Eve of London 1998*. Duke UP, 2004.

Stoler, Ann L. "Making Empire Respectable: The Politics of Race and Sexuality Morality in 20th Century Cultures." *American Ethnologist*, vol. 16, no. 4, Nov. 1989, pp. 634–60.

Sueiro, Daniel, and Bernardo Díaz-Nosty. *Historia del Franquismo*. Editorial Argos Vergara, 1985.

Sutton, Barbara. *Surviving State Terror: Women's Testimonies of Repression and Resistance in Argentina*. New York UP, 2018.

Szymborska, Wisława. "Tortures." *Women on War: Essential Voices for the Nuclear Age*, edited by Daniela Gioseffi, Simon & Schuster, 1988, pp. 258–9.

Taddonio, Patrice. "Trump the 'Bully': How Childhood & Military School Shaped the Future President." 22 Sept. 2020, https://www.pbs.org/wgbh /frontline/article/trump-the-bully-how-childhood-military-school-shaped -the-future-president/.

Taylor, Diana. *Disappearing Acts: Spectacles of Gender and Nationalism in Argentina's "Dirty War."* Duke UP, 1997.

Teixidor, E. *Pan negro* [*Black Bread*]. Editorial Seix Barral, 2011.

Theidon, Kimberly. "Reconstructing Masculinities: The Disarmament, Demobilization, and Reintegration of Former Combatants in Colombia." *Human Rights Quarterly*, vol. 31, no. 1, Johns Hopkins UP, 2009, pp. 1–34.

Theweleit, Klaus. *Das Lachen der Täter: Breivik u.a. – Psychogramm der Tötungslust* [*The Laughter of Killers: Breivik et al.; A Psychogram of Killing for Pleasure*]. Residenz Verlag, 2015.

– *Women, Floods, Bodies, History*. 1979. Vol. 1 of *Male Fantasies*, U of Minnesota P, 1987.

Thomas, Gwynn. "Working within a Gendered Political Consensus: Uneven progress on Gender and Sexuality Rights in Chile." *Seeking Rights from the Left: Gender, Sexuality, and the Latin American Pink Tide*, edited by Elisabeth Jay Friedman, Duke UP, 2019, pp. 115–43.

Torbado, Jesús, and Manuel Leguineche. *The Moles: An Account of Courage and Tenacity during the Franco Years*. Secker & Warburg, 1977.

Townsend, Brandi. "The Body and State Violence, from the Harrowing to the Mundane: Chilean Women's Oral Histories of the Augusto Pinochet Dictatorship (1973–1990)." *Journal of Women's History*, vol. 31, no. 2, 2019, pp. 33–56.

Tras el cristal. Directed by Agustí Villaronga, Cult Epics, 1986.

Triana-Toribio, Núria. "In Memoriam: Pilar Miró (1940–1997)." *Film History*, vol. 10, no. 2, 1998, pp. 231–40, www.jstor.org/stable/3815284. Accessed 25 Nov. 2020.

La trinchera infinita [*The Endless Trench*]. Directed by Jon Garaño, Aitor Arregi, and José Mari Goenaga, La Claqueta et al., 2019.

Uesseler, Rolf. *Servants of War: Private Military Corporations and the Profit of Conflict*. Soft Skull Press, 2008.

Ulises' Odyssey = La odisea de Ulises. Directed by Lorena Manríquez, Andes Media LLC, 2014.

The Unspeakable. Directed by Carolina Astudillo, España-Chile, 2012. https://www.carolinaastudillo.com/portfolio/lo-indecible/.

Urrutia, Carolina. "*Los perros*: Naturaleza muerta." *LaFuga*, 2018, http://lafuga.cl/los-perros/919.

Vargas Llosa, Mario. *La ciudad y los perros*. Punto de Lectura, 2006.

"'Viudos de Franco' homenajearon a Pinochet en España." *La Cuarta*, 12 January 2007. https://web.archive.org/web/20150205083046/http://www.lacuarta.com/diario/2007/01/12/12.14.4a.VUE.VIUDOS.html.¡*Viva Chile Mierda!* [*Long Live Chile, Damn It!*]. Directed by Adrian Goycoolea, Brighton, 2014.

La voz dormida [*The Sleeping Voice*]. Directed by Benito Zambrano, Warner Bros, 2011.

Vuong, Ocean. *On Earth We're Briefly Gorgeous*. Penguin Books, 2021.

Wallenbrock, Nicole Beth. "An Apology for French Torturers: L'Ennemi intime." *Screening the Tortured Body*, edited by Mark de Valk, 2007, pp. 89–108.

Waller, James. *Confronting Evil: Engaging Our Responsibility to Prevent Genocide*. Oxford UP, 2016.

Weld, Kirsten. "The Spanish Civil War and the Construction of a Reactionary Historical Consciousness in Augusto Pinochet's Chile." *Hispanic American Historical Review*, vol. 98, no. 1, 2018, pp. 77–115.

Willems, Emilio. *A Way of Life and Death: Three Centuries of Prussian-German Militarism; An Anthropological Approach*. Vanderbilt UP, 1986.

Williams, Raymond. *Keywords: A Vocabulary of Culture and Society*. Fontana William Collins Sons, 1976.

Winchester, Ian. "'Boys to Men': Martial Masculinity and Sexual Behaviour in Franco's Army, 1939–1944." *Spain at War: Society, Culture and Mobilization, 1936–44*, edited by James Matthews, Bloomsbury Academic, 2019, pp. 233–48.

Woolf, Virginia. *Three Guineas*. Harcourt, Brace & World, 1938. Rpt. New York, 1966.

– *A Room of One's Own*. Capstone, Wiley Brand, Feminist Classic, 2021.

Wunker, Erin. *Notes from a Feminist Killjoy: Essays on Everyday Life*. Book Thug, 2016.

Zecchi, Barbara. *La pantalla sexuada*. Ediciones Cátedra, 2014.

Index

LATINOAMERICANA

SERIES EDITORS: Susan Antebi, Department of Spanish and Portuguese, University of Toronto; Néstor E. Rodríguez, Department of Spanish and Portuguese, University of Toronto

EDITORIAL ADVISORY BOARD: Carlos J. Alonso, Department of Latin American and Iberian Cultures, Columbia University; Santa Arias, Department of Spanish and Portuguese, University of Kansas; Kim Beauchesne, Department of French, Hispanic and Italian Studies, University of British Columbia; Héctor Domínguez-Ruvalcaba, Department of Spanish and Portuguese, University of Texas at Austin; Aníbal González-Pérez, Department of Spanish and Portuguese, Yale University; Jorge Guerrero, Department of Modern Languages and Literatures, University of Ottawa; Beth Jörgensen, Department of Modern Languages and Cultures, University of Rochester; Emily Maguire, Department of Spanish and Portuguese, Northwestern University; Kerstin Oloff, Department of Hispanic Studies, Durham University